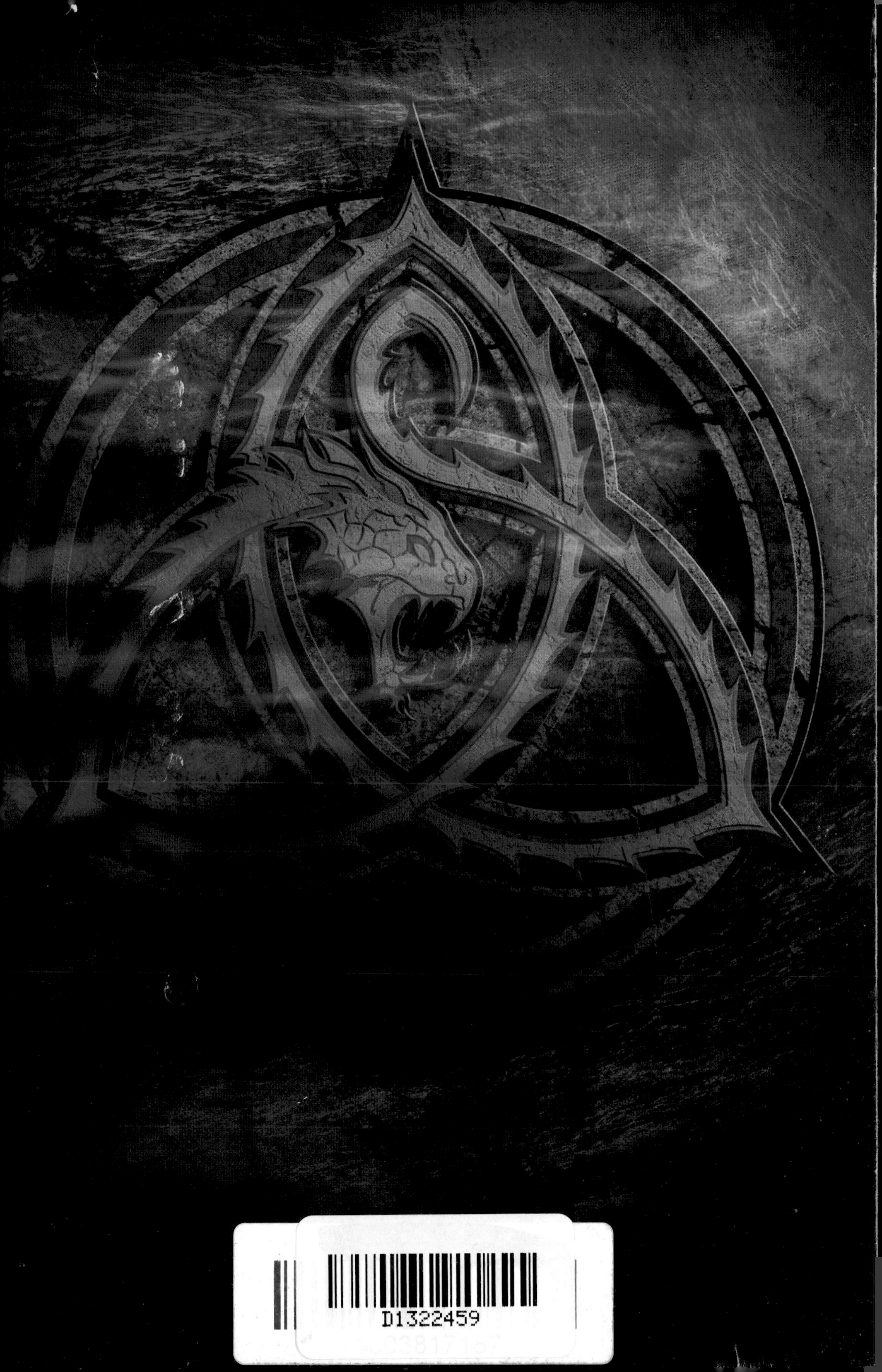

FEAR ITSELF AVENGERS ACADEMY

WRITER
CHRISTOS GAGE

PENCILERS
SEAN CHEN (ISSUES #14-14.1 & #17)
TOM RANEY (ISSUES #15-16 & #19-20)
ANDREA DI VITO (ISSUE #18)

INKERS
SCOTT HANNA (ISSUES #14-15 & #19-20)
ANDREW HENNESSY (ISSUES #15-17)
ANDREA DI VITO (ISSUE #18)

COLORIST
JEROMY COX

LETTERER
VC'S JOE CARAMAGNA

COVER ARTIST
BILLY TAN WITH LEONARDO OLEA

ASSISTANT EDITORS
JOHN DENNING & JAKE THOMAS

EDITOR
BILL ROSEMANN

COLLECTION EDITOR: CORY LEVINE • ASSISTANT EDITORS: ALEX STARBUCK & NELSON RIBEIRO
EDITORS, SPECIAL PROJECTS: JENNIFER GRÜNWALD & MARK D. BEAZLEY
SENIOR EDITOR, SPECIAL PROJECTS: JEFF YOUNGQUIST • SENIOR VICE PRESIDENT OF SALES: DAVID GABRIEL
SVP OF BRAND PLANNING & COMMUNICATIONS: MICHAEL PASCIULLO
BOOK DESIGN: JEFF POWELL

EDITOR IN CHIEF: AXEL ALONSO • CHIEF CREATIVE OFFICER: JOE QUESADA
PUBLISHER: DAN BUCKLEY • EXECUTIVE PRODUCER: ALAN FINE

FEAR ITSELF: AVENGERS ACADEMY. Contains material originally published in magazine form as AVENGERS ACADEMY #14-20 and #14.1. First printing 2012. ISBN# 978-0-7851-5201-9. Published by MARVEL WORLDWIDE, INC., a subsidiary of MARVEL ENTERTAINMENT, LLC. OFFICE OF PUBLICATION: 135 West 50th Street, New York, NY 10020. $19.99 per copy in the U.S. and $21.99 in Canada (GST #R127032852); Canadian Agreement #40668537. **Printed in the U.S.A.** ALAN FINE, EVP - Office of the President, Marvel Worldwide, Inc. and EVP & CMO Marvel Characters B.V.; DAN BUCKLEY, Publisher & President - Print, Animation & Digital Divisions; JOE QUESADA, Chief Creative Officer; TOM BREVOORT, SVP of Publishing; DAVID BOGART, SVP of Operations & Procurement, Publishing; RUWAN JAYATILLEKE, SVP & Associate Publisher, Publishing; C.B. CEBULSKI, SVP of Creator & Content Development; DAVID GABRIEL, SVP of Publishing Sales & Circulation; MICHAEL PASCIULLO, SVP of Brand Planning & Communications; JIM O'KEEFE, VP of Operations & Logistics; DAN CARR, Executive Director of Publishing Technology; SUSAN CRESPI, Editorial Operations Manager; ALEX MORALES, Publishing Operations Manager; STAN LEE, Chairman Emeritus. For information regarding advertising in Marvel Comics or on Marvel.com, please contact Niza Disla, Director of Marvel Partnerships, at ndisla@marvel.com. For Marvel subscription inquiries, please call 800-217-9158. **Manufactured between 8/22/2012 and 9/24/2012 by R.R. DONNELLEY, INC., SALEM, VA, USA.**

10 9 8 7 6 5 4 3 2 1

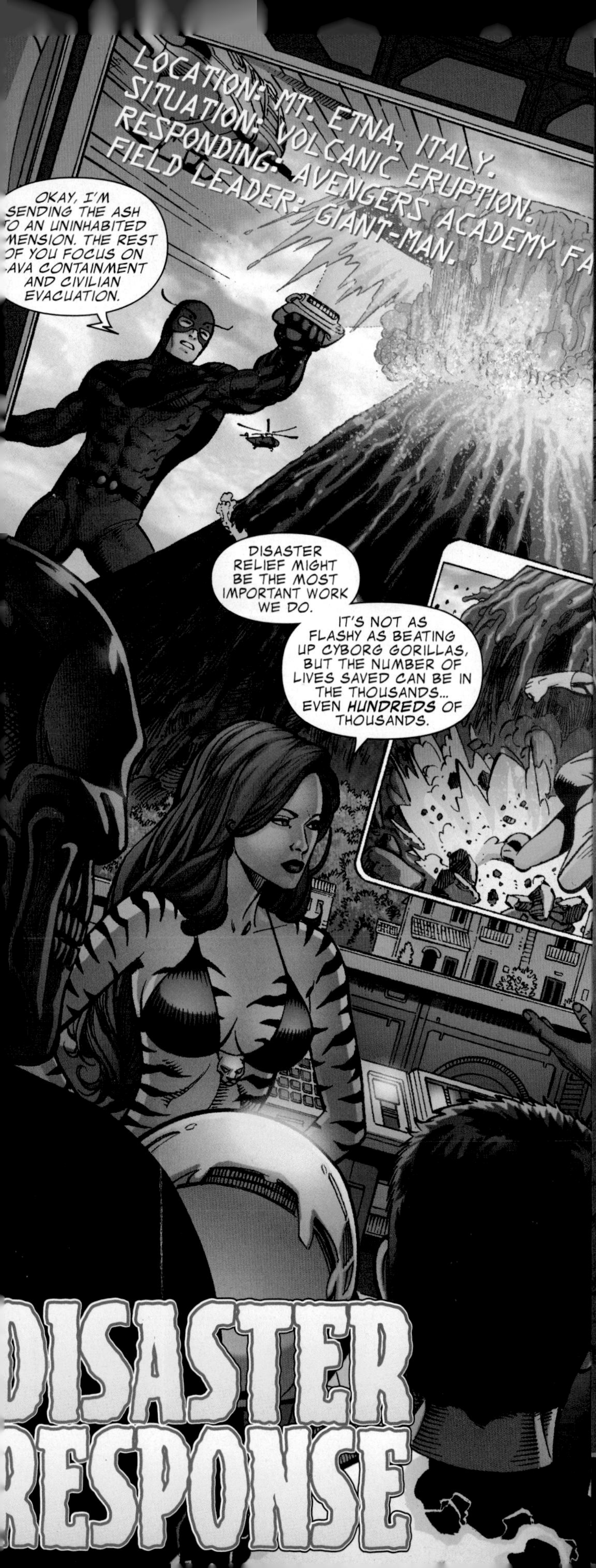
LOCATION: MT. ETNA, ITALY.
SITUATION: VOLCANIC ERUPTION.
RESPONDING: AVENGERS ACADEMY FA
FIELD LEADER: GIANT-MAN.
OKAY, I'M SENDING THE ASH TO AN UNINHABITED MENSION. THE REST OF YOU FOCUS ON AVA CONTAINMENT AND CIVILIAN EVACUATION.
DISASTER RELIEF MIGHT BE THE MOST IMPORTANT WORK WE DO.
IT'S NOT AS FLASHY AS BEATING UP CYBORG GORILLAS, BUT THE NUMBER OF LIVES SAVED CAN BE IN THE THOUSANDS... EVEN HUNDREDS OF THOUSANDS.
DISASTER RESPONSE

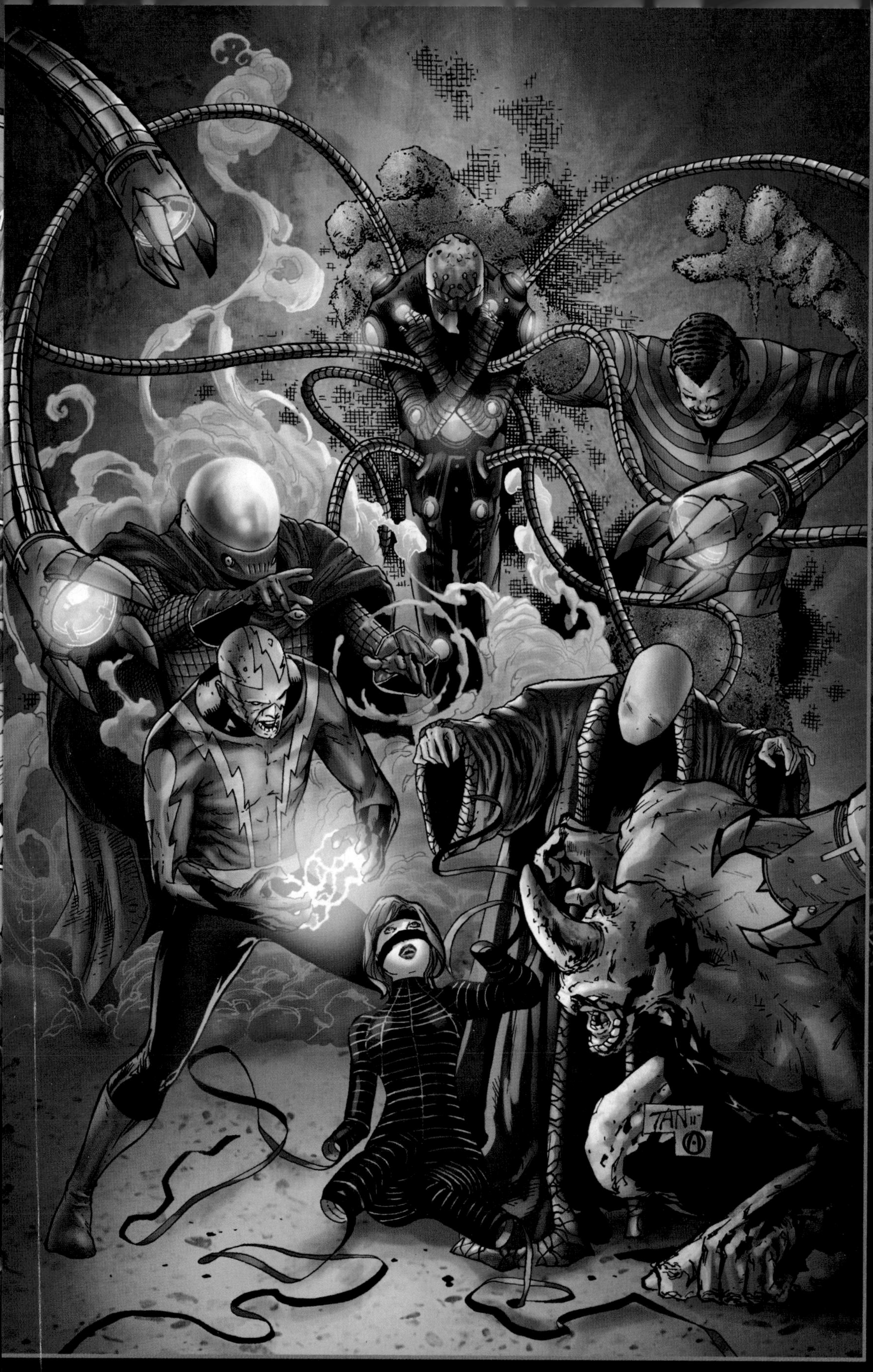

AVENGERS ACADEMY #14

AND THERE CAME A DAY, A DAY UNLIKE ANY OTHER, WHEN EARTH'S MIGHTIEST HEROES OPENED THEIR DOORS TO TEACH THE NEXT GENERATION! ON THAT DAY, THE AVENGERS ACADEMY WAS BORN, TO TRAIN YOUNG ADULTS TO FIGHT THE FOES NO SINGLE SUPER HERO COULD WITHSTAND!

FINESSE — PHOTOGRAPHIC FIGHTER. ALL HEAD, NO HEART.

HAZMAT — HUMAN TOXIC SPILL. CAUSTIC PERSONALITY.

METTLE — STEEL-SKINNED POWERHOUSE. ARMORED SHELL PROTECTING INNER FEELINGS.

REPTIL — DINOSAUR MORPHER. FUTURE HERO OR NAIVE OPTIMIST?

STRIKER — ELECTRIC DYNAMO. SELF-PROMOTES THROUGH SHOCK TACTICS.

VEIL — VARIABLE GAS GENERATOR. UNSEEN POTENTIAL... UNTIL SHE DISCORPORATES.

AVENG ACAD

ORIGINAL AVENGER H
PYM FOUNDED THE AVE
ACADEMY TO HELP GUI
NEXT GENERATION
SUPERHUMANS IN THE
TRADITION OF EART
MIGHTIEST HEROES.
INAUGURAL CLASS--
WERE PREVIOUSLY REC
AND TORTURED BY NO
OSBORN--HAS SECR
LEARNED THE SHOC
TRUTH: THEY
WERE SELECTED N
BECAUSE THEY HAVE
GREATEST POTENTIA
BECOME HEROES...
BECAUSE THEY ARE A
OF BECOMING VILLA

AFTER HAVING THEIR
TEMPORARILY TRANSPL
INTO ADULT BODIES F
POSSIBLE FUTURES,
STUDENTS DEFEATED
NEAR OMNIPOTENT KO
A FEAT WORTHY OF
AVENGERS THEMSEL
ALTHOUGH THE TEAM
VICTORIOUS, THE EXPE
LEFT THEM WITH EVEN
QUESTIONS ABOUT W
THEIR FUTURES MAY H

WY 11/12 SG 7/14

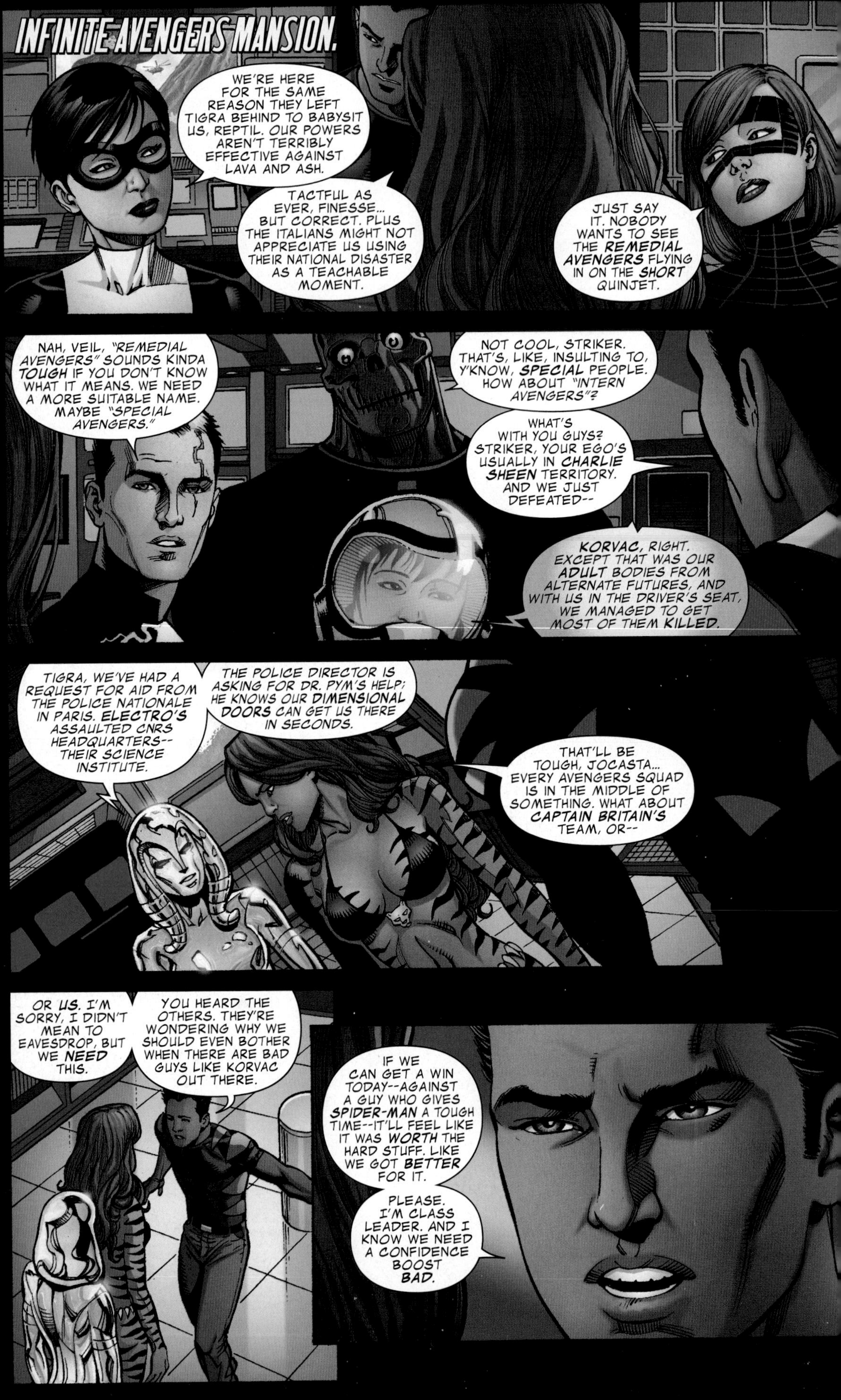

INFINITE AVENGERS MANSION.
WE'RE HERE FOR THE SAME REASON THEY LEFT TIGRA BEHIND TO BABYSIT US, REPTIL. OUR POWERS AREN'T TERRIBLY EFFECTIVE AGAINST LAVA AND ASH.
TACTFUL AS EVER, FINESSE... BUT CORRECT. PLUS THE ITALIANS MIGHT NOT APPRECIATE US USING THEIR NATIONAL DISASTER AS A TEACHABLE MOMENT.
JUST SAY IT. NOBODY WANTS TO SEE THE REMEDIAL AVENGERS FLYING IN ON THE SHORT QUINJET.
NAH, VEIL, "REMEDIAL AVENGERS" SOUNDS KINDA TOUGH IF YOU DON'T KNOW WHAT IT MEANS. WE NEED A MORE SUITABLE NAME. MAYBE "SPECIAL AVENGERS."
NOT COOL, STRIKER. THAT'S, LIKE, INSULTING TO, Y'KNOW, SPECIAL PEOPLE. HOW ABOUT "INTERN AVENGERS"?
WHAT'S WITH YOU GUYS? STRIKER, YOUR EGO'S USUALLY IN CHARLIE SHEEN TERRITORY. AND WE JUST DEFEATED--
KORVAC, RIGHT. EXCEPT THAT WAS OUR ADULT BODIES FROM ALTERNATE FUTURES, AND WITH US IN THE DRIVER'S SEAT, WE MANAGED TO GET MOST OF THEM KILLED.
TIGRA, WE'VE HAD A REQUEST FOR AID FROM THE POLICE NATIONALE IN PARIS. ELECTRO'S ASSAULTED CNRS HEADQUARTERS-- THEIR SCIENCE INSTITUTE.
THE POLICE DIRECTOR IS ASKING FOR DR. PYM'S HELP; HE KNOWS OUR DIMENSIONAL DOORS CAN GET US THERE IN SECONDS.
THAT'LL BE TOUGH, JOCASTA... EVERY AVENGERS SQUAD IS IN THE MIDDLE OF SOMETHING. WHAT ABOUT CAPTAIN BRITAIN'S TEAM, OR--
OR US. I'M SORRY, I DIDN'T MEAN TO EAVESDROP, BUT WE NEED THIS.
YOU HEARD THE OTHERS. THEY'RE WONDERING WHY WE SHOULD EVEN BOTHER WHEN THERE ARE BAD GUYS LIKE KORVAC OUT THERE.
IF WE CAN GET A WIN TODAY--AGAINST A GUY WHO GIVES SPIDER-MAN A TOUGH TIME--IT'LL FEEL LIKE IT WAS WORTH THE HARD STUFF. LIKE WE GOT BETTER FOR IT.
PLEASE. I'M CLASS LEADER. AND I KNOW WE NEED A CONFIDENCE BOOST BAD.

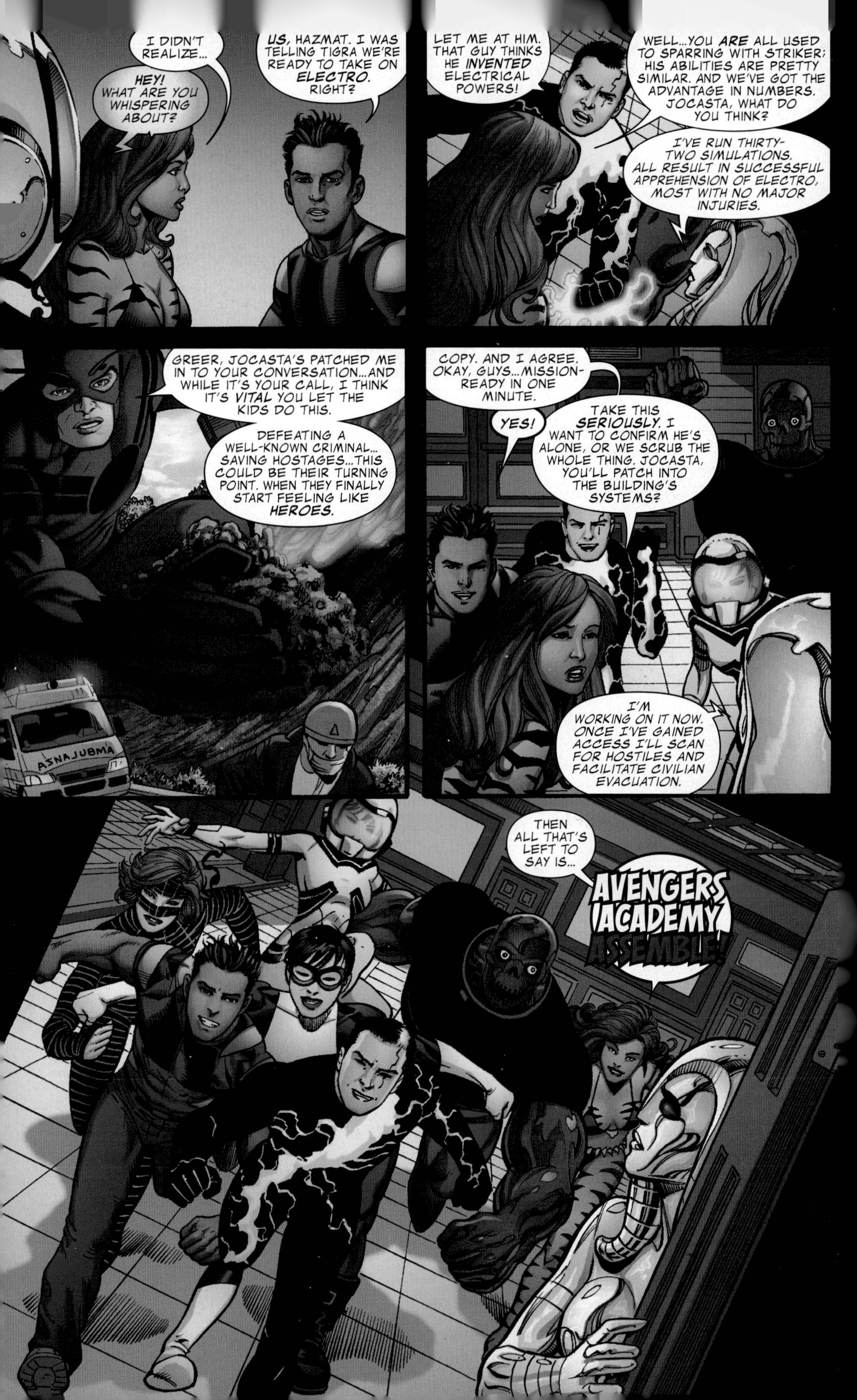
I DIDN'T REALIZE...
HEY! WHAT ARE YOU WHISPERING ABOUT?
US, HAZMAT. I WAS TELLING TIGRA WE'RE READY TO TAKE ON ELECTRO. RIGHT?
LET ME AT HIM. THAT GUY THINKS HE INVENTED ELECTRICAL POWERS!
WELL...YOU ARE ALL USED TO SPARRING WITH STRIKER; HIS ABILITIES ARE PRETTY SIMILAR. AND WE'VE GOT THE ADVANTAGE IN NUMBERS. JOCASTA, WHAT DO YOU THINK?
I'VE RUN THIRTY-TWO SIMULATIONS. ALL RESULT IN SUCCESSFUL APPREHENSION OF ELECTRO, MOST WITH NO MAJOR INJURIES.
GREER, JOCASTA'S PATCHED ME IN TO YOUR CONVERSATION...AND WHILE IT'S YOUR CALL, I THINK IT'S VITAL YOU LET THE KIDS DO THIS.
DEFEATING A WELL-KNOWN CRIMINAL... SAVING HOSTAGES...THIS COULD BE THEIR TURNING POINT. WHEN THEY FINALLY START FEELING LIKE HEROES.
AMBULANCE
COPY. AND I AGREE. OKAY, GUYS...MISSION-READY IN ONE MINUTE.
YES!
TAKE THIS SERIOUSLY. I WANT TO CONFIRM HE'S ALONE, OR WE SCRUB THE WHOLE THING. JOCASTA, YOU'LL PATCH INTO THE BUILDING'S SYSTEMS?
I'M WORKING ON IT NOW. ONCE I'VE GAINED ACCESS I'LL SCAN FOR HOSTILES AND FACILITATE CIVILIAN EVACUATION.
THEN ALL THAT'S LEFT TO SAY IS...
AVENGERS ACADEMY ASSEMBLE!

PARIS.
CENTRE NATIONAL DE LA
RECHERCHE SCIENTIFIQUE.

DUDE! DOES DR. PYM HAVE DIMENSIONAL DOORS TO EVERY LAB IN THE WORLD?

ONLY THE TOP TWO THOUSAND. JOCASTA, WE'RE IN. DO YOU COPY?

IT APPEARS ELECTRO SHORTED OUT THE DOOR RELEASE CONTROLS, AS WELL AS ALL FAIL-SAFES, SEALING THE BUILDING.

FORTUNATELY, IT'S A SIMPLE MATTER FOR ME TO REROUTE THE SYSTEMS. ALL EXIT DOORS ARE NOW OPEN.

JUDGING FROM THE TRAIL OF DISABLED SECURITY CAMERAS, ELECTRO IS TWO LEVELS DOWN FROM YOU, IN A SECTOR THAT'S ISOLATED DUE TO THE USE OF HAZARDOUS MATERIALS.

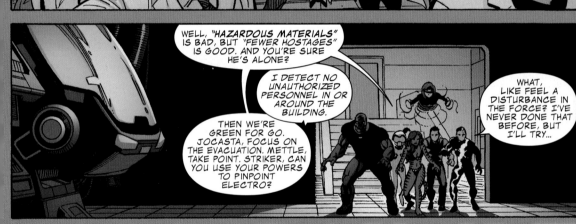

WELL, "HAZARDOUS MATERIALS" IS BAD, BUT "FEWER HOSTAGES" IS GOOD. AND YOU'RE SURE HE'S ALONE?

I DETECT NO UNAUTHORIZED PERSONNEL IN OR AROUND THE BUILDING.

THEN WE'RE GREEN FOR GO. JOCASTA, FOCUS ON THE EVACUATION. METTLE, TAKE POINT. STRIKER, CAN YOU USE YOUR POWERS TO PINPOINT ELECTRO?

WHAT, LIKE FEEL A DISTURBANCE IN THE FORCE? I'VE NEVER DONE THAT BEFORE, BUT I'LL TRY...

IT'S EASY IF YOU PRACTICE.

YOU LED ME HERE LIKE A BEACON.

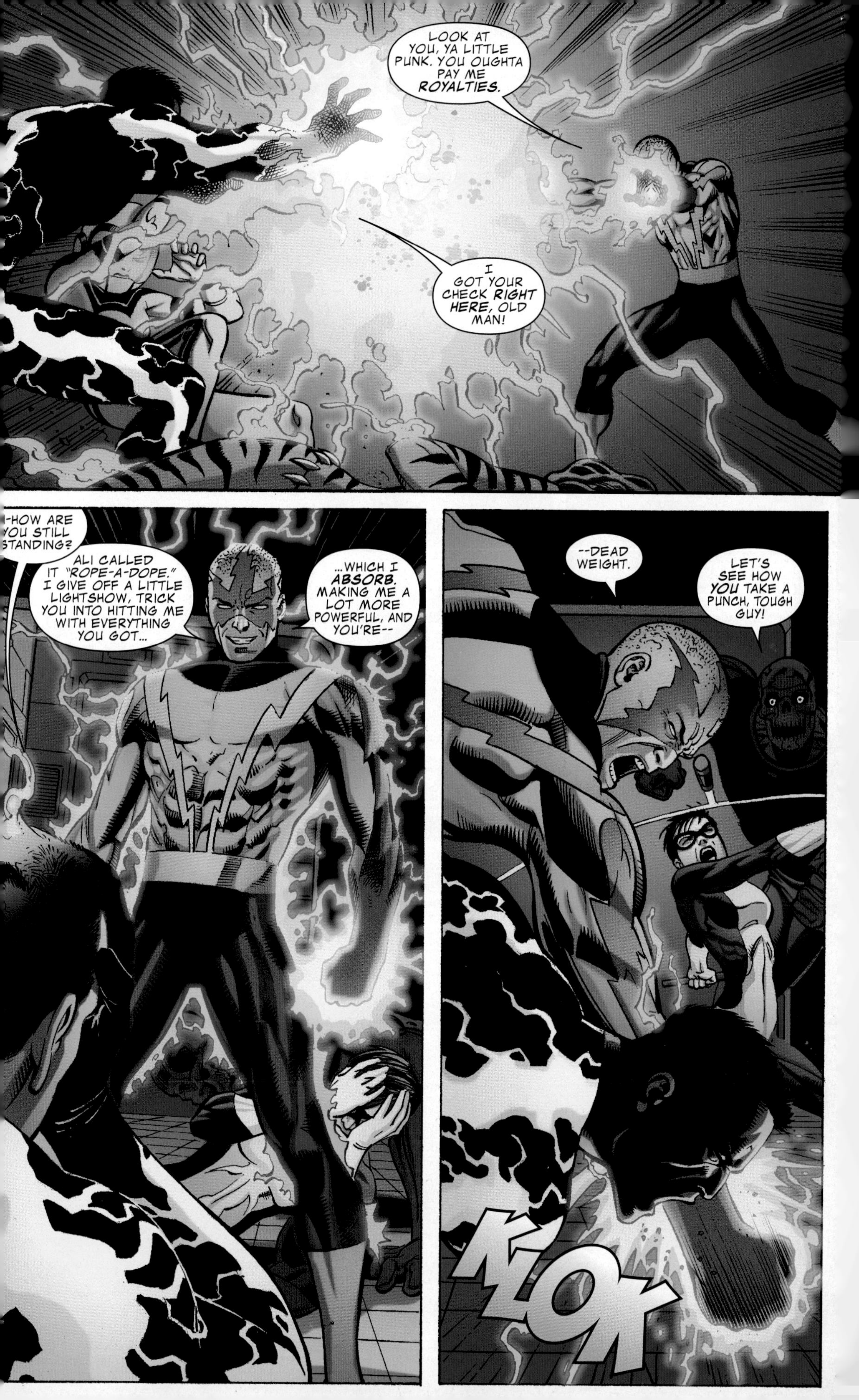
LOOK AT YOU, YA LITTLE PUNK. YOU OUGHTA PAY ME ROYALTIES.
I GOT YOUR CHECK RIGHT HERE, OLD MAN!
-HOW ARE YOU STILL STANDING?
ALI CALLED IT "ROPE-A-DOPE." I GIVE OFF A LITTLE LIGHTSHOW, TRICK YOU INTO HITTING ME WITH EVERYTHING YOU GOT...
...WHICH I ABSORB. MAKING ME A LOT MORE POWERFUL, AND YOU'RE--
--DEAD WEIGHT.
LET'S SEE HOW YOU TAKE A PUNCH, TOUGH GUY!
KLOK

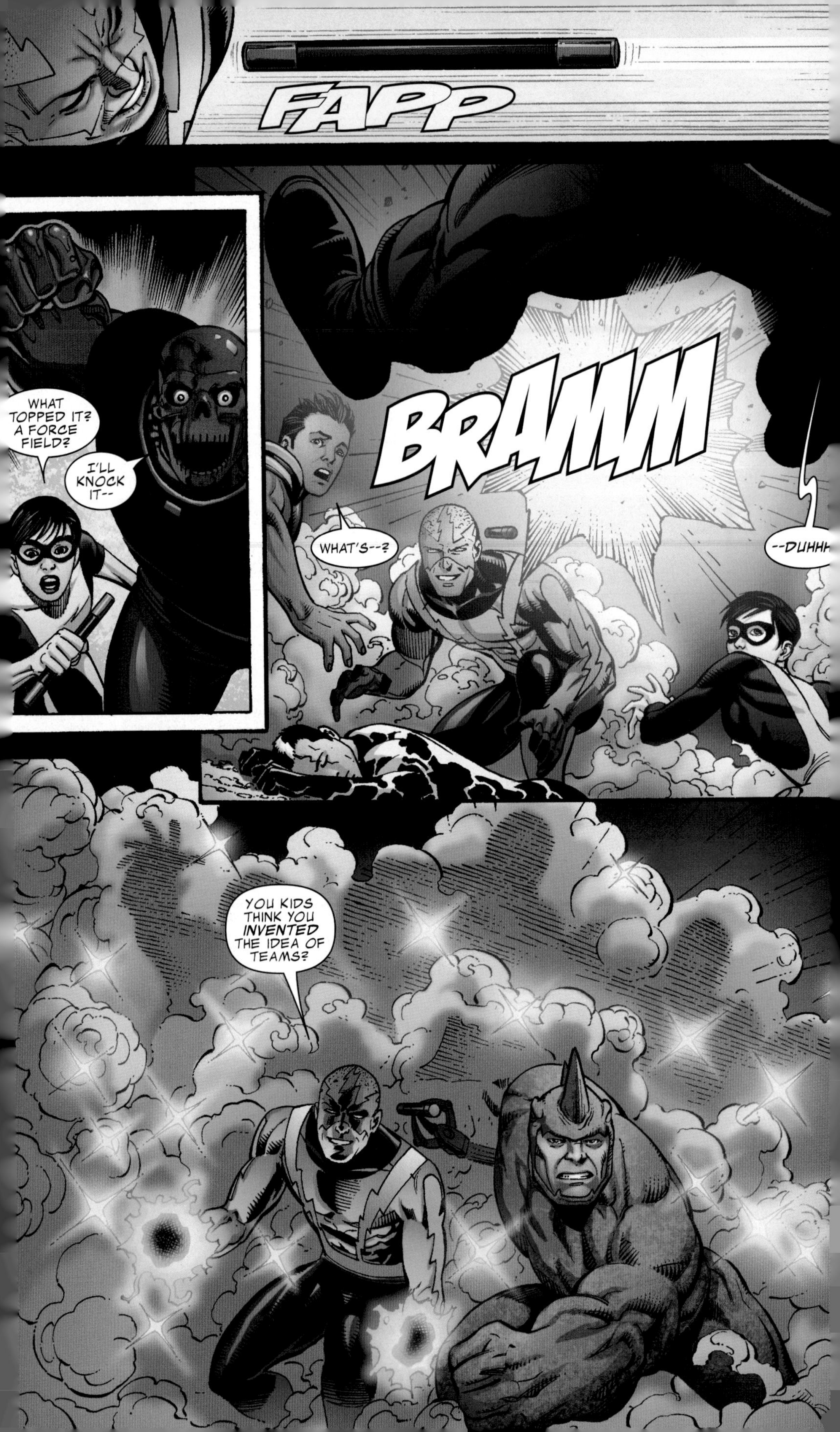
FAPP
WHAT TOPPED IT? A FORCE FIELD?
I'LL KNOCK IT--
BRAMM
WHAT'S--?
--DUHHH
YOU KIDS THINK YOU INVENTED THE IDEA OF TEAMS?

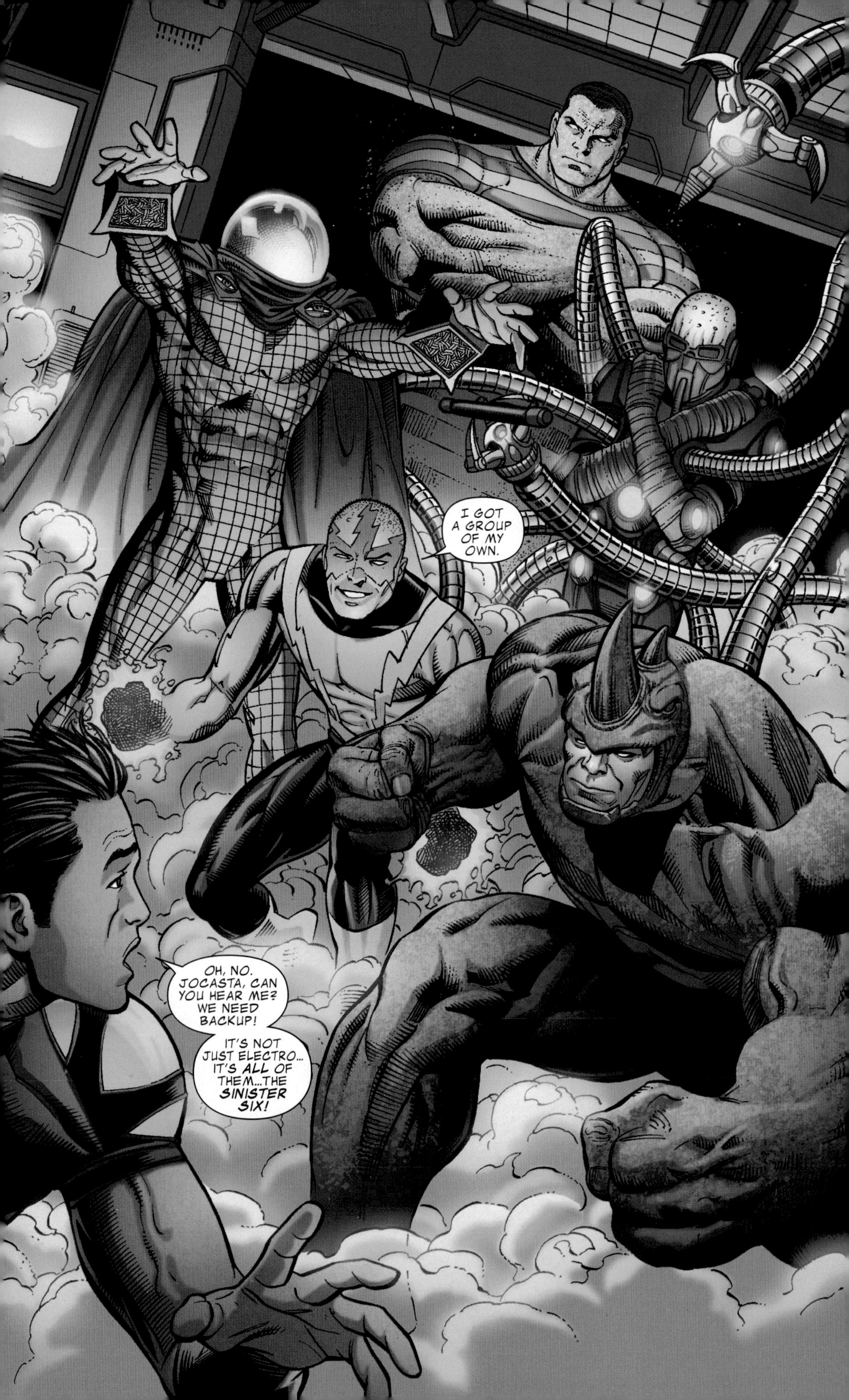
I GOT A GROUP OF MY OWN.
OH, NO. JOCASTA, CAN YOU HEAR ME? WE NEED BACKUP!
IT'S NOT JUST ELECTRO... IT'S ALL OF THEM...THE SINISTER SIX!

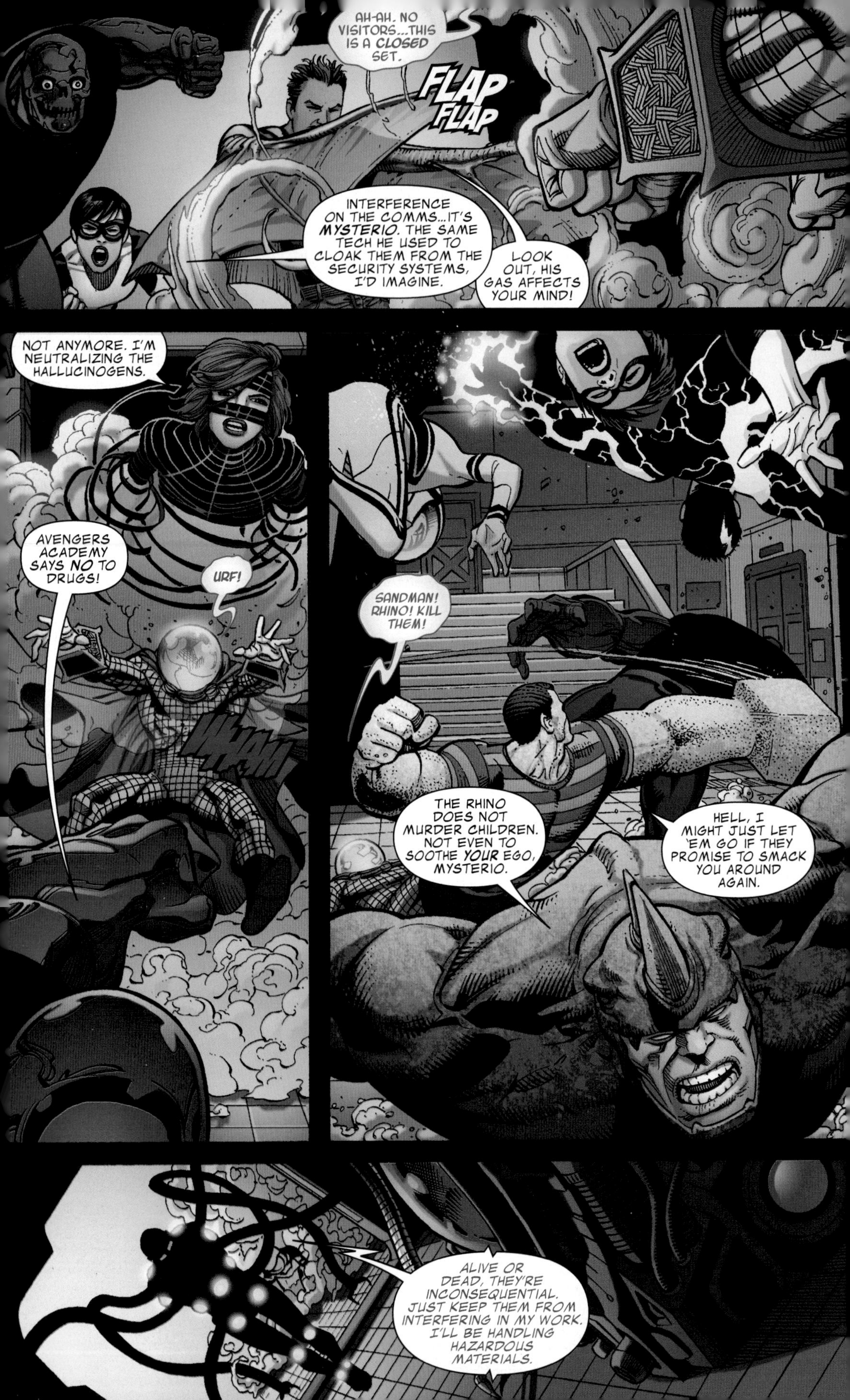
AH-AH. NO VISITORS...THIS IS A CLOSED SET.
FLAP FLAP
INTERFERENCE ON THE COMMS...IT'S MYSTERIO. THE SAME TECH HE USED TO CLOAK THEM FROM THE SECURITY SYSTEMS, I'D IMAGINE.
LOOK OUT, HIS GAS AFFECTS YOUR MIND!
NOT ANYMORE. I'M NEUTRALIZING THE HALLUCINOGENS.
AVENGERS ACADEMY SAYS NO TO DRUGS!
URF!
SANDMAN! RHINO! KILL THEM!
THE RHINO DOES NOT MURDER CHILDREN. NOT EVEN TO SOOTHE YOUR EGO, MYSTERIO.
HELL, I MIGHT JUST LET 'EM GO IF THEY PROMISE TO SMACK YOU AROUND AGAIN.
ALIVE OR DEAD, THEY'RE INCONSEQUENTIAL. JUST KEEP THEM FROM INTERFERING IN MY WORK. I'LL BE HANDLING HAZARDOUS MATERIALS.

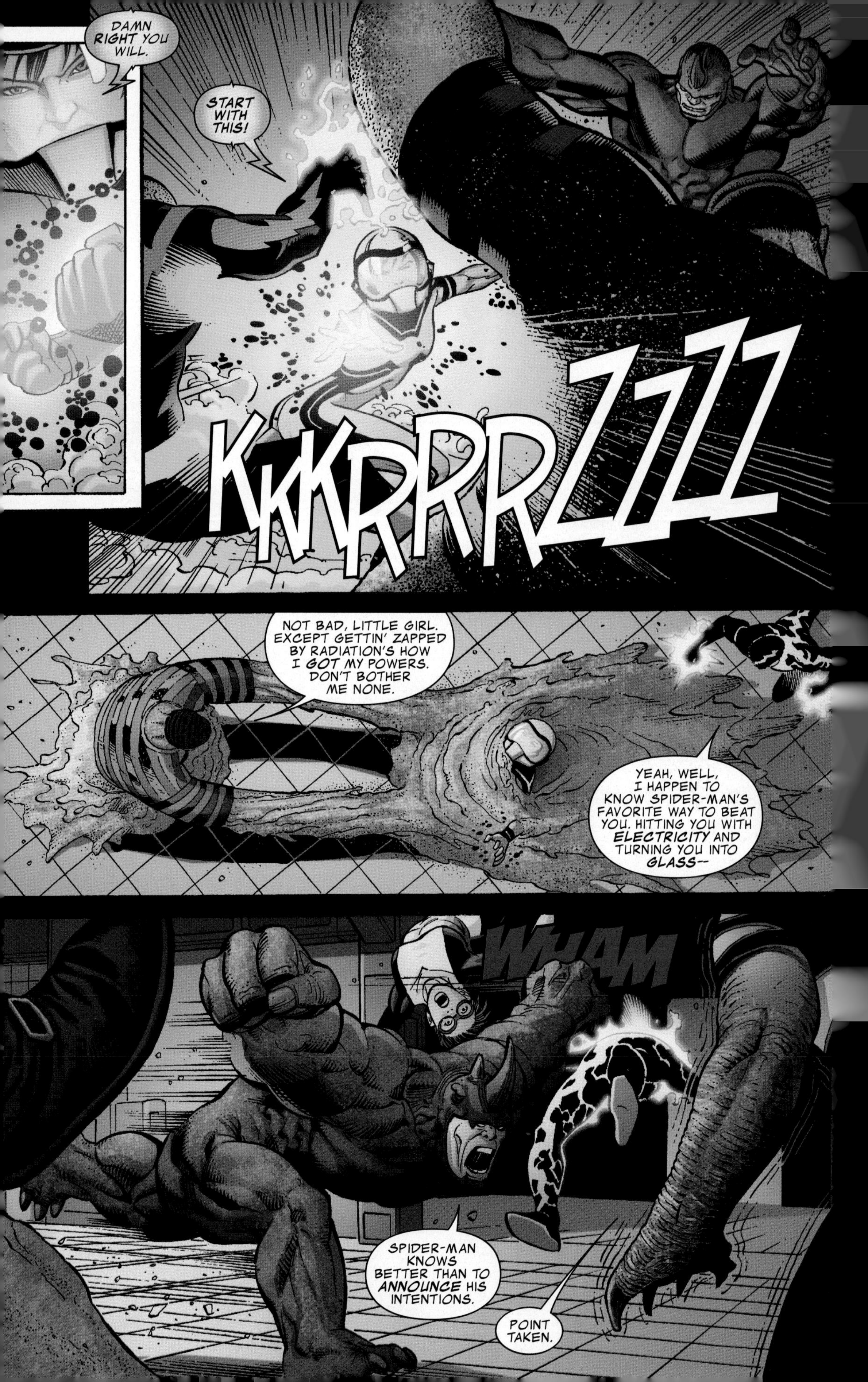
DAMN RIGHT YOU WILL.
START WITH THIS!
KKKRRRRZZZZ
NOT BAD, LITTLE GIRL. EXCEPT GETTIN' ZAPPED BY RADIATION'S HOW I GOT MY POWERS. DON'T BOTHER ME NONE.
YEAH, WELL, I HAPPEN TO KNOW SPIDER-MAN'S FAVORITE WAY TO BEAT YOU. HITTING YOU WITH ELECTRICITY AND TURNING YOU INTO GLASS--
WHAM
SPIDER-MAN KNOWS BETTER THAN TO ANNOUNCE HIS INTENTIONS.
POINT TAKEN.

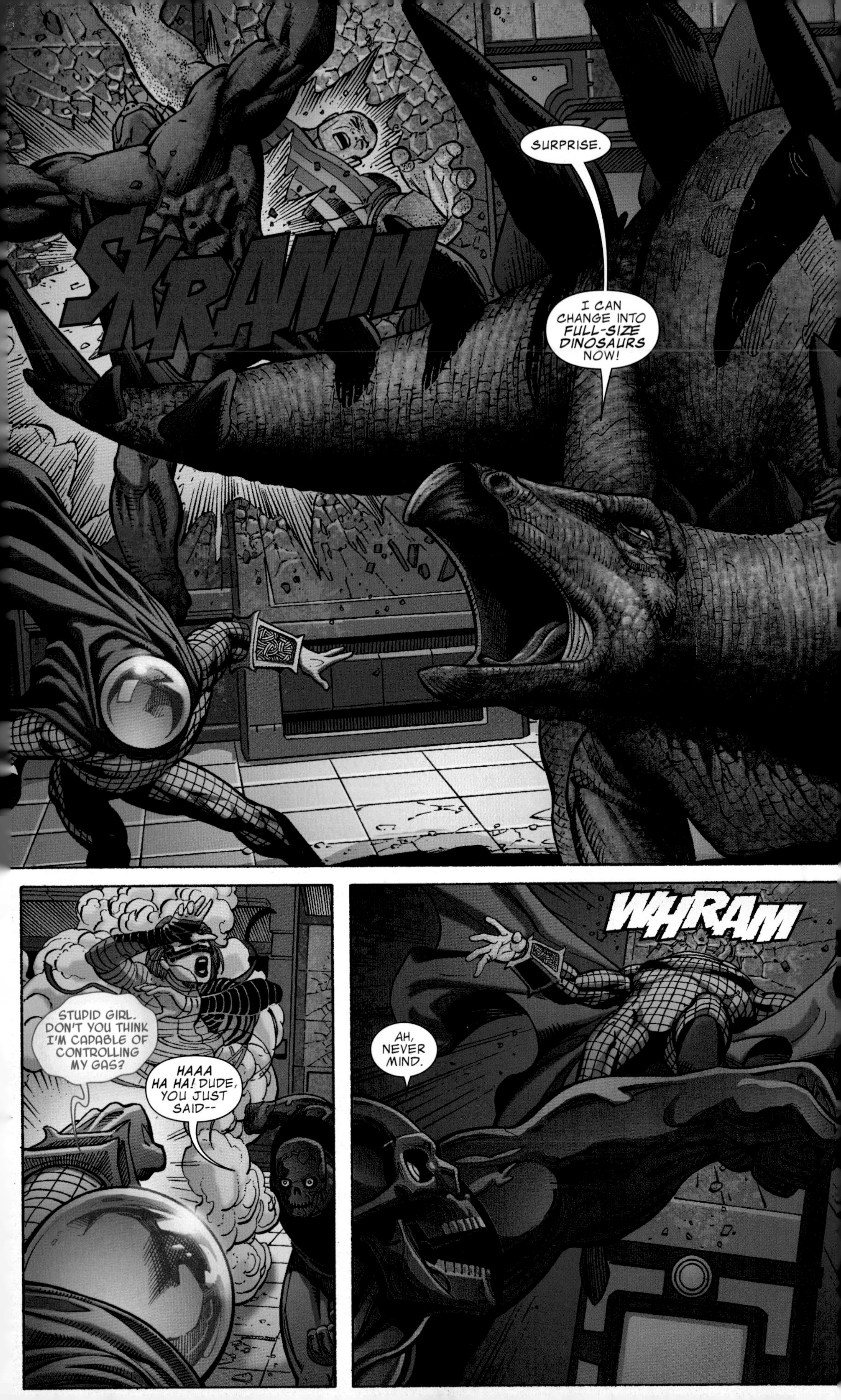
SKRAMM
SURPRISE.
I CAN CHANGE INTO FULL-SIZE DINOSAURS NOW!
STUPID GIRL. DON'T YOU THINK I'M CAPABLE OF CONTROLLING MY GAS?
HAAA HA HA! DUDE, YOU JUST SAID--
WHRAM
AH, NEVER MIND.

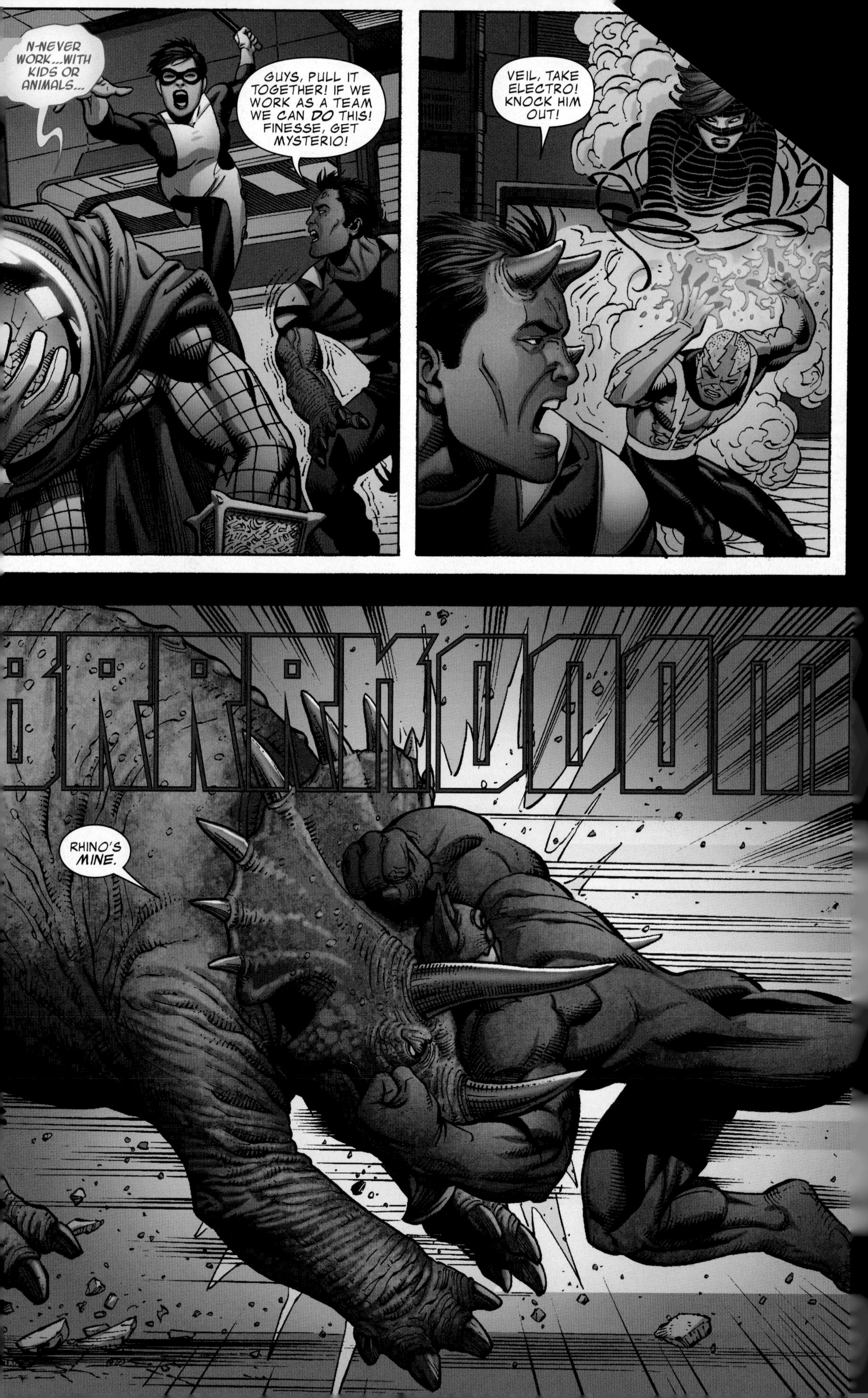
N-NEVER WORK...WITH KIDS OR ANIMALS...
GUYS, PULL IT TOGETHER! IF WE WORK AS A TEAM WE CAN *DO* THIS! FINESSE, GET MYSTERIO!
VEIL, TAKE ELECTRO! KNOCK HIM OUT!
RHINO'S *MINE*.

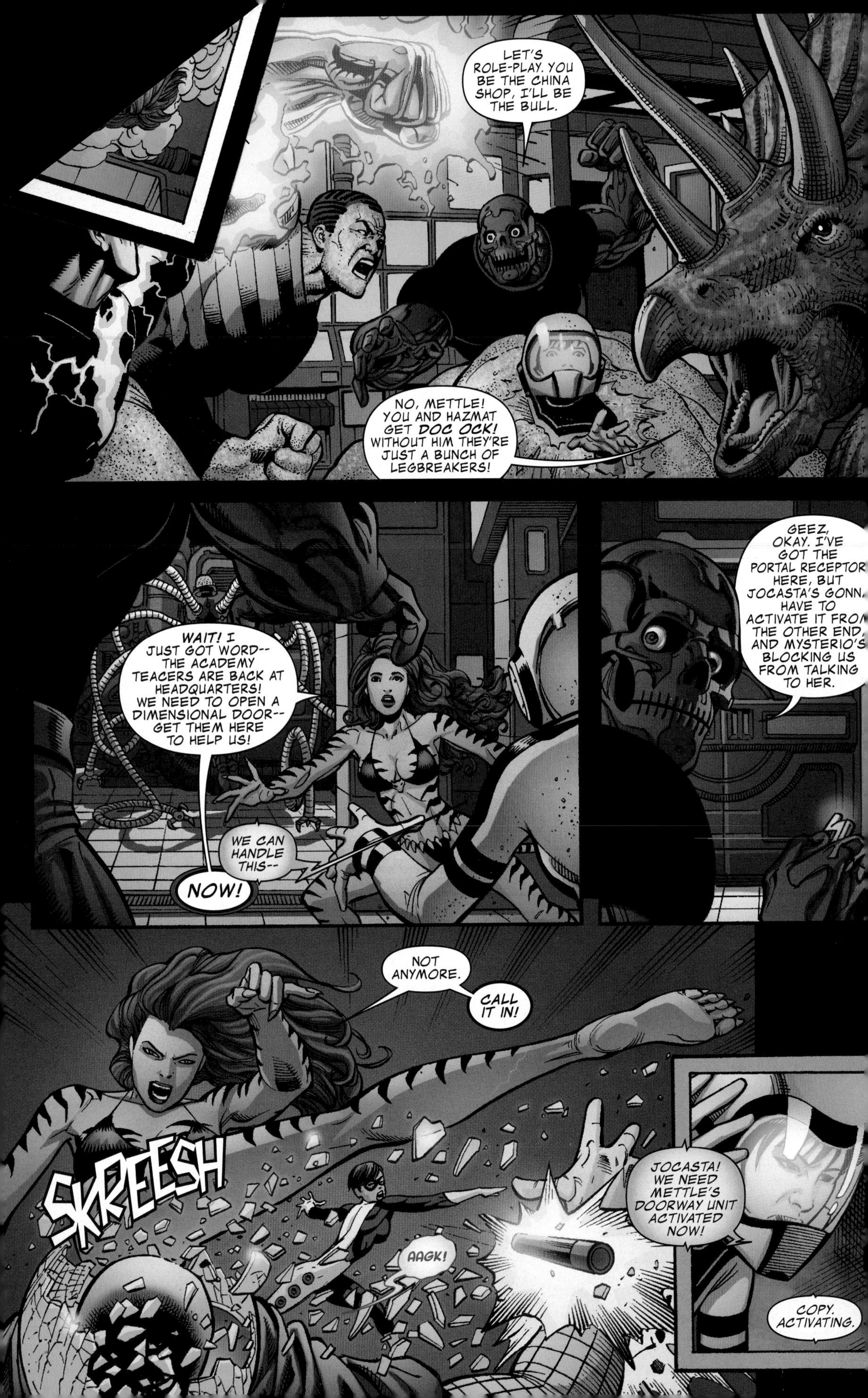
LET'S ROLE-PLAY. YOU BE THE CHINA SHOP, I'LL BE THE BULL.
NO, METTLE! YOU AND HAZMAT GET DOC OCK! WITHOUT HIM THEY'RE JUST A BUNCH OF LEGBREAKERS!
WAIT! I JUST GOT WORD-- THE ACADEMY TEACERS ARE BACK AT HEADQUARTERS! WE NEED TO OPEN A DIMENSIONAL DOOR-- GET THEM HERE TO HELP US!
WE CAN HANDLE THIS--
NOW!
GEEZ, OKAY. I'VE GOT THE PORTAL RECEPTOR HERE, BUT JOCASTA'S GONN HAVE TO ACTIVATE IT FRO THE OTHER END, AND MYSTERIO'S BLOCKING US FROM TALKING TO HER.
NOT ANYMORE.
CALL IT IN!
SKREESH
AAGK!
JOCASTA! WE NEED METTLE'S DOORWAY UNIT ACTIVATED NOW!
COPY. ACTIVATING.

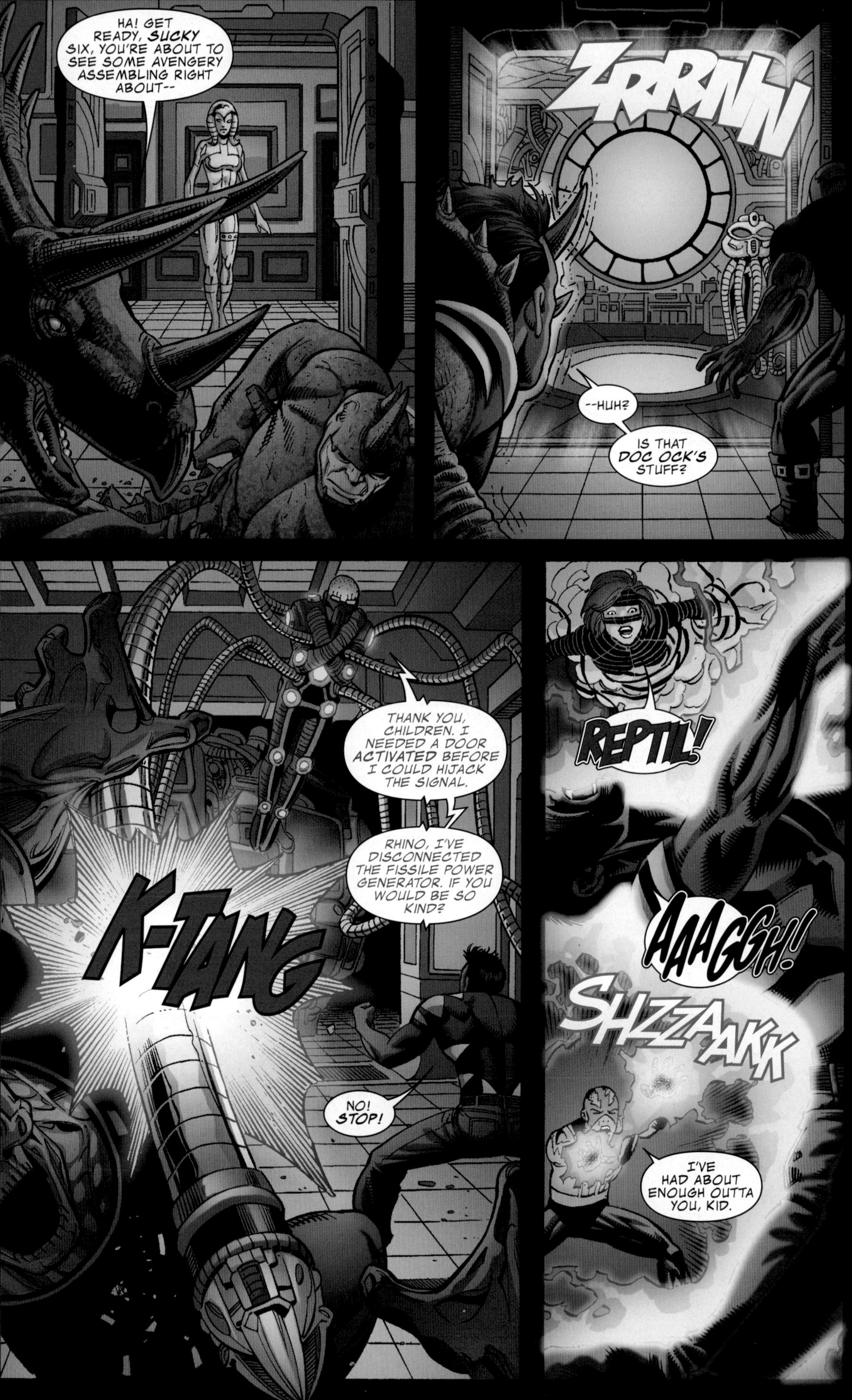
HA! GET READY, SUCKY SIX, YOU'RE ABOUT TO SEE SOME AVENGERY ASSEMBLING RIGHT ABOUT--
ZRRRMM
--HUH?
IS THAT DOC OCK'S STUFF?
THANK YOU, CHILDREN. I NEEDED A DOOR ACTIVATED BEFORE I COULD HIJACK THE SIGNAL.
RHINO, I'VE DISCONNECTED THE FISSILE POWER GENERATOR. IF YOU WOULD BE SO KIND?
K-TANG
NO! STOP!
REPTIL!
AAAGGH!
SHZZAKK
I'VE HAD ABOUT ENOUGH OUTTA YOU, KID.

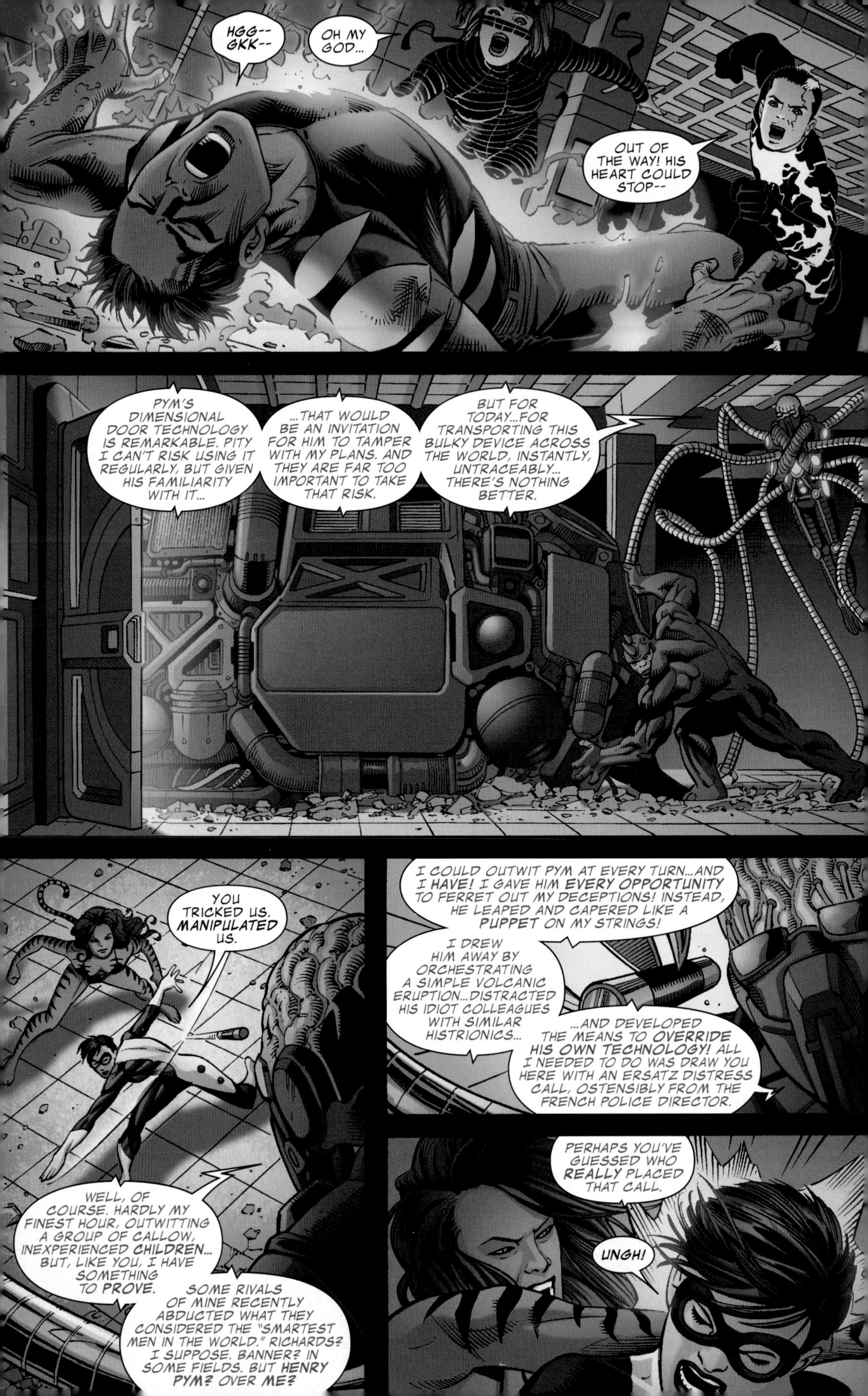
HGG-- GKK--
OH MY GOD...
OUT OF THE WAY! HIS HEART COULD STOP--
PYM'S DIMENSIONAL DOOR TECHNOLOGY IS REMARKABLE. PITY I CAN'T RISK USING IT REGULARLY, BUT GIVEN HIS FAMILIARITY WITH IT...
...THAT WOULD BE AN INVITATION FOR HIM TO TAMPER WITH MY PLANS. AND THEY ARE FAR TOO IMPORTANT TO TAKE THAT RISK.
BUT FOR TODAY...FOR TRANSPORTING THIS BULKY DEVICE ACROSS THE WORLD, INSTANTLY, UNTRACEABLY... THERE'S NOTHING BETTER.
YOU TRICKED US. MANIPULATED US.
WELL, OF COURSE. HARDLY MY FINEST HOUR, OUTWITTING A GROUP OF CALLOW, INEXPERIENCED CHILDREN... BUT, LIKE YOU, I HAVE SOMETHING TO PROVE.
SOME RIVALS OF MINE RECENTLY ABDUCTED WHAT THEY CONSIDERED THE "SMARTEST MEN IN THE WORLD." RICHARDS? I SUPPOSE. BANNER? IN SOME FIELDS. BUT HENRY PYM? OVER ME?
I COULD OUTWIT PYM AT EVERY TURN...AND I HAVE! I GAVE HIM EVERY OPPORTUNITY TO FERRET OUT MY DECEPTIONS! INSTEAD, HE LEAPED AND CAPERED LIKE A PUPPET ON MY STRINGS!
I DREW HIM AWAY BY ORCHESTRATING A SIMPLE VOLCANIC ERUPTION...DISTRACTED HIS IDIOT COLLEAGUES WITH SIMILAR HISTRIONICS...
...AND DEVELOPED THE MEANS TO OVERRIDE HIS OWN TECHNOLOGY! ALL I NEEDED TO DO WAS DRAW YOU HERE WITH AN ERSATZ DISTRESS CALL, OSTENSIBLY FROM THE FRENCH POLICE DIRECTOR.
PERHAPS YOU'VE GUESSED WHO REALLY PLACED THAT CALL.
UNGH!

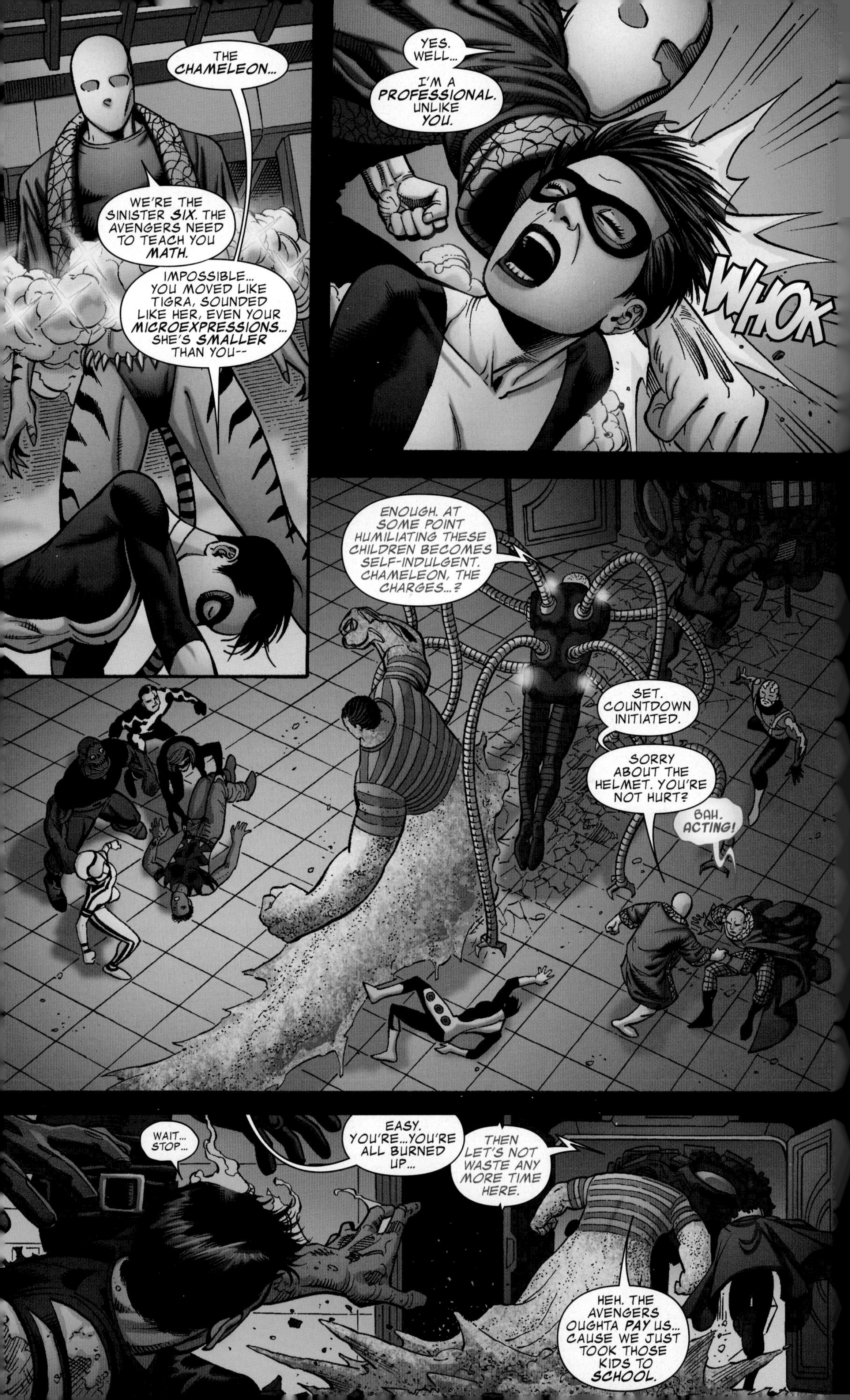
THE CHAMELEON...
WE'RE THE SINISTER SIX. THE AVENGERS NEED TO TEACH YOU MATH.
IMPOSSIBLE... YOU MOVED LIKE TIGRA, SOUNDED LIKE HER, EVEN YOUR MICROEXPRESSIONS... SHE'S SMALLER THAN YOU--
YES. WELL...
I'M A PROFESSIONAL. UNLIKE YOU.
WHOK
ENOUGH. AT SOME POINT HUMILIATING THESE CHILDREN BECOMES SELF-INDULGENT. CHAMELEON, THE CHARGES...?
SET. COUNTDOWN INITIATED.
SORRY ABOUT THE HELMET. YOU'RE NOT HURT?
BAH. ACTING!
WAIT... STOP...
EASY. YOU'RE...YOU'RE ALL BURNED UP...
THEN LET'S NOT WASTE ANY MORE TIME HERE.
HEH. THE AVENGERS OUGHTA PAY US... CAUSE WE JUST TOOK THOSE KIDS TO SCHOOL.

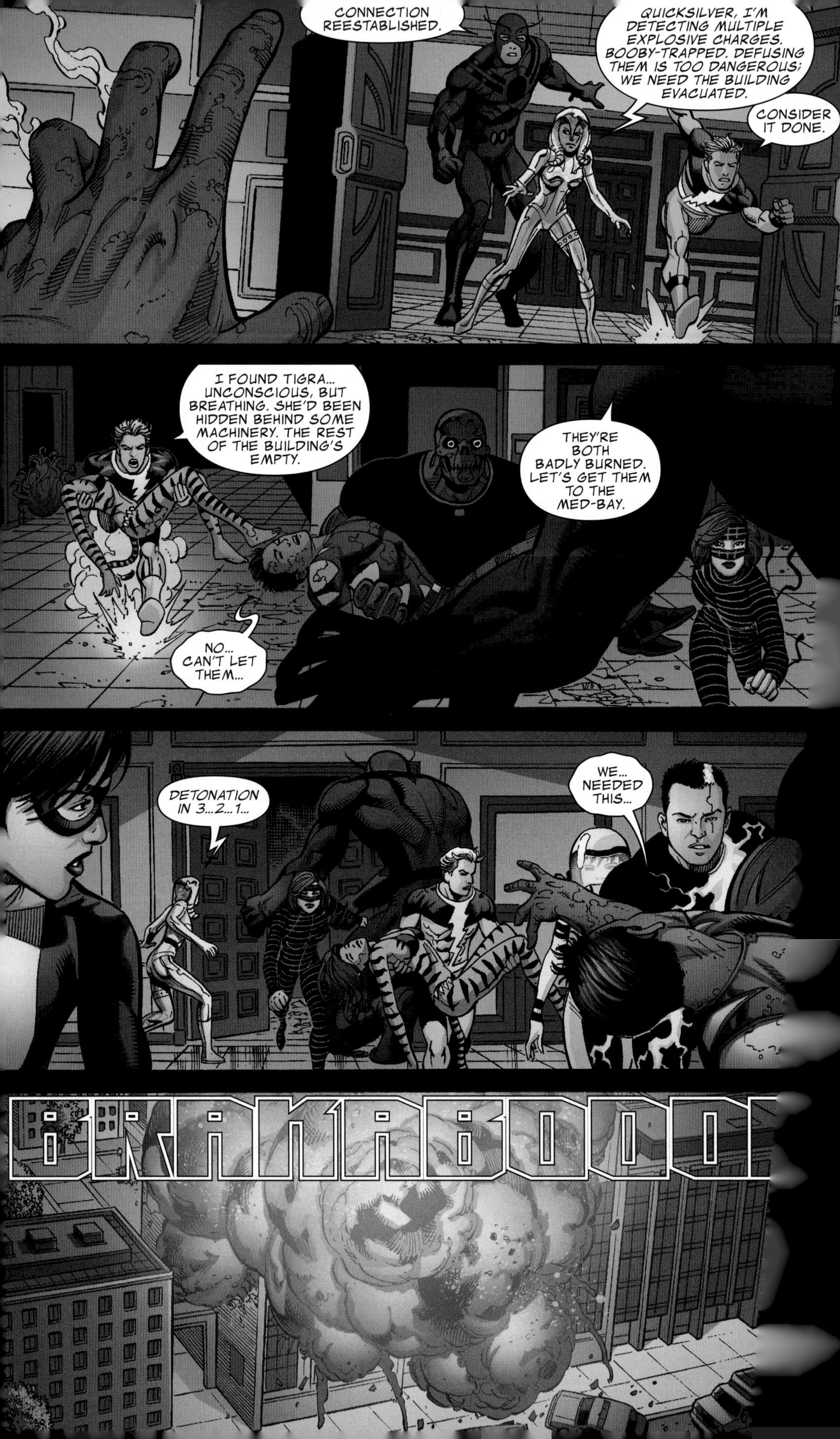
CONNECTION REESTABLISHED.
QUICKSILVER, I'M DETECTING MULTIPLE EXPLOSIVE CHARGES. BOOBY-TRAPPED. DEFUSING THEM IS TOO DANGEROUS; WE NEED THE BUILDING EVACUATED.
CONSIDER IT DONE.
I FOUND TIGRA... UNCONSCIOUS, BUT BREATHING. SHE'D BEEN HIDDEN BEHIND SOME MACHINERY. THE REST OF THE BUILDING'S EMPTY.
THEY'RE BOTH BADLY BURNED. LET'S GET THEM TO THE MED-BAY.
NO... CAN'T LET THEM...
DETONATION IN 3...2...1...
WE... NEEDED THIS...

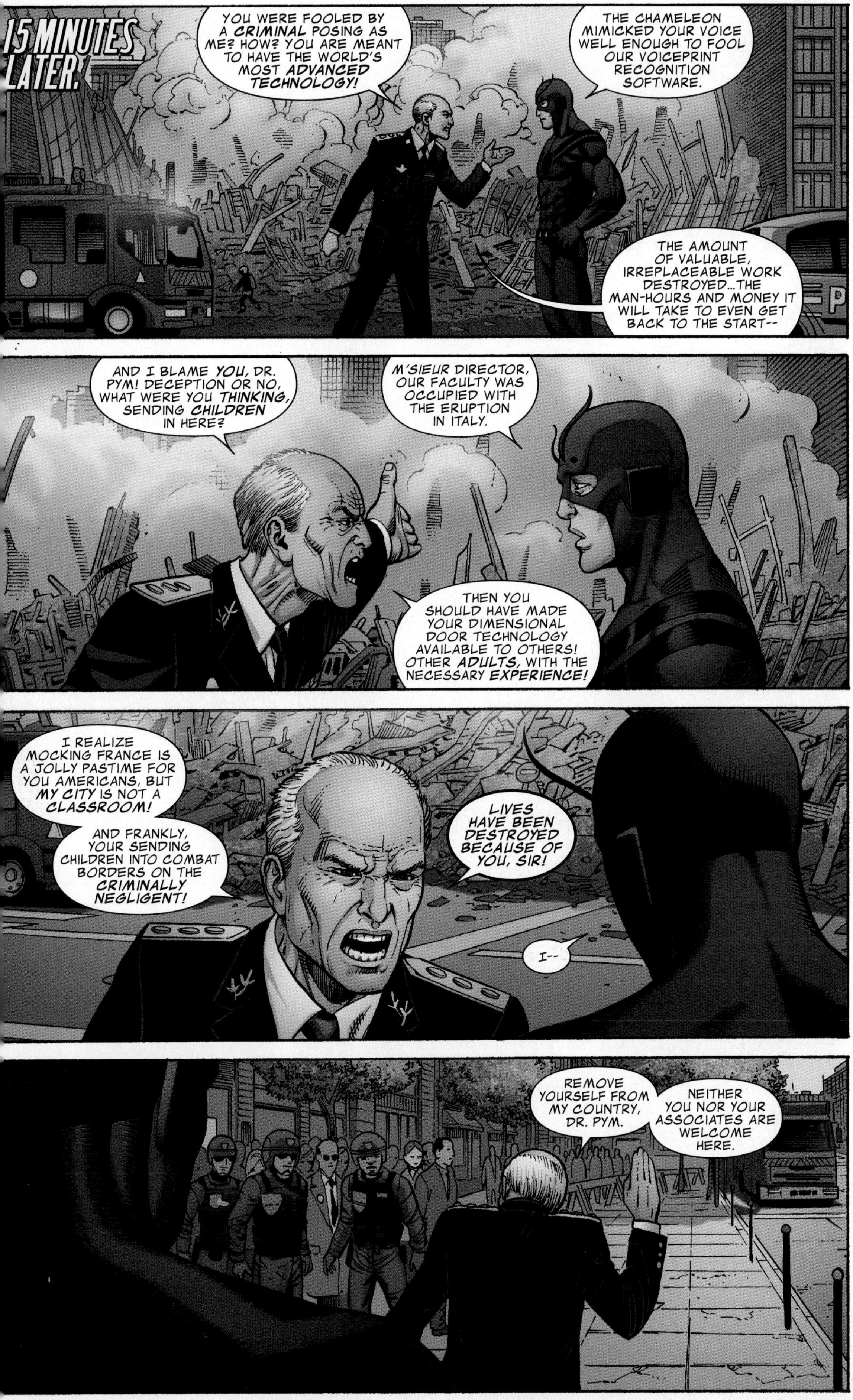
15 MINUTES LATER:
YOU WERE FOOLED BY A CRIMINAL POSING AS ME? HOW? YOU ARE MEANT TO HAVE THE WORLD'S MOST ADVANCED TECHNOLOGY!
THE CHAMELEON MIMICKED YOUR VOICE WELL ENOUGH TO FOOL OUR VOICEPRINT RECOGNITION SOFTWARE.
THE AMOUNT OF VALUABLE, IRREPLACEABLE WORK DESTROYED...THE MAN-HOURS AND MONEY IT WILL TAKE TO EVEN GET BACK TO THE START--
AND I BLAME YOU, DR. PYM! DECEPTION OR NO, WHAT WERE YOU THINKING, SENDING CHILDREN IN HERE?
M'SIEUR DIRECTOR, OUR FACULTY WAS OCCUPIED WITH THE ERUPTION IN ITALY.
THEN YOU SHOULD HAVE MADE YOUR DIMENSIONAL DOOR TECHNOLOGY AVAILABLE TO OTHERS! OTHER ADULTS, WITH THE NECESSARY EXPERIENCE!
I REALIZE MOCKING FRANCE IS A JOLLY PASTIME FOR YOU AMERICANS, BUT MY CITY IS NOT A CLASSROOM!
AND FRANKLY, YOUR SENDING CHILDREN INTO COMBAT BORDERS ON THE CRIMINALLY NEGLIGENT!
LIVES HAVE BEEN DESTROYED BECAUSE OF YOU, SIR!
I--
REMOVE YOURSELF FROM MY COUNTRY, DR. PYM.
NEITHER YOU NOR YOUR ASSOCIATES ARE WELCOME HERE.

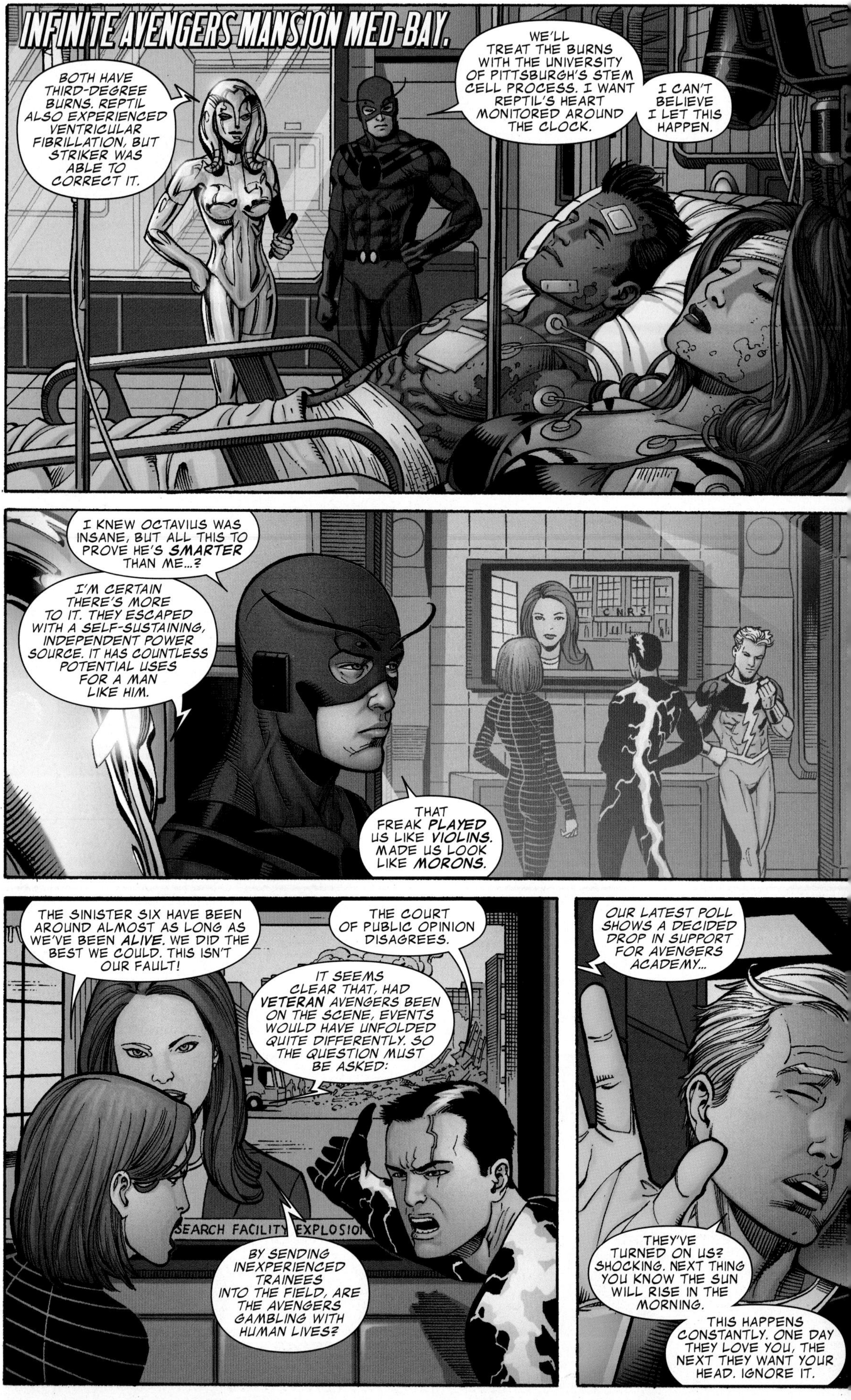
INFINITE AVENGERS MANSION MED-BAY.
BOTH HAVE THIRD-DEGREE BURNS. REPTIL ALSO EXPERIENCED VENTRICULAR FIBRILLATION, BUT STRIKER WAS ABLE TO CORRECT IT.
WE'LL TREAT THE BURNS WITH THE UNIVERSITY OF PITTSBURGH'S STEM CELL PROCESS. I WANT REPTIL'S HEART MONITORED AROUND THE CLOCK.
I CAN'T BELIEVE I LET THIS HAPPEN.
I KNEW OCTAVIUS WAS INSANE, BUT ALL THIS TO PROVE HE'S SMARTER THAN ME...?
I'M CERTAIN THERE'S MORE TO IT. THEY ESCAPED WITH A SELF-SUSTAINING, INDEPENDENT POWER SOURCE. IT HAS COUNTLESS POTENTIAL USES FOR A MAN LIKE HIM.
CNRS
THAT FREAK PLAYED US LIKE VIOLINS. MADE US LOOK LIKE MORONS.
THE SINISTER SIX HAVE BEEN AROUND ALMOST AS LONG AS WE'VE BEEN ALIVE. WE DID THE BEST WE COULD. THIS ISN'T OUR FAULT!
THE COURT OF PUBLIC OPINION DISAGREES.
IT SEEMS CLEAR THAT, HAD VETERAN AVENGERS BEEN ON THE SCENE, EVENTS WOULD HAVE UNFOLDED QUITE DIFFERENTLY. SO THE QUESTION MUST BE ASKED:
SEARCH FACILITY EXPLOSIO
BY SENDING INEXPERIENCED TRAINEES INTO THE FIELD, ARE THE AVENGERS GAMBLING WITH HUMAN LIVES?
OUR LATEST POLL SHOWS A DECIDED DROP IN SUPPORT FOR AVENGERS ACADEMY...
THEY'VE TURNED ON US? SHOCKING. NEXT THING YOU KNOW THE SUN WILL RISE IN THE MORNING.
THIS HAPPENS CONSTANTLY. ONE DAY THEY LOVE YOU, THE NEXT THEY WANT YOUR HEAD. IGNORE IT.

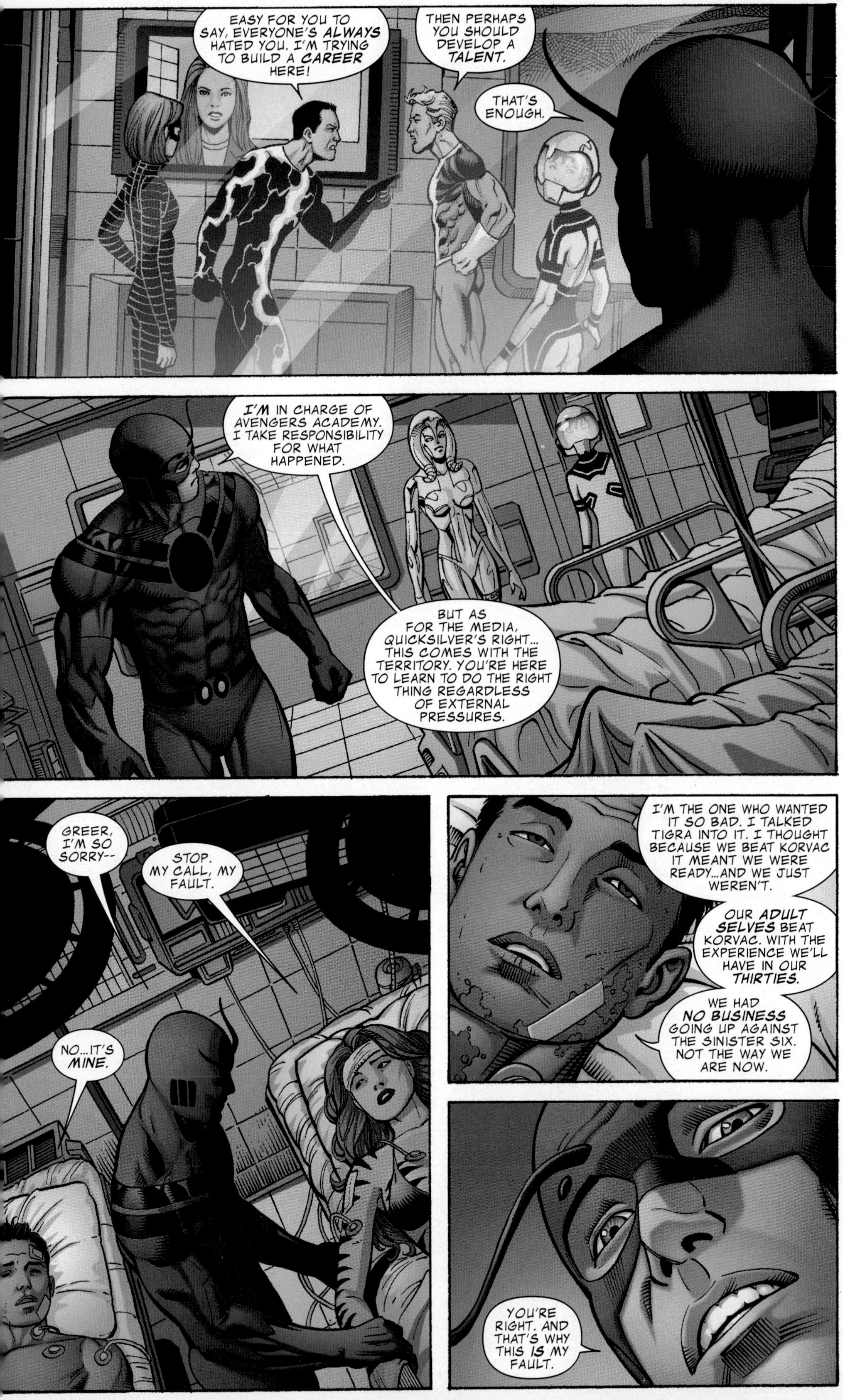

EASY FOR YOU TO SAY, EVERYONE'S ALWAYS HATED YOU. I'M TRYING TO BUILD A CAREER HERE!
THEN PERHAPS YOU SHOULD DEVELOP A TALENT.
THAT'S ENOUGH.
I'M IN CHARGE OF AVENGERS ACADEMY. I TAKE RESPONSIBILITY FOR WHAT HAPPENED.
BUT AS FOR THE MEDIA, QUICKSILVER'S RIGHT... THIS COMES WITH THE TERRITORY. YOU'RE HERE TO LEARN TO DO THE RIGHT THING REGARDLESS OF EXTERNAL PRESSURES.
GREER, I'M SO SORRY--
STOP. MY CALL, MY FAULT.
NO...IT'S MINE.
I'M THE ONE WHO WANTED IT SO BAD. I TALKED TIGRA INTO IT. I THOUGHT BECAUSE WE BEAT KORVAC IT MEANT WE WERE READY...AND WE JUST WEREN'T.
OUR ADULT SELVES BEAT KORVAC. WITH THE EXPERIENCE WE'LL HAVE IN OUR THIRTIES.
WE HAD NO BUSINESS GOING UP AGAINST THE SINISTER SIX. NOT THE WAY WE ARE NOW.
YOU'RE RIGHT. AND THAT'S WHY THIS IS MY FAULT.

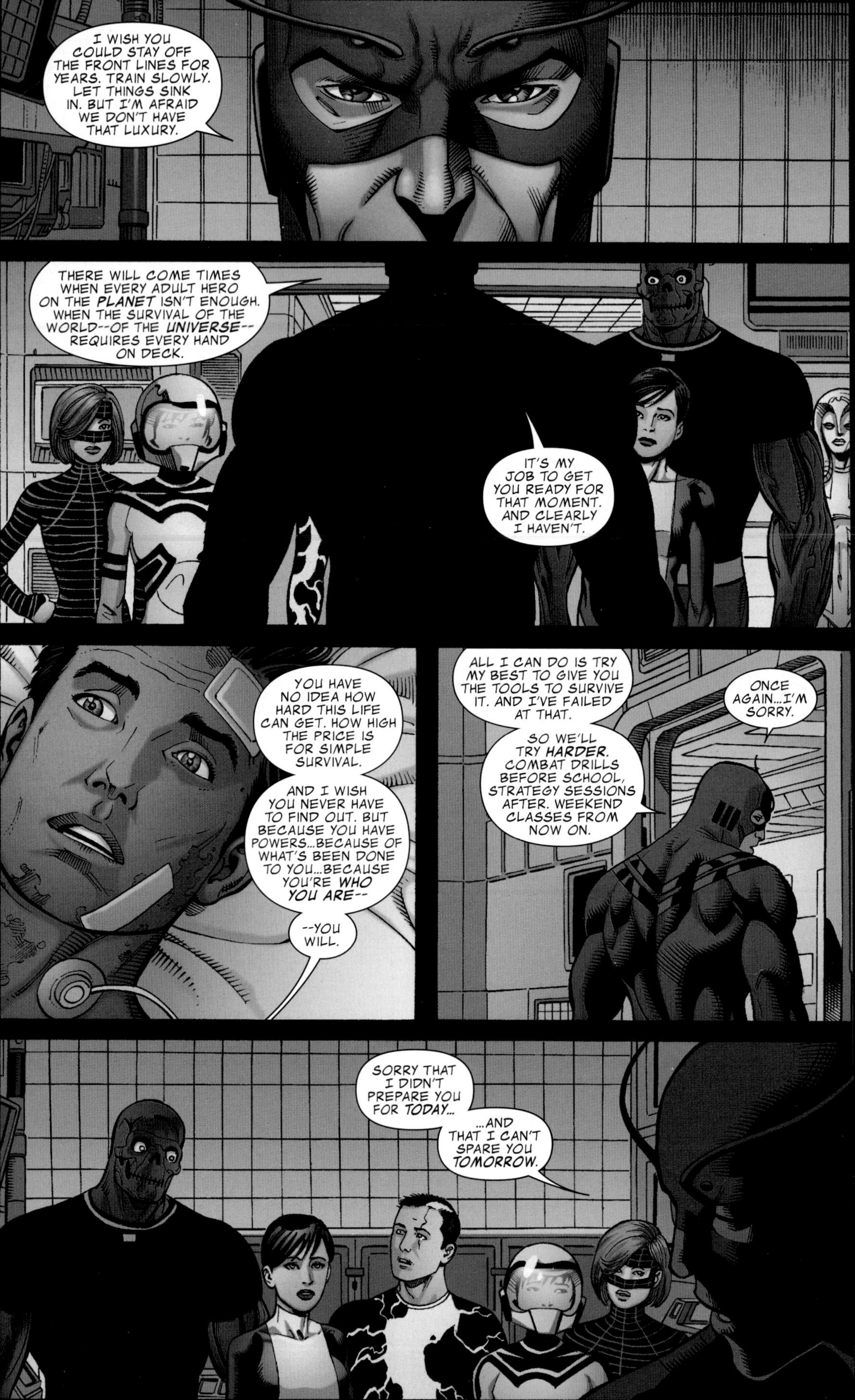
I WISH YOU COULD STAY OFF THE FRONT LINES FOR YEARS. TRAIN SLOWLY. LET THINGS SINK IN. BUT I'M AFRAID WE DON'T HAVE THAT LUXURY.
THERE WILL COME TIMES WHEN EVERY ADULT HERO ON THE PLANET ISN'T ENOUGH. WHEN THE SURVIVAL OF THE WORLD--OF THE UNIVERSE-- REQUIRES EVERY HAND ON DECK.
IT'S MY JOB TO GET YOU READY FOR THAT MOMENT. AND CLEARLY I HAVEN'T.
YOU HAVE NO IDEA HOW HARD THIS LIFE CAN GET. HOW HIGH THE PRICE IS FOR SIMPLE SURVIVAL.
AND I WISH YOU NEVER HAVE TO FIND OUT. BUT BECAUSE YOU HAVE POWERS...BECAUSE OF WHAT'S BEEN DONE TO YOU...BECAUSE YOU'RE WHO YOU ARE--
--YOU WILL.
ALL I CAN DO IS TRY MY BEST TO GIVE YOU THE TOOLS TO SURVIVE IT. AND I'VE FAILED AT THAT.
SO WE'LL TRY HARDER. COMBAT DRILLS BEFORE SCHOOL, STRATEGY SESSIONS AFTER. WEEKEND CLASSES FROM NOW ON.
ONCE AGAIN...I'M SORRY.
SORRY THAT I DIDN'T PREPARE YOU FOR TODAY...
...AND THAT I CAN'T SPARE YOU TOMORROW.

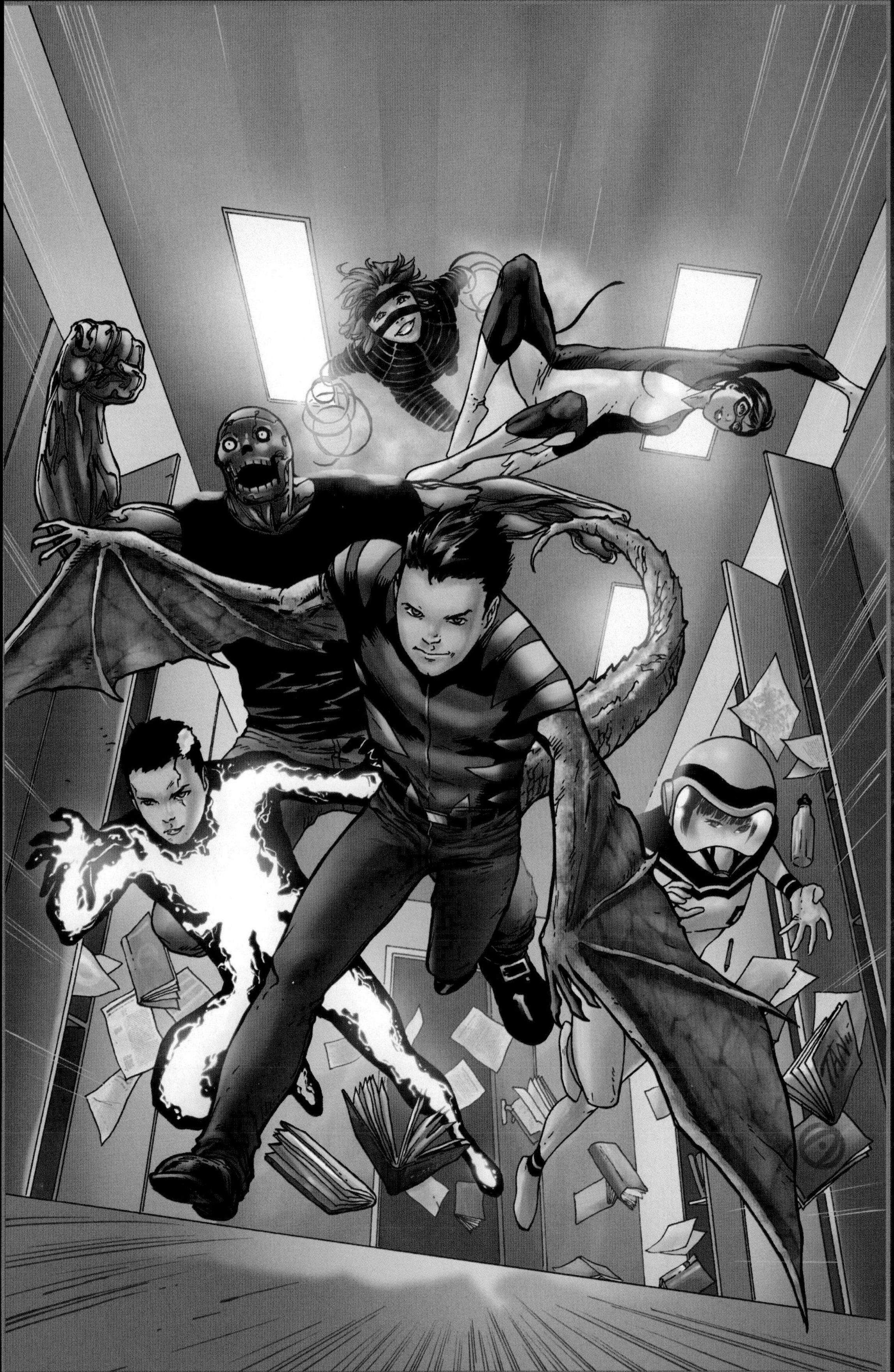

AVENGERS ACADEMY #14.1

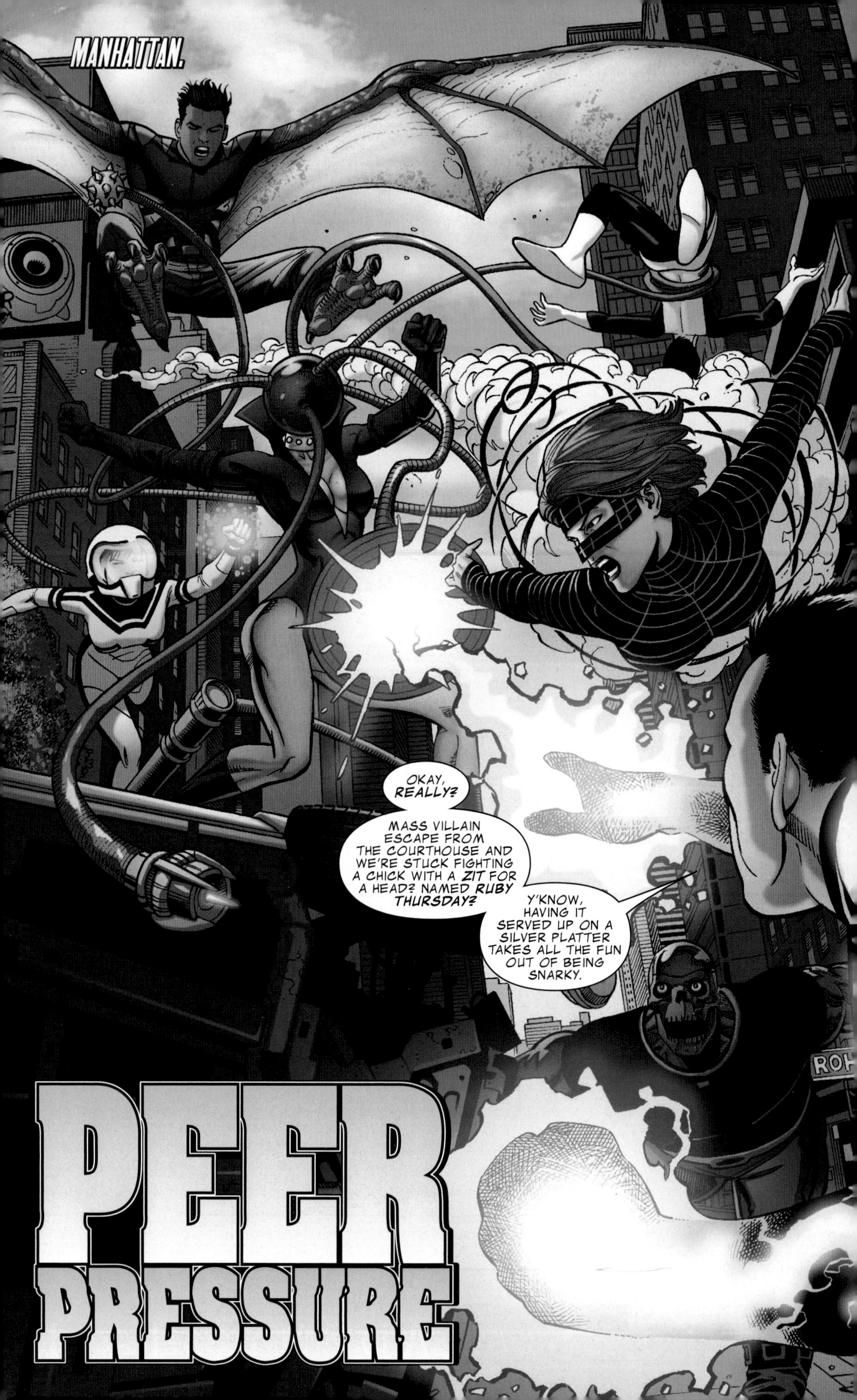
MANHATTAN.
OKAY, REALLY?
MASS VILLAIN ESCAPE FROM THE COURTHOUSE AND WE'RE STUCK FIGHTING A CHICK WITH A ZIT FOR A HEAD? NAMED RUBY THURSDAY?
Y'KNOW, HAVING IT SERVED UP ON A SILVER PLATTER TAKES ALL THE FUN OUT OF BEING SNARKY.
PEER PRESSURE

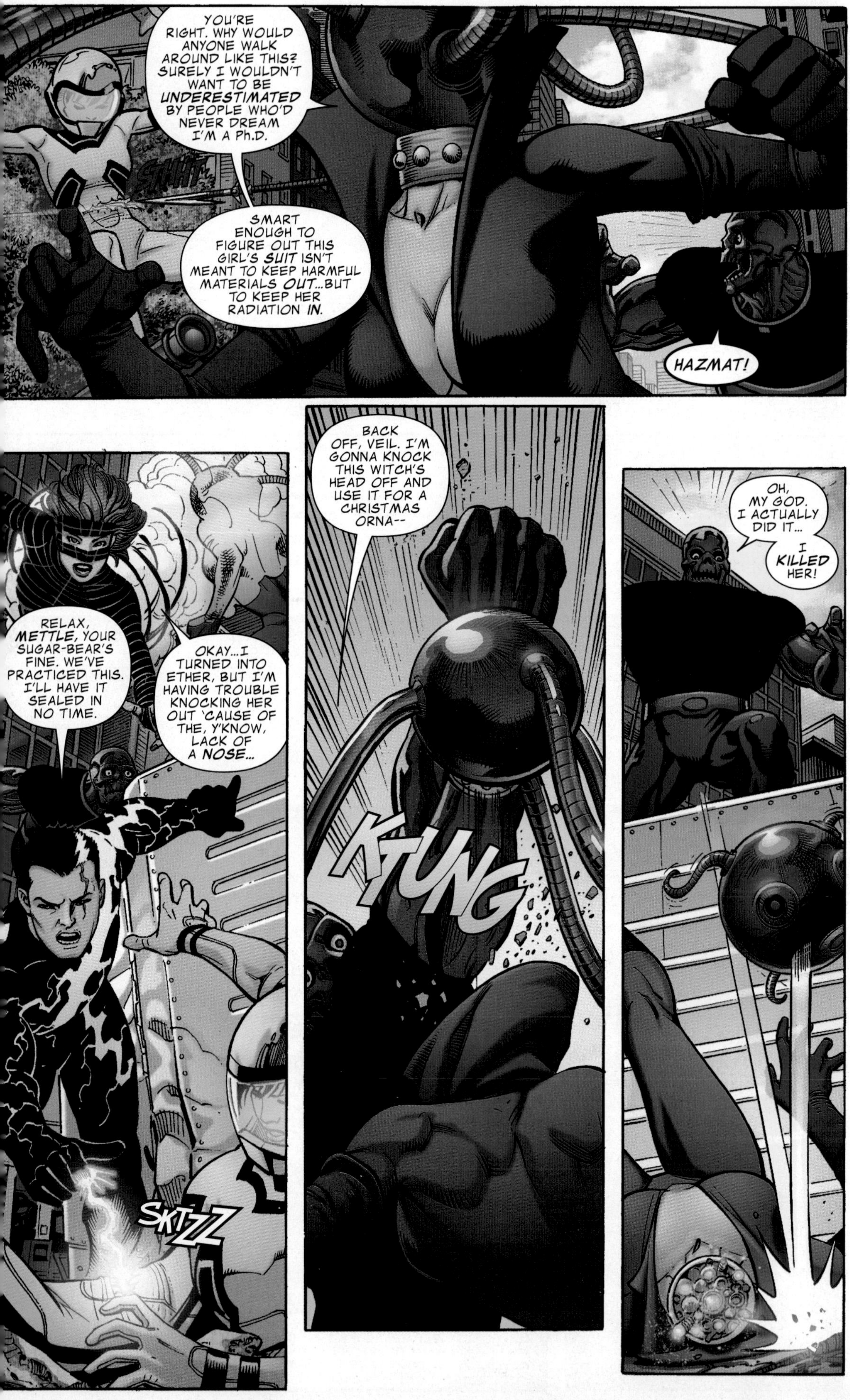
YOU'RE RIGHT. WHY WOULD ANYONE WALK AROUND LIKE THIS? SURELY I WOULDN'T WANT TO BE UNDERESTIMATED BY PEOPLE WHO'D NEVER DREAM I'M A Ph.D.
SHHT
SMART ENOUGH TO FIGURE OUT THIS GIRL'S SUIT ISN'T MEANT TO KEEP HARMFUL MATERIALS OUT...BUT TO KEEP HER RADIATION IN.
HAZMAT!
RELAX, METTLE, YOUR SUGAR-BEAR'S FINE. WE'VE PRACTICED THIS. I'LL HAVE IT SEALED IN NO TIME.
OKAY...I TURNED INTO ETHER, BUT I'M HAVING TROUBLE KNOCKING HER OUT 'CAUSE OF THE, Y'KNOW, LACK OF A NOSE...
SKTZZZ
BACK OFF, VEIL. I'M GONNA KNOCK THIS WITCH'S HEAD OFF AND USE IT FOR A CHRISTMAS ORNA--
KTUNG
OH, MY GOD. I ACTUALLY DID IT... I KILLED HER!

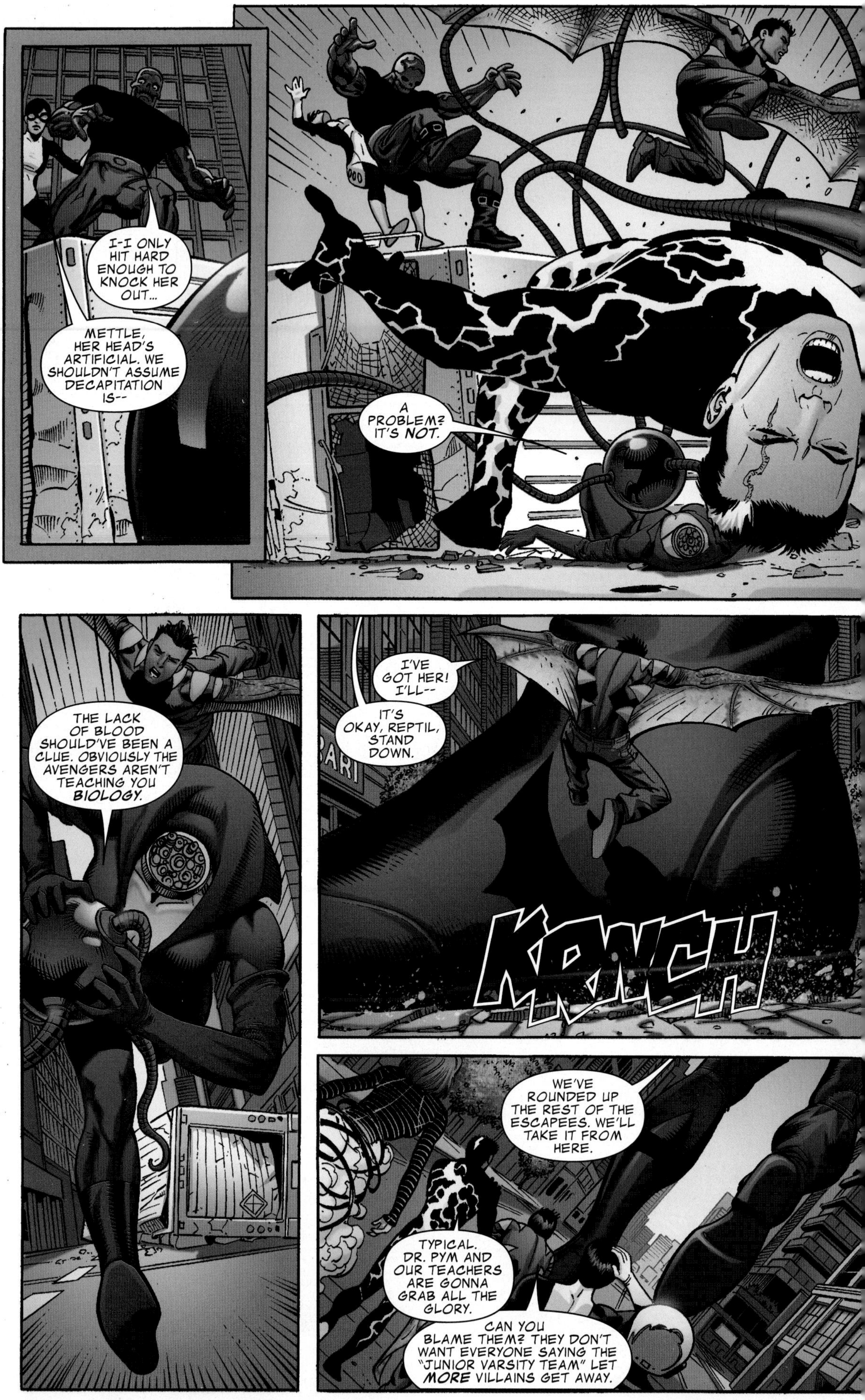
I-I ONLY HIT HARD ENOUGH TO KNOCK HER OUT...
METTLE, HER HEAD'S ARTIFICIAL. WE SHOULDN'T ASSUME DECAPITATION IS--
A PROBLEM? IT'S **NOT**.
THE LACK OF BLOOD SHOULD'VE BEEN A CLUE. OBVIOUSLY THE AVENGERS AREN'T TEACHING YOU ***BIOLOGY***.
I'VE GOT HER! I'LL--
IT'S OKAY, REPTIL, STAND DOWN.
KRNCH
WE'VE ROUNDED UP THE REST OF THE ESCAPEES. WE'LL TAKE IT FROM HERE.
TYPICAL. DR. PYM AND OUR TEACHERS ARE GONNA GRAB ALL THE GLORY.
CAN YOU BLAME THEM? THEY DON'T WANT EVERYONE SAYING THE "JUNIOR VARSITY TEAM" LET ***MORE*** VILLAINS GET AWAY.

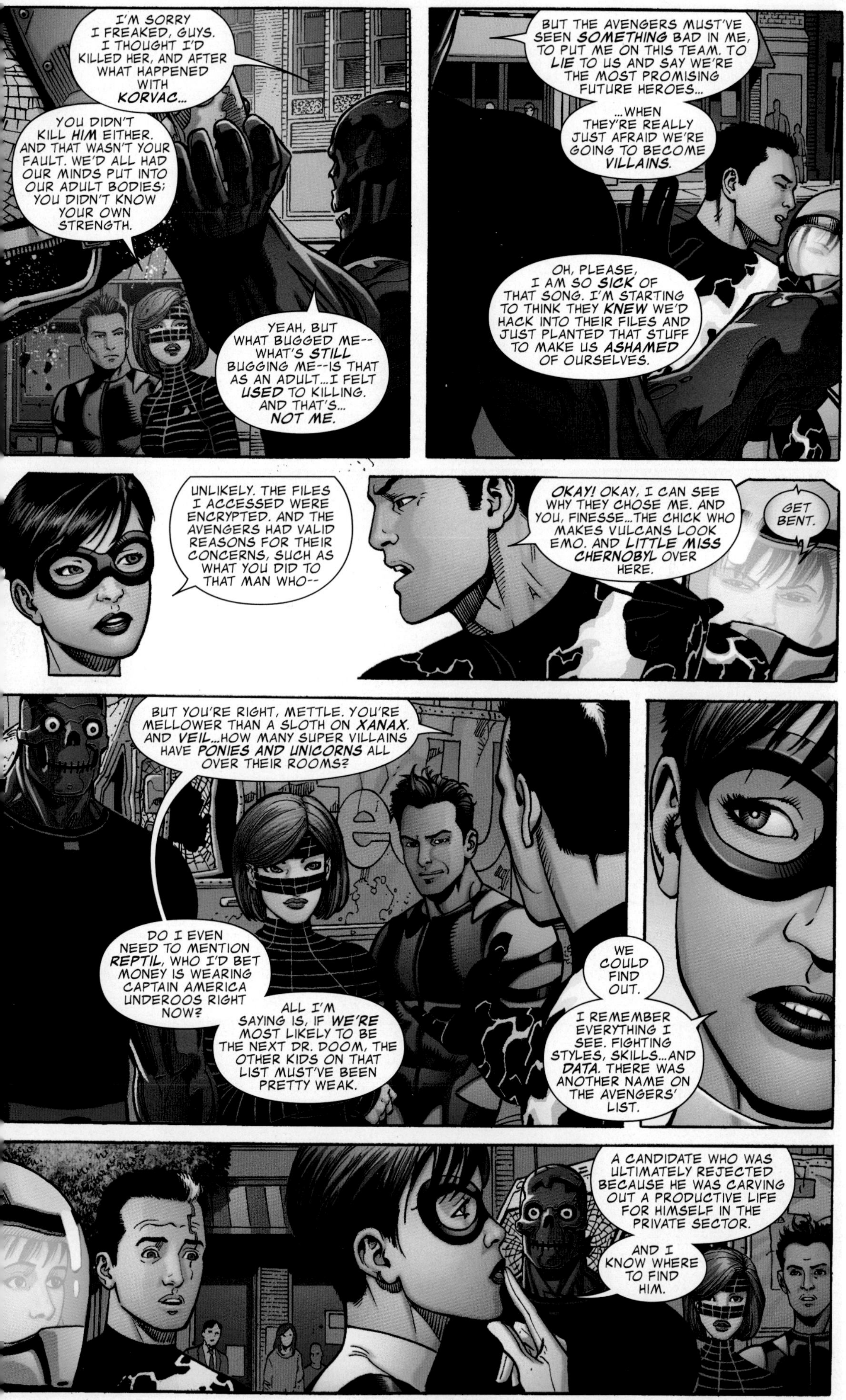

I'M SORRY I FREAKED, GUYS. I THOUGHT I'D KILLED HER, AND AFTER WHAT HAPPENED WITH KORVAC...
YOU DIDN'T KILL HIM EITHER. AND THAT WASN'T YOUR FAULT. WE'D ALL HAD OUR MINDS PUT INTO OUR ADULT BODIES; YOU DIDN'T KNOW YOUR OWN STRENGTH.
YEAH, BUT WHAT BUGGED ME--WHAT'S STILL BUGGING ME--IS THAT AS AN ADULT...I FELT USED TO KILLING. AND THAT'S... NOT ME.
BUT THE AVENGERS MUST'VE SEEN SOMETHING BAD IN ME, TO PUT ME ON THIS TEAM. TO LIE TO US AND SAY WE'RE THE MOST PROMISING FUTURE HEROES...
...WHEN THEY'RE REALLY JUST AFRAID WE'RE GOING TO BECOME VILLAINS.
OH, PLEASE, I AM SO SICK OF THAT SONG. I'M STARTING TO THINK THEY KNEW WE'D HACK INTO THEIR FILES AND JUST PLANTED THAT STUFF TO MAKE US ASHAMED OF OURSELVES.
UNLIKELY. THE FILES I ACCESSED WERE ENCRYPTED. AND THE AVENGERS HAD VALID REASONS FOR THEIR CONCERNS, SUCH AS WHAT YOU DID TO THAT MAN WHO--
OKAY! OKAY, I CAN SEE WHY THEY CHOSE ME. AND YOU, FINESSE...THE CHICK WHO MAKES VULCANS LOOK EMO. AND LITTLE MISS CHERNOBYL OVER HERE.
GET BENT.
BUT YOU'RE RIGHT, METTLE. YOU'RE MELLOWER THAN A SLOTH ON XANAX. AND VEIL...HOW MANY SUPER VILLAINS HAVE PONIES AND UNICORNS ALL OVER THEIR ROOMS?
DO I EVEN NEED TO MENTION REPTIL, WHO I'D BET MONEY IS WEARING CAPTAIN AMERICA UNDEROOS RIGHT NOW?
ALL I'M SAYING IS, IF WE'RE MOST LIKELY TO BE THE NEXT DR. DOOM, THE OTHER KIDS ON THAT LIST MUST'VE BEEN PRETTY WEAK.
WE COULD FIND OUT.
I REMEMBER EVERYTHING I SEE. FIGHTING STYLES, SKILLS...AND DATA. THERE WAS ANOTHER NAME ON THE AVENGERS' LIST.
A CANDIDATE WHO WAS ULTIMATELY REJECTED BECAUSE HE WAS CARVING OUT A PRODUCTIVE LIFE FOR HIMSELF IN THE PRIVATE SECTOR.
AND I KNOW WHERE TO FIND HIM.

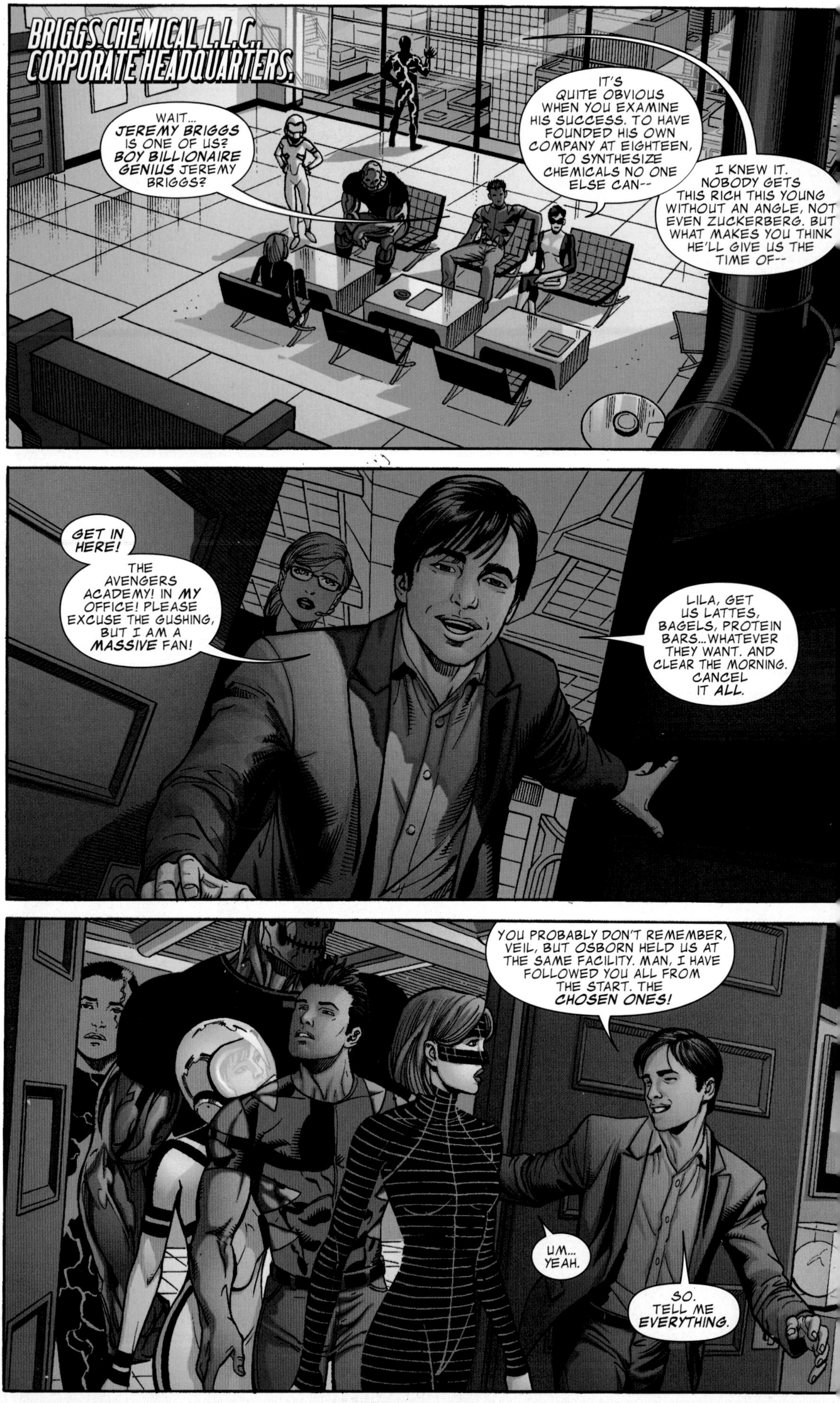
BRIGGS CHEMICAL L.L.C., CORPORATE HEADQUARTERS.
WAIT... JEREMY BRIGGS IS ONE OF US? BOY BILLIONAIRE GENIUS JEREMY BRIGGS?
IT'S QUITE OBVIOUS WHEN YOU EXAMINE HIS SUCCESS. TO HAVE FOUNDED HIS OWN COMPANY AT EIGHTEEN, TO SYNTHESIZE CHEMICALS NO ONE ELSE CAN--
I KNEW IT. NOBODY GETS THIS RICH THIS YOUNG WITHOUT AN ANGLE, NOT EVEN ZUCKERBERG. BUT WHAT MAKES YOU THINK HE'LL GIVE US THE TIME OF--
GET IN HERE!
THE AVENGERS ACADEMY! IN MY OFFICE! PLEASE EXCUSE THE GUSHING, BUT I AM A MASSIVE FAN!
LILA, GET US LATTES, BAGELS, PROTEIN BARS...WHATEVER THEY WANT. AND CLEAR THE MORNING. CANCEL IT ALL.
YOU PROBABLY DON'T REMEMBER, VEIL, BUT OSBORN HELD US AT THE SAME FACILITY. MAN, I HAVE FOLLOWED YOU ALL FROM THE START. THE CHOSEN ONES!
UM... YEAH.
SO. TELL ME EVERYTHING.

...SO AFTER OSBORN'S INITIATIVE PROGRAM WAS SHUT DOWN, I WASN'T SURE WHAT TO DO WITH MYSELF. I MEAN, HE'D JACKED UP MY POWERS. A *LOT*.

I CAN CHANGE THE CHEMICAL MAKEUP OF MOST ANYTHING. THE MORE COMPLEX IT IS, THE TOUGHER IT GETS, BUT I'M STILL LEARNING.

I THOUGHT ABOUT CALLING MYSELF *"THE ALCHEMIST"*... PUTTING ON A COSTUME. EVEN HAD ONE MADE. THEN I TOOK ONE LOOK AT MYSELF IN IT AND FELL OVER *LAUGHING*.

I MEAN, I HATE WHAT NORMAN OSBORN DID TO US... ROUNDING UP KIDS WITH POWERS, EXPERIMENTING ON US...IT WAS TORTURE. BUT I HAD TO ADMIRE HIS *VISION*.

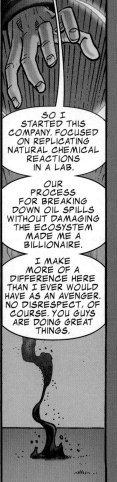

HE WANTED TO CHANGE THE WAY THE *WORLD* WORKS. HIS PROBLEM WAS HE STILL THOUGHT IN TERMS OF TIGHTS AND CAPES. ACTION FIGURES SMASHING INTO EACH OTHER.

NOW, ME... I DIDN'T GRADUATE M.I.T. AT SEVENTEEN BY THINKING *INSIDE* THE BOX.

SO I STARTED THIS COMPANY. FOCUSED ON REPLICATING NATURAL CHEMICAL REACTIONS IN A LAB.

OUR PROCESS FOR BREAKING DOWN OIL SPILLS WITHOUT DAMAGING THE ECOSYSTEM MADE ME A BILLIONAIRE.

I MAKE MORE OF A DIFFERENCE HERE THAN I EVER WOULD HAVE AS AN AVENGER. NO DISRESPECT, OF COURSE. YOU GUYS ARE DOING GREAT THINGS.

YEAH... FIGHTING WOMEN WHOSE HEADS ARE MADE OF RED SILLY PUTTY. AND LETTING THEM GET *AWAY*.

I REMEMBER SEEING OTHER KIDS AT OSBORN'S LAB. THEY HAD POWERS TOO. SOMETIMES I WONDER WHO'S BETTER OFF...

...US, RECRUITED TO AVENGERS ACADEMY... OR THEM, LEFT TO WORK OUT THEIR OWN LIVES?

WELL, I CAN SHOW YOU IF YOU WANT. I KEEP TRACK OF ALL THE ALUMS OF OSBORN U.

DON'T LOOK SO SURPRISED... WHEN YOU'RE RICH THE WORLD'S AN OPEN BOOK. COME BY AFTER CLASS NEXT WEEK. I'LL CLEAR SOME SPACE ON MY SCHEDULE.

WE'LL LOOK UP SOME OLD FRIENDS.

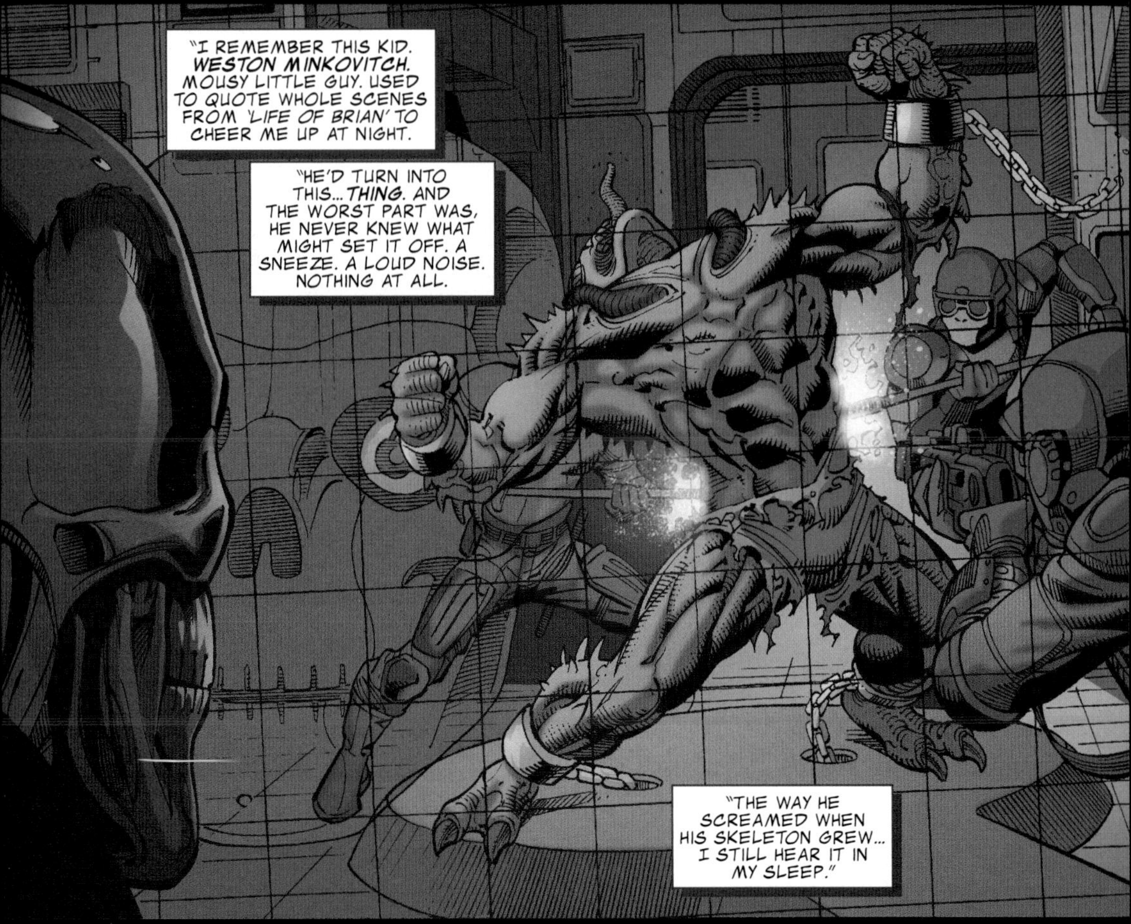
"I REMEMBER THIS KID. WESTON MINKOVITCH. MOUSY LITTLE GUY. USED TO QUOTE WHOLE SCENES FROM 'LIFE OF BRIAN' TO CHEER ME UP AT NIGHT.
"HE'D TURN INTO THIS... THING. AND THE WORST PART WAS, HE NEVER KNEW WHAT MIGHT SET IT OFF. A SNEEZE. A LOUD NOISE. NOTHING AT ALL.
"THE WAY HE SCREAMED WHEN HIS SKELETON GREW... I STILL HEAR IT IN MY SLEEP."
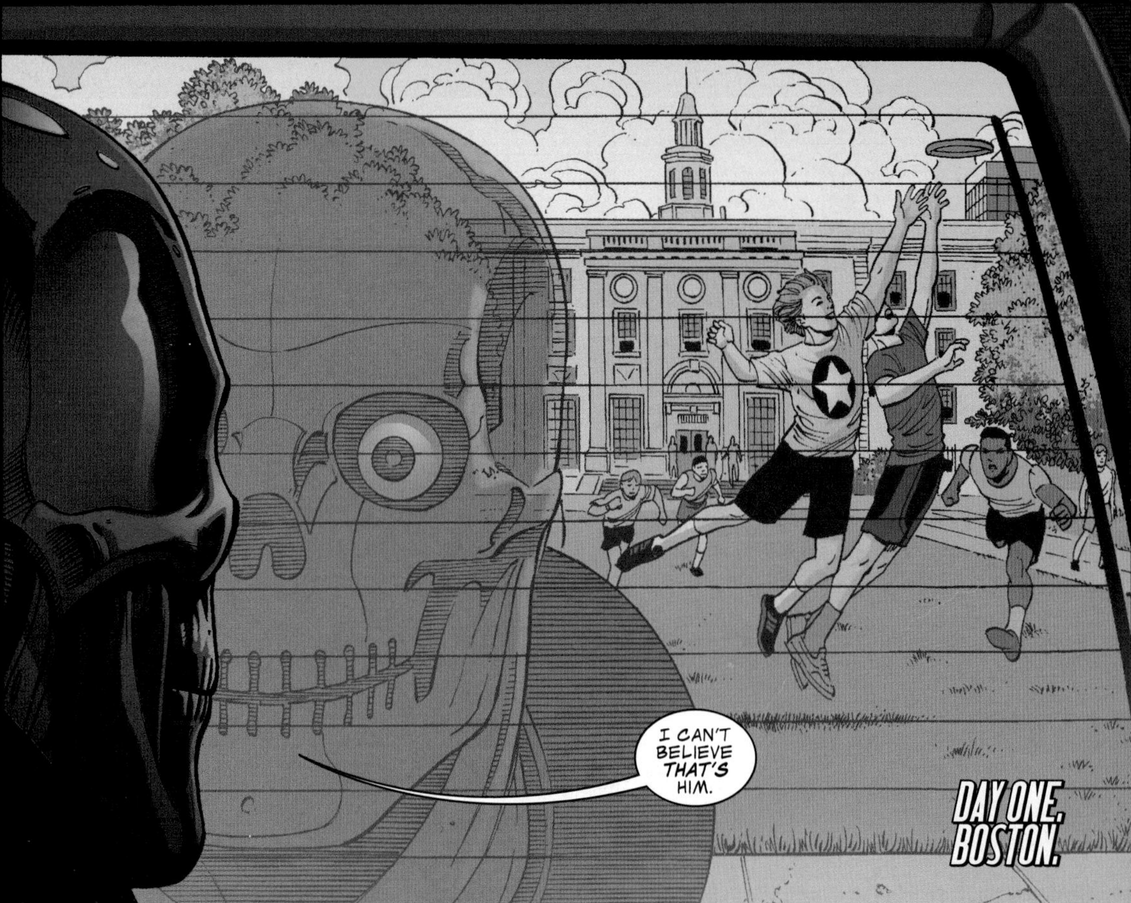
DAY ONE. BOSTON.
I CAN'T BELIEVE THAT'S HIM.

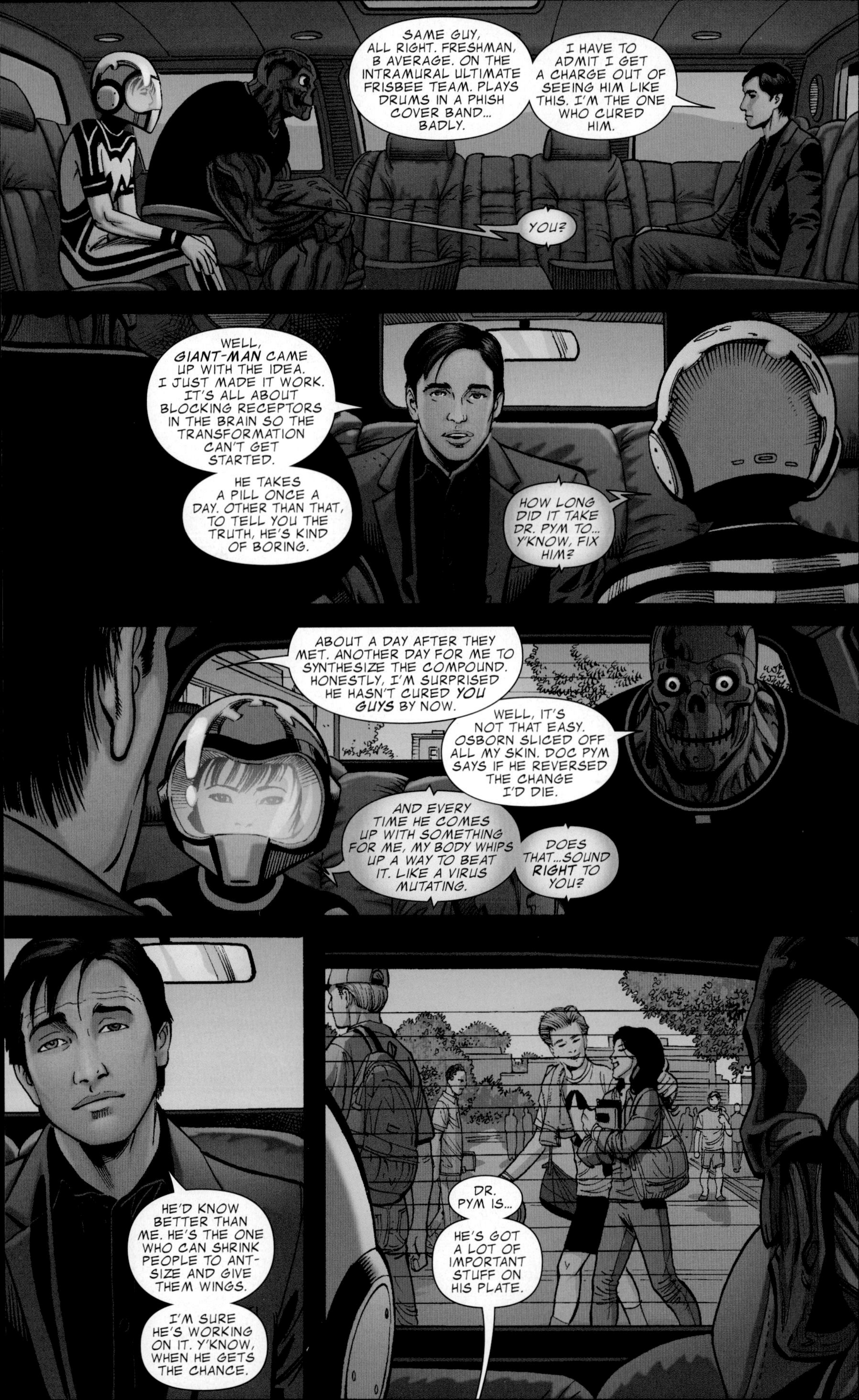
SAME GUY, ALL RIGHT. FRESHMAN, B AVERAGE. ON THE INTRAMURAL ULTIMATE FRISBEE TEAM. PLAYS DRUMS IN A PHISH COVER BAND... BADLY.
I HAVE TO ADMIT I GET A CHARGE OUT OF SEEING HIM LIKE THIS. I'M THE ONE WHO CURED HIM.
YOU?
WELL, GIANT-MAN CAME UP WITH THE IDEA. I JUST MADE IT WORK. IT'S ALL ABOUT BLOCKING RECEPTORS IN THE BRAIN SO THE TRANSFORMATION CAN'T GET STARTED.
HE TAKES A PILL ONCE A DAY. OTHER THAN THAT, TO TELL YOU THE TRUTH, HE'S KIND OF BORING.
HOW LONG DID IT TAKE DR. PYM TO... Y'KNOW, FIX HIM?
ABOUT A DAY AFTER THEY MET. ANOTHER DAY FOR ME TO SYNTHESIZE THE COMPOUND. HONESTLY, I'M SURPRISED HE HASN'T CURED YOU GUYS BY NOW.
WELL, IT'S NOT THAT EASY. OSBORN SLICED OFF ALL MY SKIN. DOC PYM SAYS IF HE REVERSED THE CHANGE I'D DIE.
AND EVERY TIME HE COMES UP WITH SOMETHING FOR ME, MY BODY WHIPS UP A WAY TO BEAT IT. LIKE A VIRUS MUTATING.
DOES THAT...SOUND RIGHT TO YOU?
HE'D KNOW BETTER THAN ME. HE'S THE ONE WHO CAN SHRINK PEOPLE TO ANT-SIZE AND GIVE THEM WINGS.
I'M SURE HE'S WORKING ON IT. Y'KNOW, WHEN HE GETS THE CHANCE.
DR. PYM IS...
HE'S GOT A LOT OF IMPORTANT STUFF ON HIS PLATE.

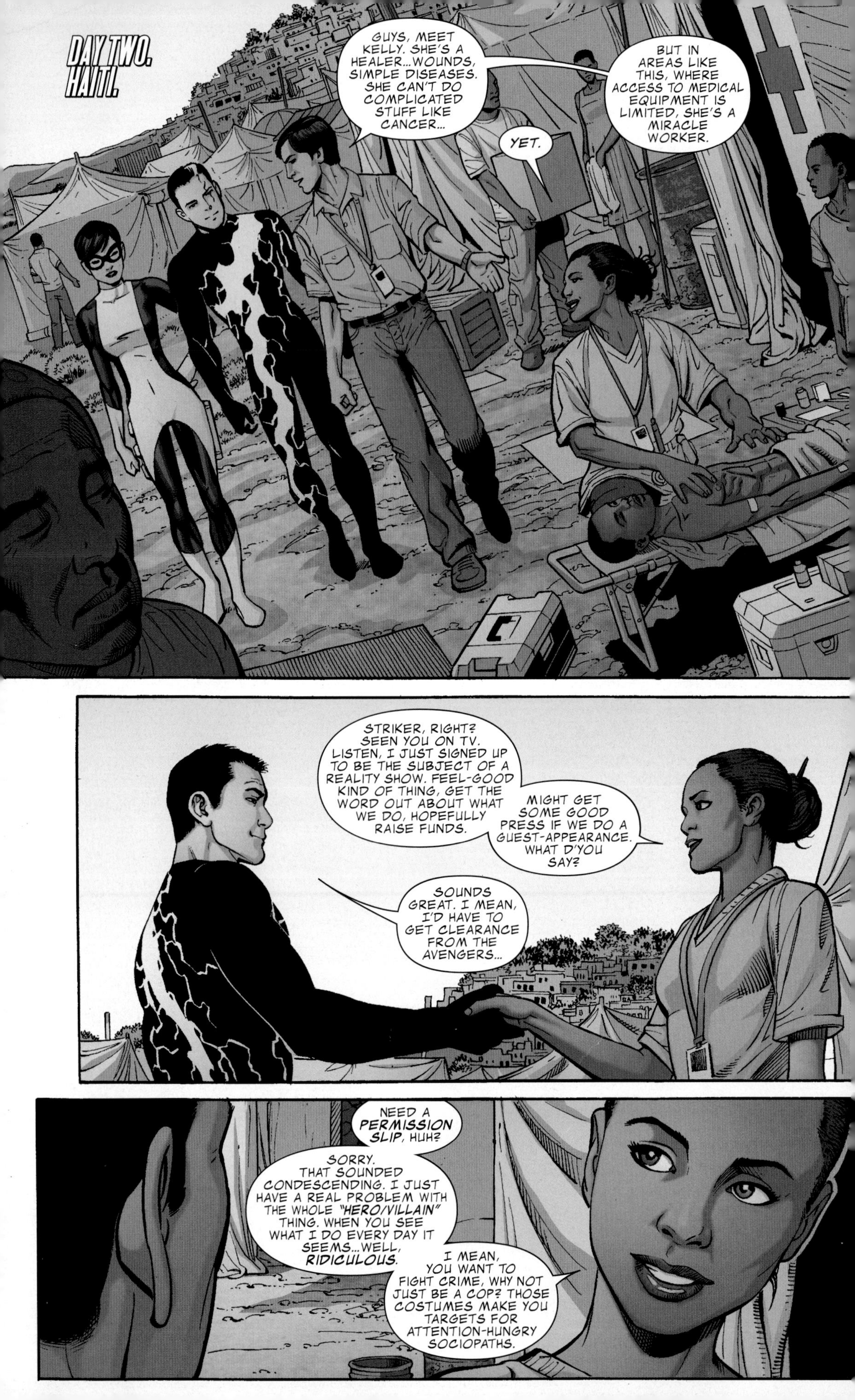
DAY TWO. HAITI.
GUYS, MEET KELLY. SHE'S A HEALER...WOUNDS, SIMPLE DISEASES. SHE CAN'T DO COMPLICATED STUFF LIKE CANCER...
YET.
BUT IN AREAS LIKE THIS, WHERE ACCESS TO MEDICAL EQUIPMENT IS LIMITED, SHE'S A MIRACLE WORKER.
STRIKER, RIGHT? SEEN YOU ON TV. LISTEN, I JUST SIGNED UP TO BE THE SUBJECT OF A REALITY SHOW. FEEL-GOOD KIND OF THING, GET THE WORD OUT ABOUT WHAT WE DO, HOPEFULLY RAISE FUNDS.
MIGHT GET SOME GOOD PRESS IF WE DO A GUEST-APPEARANCE. WHAT D'YOU SAY?
SOUNDS GREAT. I MEAN, I'D HAVE TO GET CLEARANCE FROM THE AVENGERS...
NEED A PERMISSION SLIP, HUH?
SORRY. THAT SOUNDED CONDESCENDING. I JUST HAVE A REAL PROBLEM WITH THE WHOLE "HERO/VILLAIN" THING. WHEN YOU SEE WHAT I DO EVERY DAY IT SEEMS...WELL, RIDICULOUS.
I MEAN, YOU WANT TO FIGHT CRIME, WHY NOT JUST BE A COP? THOSE COSTUMES MAKE YOU TARGETS FOR ATTENTION-HUNGRY SOCIOPATHS.

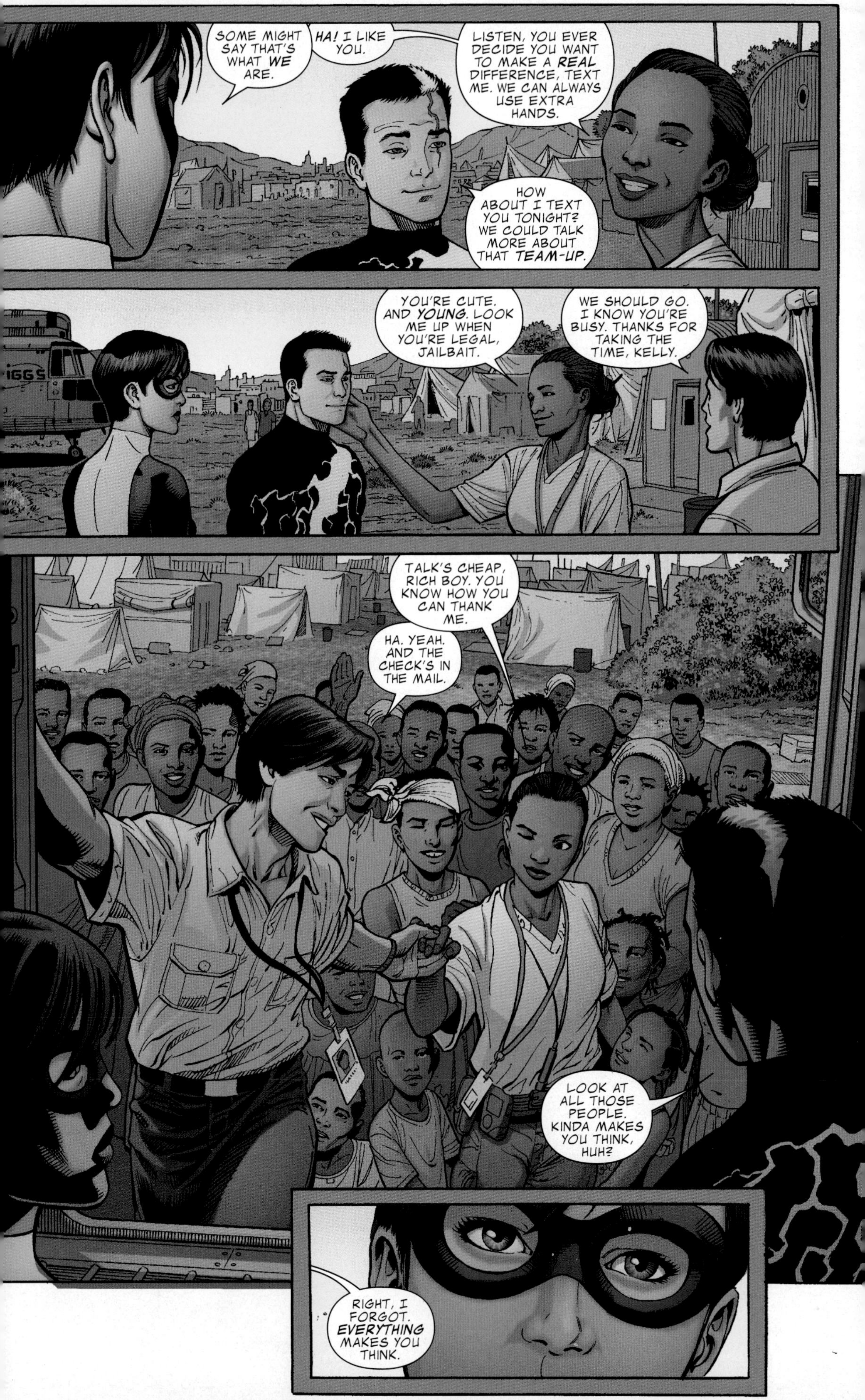
SOME MIGHT SAY THAT'S WHAT **WE** ARE.
HA! I LIKE YOU.
LISTEN, YOU EVER DECIDE YOU WANT TO MAKE A **REAL** DIFFERENCE, TEXT ME. WE CAN ALWAYS USE EXTRA HANDS.
HOW ABOUT I TEXT YOU TONIGHT? WE COULD TALK MORE ABOUT THAT **TEAM-UP**.
YOU'RE CUTE. AND **YOUNG**. LOOK ME UP WHEN YOU'RE LEGAL, JAILBAIT.
WE SHOULD GO. I KNOW YOU'RE BUSY. THANKS FOR TAKING THE TIME, KELLY.
TALK'S CHEAP, RICH BOY. YOU KNOW HOW YOU CAN THANK ME.
HA. YEAH. AND THE CHECK'S IN THE MAIL.
LOOK AT ALL THOSE PEOPLE. KINDA MAKES YOU THINK, HUH?
RIGHT, I FORGOT. **EVERYTHING** MAKES YOU THINK.

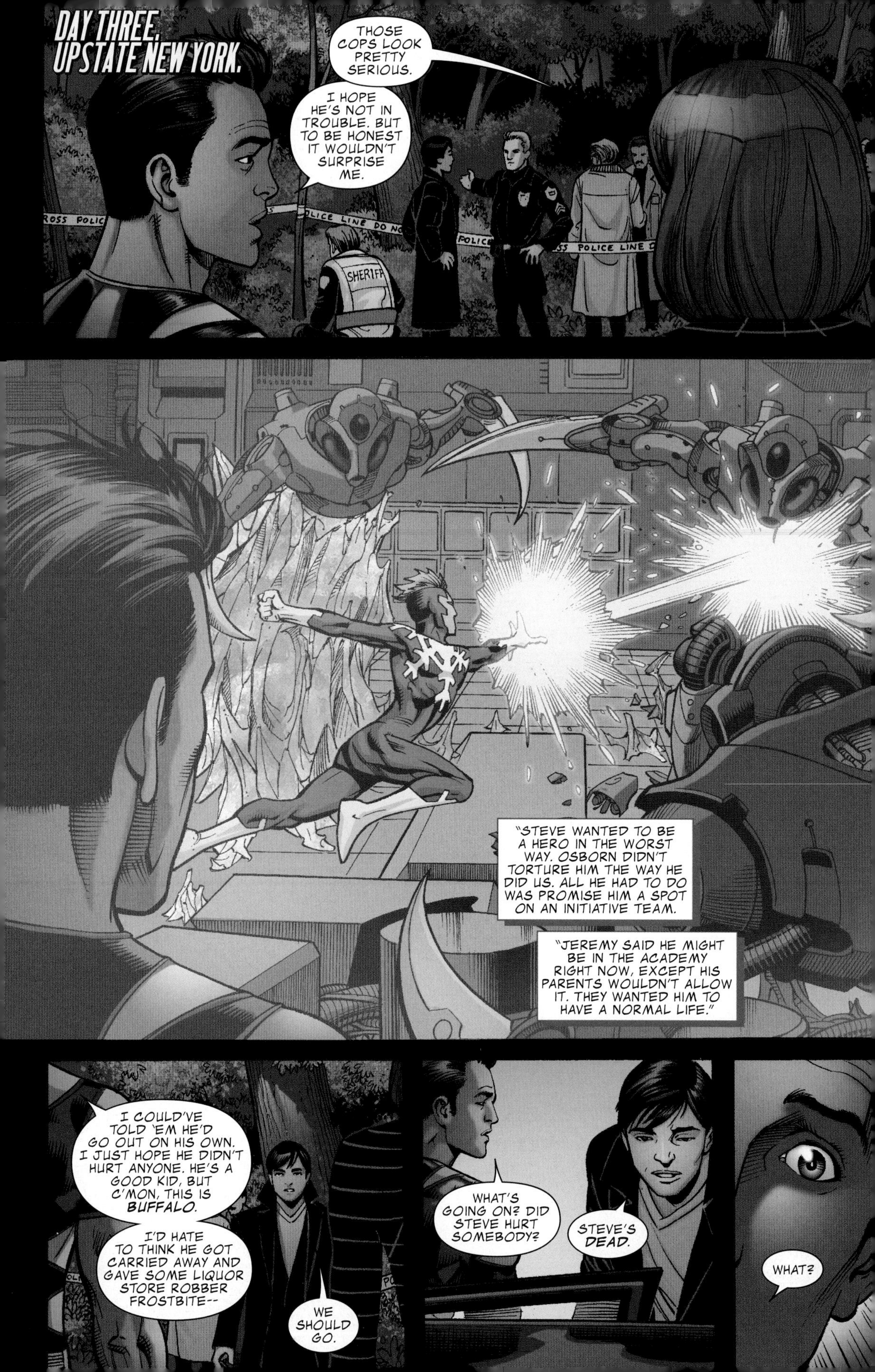
DAY THREE.
UPSTATE NEW YORK.
THOSE COPS LOOK PRETTY SERIOUS.
I HOPE HE'S NOT IN TROUBLE. BUT TO BE HONEST IT WOULDN'T SURPRISE ME.
POLICE LINE DO NOT CROSS
SHERIFF
"STEVE WANTED TO BE A HERO IN THE WORST WAY. OSBORN DIDN'T TORTURE HIM THE WAY HE DID US. ALL HE HAD TO DO WAS PROMISE HIM A SPOT ON AN INITIATIVE TEAM.
"JEREMY SAID HE MIGHT BE IN THE ACADEMY RIGHT NOW, EXCEPT HIS PARENTS WOULDN'T ALLOW IT. THEY WANTED HIM TO HAVE A NORMAL LIFE."
I COULD'VE TOLD 'EM HE'D GO OUT ON HIS OWN. I JUST HOPE HE DIDN'T HURT ANYONE. HE'S A GOOD KID, BUT C'MON, THIS IS BUFFALO.
I'D HATE TO THINK HE GOT CARRIED AWAY AND GAVE SOME LIQUOR STORE ROBBER FROSTBITE--
WE SHOULD GO.
WHAT'S GOING ON? DID STEVE HURT SOMEBODY?
STEVE'S DEAD.
WHAT?

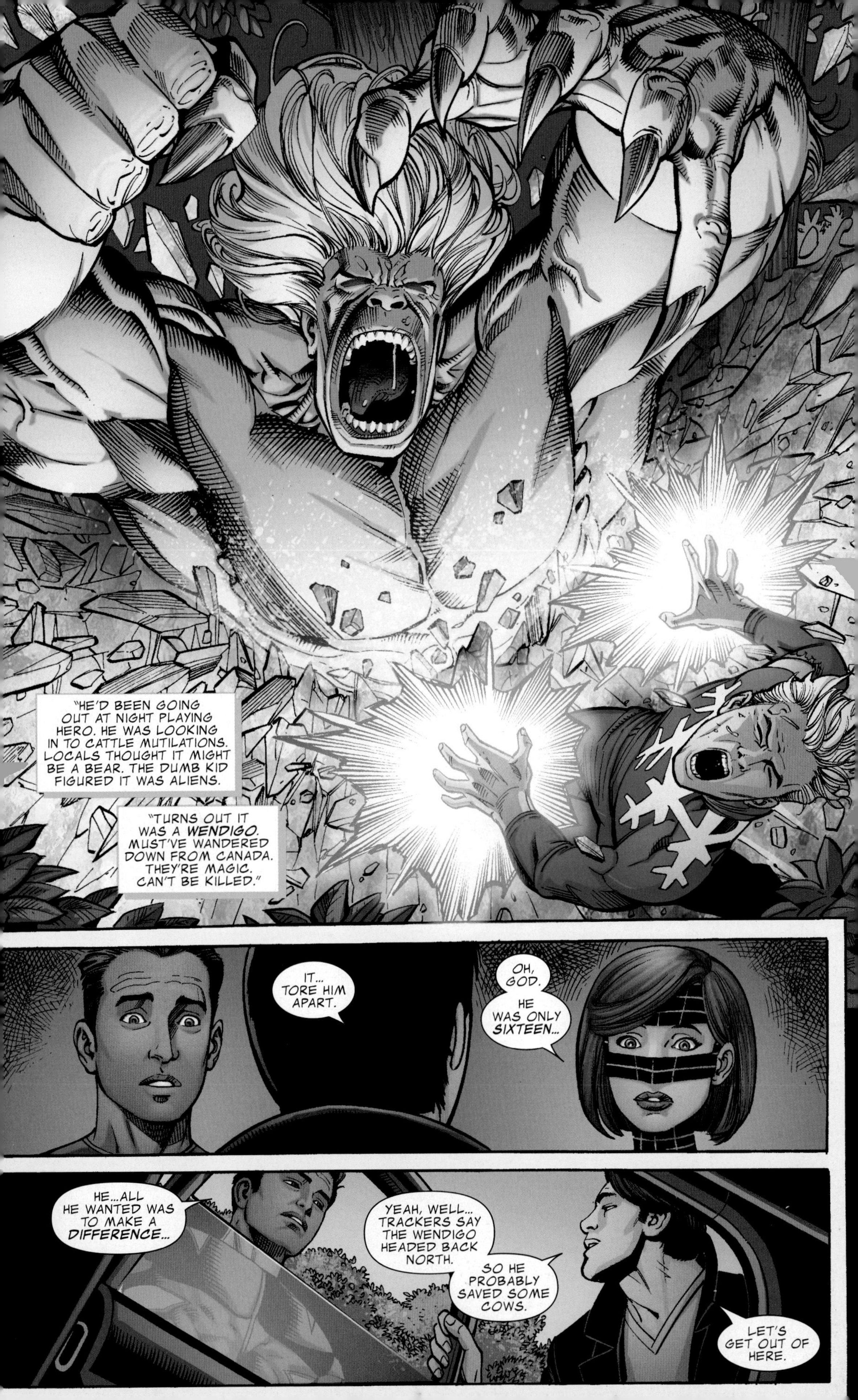

"HE'D BEEN GOING OUT AT NIGHT PLAYING HERO. HE WAS LOOKING IN TO CATTLE MUTILATIONS. LOCALS THOUGHT IT MIGHT BE A BEAR. THE DUMB KID FIGURED IT WAS ALIENS.
"TURNS OUT IT WAS A WENDIGO. MUST'VE WANDERED DOWN FROM CANADA. THEY'RE MAGIC. CAN'T BE KILLED."
IT... TORE HIM APART.
OH, GOD.
HE WAS ONLY SIXTEEN...
HE...ALL HE WANTED WAS TO MAKE A DIFFERENCE...
YEAH, WELL... TRACKERS SAY THE WENDIGO HEADED BACK NORTH.
SO HE PROBABLY SAVED SOME COWS.
LET'S GET OUT OF HERE.

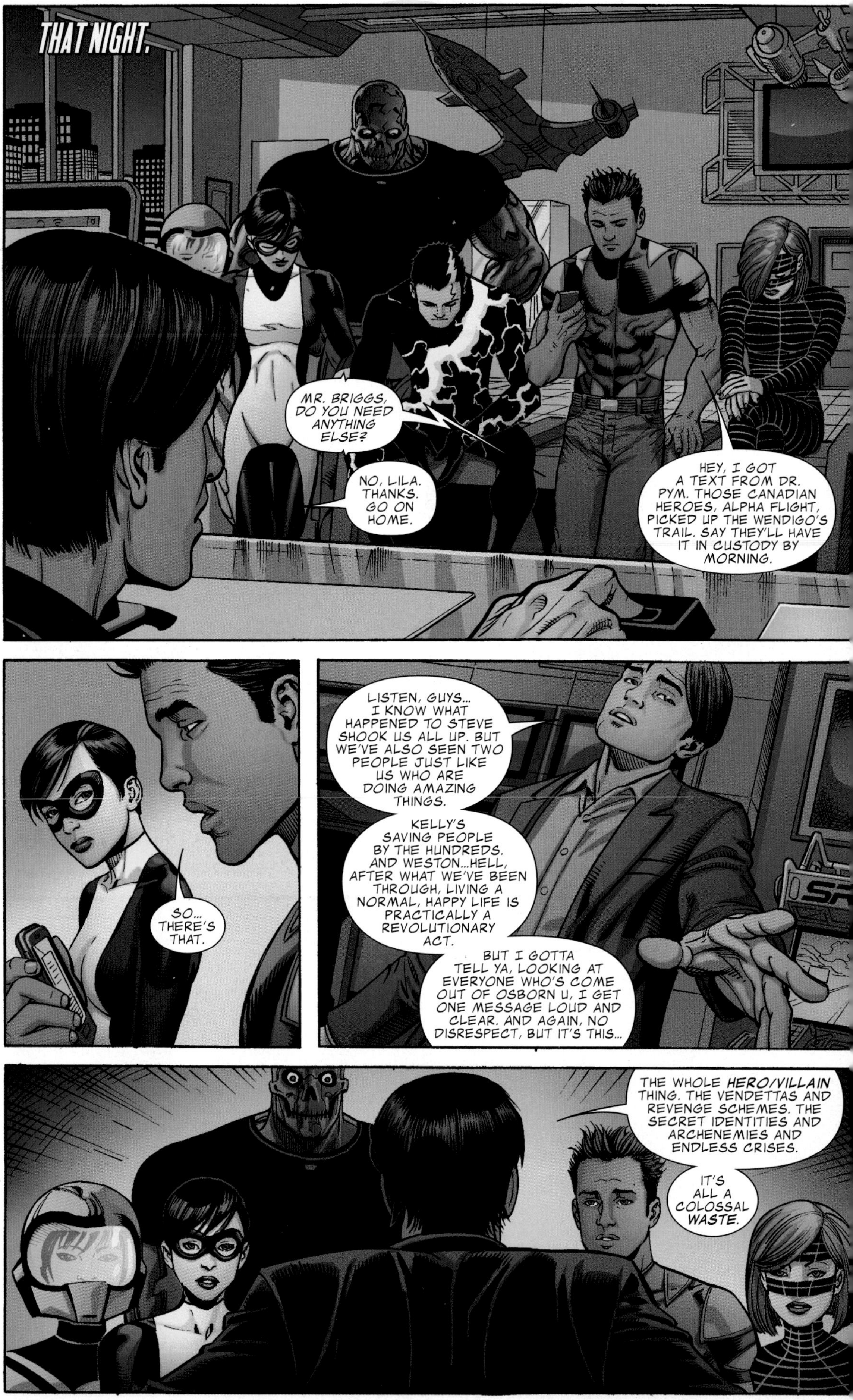
THAT NIGHT.
MR. BRIGGS, DO YOU NEED ANYTHING ELSE?
NO, LILA. THANKS. GO ON HOME.
HEY, I GOT A TEXT FROM DR. PYM. THOSE CANADIAN HEROES, ALPHA FLIGHT, PICKED UP THE WENDIGO'S TRAIL. SAY THEY'LL HAVE IT IN CUSTODY BY MORNING.
SO... THERE'S THAT.
LISTEN, GUYS... I KNOW WHAT HAPPENED TO STEVE SHOOK US ALL UP. BUT WE'VE ALSO SEEN TWO PEOPLE JUST LIKE US WHO ARE DOING AMAZING THINGS.
KELLY'S SAVING PEOPLE BY THE HUNDREDS. AND WESTON...HELL, AFTER WHAT WE'VE BEEN THROUGH, LIVING A NORMAL, HAPPY LIFE IS PRACTICALLY A REVOLUTIONARY ACT.
BUT I GOTTA TELL YA, LOOKING AT EVERYONE WHO'S COME OUT OF OSBORN U, I GET ONE MESSAGE LOUD AND CLEAR. AND AGAIN, NO DISRESPECT, BUT IT'S THIS...
THE WHOLE HERO/VILLAIN THING. THE VENDETTAS AND REVENGE SCHEMES. THE SECRET IDENTITIES AND ARCHENEMIES AND ENDLESS CRISES.
IT'S ALL A COLOSSAL WASTE.

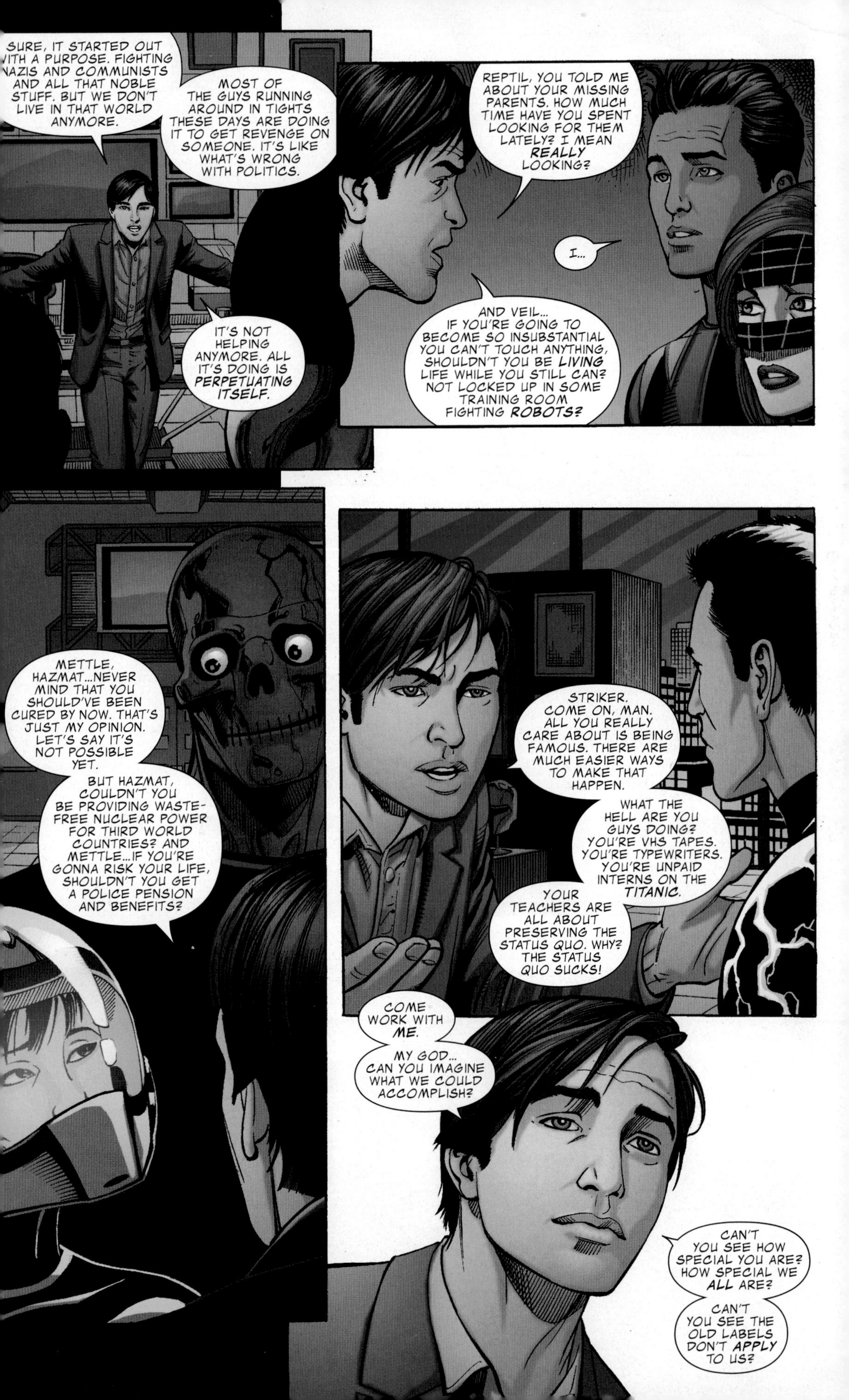
SURE, IT STARTED OUT WITH A PURPOSE. FIGHTING NAZIS AND COMMUNISTS AND ALL THAT NOBLE STUFF. BUT WE DON'T LIVE IN THAT WORLD ANYMORE.
MOST OF THE GUYS RUNNING AROUND IN TIGHTS THESE DAYS ARE DOING IT TO GET REVENGE ON SOMEONE. IT'S LIKE WHAT'S WRONG WITH POLITICS.
IT'S NOT HELPING ANYMORE. ALL IT'S DOING IS *PERPETUATING ITSELF*.
REPTIL, YOU TOLD ME ABOUT YOUR MISSING PARENTS. HOW MUCH TIME HAVE YOU SPENT LOOKING FOR THEM LATELY? I MEAN *REALLY* LOOKING?
I...
AND VEIL... IF YOU'RE GOING TO BECOME SO INSUBSTANTIAL YOU CAN'T TOUCH ANYTHING, SHOULDN'T YOU BE *LIVING* LIFE WHILE YOU STILL CAN? NOT LOCKED UP IN SOME TRAINING ROOM FIGHTING *ROBOTS?*
METTLE, HAZMAT...NEVER MIND THAT YOU SHOULD'VE BEEN CURED BY NOW. THAT'S JUST MY OPINION. LET'S SAY IT'S NOT POSSIBLE YET.
BUT HAZMAT, COULDN'T YOU BE PROVIDING WASTE-FREE NUCLEAR POWER FOR THIRD WORLD COUNTRIES? AND METTLE...IF YOU'RE GONNA RISK YOUR LIFE, SHOULDN'T YOU GET A POLICE PENSION AND BENEFITS?
STRIKER. COME ON, MAN. ALL YOU REALLY CARE ABOUT IS BEING FAMOUS. THERE ARE MUCH EASIER WAYS TO MAKE THAT HAPPEN.
WHAT THE HELL ARE YOU GUYS DOING? YOU'RE VHS TAPES. YOU'RE TYPEWRITERS. YOU'RE UNPAID INTERNS ON THE *TITANIC*.
YOUR TEACHERS ARE ALL ABOUT PRESERVING THE STATUS QUO. WHY? THE STATUS QUO SUCKS!
COME WORK WITH *ME*.
MY GOD... CAN YOU IMAGINE WHAT WE COULD ACCOMPLISH?
CAN'T YOU SEE HOW SPECIAL YOU ARE? HOW SPECIAL WE *ALL* ARE?
CAN'T YOU SEE THE OLD LABELS DON'T *APPLY* TO US?

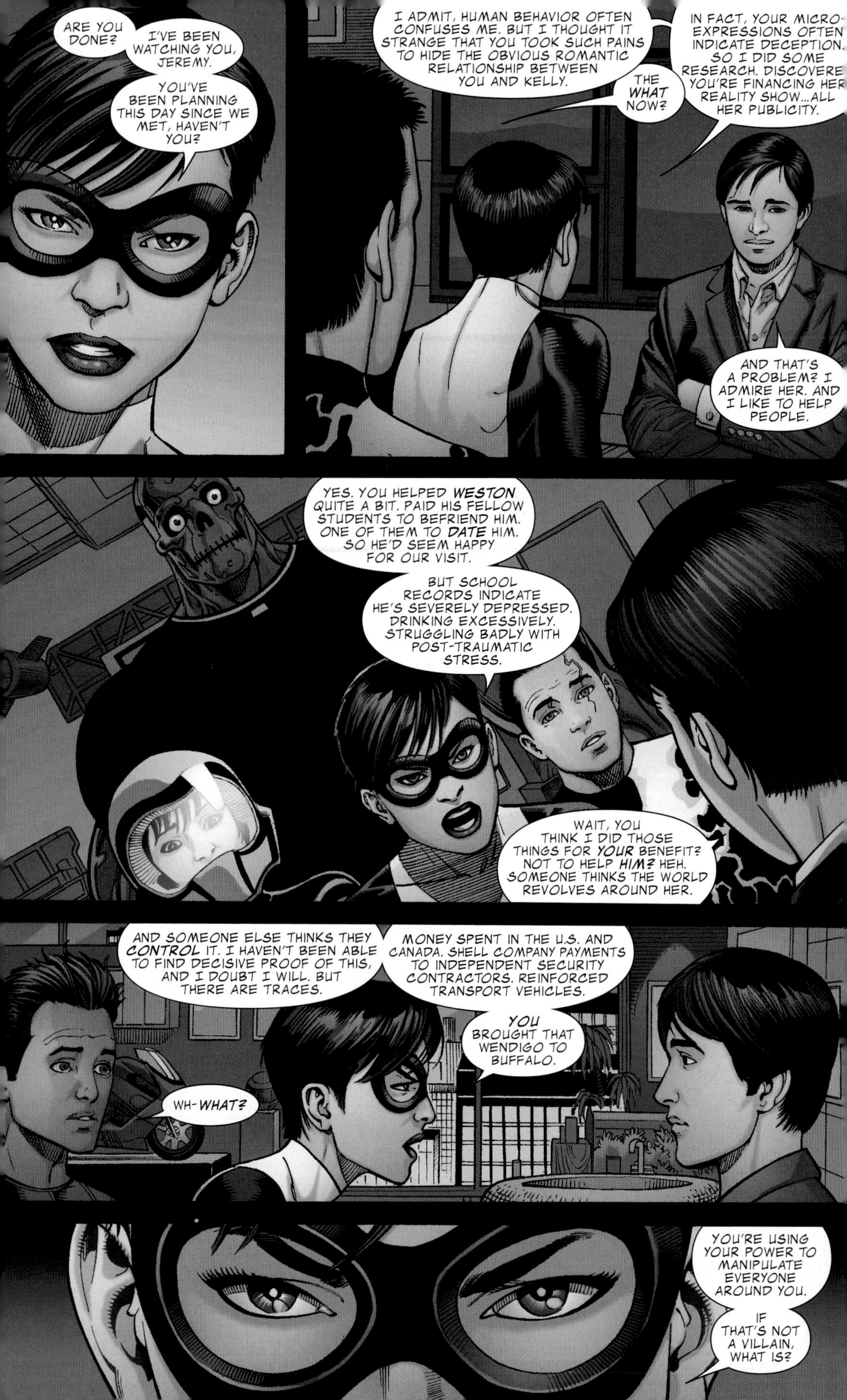

ARE YOU DONE?
I'VE BEEN WATCHING YOU, JEREMY.
YOU'VE BEEN PLANNING THIS DAY SINCE WE MET, HAVEN'T YOU?
I ADMIT, HUMAN BEHAVIOR OFTEN CONFUSES ME. BUT I THOUGHT IT STRANGE THAT YOU TOOK SUCH PAINS TO HIDE THE OBVIOUS ROMANTIC RELATIONSHIP BETWEEN YOU AND KELLY.
THE WHAT NOW?
IN FACT, YOUR MICRO-EXPRESSIONS OFTEN INDICATE DECEPTION. SO I DID SOME RESEARCH. DISCOVERED YOU'RE FINANCING HER REALITY SHOW...ALL HER PUBLICITY.
AND THAT'S A PROBLEM? I ADMIRE HER. AND I LIKE TO HELP PEOPLE.
YES. YOU HELPED WESTON QUITE A BIT. PAID HIS FELLOW STUDENTS TO BEFRIEND HIM. ONE OF THEM TO DATE HIM. SO HE'D SEEM HAPPY FOR OUR VISIT.
BUT SCHOOL RECORDS INDICATE HE'S SEVERELY DEPRESSED. DRINKING EXCESSIVELY. STRUGGLING BADLY WITH POST-TRAUMATIC STRESS.
WAIT, YOU THINK I DID THOSE THINGS FOR YOUR BENEFIT? NOT TO HELP HIM? HEH. SOMEONE THINKS THE WORLD REVOLVES AROUND HER.
AND SOMEONE ELSE THINKS THEY CONTROL IT. I HAVEN'T BEEN ABLE TO FIND DECISIVE PROOF OF THIS, AND I DOUBT I WILL. BUT THERE ARE TRACES.
MONEY SPENT IN THE U.S. AND CANADA. SHELL COMPANY PAYMENTS TO INDEPENDENT SECURITY CONTRACTORS. REINFORCED TRANSPORT VEHICLES.
YOU BROUGHT THAT WENDIGO TO BUFFALO.
WH-WHAT?
YOU'RE USING YOUR POWER TO MANIPULATE EVERYONE AROUND YOU.
IF THAT'S NOT A VILLAIN, WHAT IS?

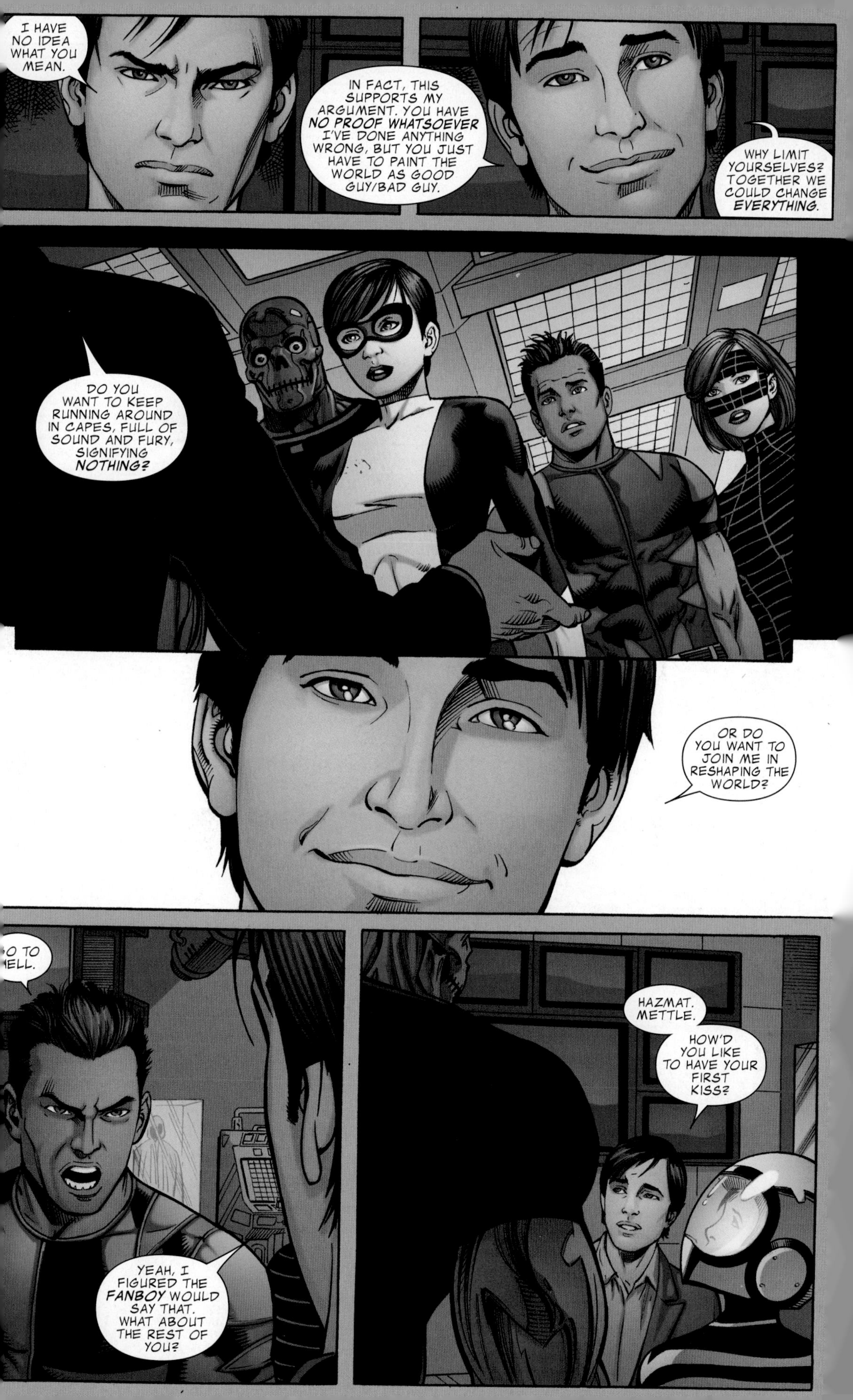
I HAVE NO IDEA WHAT YOU MEAN.
IN FACT, THIS SUPPORTS MY ARGUMENT. YOU HAVE NO PROOF WHATSOEVER I'VE DONE ANYTHING WRONG, BUT YOU JUST HAVE TO PAINT THE WORLD AS GOOD GUY/BAD GUY.
WHY LIMIT YOURSELVES? TOGETHER WE COULD CHANGE EVERYTHING.
DO YOU WANT TO KEEP RUNNING AROUND IN CAPES, FULL OF SOUND AND FURY, SIGNIFYING NOTHING?
OR DO YOU WANT TO JOIN ME IN RESHAPING THE WORLD?
O TO ELL.
YEAH, I FIGURED THE FANBOY WOULD SAY THAT. WHAT ABOUT THE REST OF YOU?
HAZMAT. METTLE.
HOW'D YOU LIKE TO HAVE YOUR FIRST KISS?

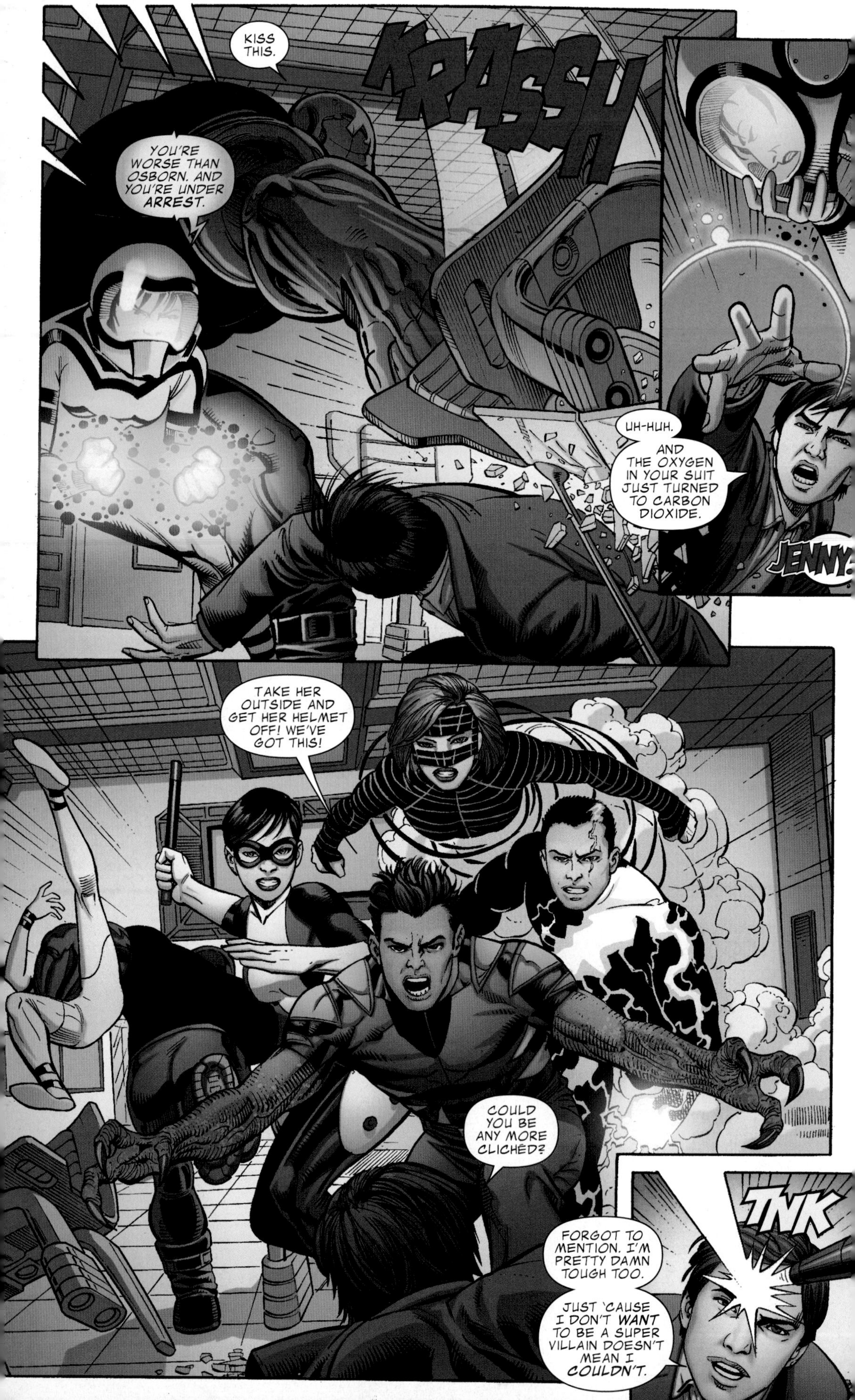
KISS THIS.
KRASSH
YOU'RE WORSE THAN OSBORN. AND YOU'RE UNDER ARREST.
UH-HUH.
AND THE OXYGEN IN YOUR SUIT JUST TURNED TO CARBON DIOXIDE.
JENNY!
TAKE HER OUTSIDE AND GET HER HELMET OFF! WE'VE GOT THIS!
COULD YOU BE ANY MORE CLICHéD?
TNK
FORGOT TO MENTION. I'M PRETTY DAMN TOUGH TOO.
JUST 'CAUSE I DON'T WANT TO BE A SUPER VILLAIN DOESN'T MEAN I COULDN'T.

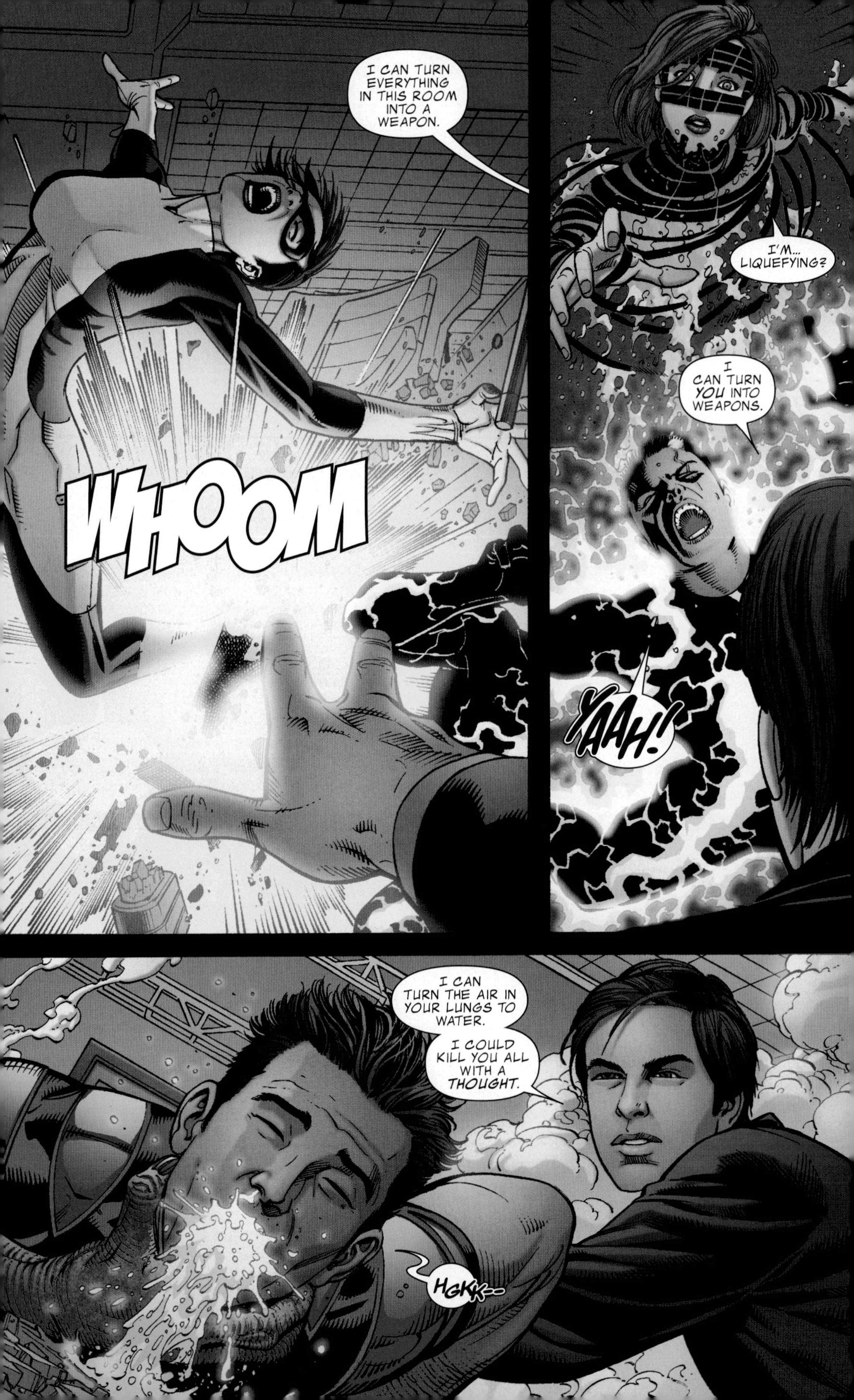
I CAN TURN EVERYTHING IN THIS ROOM INTO A WEAPON.
WHOOM
I'M... LIQUEFYING?
I CAN TURN YOU INTO WEAPONS.
YAAH!
I CAN TURN THE AIR IN YOUR LUNGS TO WATER.
I COULD KILL YOU ALL WITH A THOUGHT.
HGKK--

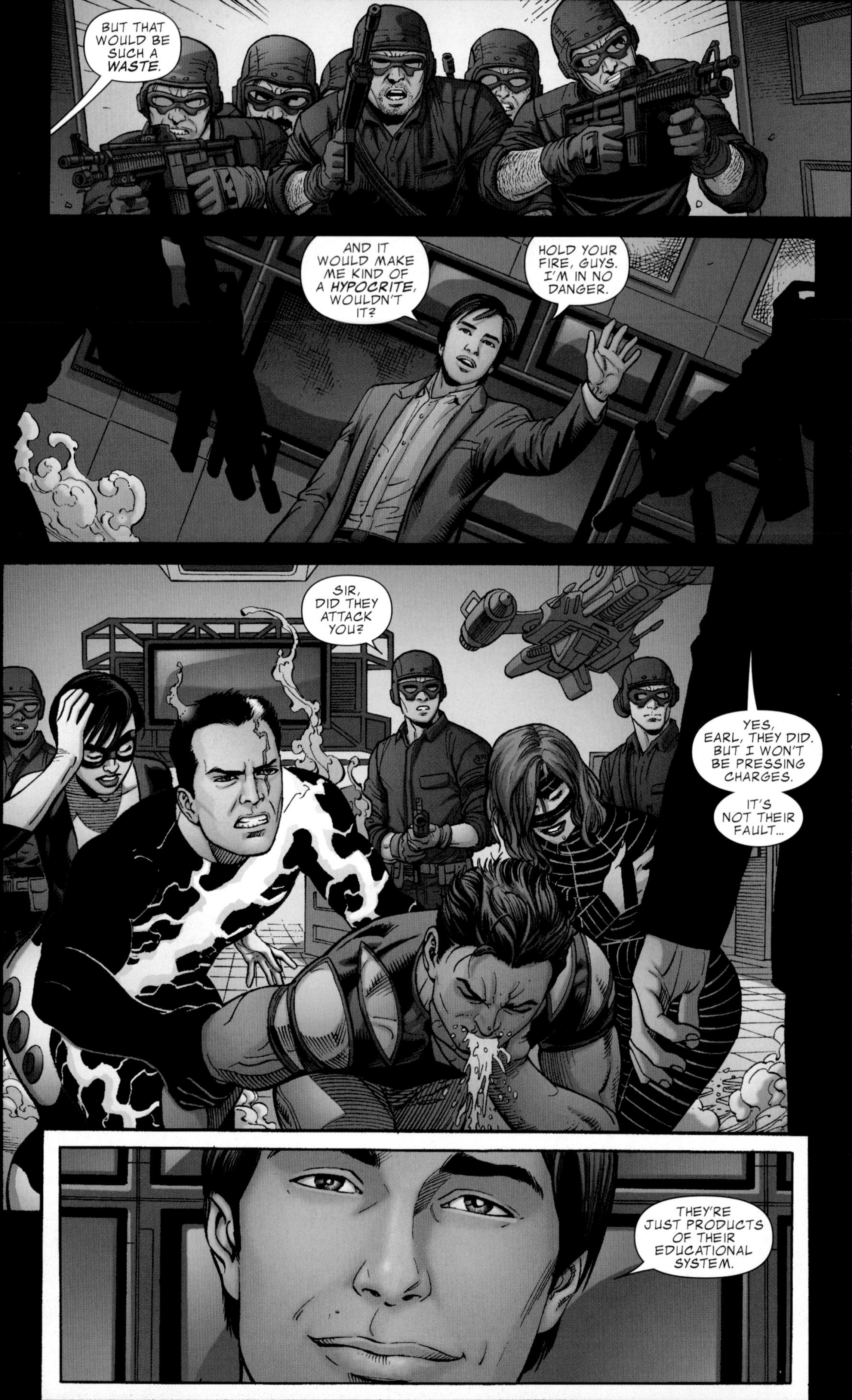
BUT THAT WOULD BE SUCH A *WASTE*.
AND IT WOULD MAKE ME KIND OF A *HYPOCRITE*, WOULDN'T IT?
HOLD YOUR FIRE, GUYS. I'M IN NO DANGER.
SIR, DID THEY ATTACK YOU?
YES, EARL, THEY DID. BUT I WON'T BE PRESSING CHARGES.
IT'S NOT THEIR FAULT...
THEY'RE JUST PRODUCTS OF THEIR EDUCATIONAL SYSTEM.

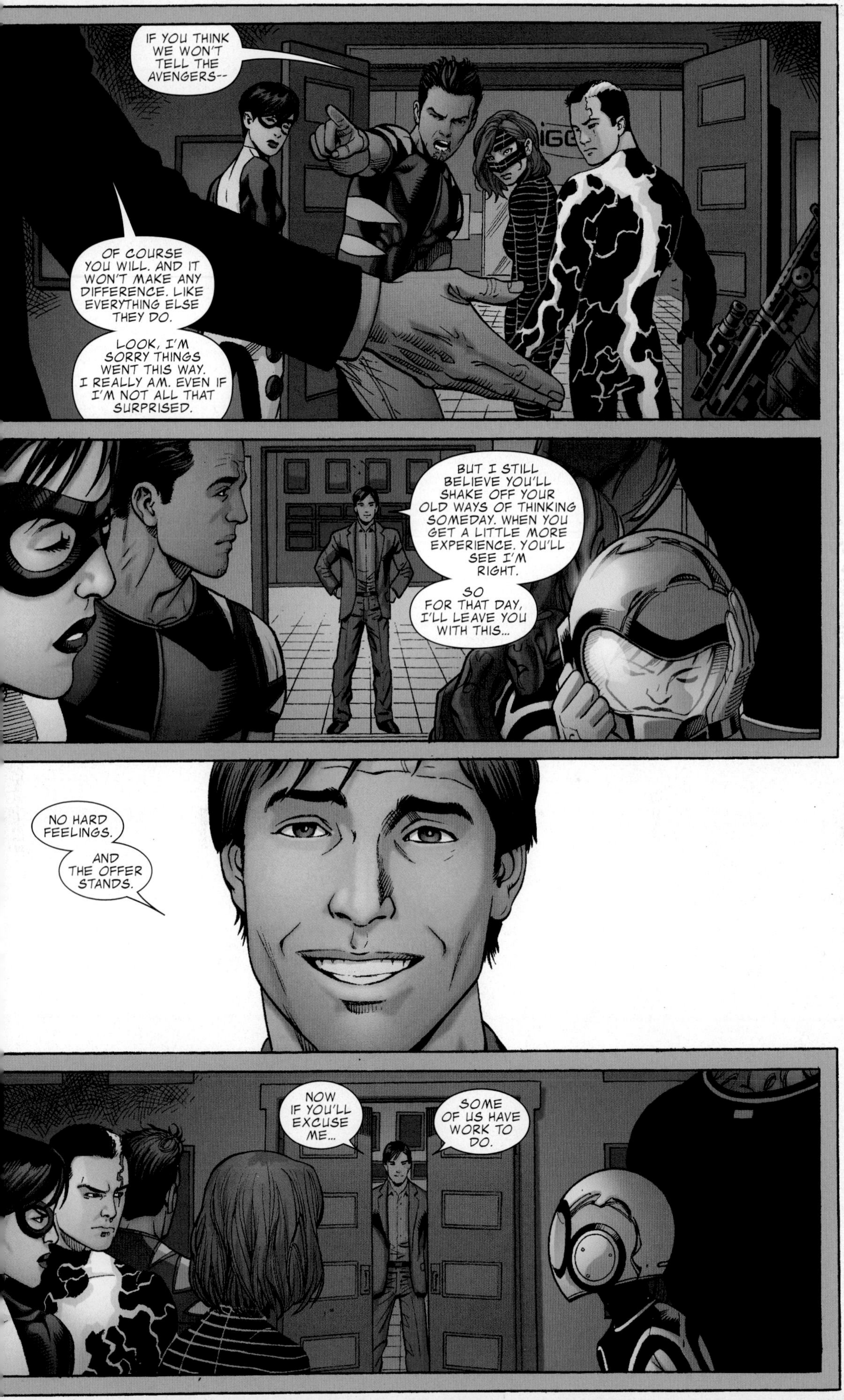
IF YOU THINK WE WON'T TELL THE AVENGERS--
OF COURSE YOU WILL. AND IT WON'T MAKE ANY DIFFERENCE. LIKE EVERYTHING ELSE THEY DO.
LOOK, I'M SORRY THINGS WENT THIS WAY. I REALLY AM. EVEN IF I'M NOT ALL THAT SURPRISED.
BUT I STILL BELIEVE YOU'LL SHAKE OFF YOUR OLD WAYS OF THINKING SOMEDAY. WHEN YOU GET A LITTLE MORE EXPERIENCE. YOU'LL SEE I'M RIGHT.
SO FOR THAT DAY, I'LL LEAVE YOU WITH THIS...
NO HARD FEELINGS.
AND THE OFFER STANDS.
NOW IF YOU'LL EXCUSE ME...
SOME OF US HAVE WORK TO DO.

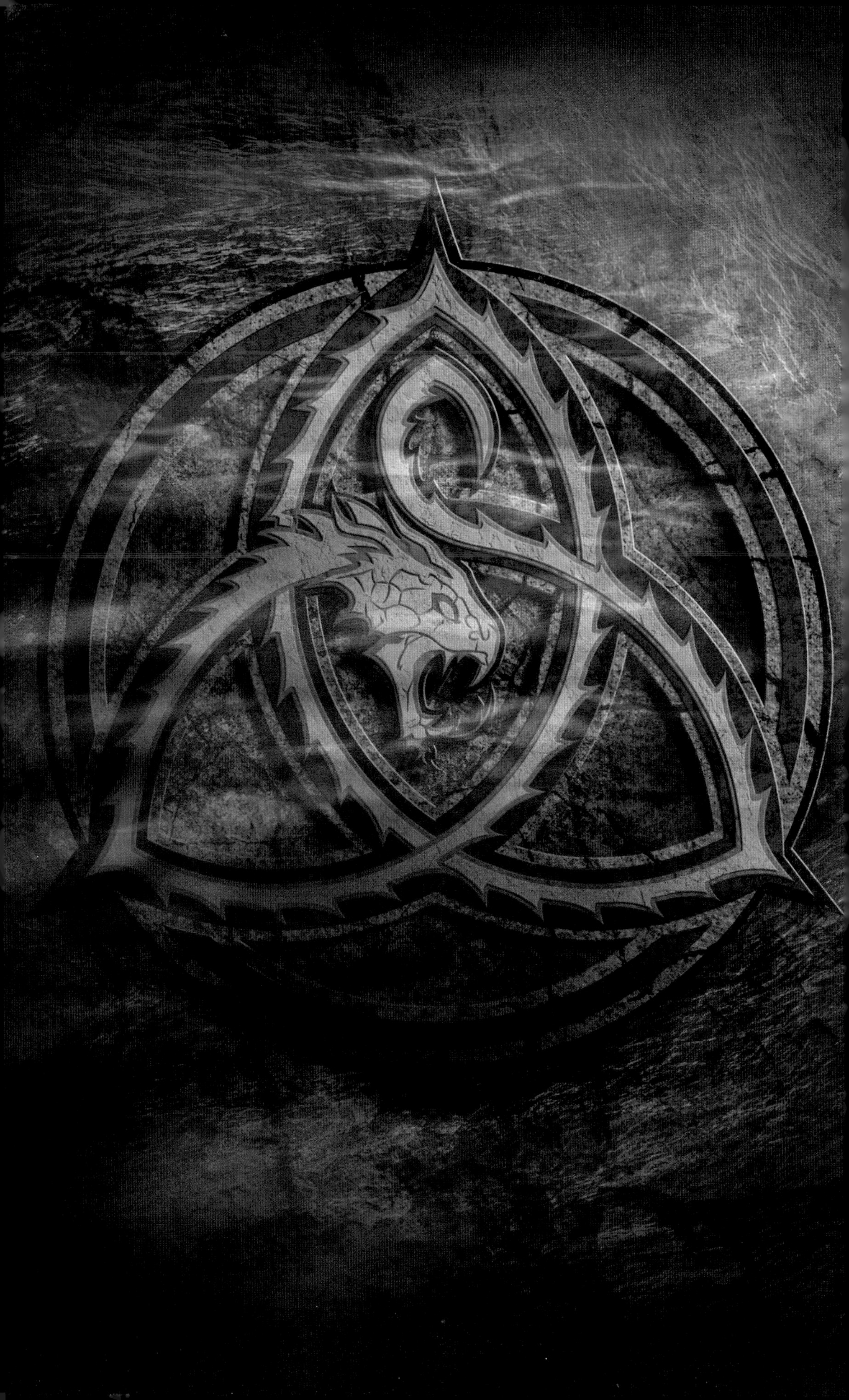

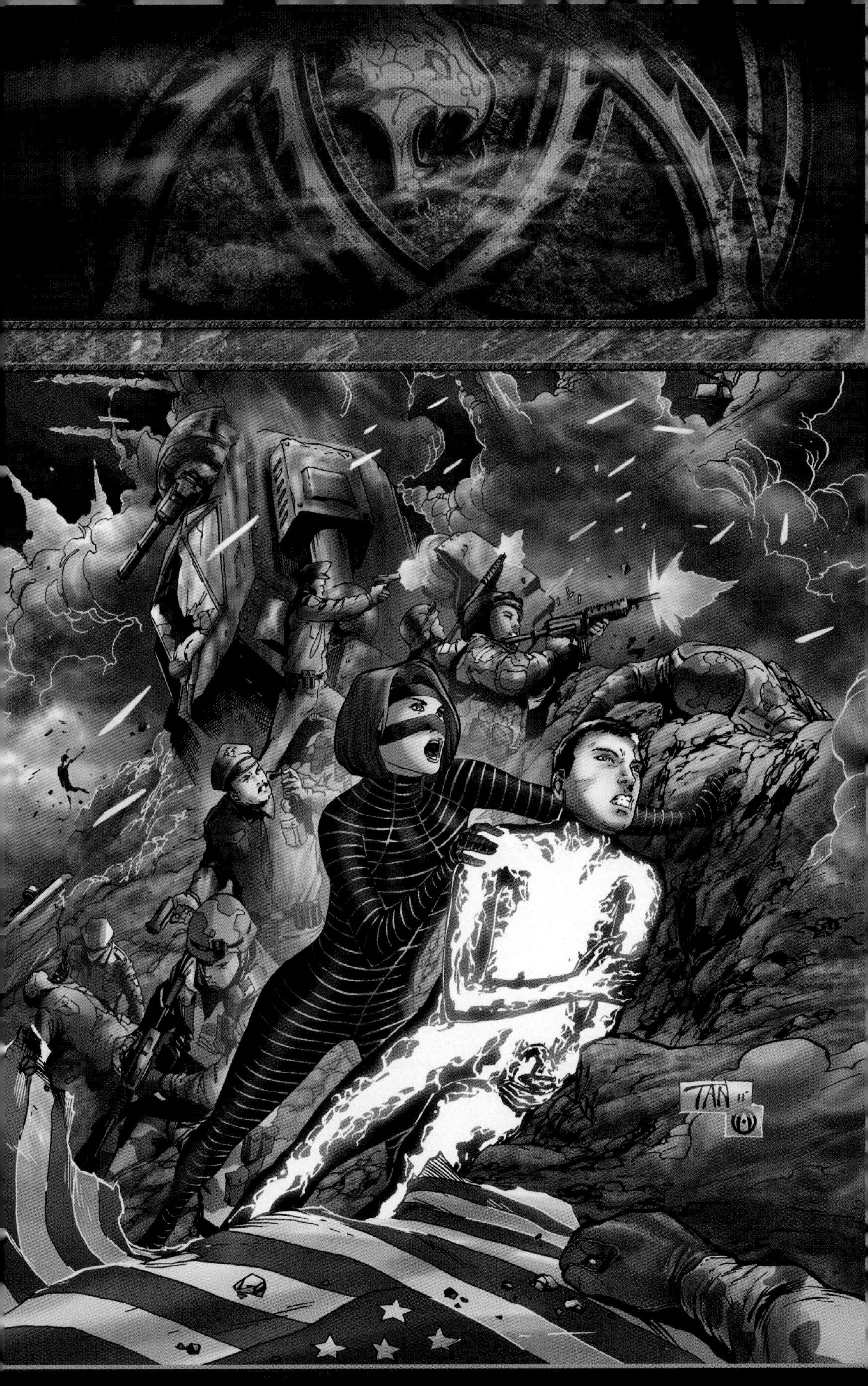

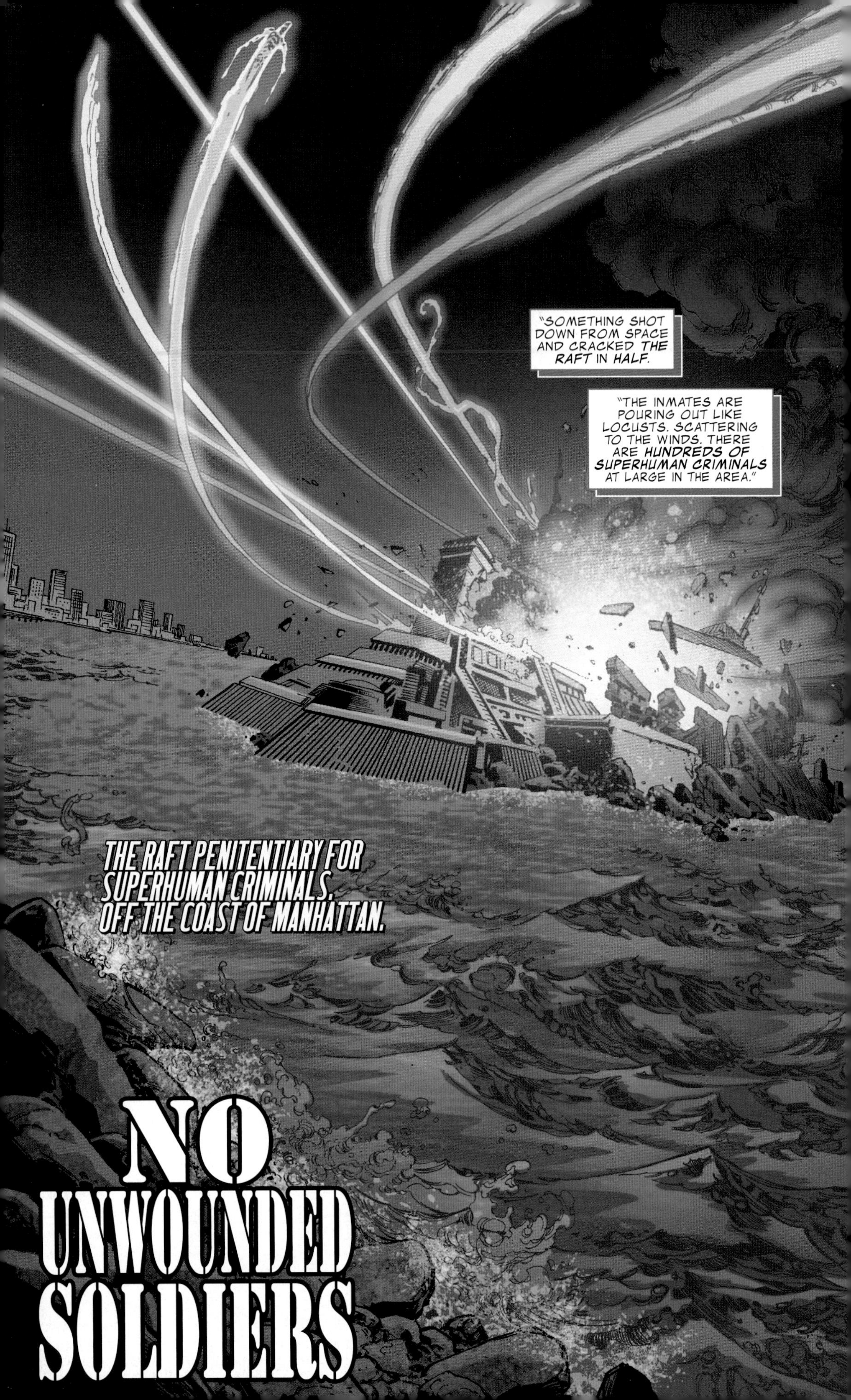

"SOMETHING SHOT DOWN FROM SPACE AND CRACKED THE RAFT IN HALF.
"THE INMATES ARE POURING OUT LIKE LOCUSTS. SCATTERING TO THE WINDS. THERE ARE HUNDREDS OF SUPERHUMAN CRIMINALS AT LARGE IN THE AREA."
THE RAFT PENITENTIARY FOR SUPERHUMAN CRIMINALS. OFF THE COAST OF MANHATTAN.
NO UNWOUNDED SOLDIERS

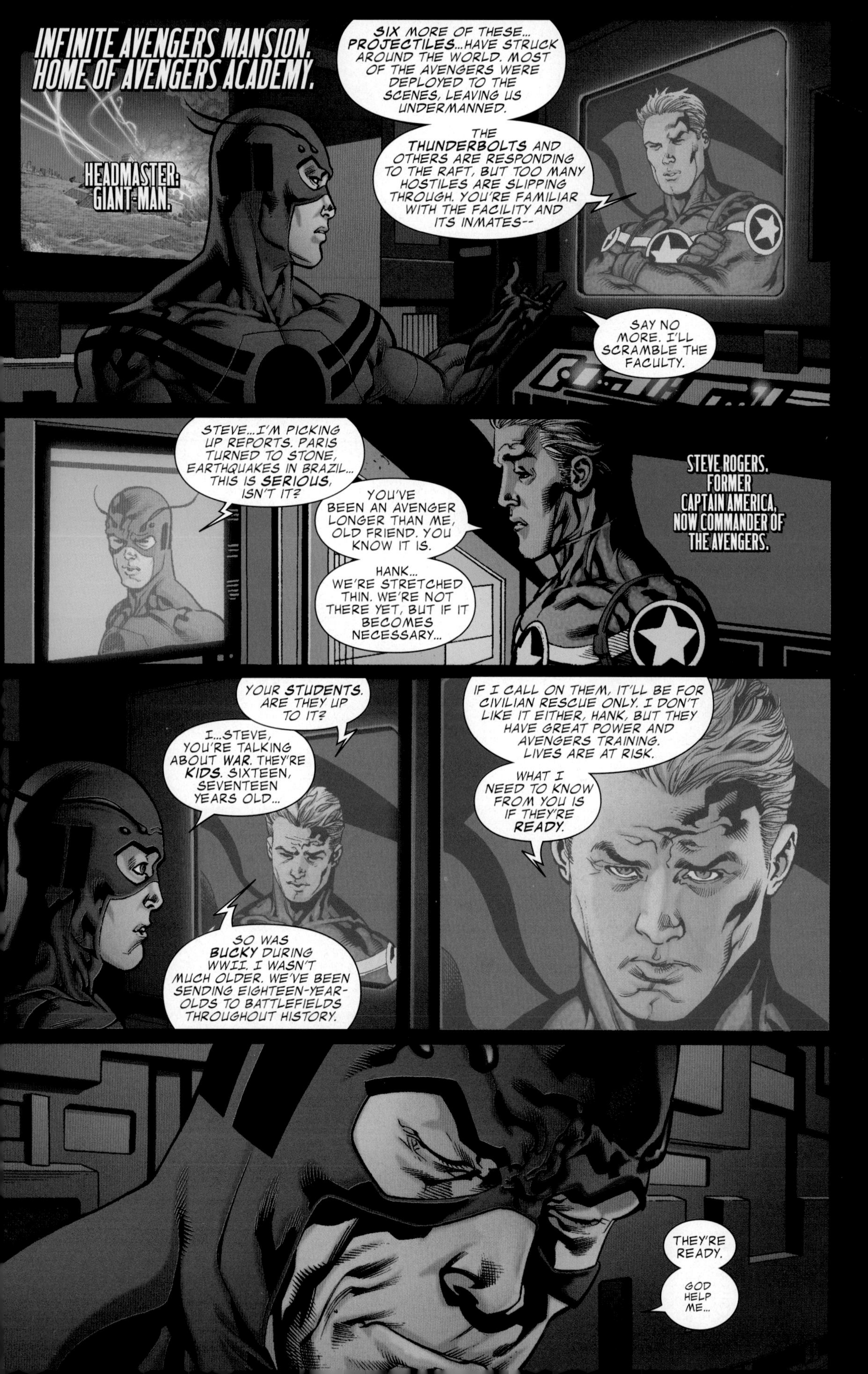
INFINITE AVENGERS MANSION. HOME OF AVENGERS ACADEMY.
HEADMASTER: GIANT-MAN.
SIX MORE OF THESE... PROJECTILES...HAVE STRUCK AROUND THE WORLD. MOST OF THE AVENGERS WERE DEPLOYED TO THE SCENES, LEAVING US UNDERMANNED.
THE THUNDERBOLTS AND OTHERS ARE RESPONDING TO THE RAFT, BUT TOO MANY HOSTILES ARE SLIPPING THROUGH. YOU'RE FAMILIAR WITH THE FACILITY AND ITS INMATES--
SAY NO MORE. I'LL SCRAMBLE THE FACULTY.
STEVE...I'M PICKING UP REPORTS. PARIS TURNED TO STONE, EARTHQUAKES IN BRAZIL... THIS IS SERIOUS, ISN'T IT?
STEVE ROGERS. FORMER CAPTAIN AMERICA, NOW COMMANDER OF THE AVENGERS.
YOU'VE BEEN AN AVENGER LONGER THAN ME, OLD FRIEND. YOU KNOW IT IS.
HANK... WE'RE STRETCHED THIN. WE'RE NOT THERE YET, BUT IF IT BECOMES NECESSARY...
YOUR STUDENTS. ARE THEY UP TO IT?
I...STEVE, YOU'RE TALKING ABOUT WAR. THEY'RE KIDS. SIXTEEN, SEVENTEEN YEARS OLD...
SO WAS BUCKY DURING WWII. I WASN'T MUCH OLDER. WE'VE BEEN SENDING EIGHTEEN-YEAR-OLDS TO BATTLEFIELDS THROUGHOUT HISTORY.
IF I CALL ON THEM, IT'LL BE FOR CIVILIAN RESCUE ONLY. I DON'T LIKE IT EITHER, HANK, BUT THEY HAVE GREAT POWER AND AVENGERS TRAINING. LIVES ARE AT RISK.
WHAT I NEED TO KNOW FROM YOU IS IF THEY'RE READY.
THEY'RE READY.
GOD HELP ME...

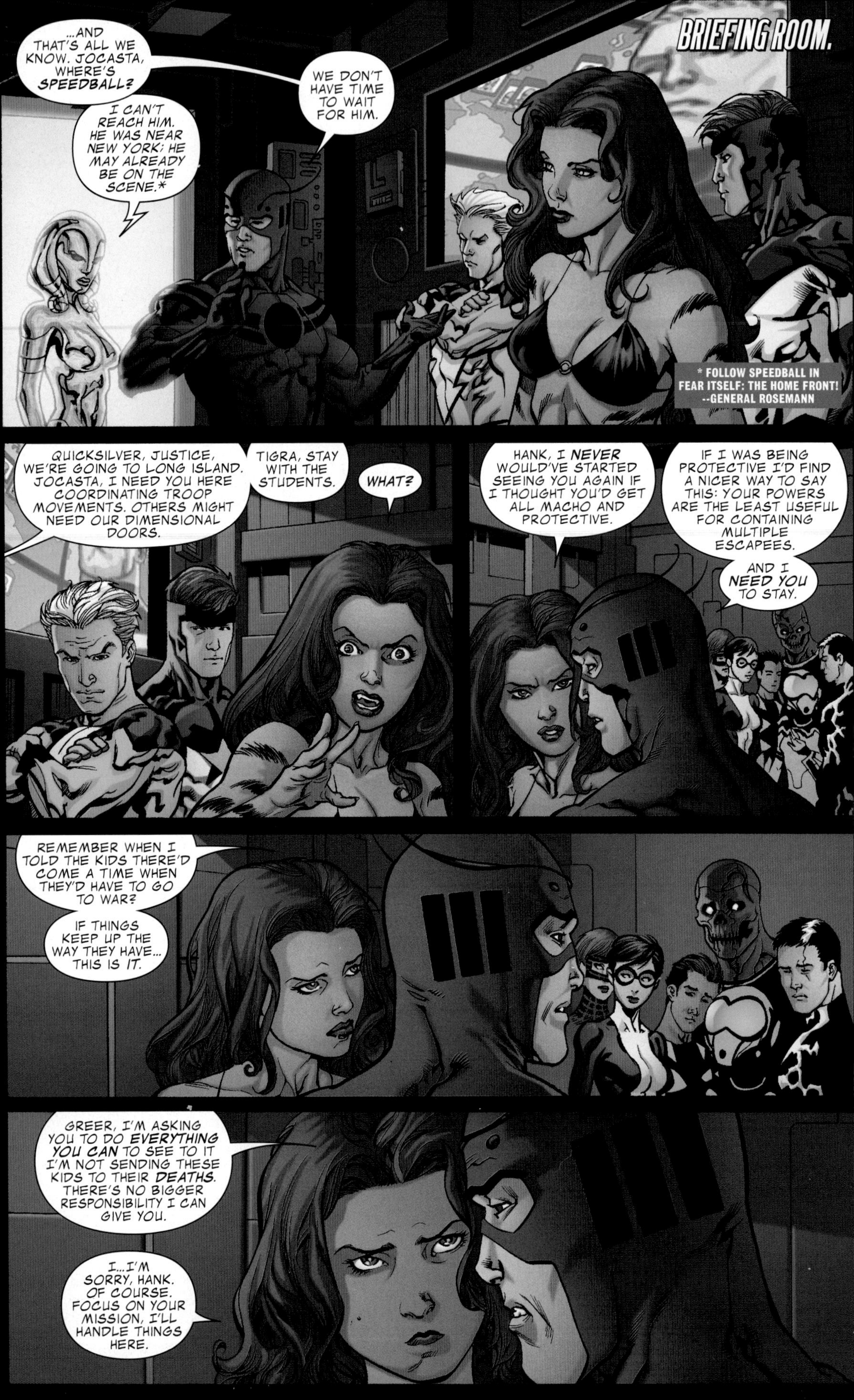
BRIEFING ROOM.
...AND THAT'S ALL WE KNOW. JOCASTA, WHERE'S SPEEDBALL?
I CAN'T REACH HIM. HE WAS NEAR NEW YORK; HE MAY ALREADY BE ON THE SCENE.*
WE DON'T HAVE TIME TO WAIT FOR HIM.
* FOLLOW SPEEDBALL IN FEAR ITSELF: THE HOME FRONT! --GENERAL ROSEMANN
QUICKSILVER, JUSTICE, WE'RE GOING TO LONG ISLAND. JOCASTA, I NEED YOU HERE COORDINATING TROOP MOVEMENTS. OTHERS MIGHT NEED OUR DIMENSIONAL DOORS.
TIGRA, STAY WITH THE STUDENTS.
WHAT?
HANK, I NEVER WOULD'VE STARTED SEEING YOU AGAIN IF I THOUGHT YOU'D GET ALL MACHO AND PROTECTIVE.
IF I WAS BEING PROTECTIVE I'D FIND A NICER WAY TO SAY THIS: YOUR POWERS ARE THE LEAST USEFUL FOR CONTAINING MULTIPLE ESCAPEES.
AND I NEED YOU TO STAY.
REMEMBER WHEN I TOLD THE KIDS THERE'D COME A TIME WHEN THEY'D HAVE TO GO TO WAR?
IF THINGS KEEP UP THE WAY THEY HAVE... THIS IS IT.
GREER, I'M ASKING YOU TO DO EVERYTHING YOU CAN TO SEE TO IT I'M NOT SENDING THESE KIDS TO THEIR DEATHS. THERE'S NO BIGGER RESPONSIBILITY I CAN GIVE YOU.
I...I'M SORRY, HANK. OF COURSE. FOCUS ON YOUR MISSION, I'LL HANDLE THINGS HERE.

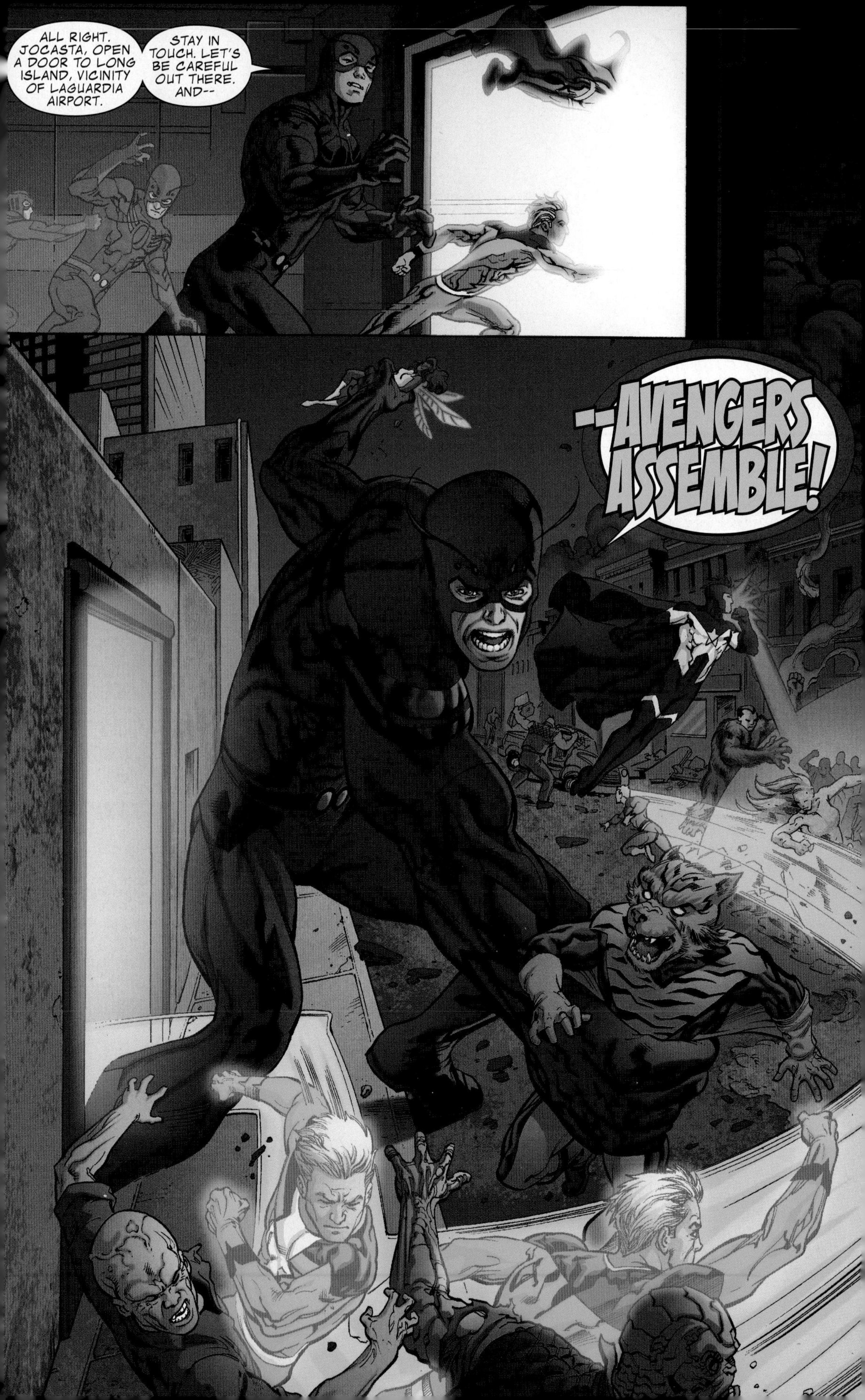
ALL RIGHT. JOCASTA, OPEN A DOOR TO LONG ISLAND, VICINITY OF LAGUARDIA AIRPORT.
STAY IN TOUCH. LET'S BE CAREFUL OUT THERE. AND--
--AVENGERS ASSEMBLE!

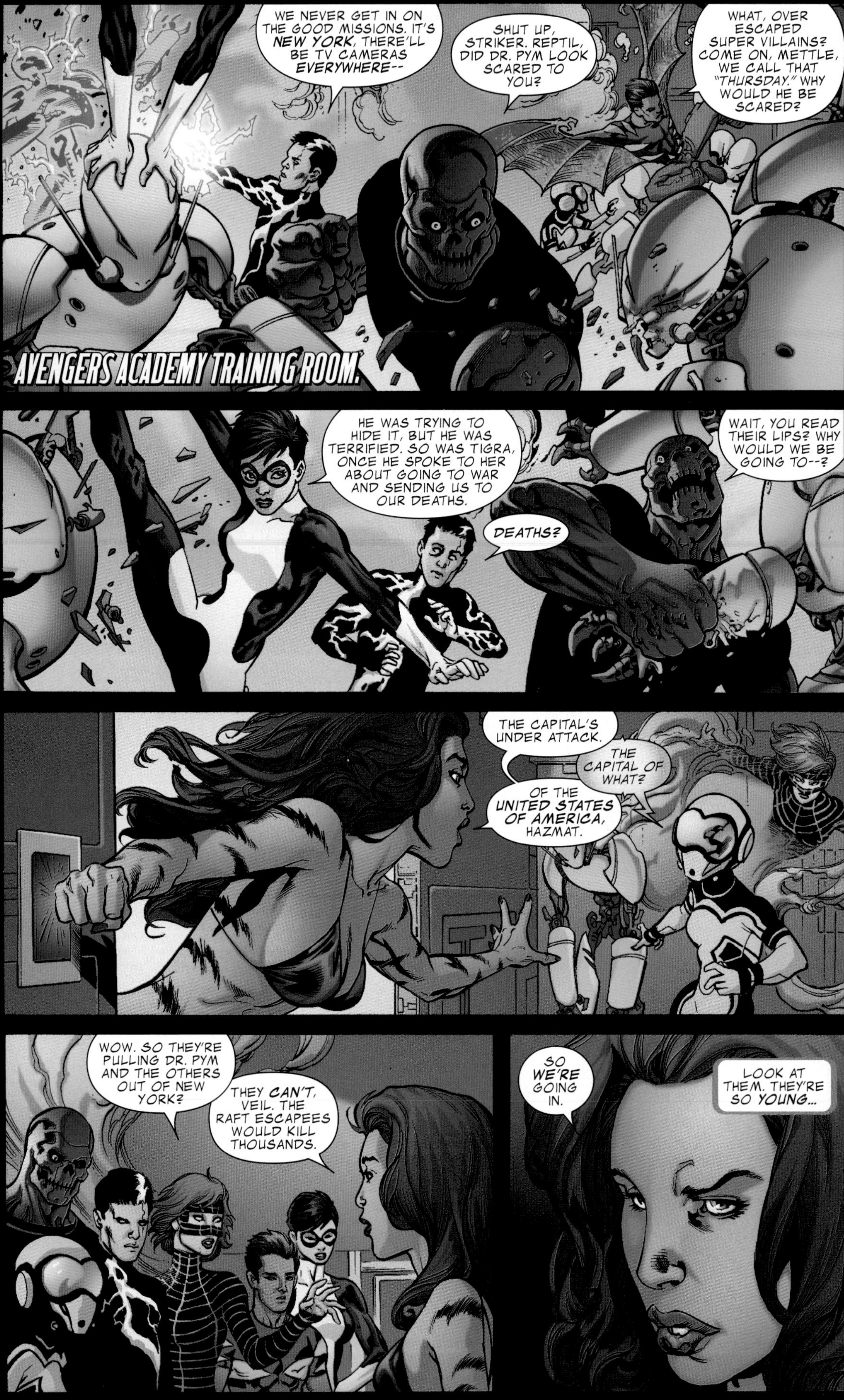
WE NEVER GET IN ON THE GOOD MISSIONS. IT'S NEW YORK, THERE'LL BE TV CAMERAS EVERYWHERE--
SHUT UP, STRIKER. REPTIL, DID DR. PYM LOOK SCARED TO YOU?
WHAT, OVER ESCAPED SUPER VILLAINS? COME ON, METTLE, WE CALL THAT "THURSDAY." WHY WOULD HE BE SCARED?
AVENGERS ACADEMY TRAINING ROOM.
HE WAS TRYING TO HIDE IT, BUT HE WAS TERRIFIED. SO WAS TIGRA, ONCE HE SPOKE TO HER ABOUT GOING TO WAR AND SENDING US TO OUR DEATHS.
DEATHS?
WAIT, YOU READ THEIR LIPS? WHY WOULD WE BE GOING TO--?
THE CAPITAL'S UNDER ATTACK.
THE CAPITAL OF WHAT?
OF THE UNITED STATES OF AMERICA, HAZMAT.
WOW. SO THEY'RE PULLING DR. PYM AND THE OTHERS OUT OF NEW YORK?
THEY CAN'T, VEIL. THE RAFT ESCAPEES WOULD KILL THOUSANDS.
SO WE'RE GOING IN.
LOOK AT THEM. THEY'RE SO YOUNG...

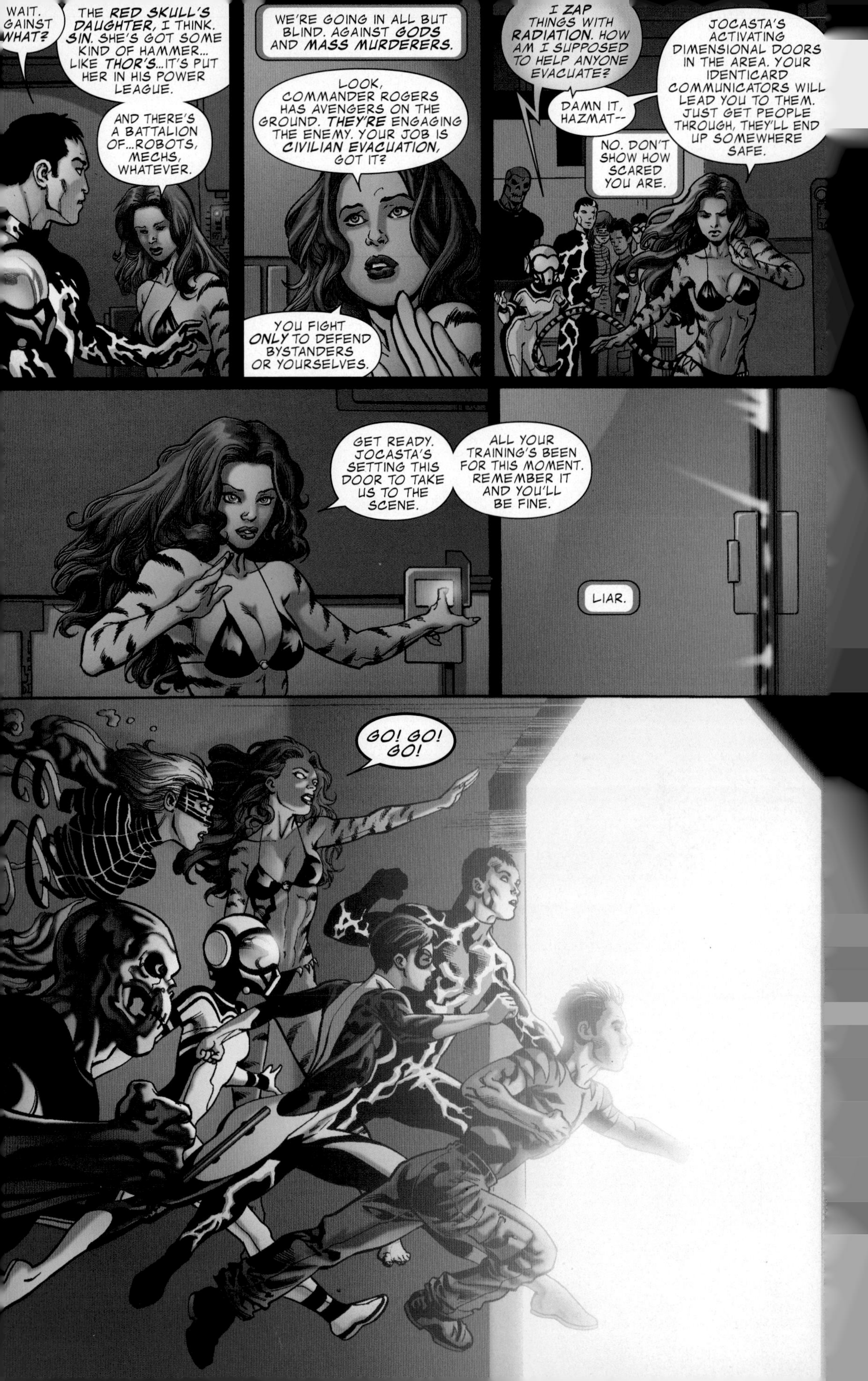

WAIT. GAINST WHAT?
THE RED SKULL'S DAUGHTER, I THINK. SIN. SHE'S GOT SOME KIND OF HAMMER... LIKE THOR'S...IT'S PUT HER IN HIS POWER LEAGUE.
AND THERE'S A BATTALION OF...ROBOTS, MECHS, WHATEVER.
WE'RE GOING IN ALL BUT BLIND. AGAINST GODS AND MASS MURDERERS.
LOOK, COMMANDER ROGERS HAS AVENGERS ON THE GROUND. THEY'RE ENGAGING THE ENEMY. YOUR JOB IS CIVILIAN EVACUATION, GOT IT?
YOU FIGHT ONLY TO DEFEND BYSTANDERS OR YOURSELVES.
I ZAP THINGS WITH RADIATION. HOW AM I SUPPOSED TO HELP ANYONE EVACUATE?
DAMN IT, HAZMAT--
NO. DON'T SHOW HOW SCARED YOU ARE.
JOCASTA'S ACTIVATING DIMENSIONAL DOORS IN THE AREA. YOUR IDENTICARD COMMUNICATORS WILL LEAD YOU TO THEM. JUST GET PEOPLE THROUGH, THEY'LL END UP SOMEWHERE SAFE.
GET READY. JOCASTA'S SETTING THIS DOOR TO TAKE US TO THE SCENE.
ALL YOUR TRAINING'S BEEN FOR THIS MOMENT. REMEMBER IT AND YOU'LL BE FINE.
LIAR.
GO! GO! GO!

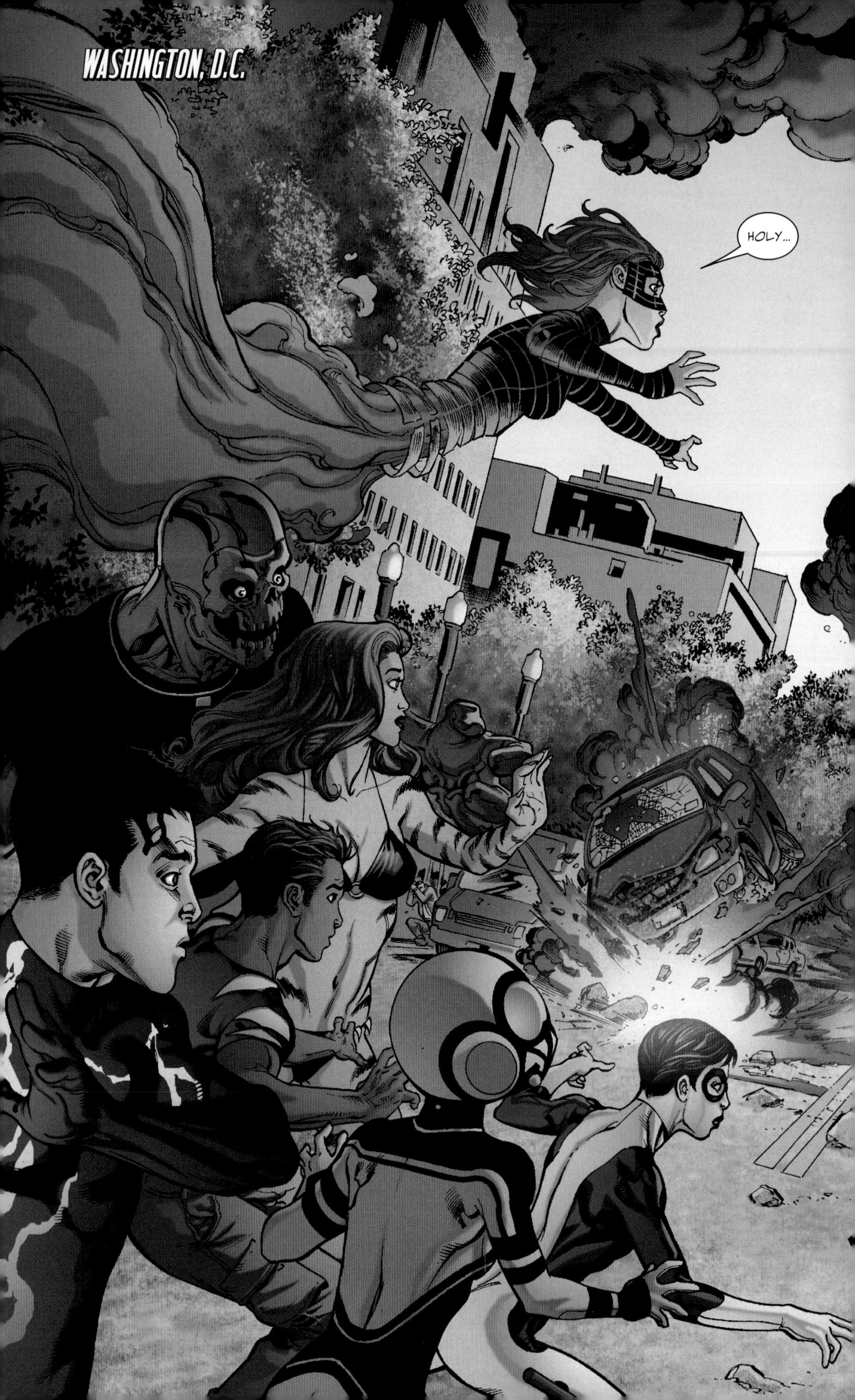
WASHINGTON, D.C.
HOLY...

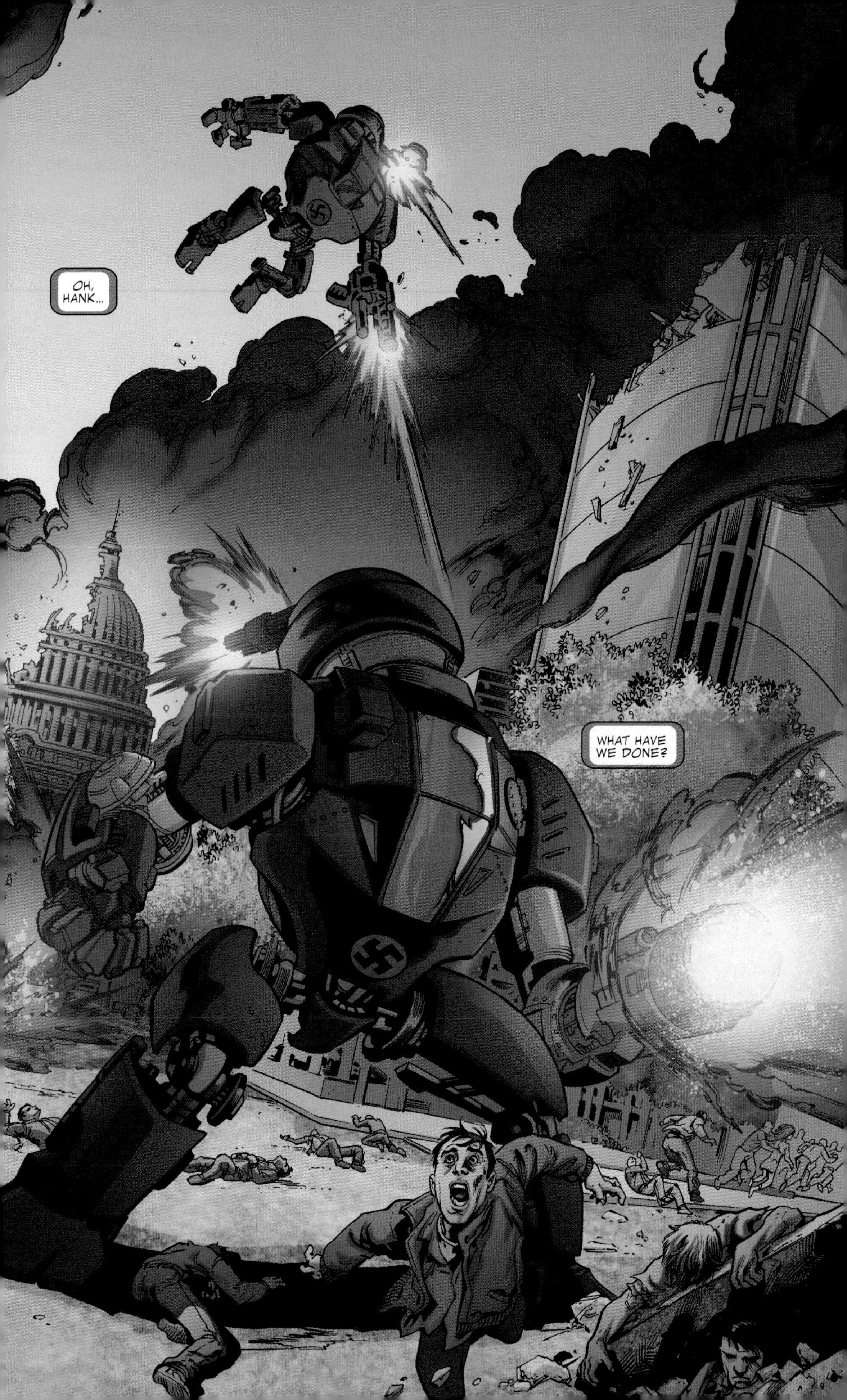
OH, HANK...
WHAT HAVE WE DONE?

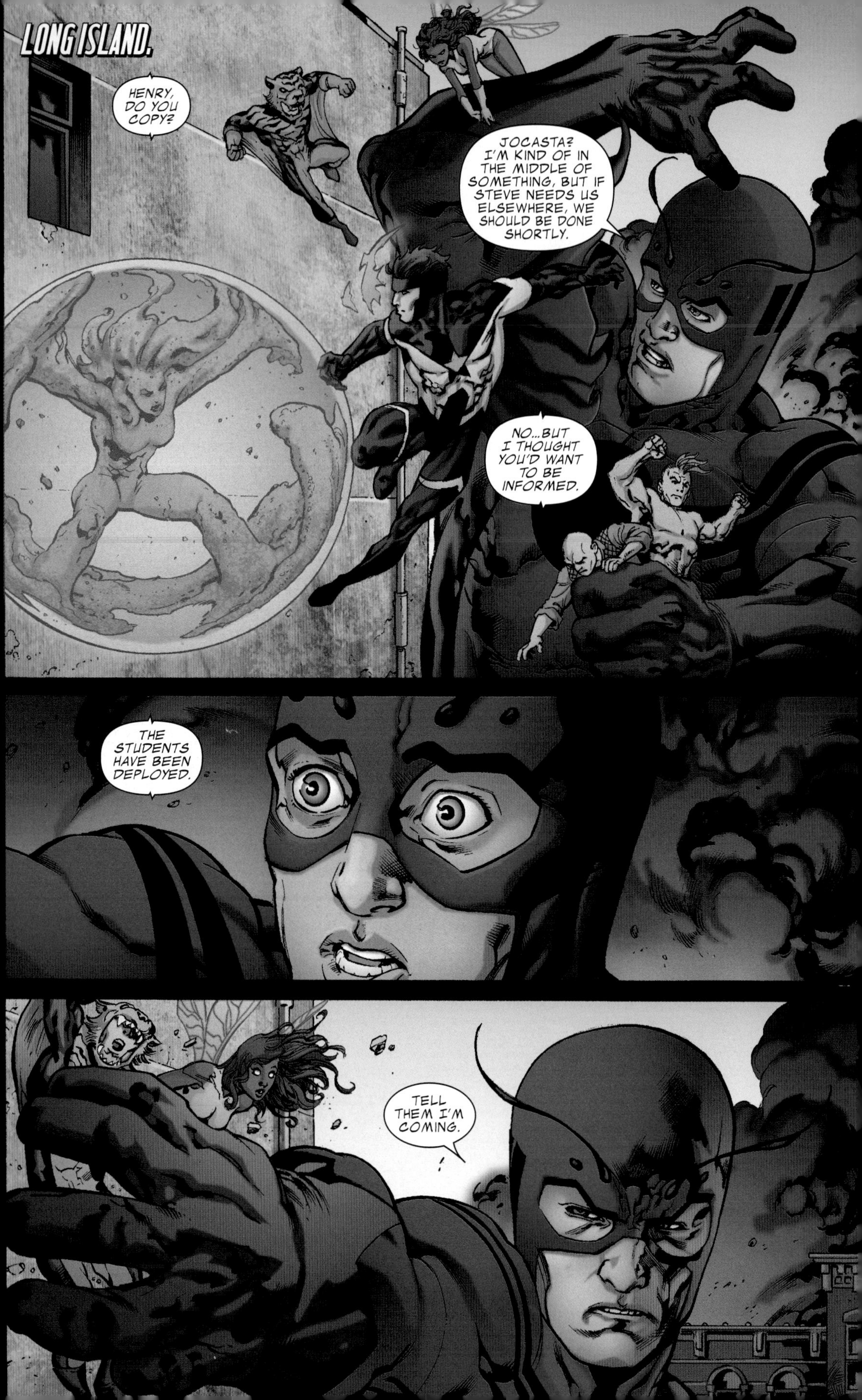
LONG ISLAND.
HENRY, DO YOU COPY?
JOCASTA? I'M KIND OF IN THE MIDDLE OF SOMETHING, BUT IF STEVE NEEDS US ELSEWHERE, WE SHOULD BE DONE SHORTLY.
NO...BUT I THOUGHT YOU'D WANT TO BE INFORMED.
THE STUDENTS HAVE BEEN DEPLOYED.
TELL THEM I'M COMING.

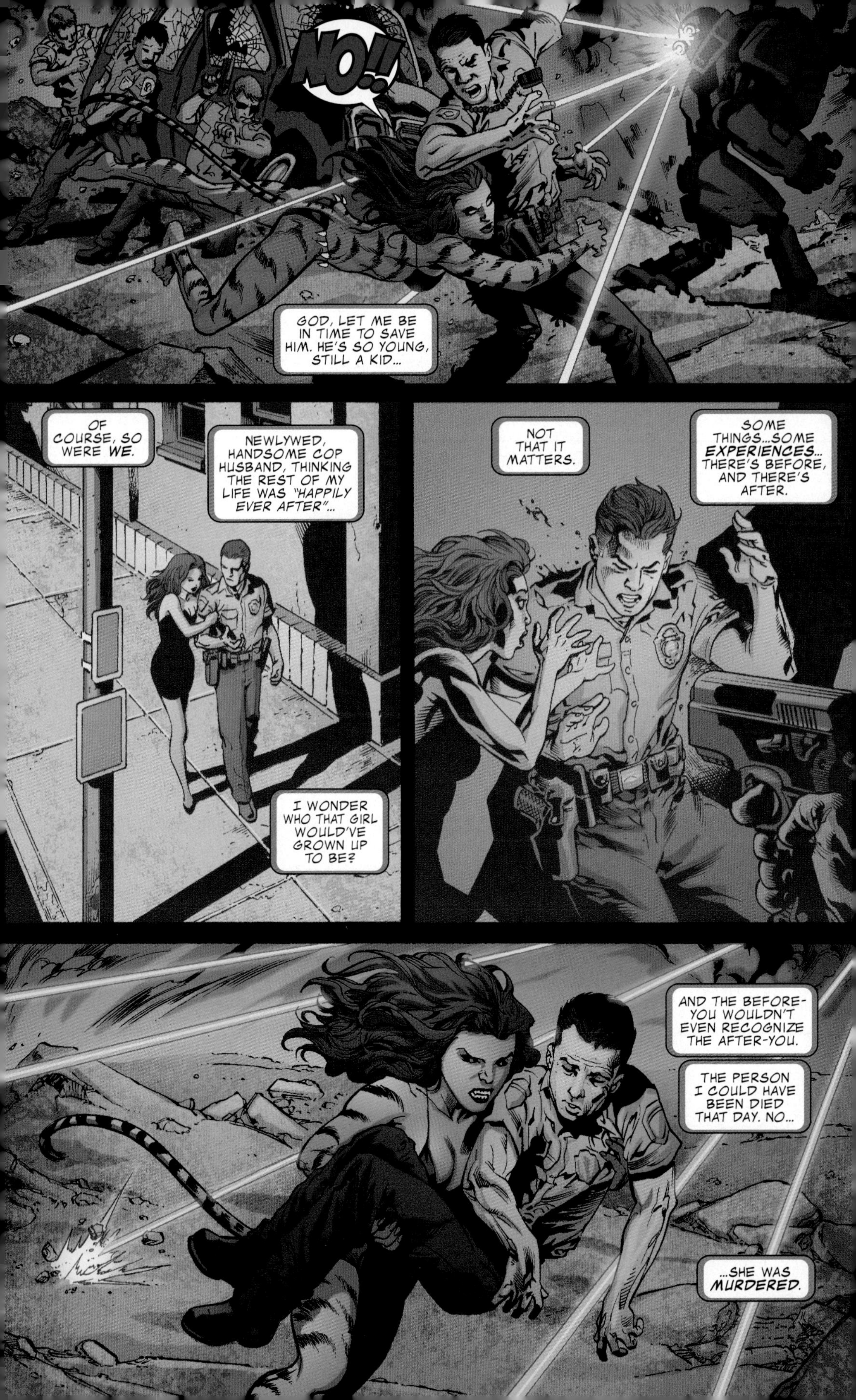
NO!!
GOD, LET ME BE IN TIME TO SAVE HIM. HE'S SO YOUNG, STILL A KID...
OF COURSE, SO WERE *WE*.
NEWLYWED, HANDSOME COP HUSBAND, THINKING THE REST OF MY LIFE WAS *"HAPPILY EVER AFTER"*...
I WONDER WHO THAT GIRL WOULD'VE GROWN UP TO BE?
NOT THAT IT MATTERS.
SOME THINGS...SOME ***EXPERIENCES***... THERE'S BEFORE, AND THERE'S AFTER.
AND THE BEFORE-YOU WOULDN'T EVEN RECOGNIZE THE AFTER-YOU.
THE PERSON I COULD HAVE BEEN DIED THAT DAY. NO...
...SHE WAS ***MURDERED***.

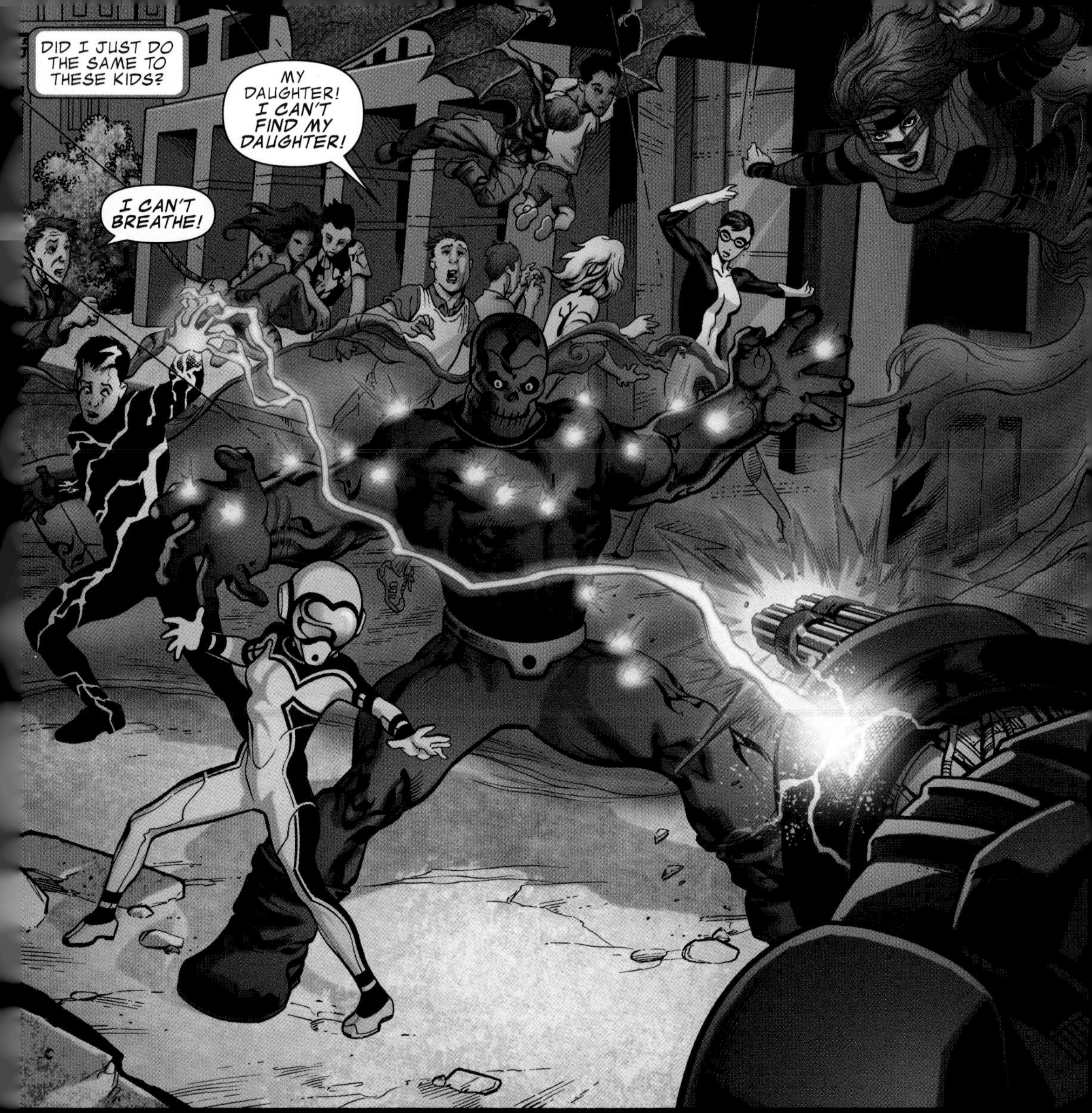
DID I JUST DO THE SAME TO THESE KIDS?
MY DAUGHTER! I CAN'T FIND MY DAUGHTER!
I CAN'T BREATHE!

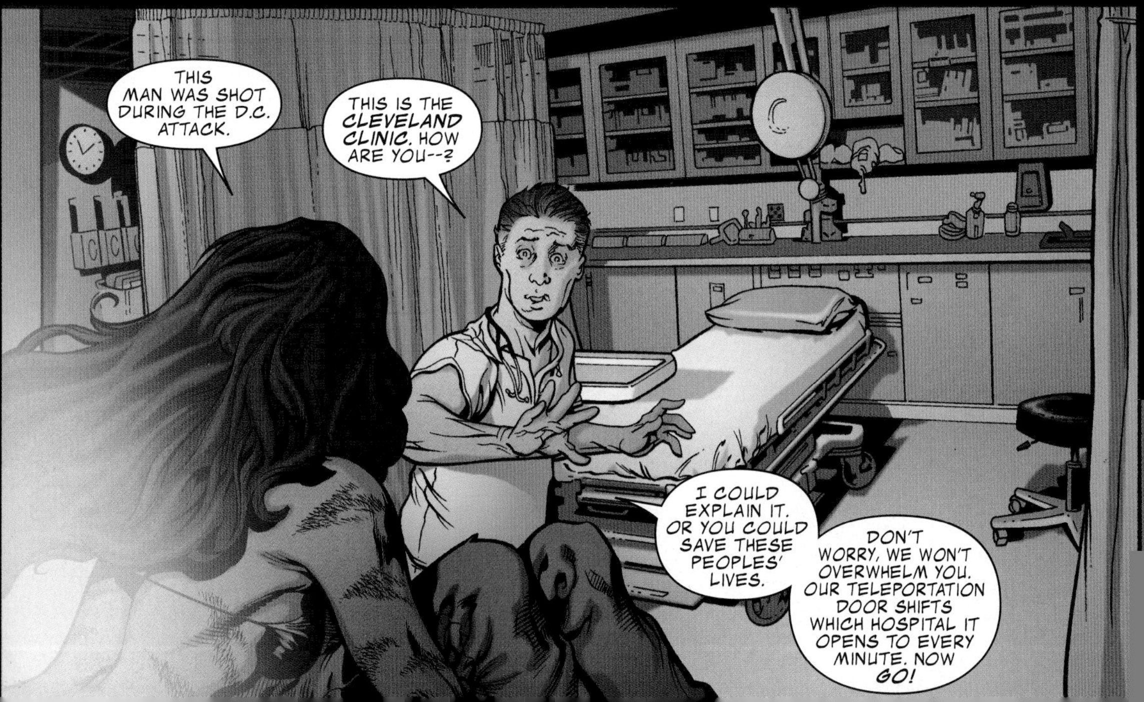
THIS MAN WAS SHOT DURING THE D.C. ATTACK.
THIS IS THE CLEVELAND CLINIC. HOW ARE YOU--?
I COULD EXPLAIN IT. OR YOU COULD SAVE THESE PEOPLES' LIVES.
DON'T WORRY, WE WON'T OVERWHELM YOU. OUR TELEPORTATION DOOR SHIFTS WHICH HOSPITAL IT OPENS TO EVERY MINUTE. NOW GO!

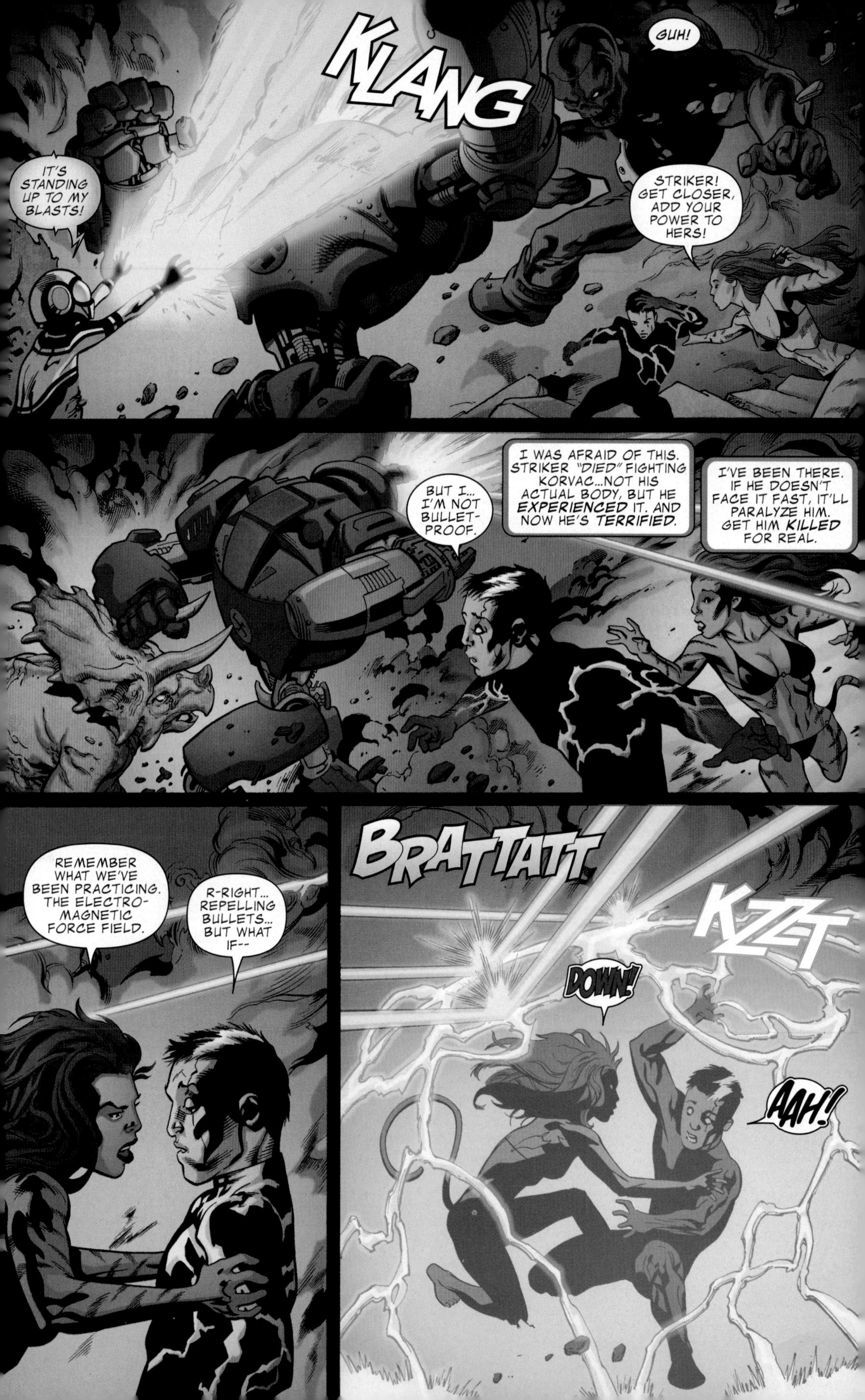
KLANG
GUH!
IT'S STANDING UP TO MY BLASTS!
STRIKER! GET CLOSER, ADD YOUR POWER TO HERS!
BUT I... I'M NOT BULLET-PROOF.
I WAS AFRAID OF THIS. STRIKER "DIED" FIGHTING KORVAC...NOT HIS ACTUAL BODY, BUT HE EXPERIENCED IT. AND NOW HE'S TERRIFIED.
I'VE BEEN THERE. IF HE DOESN'T FACE IT FAST, IT'LL PARALYZE HIM. GET HIM KILLED FOR REAL.
REMEMBER WHAT WE'VE BEEN PRACTICING. THE ELECTRO-MAGNETIC FORCE FIELD.
R-RIGHT... REPELLING BULLETS... BUT WHAT IF--
BRATTATT
KZZT
DOWN!
AAH!

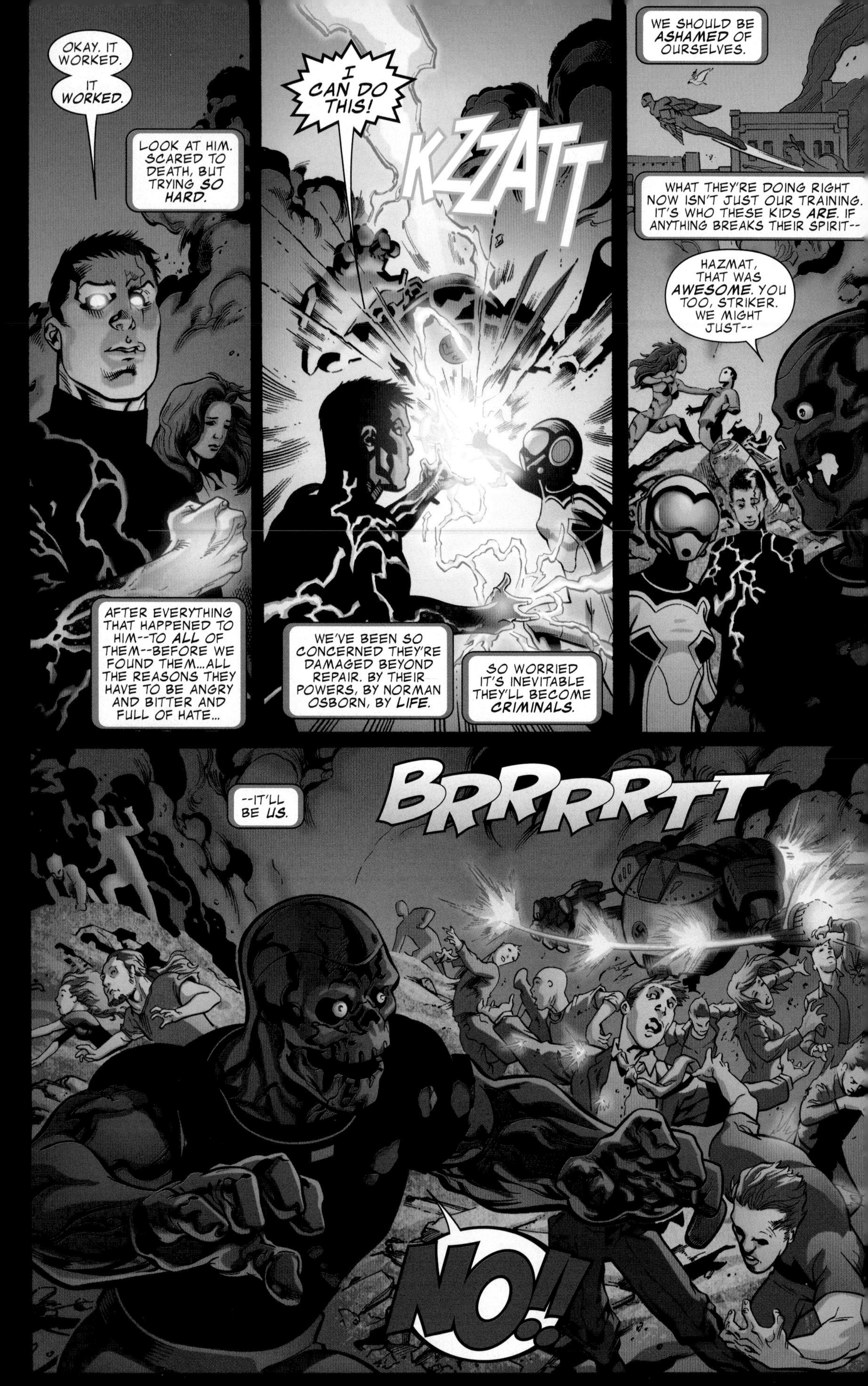
OKAY. IT WORKED.
IT WORKED.
LOOK AT HIM. SCARED TO DEATH, BUT TRYING SO HARD.
AFTER EVERYTHING THAT HAPPENED TO HIM--TO ALL OF THEM--BEFORE WE FOUND THEM...ALL THE REASONS THEY HAVE TO BE ANGRY AND BITTER AND FULL OF HATE...
I CAN DO THIS!
KKZZATT
WE'VE BEEN SO CONCERNED THEY'RE DAMAGED BEYOND REPAIR. BY THEIR POWERS, BY NORMAN OSBORN, BY LIFE.
SO WORRIED IT'S INEVITABLE THEY'LL BECOME CRIMINALS.
WE SHOULD BE ASHAMED OF OURSELVES.
WHAT THEY'RE DOING RIGHT NOW ISN'T JUST OUR TRAINING. IT'S WHO THESE KIDS ARE. IF ANYTHING BREAKS THEIR SPIRIT--
HAZMAT, THAT WAS AWESOME. YOU TOO, STRIKER. WE MIGHT JUST--
--IT'LL BE US.
BRRRRTT
NO!!

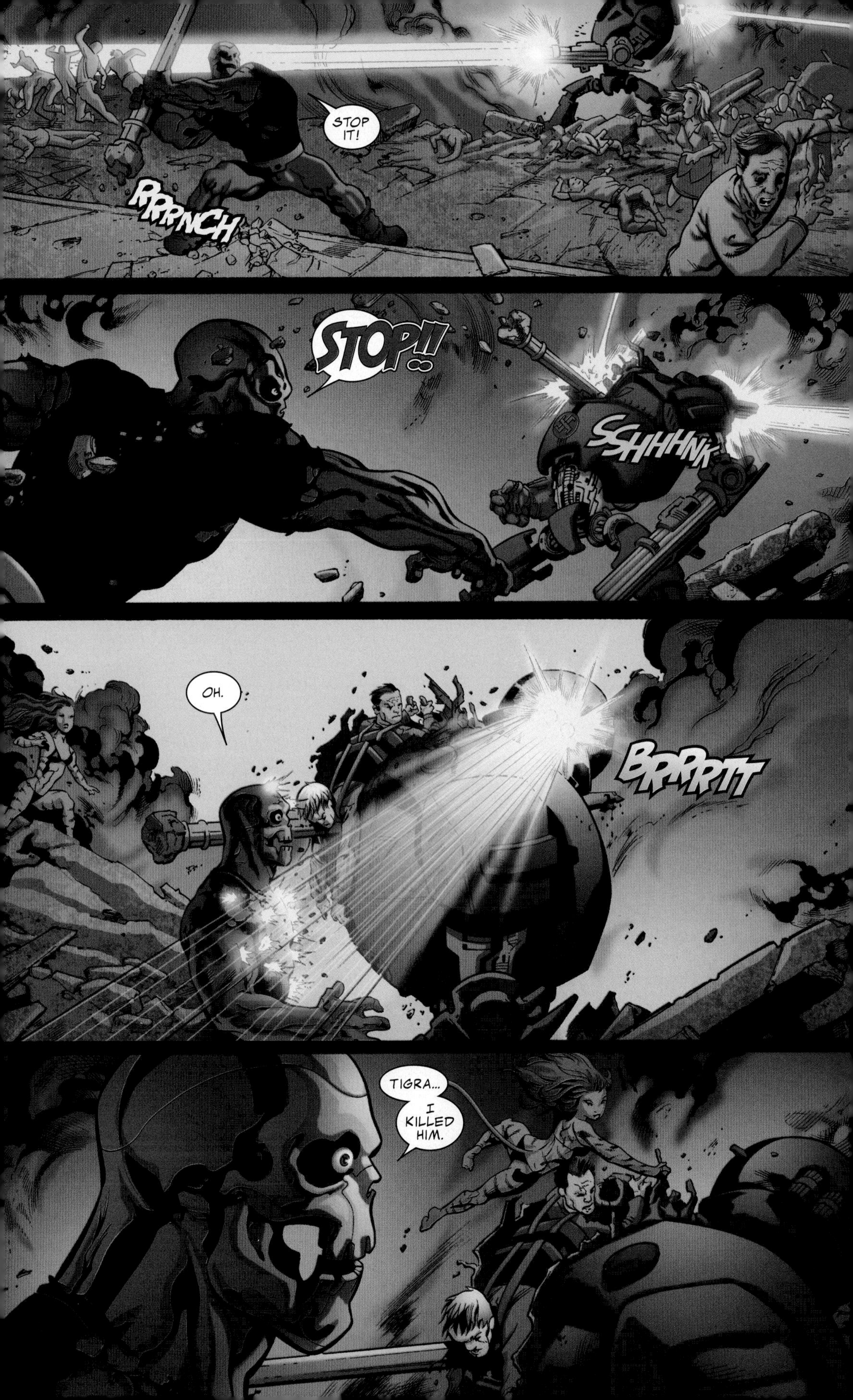
STOP IT!
RRRNCH
STOP!!
SSHHHNK
OH.
BRRRTT
TIGRA...
I KILLED HIM.

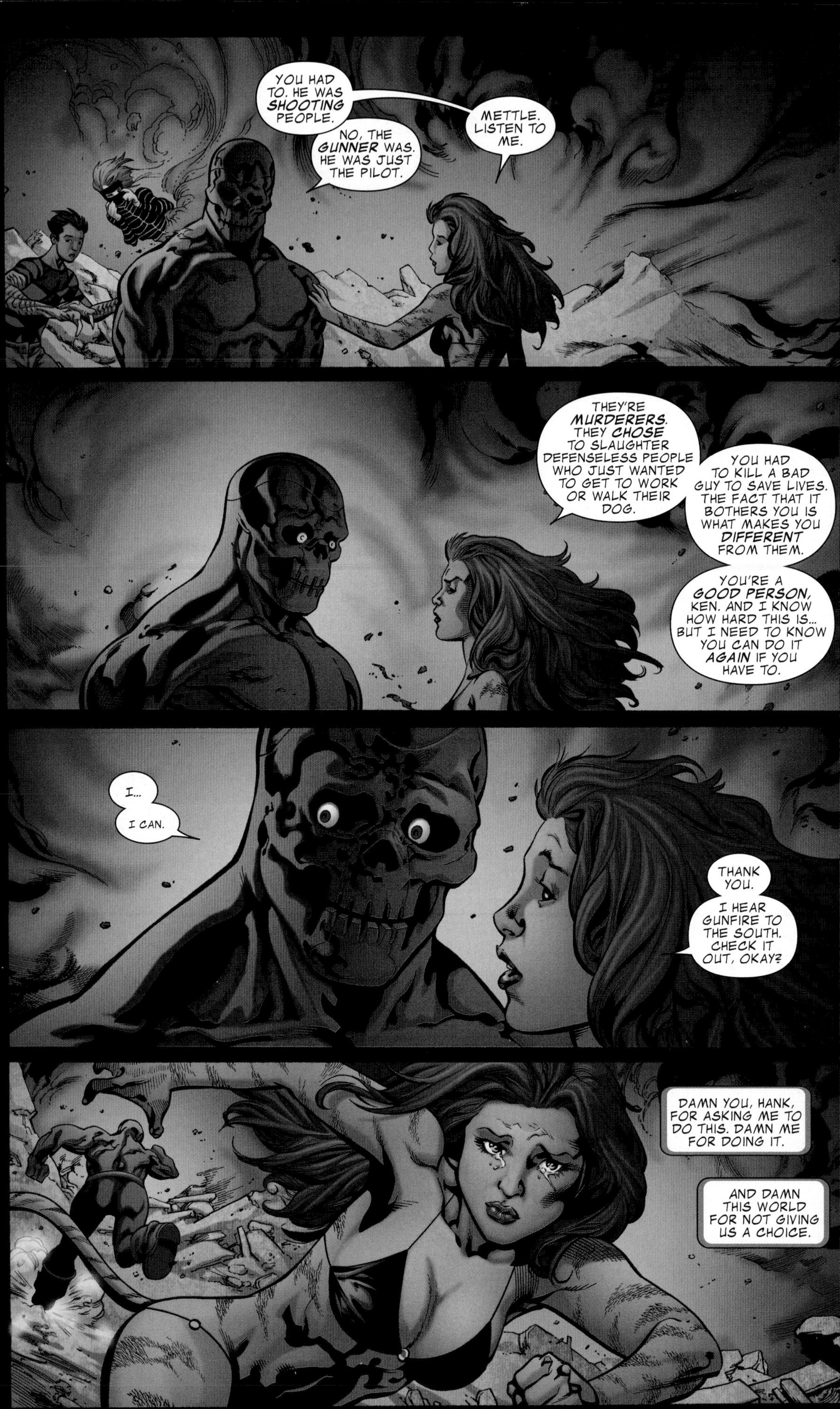

YOU HAD TO. HE WAS SHOOTING PEOPLE.
NO, THE GUNNER WAS. HE WAS JUST THE PILOT.
METTLE. LISTEN TO ME.
THEY'RE MURDERERS. THEY CHOSE TO SLAUGHTER DEFENSELESS PEOPLE WHO JUST WANTED TO GET TO WORK OR WALK THEIR DOG.
YOU HAD TO KILL A BAD GUY TO SAVE LIVES. THE FACT THAT IT BOTHERS YOU IS WHAT MAKES YOU DIFFERENT FROM THEM.
YOU'RE A GOOD PERSON, KEN. AND I KNOW HOW HARD THIS IS... BUT I NEED TO KNOW YOU CAN DO IT AGAIN IF YOU HAVE TO.
I...
I CAN.
THANK YOU.
I HEAR GUNFIRE TO THE SOUTH. CHECK IT OUT, OKAY?
DAMN YOU, HANK, FOR ASKING ME TO DO THIS. DAMN ME FOR DOING IT.
AND DAMN THIS WORLD FOR NOT GIVING US A CHOICE.

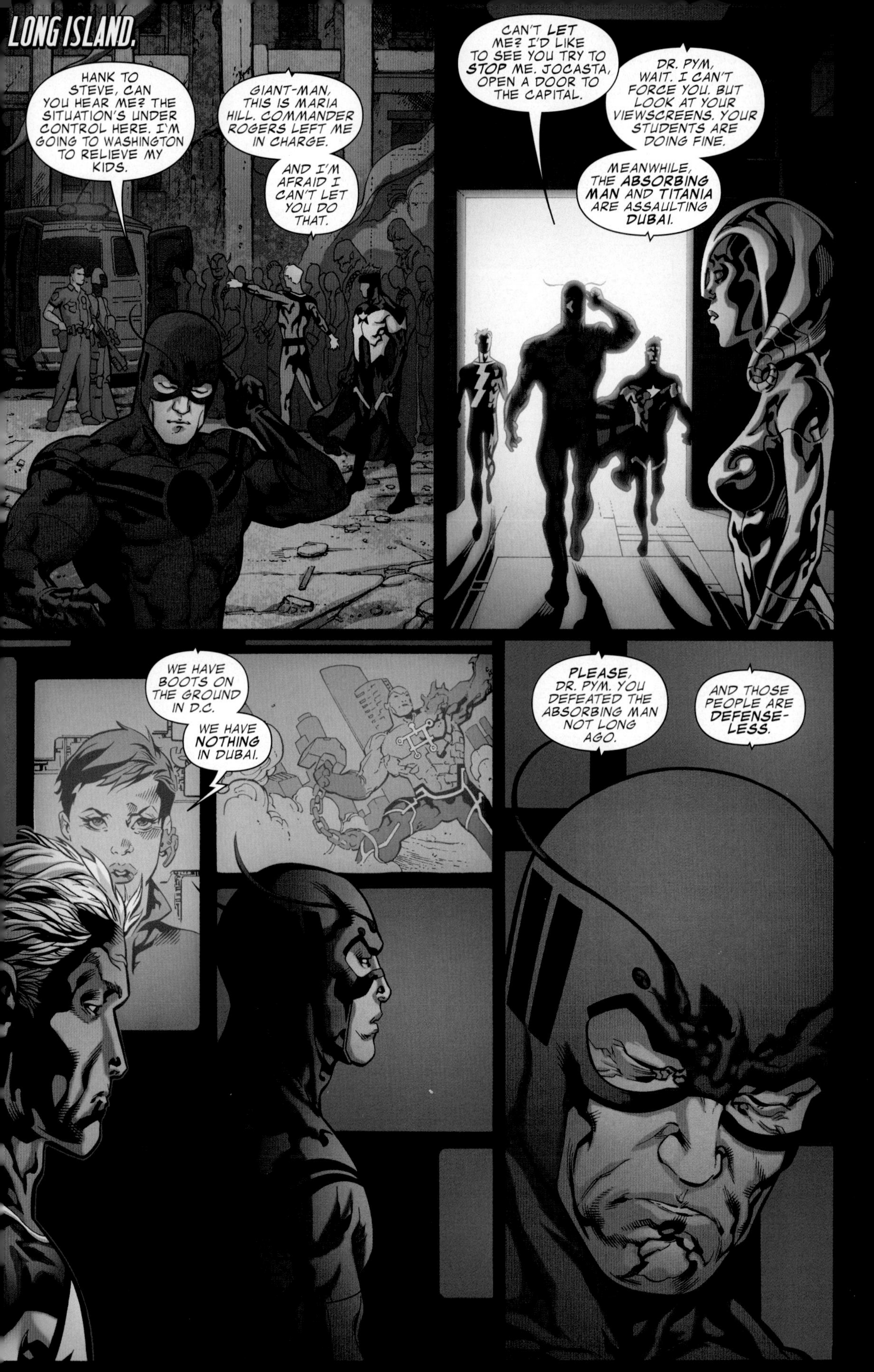
LONG ISLAND.
HANK TO STEVE, CAN YOU HEAR ME? THE SITUATION'S UNDER CONTROL HERE. I'M GOING TO WASHINGTON TO RELIEVE MY KIDS.
GIANT-MAN, THIS IS MARIA HILL. COMMANDER ROGERS LEFT ME IN CHARGE.
AND I'M AFRAID I CAN'T LET YOU DO THAT.
CAN'T LET ME? I'D LIKE TO SEE YOU TRY TO STOP ME. JOCASTA, OPEN A DOOR TO THE CAPITAL.
DR. PYM, WAIT. I CAN'T FORCE YOU. BUT LOOK AT YOUR VIEWSCREENS. YOUR STUDENTS ARE DOING FINE.
MEANWHILE, THE ABSORBING MAN AND TITANIA ARE ASSAULTING DUBAI.
WE HAVE BOOTS ON THE GROUND IN D.C.
WE HAVE NOTHING IN DUBAI.
PLEASE, DR. PYM. YOU DEFEATED THE ABSORBING MAN NOT LONG AGO.
AND THOSE PEOPLE ARE DEFENSE-LESS.

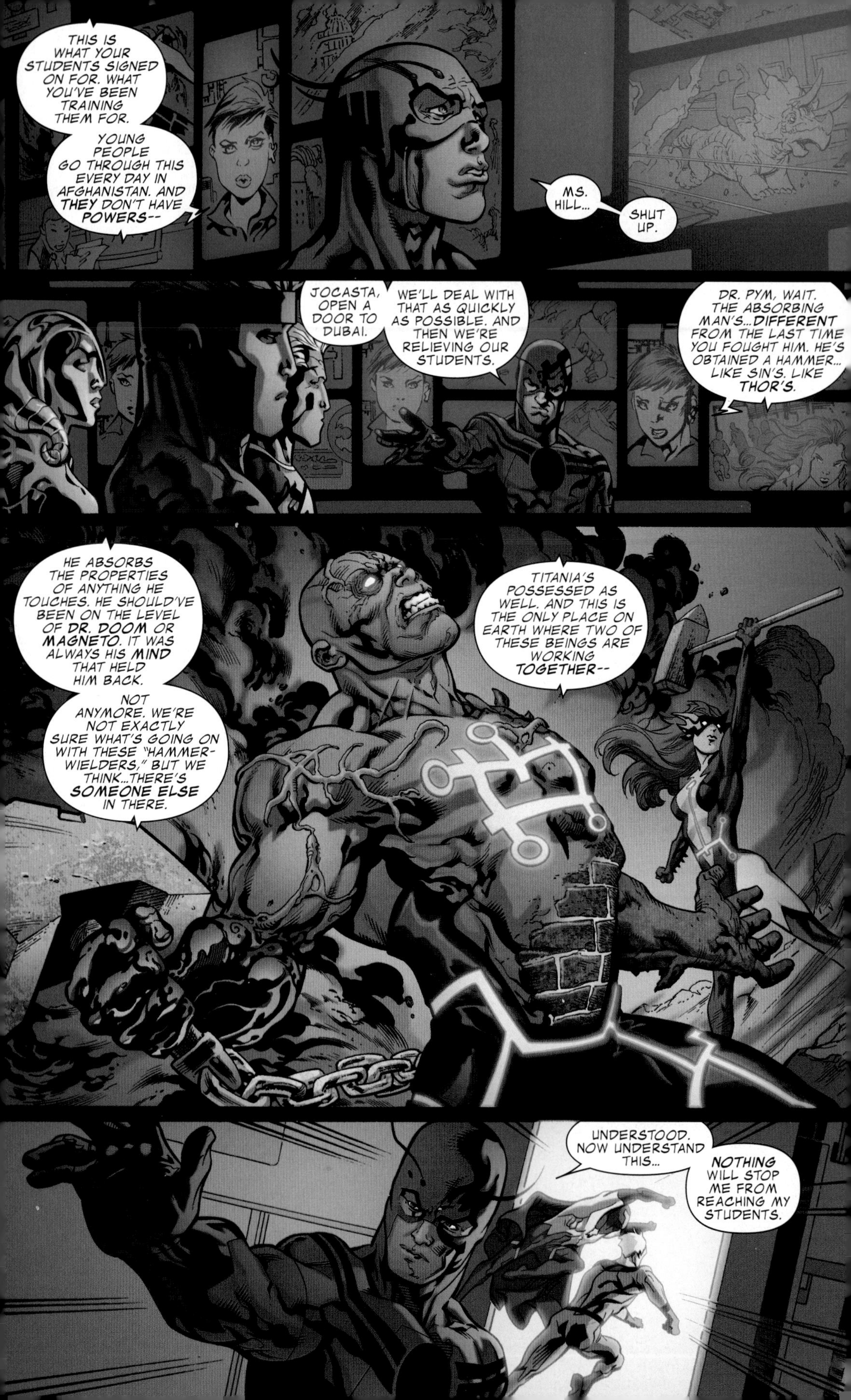
THIS IS WHAT YOUR STUDENTS SIGNED ON FOR. WHAT YOU'VE BEEN TRAINING THEM FOR.
YOUNG PEOPLE GO THROUGH THIS EVERY DAY IN AFGHANISTAN. AND THEY DON'T HAVE POWERS--
MS. HILL...
SHUT UP.
JOCASTA, OPEN A DOOR TO DUBAI.
WE'LL DEAL WITH THAT AS QUICKLY AS POSSIBLE. AND THEN WE'RE RELIEVING OUR STUDENTS.
DR. PYM, WAIT. THE ABSORBING MAN'S...DIFFERENT FROM THE LAST TIME YOU FOUGHT HIM. HE'S OBTAINED A HAMMER... LIKE SIN'S. LIKE THOR'S.
HE ABSORBS THE PROPERTIES OF ANYTHING HE TOUCHES. HE SHOULD'VE BEEN ON THE LEVEL OF DR. DOOM OR MAGNETO. IT WAS ALWAYS HIS MIND THAT HELD HIM BACK.
NOT ANYMORE. WE'RE NOT EXACTLY SURE WHAT'S GOING ON WITH THESE "HAMMER-WIELDERS," BUT WE THINK...THERE'S SOMEONE ELSE IN THERE.
TITANIA'S POSSESSED AS WELL. AND THIS IS THE ONLY PLACE ON EARTH WHERE TWO OF THESE BEINGS ARE WORKING TOGETHER--
UNDERSTOOD. NOW UNDERSTAND THIS...
NOTHING WILL STOP ME FROM REACHING MY STUDENTS.

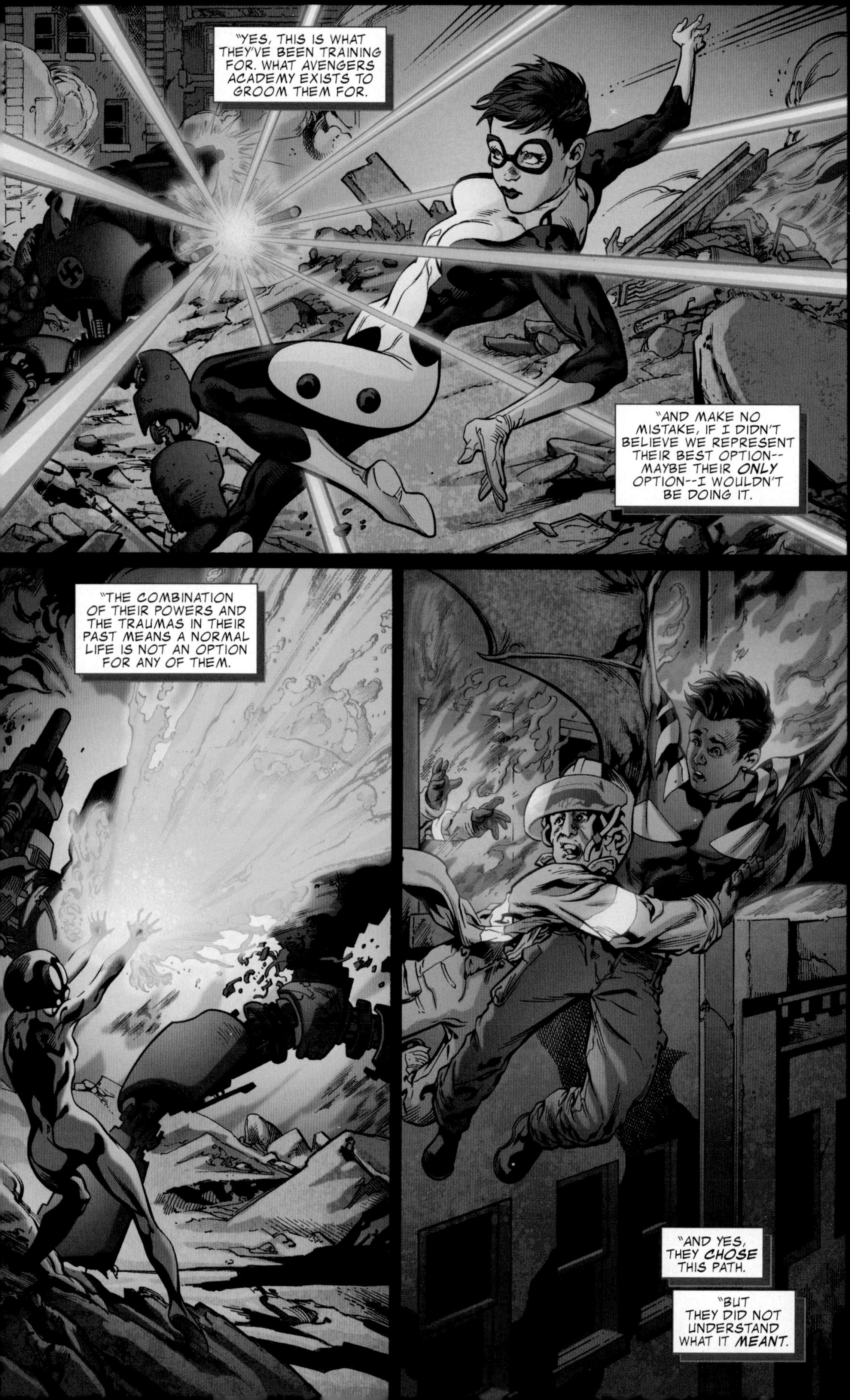
"YES, THIS IS WHAT THEY'VE BEEN TRAINING FOR. WHAT AVENGERS ACADEMY EXISTS TO GROOM THEM FOR.
"AND MAKE NO MISTAKE, IF I DIDN'T BELIEVE WE REPRESENT THEIR BEST OPTION-- MAYBE THEIR ONLY OPTION--I WOULDN'T BE DOING IT.
"THE COMBINATION OF THEIR POWERS AND THE TRAUMAS IN THEIR PAST MEANS A NORMAL LIFE IS NOT AN OPTION FOR ANY OF THEM.
"AND YES, THEY CHOSE THIS PATH.
"BUT THEY DID NOT UNDERSTAND WHAT IT MEANT.

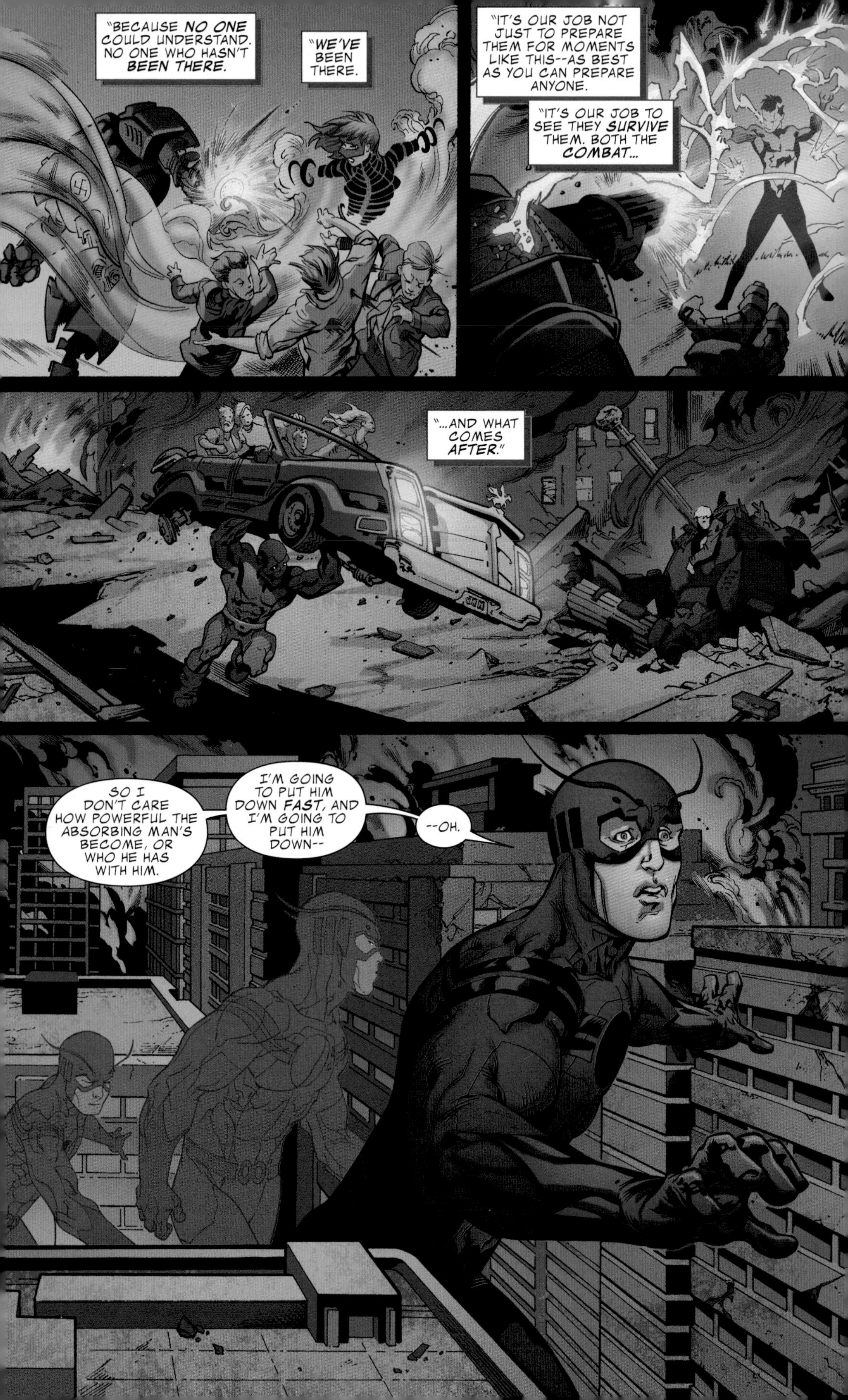
"BECAUSE NO ONE COULD UNDERSTAND. NO ONE WHO HASN'T BEEN THERE.
"WE'VE BEEN THERE.
"IT'S OUR JOB NOT JUST TO PREPARE THEM FOR MOMENTS LIKE THIS--AS BEST AS YOU CAN PREPARE ANYONE.
"IT'S OUR JOB TO SEE THEY SURVIVE THEM. BOTH THE COMBAT...
"...AND WHAT COMES AFTER."
SO I DON'T CARE HOW POWERFUL THE ABSORBING MAN'S BECOME, OR WHO HE HAS WITH HIM.
I'M GOING TO PUT HIM DOWN FAST, AND I'M GOING TO PUT HIM DOWN--
--OH.

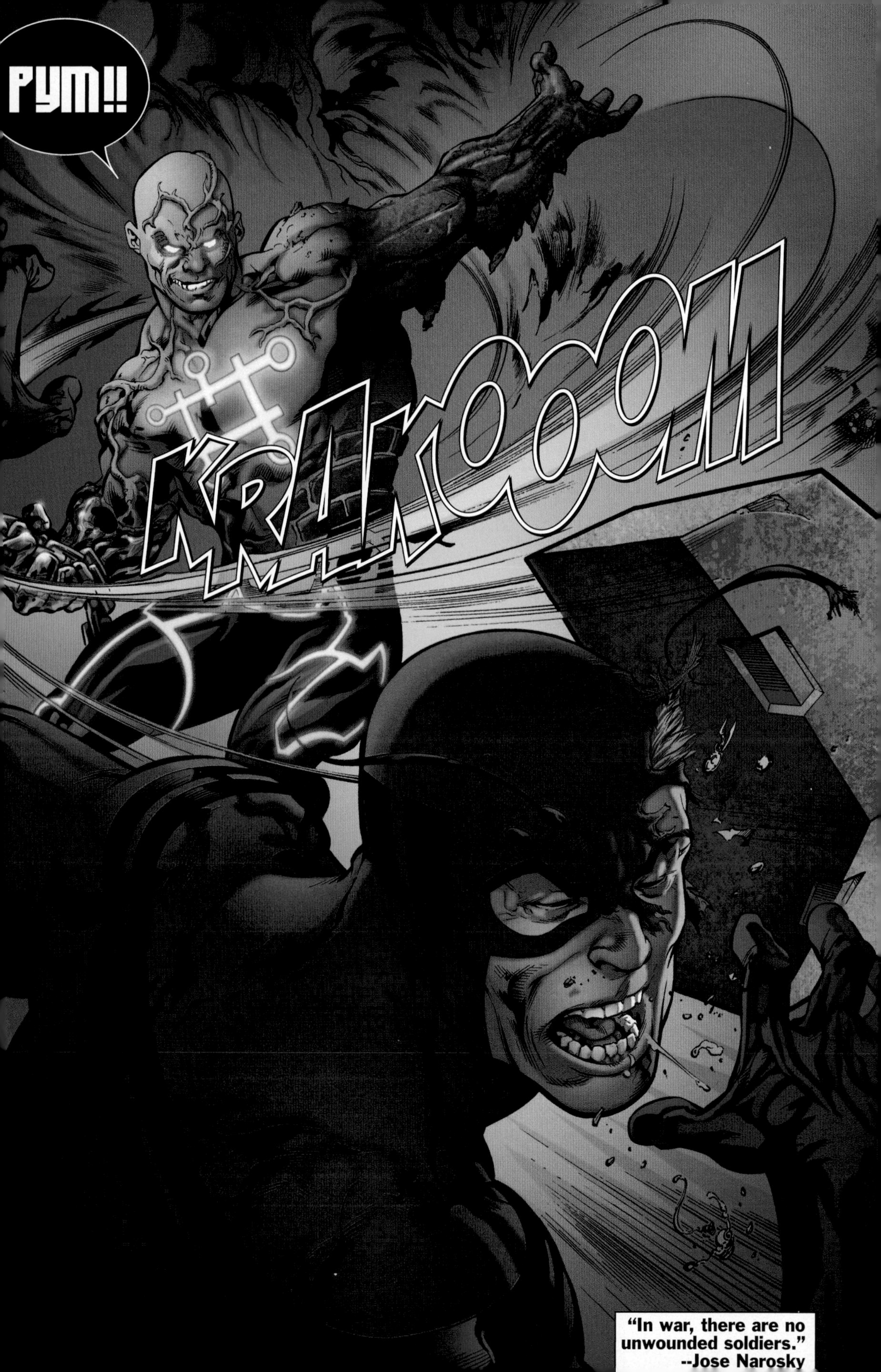
PYM!!
KRAKOOOM
"In war, there are no unwounded soldiers."
--Jose Narosky

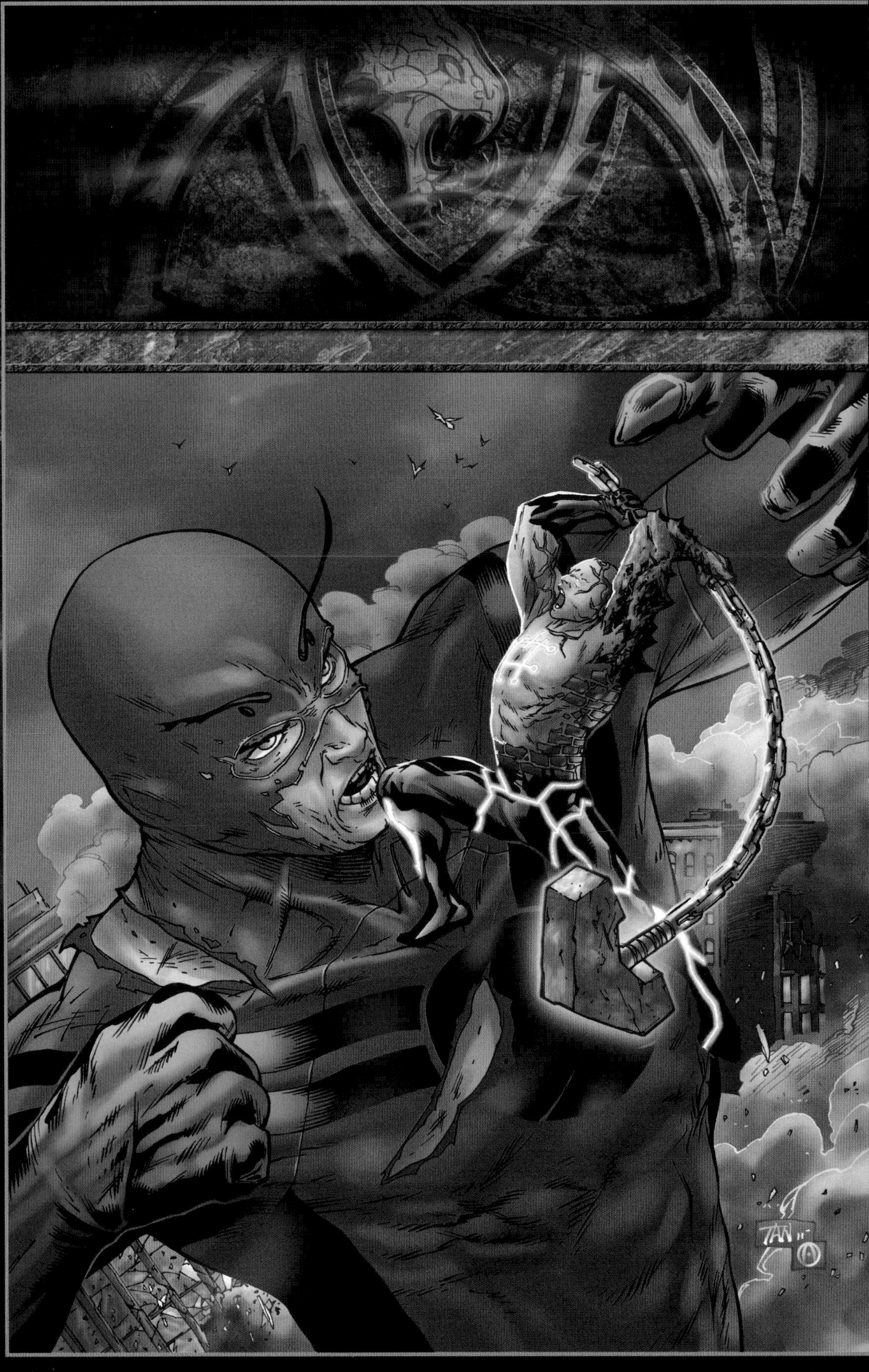
TAN

AVENGERS ACADEMY #16

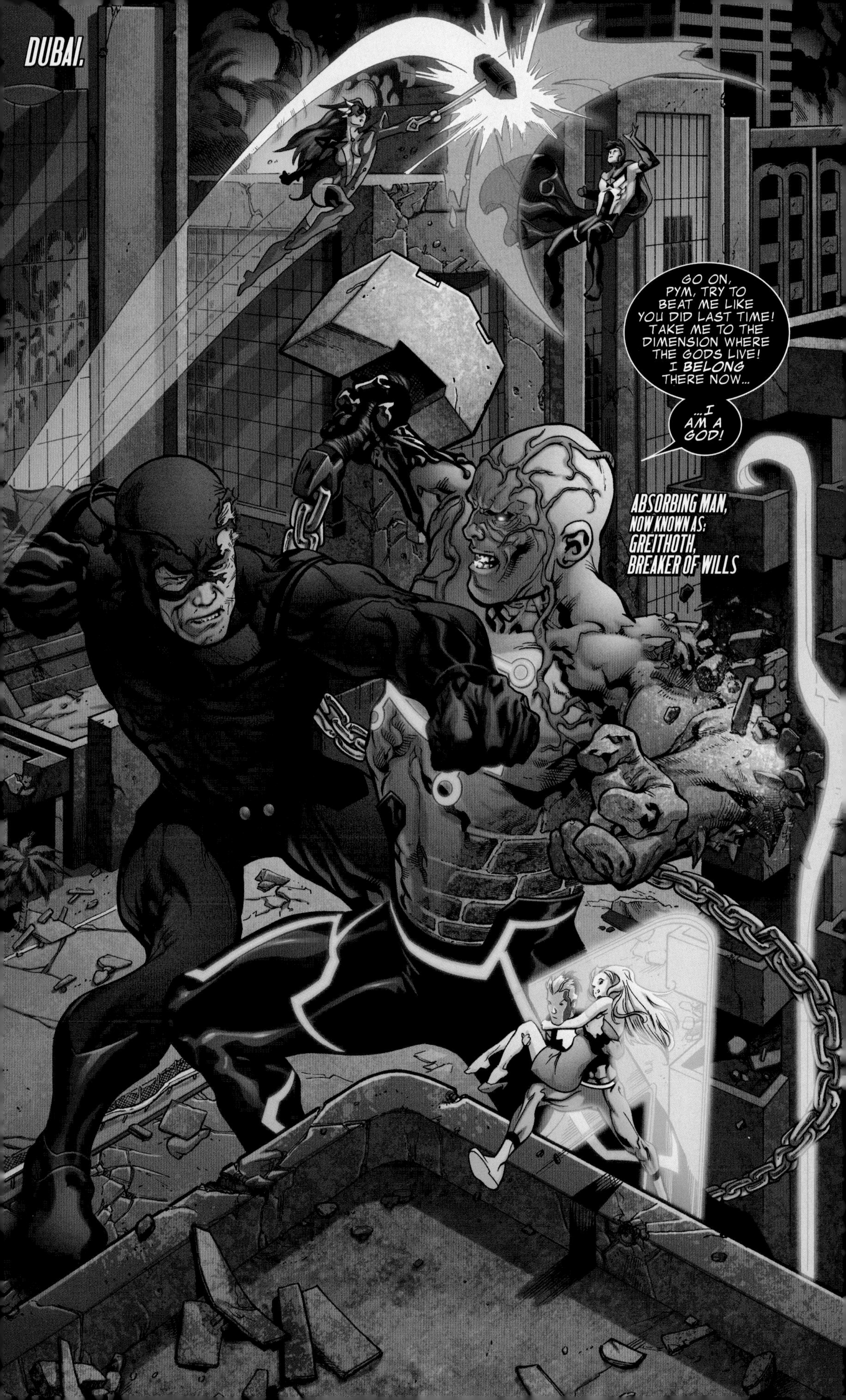
DUBAI.
GO ON, PYM, TRY TO BEAT ME LIKE YOU DID LAST TIME! TAKE ME TO THE DIMENSION WHERE THE GODS LIVE! I BELONG THERE NOW...
...I AM A GOD!
ABSORBING MAN, NOW KNOWN AS: GREITHOTH, BREAKER OF WILLS

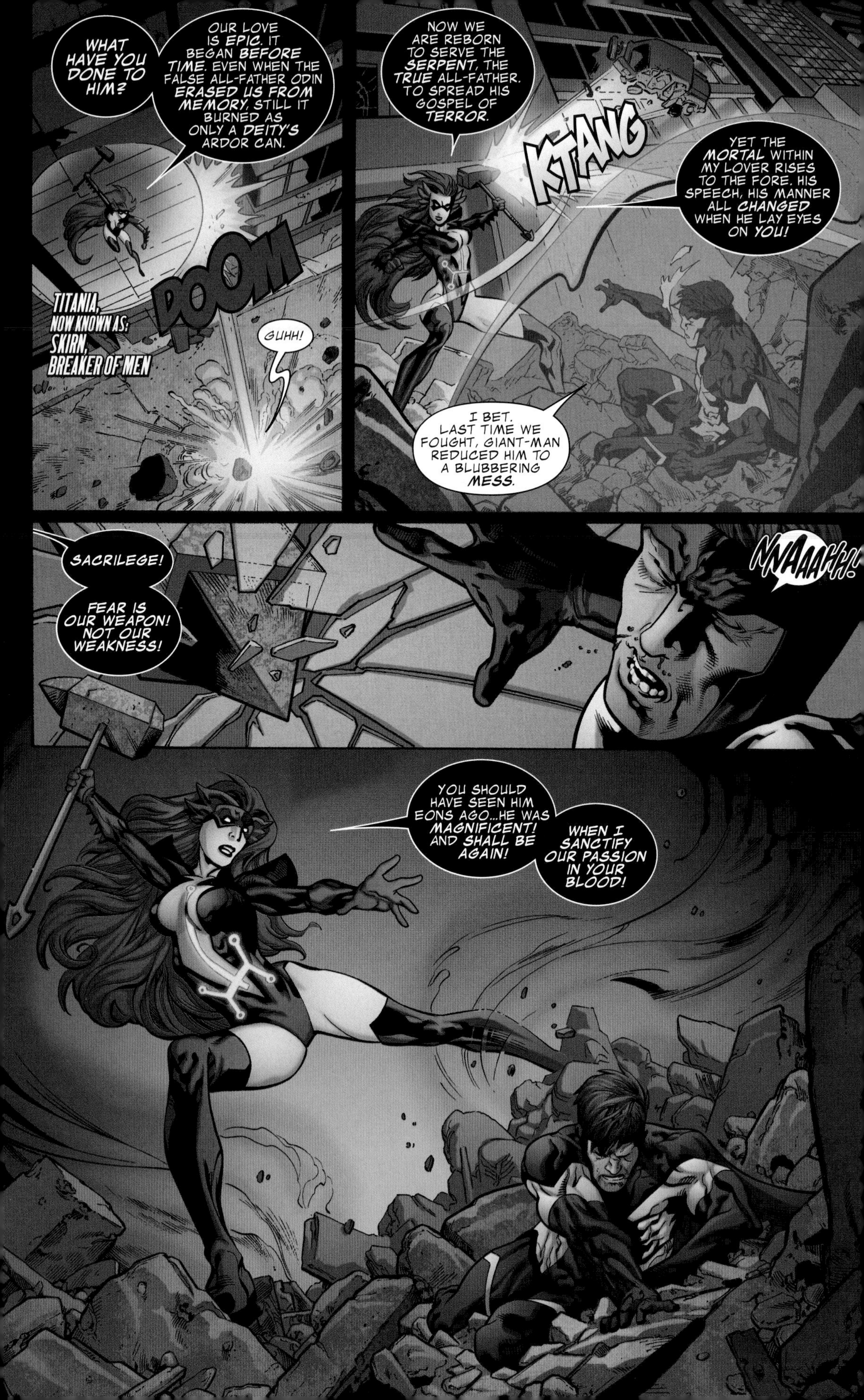
WHAT HAVE YOU DONE TO HIM?
OUR LOVE IS EPIC. IT BEGAN BEFORE TIME. EVEN WHEN THE FALSE ALL-FATHER ODIN ERASED US FROM MEMORY, STILL IT BURNED AS ONLY A DEITY'S ARDOR CAN.
DOOM
TITANIA, NOW KNOWN AS: SKIRN, BREAKER OF MEN
GUHH!
NOW WE ARE REBORN TO SERVE THE SERPENT, THE TRUE ALL-FATHER. TO SPREAD HIS GOSPEL OF TERROR.
KTANG
YET THE MORTAL WITHIN MY LOVER RISES TO THE FORE. HIS SPEECH, HIS MANNER ALL CHANGED WHEN HE LAY EYES ON YOU!
I BET. LAST TIME WE FOUGHT, GIANT-MAN REDUCED HIM TO A BLUBBERING MESS.
SACRILEGE!
FEAR IS OUR WEAPON! NOT OUR WEAKNESS!
NNAAAHH!
YOU SHOULD HAVE SEEN HIM EONS AGO...HE WAS MAGNIFICENT! AND SHALL BE AGAIN!
WHEN I SANCTIFY OUR PASSION IN YOUR BLOOD!

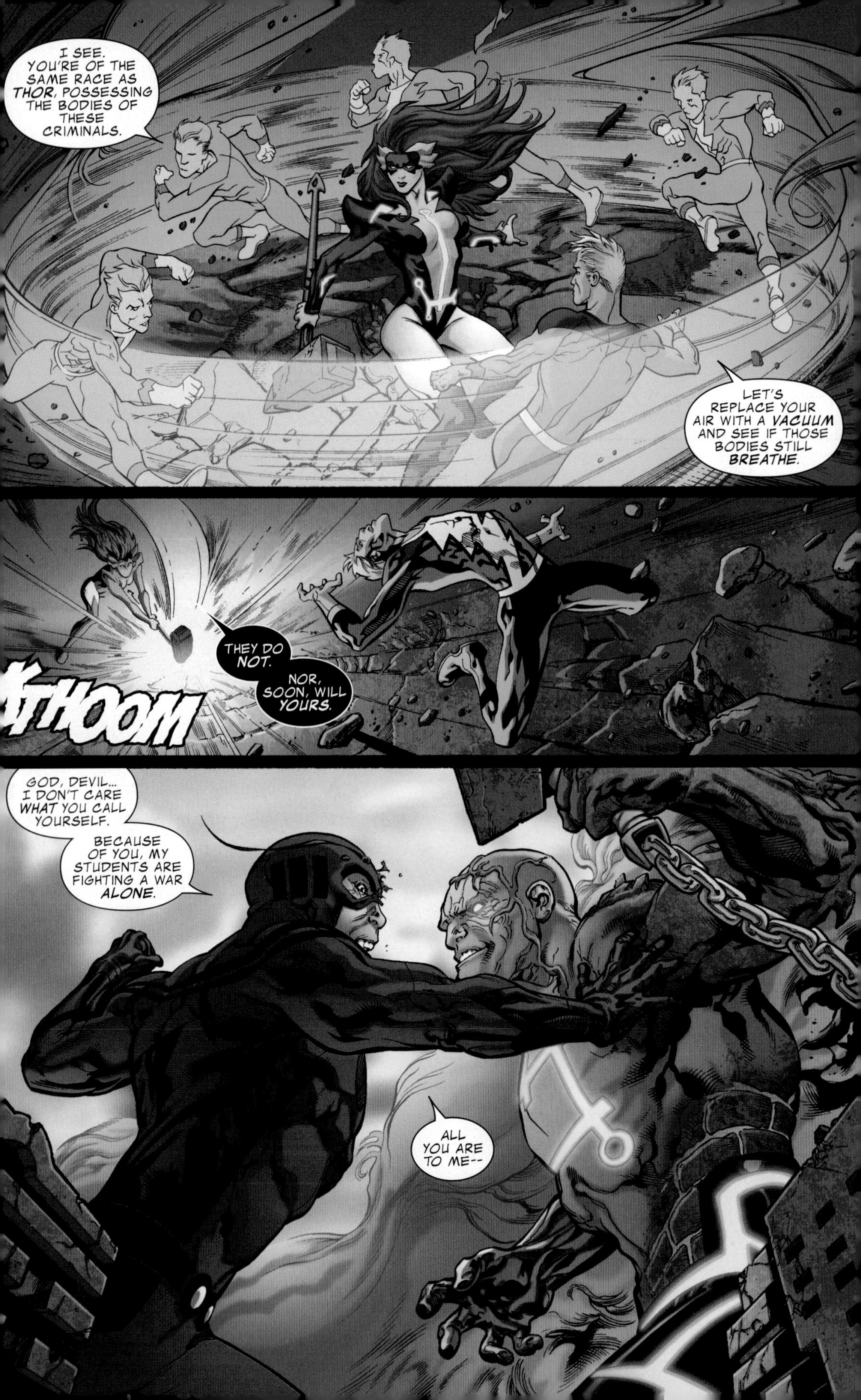
I SEE. YOU'RE OF THE SAME RACE AS THOR, POSSESSING THE BODIES OF THESE CRIMINALS.
LET'S REPLACE YOUR AIR WITH A VACUUM AND SEE IF THOSE BODIES STILL BREATHE.
THOOM
THEY DO NOT.
NOR, SOON, WILL YOURS.
GOD, DEVIL... I DON'T CARE WHAT YOU CALL YOURSELF.
BECAUSE OF YOU, MY STUDENTS ARE FIGHTING A WAR ALONE.
ALL YOU ARE TO ME--

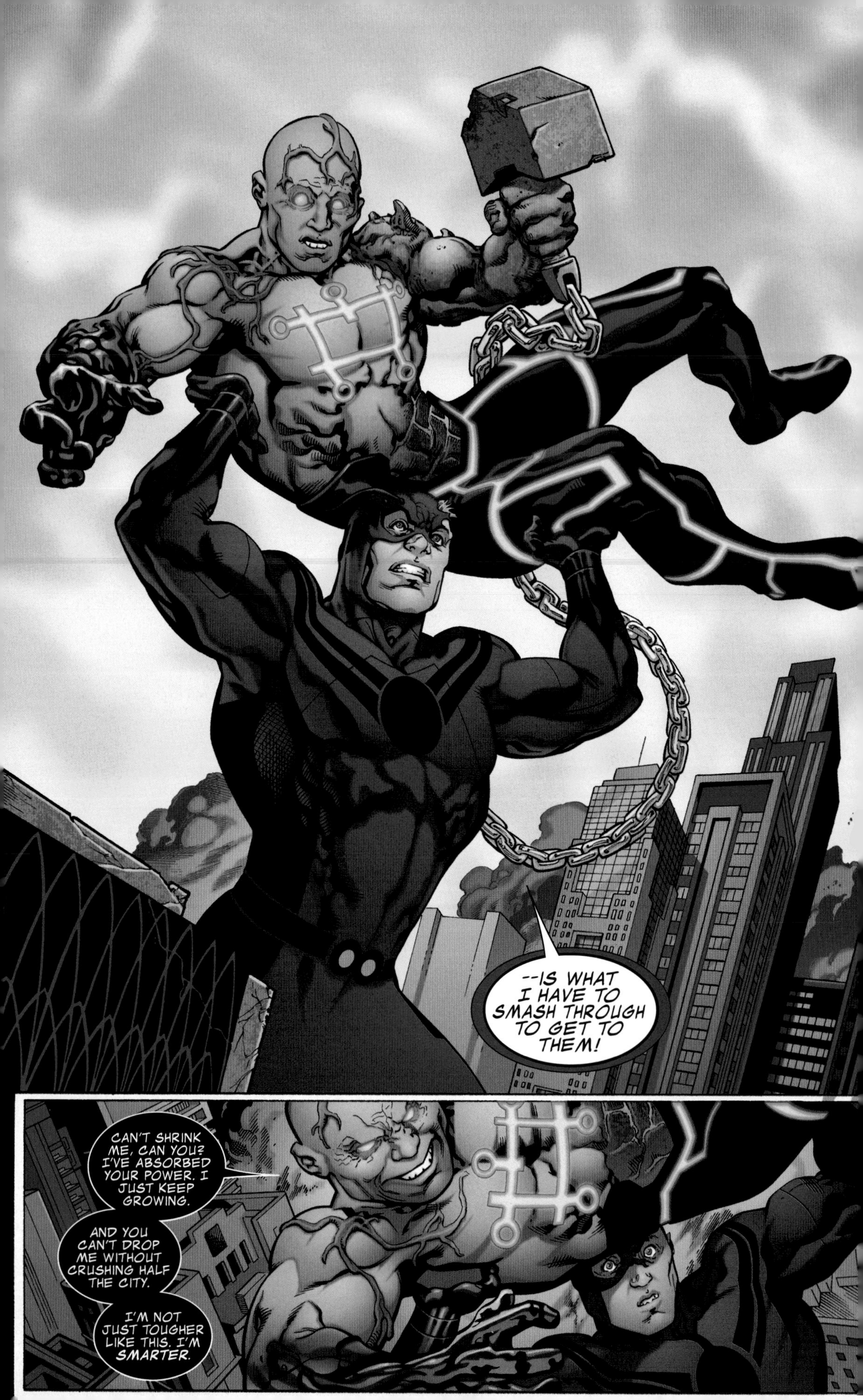
--IS WHAT I HAVE TO SMASH THROUGH TO GET TO THEM!
CAN'T SHRINK ME, CAN YOU? I'VE ABSORBED YOUR POWER. I JUST KEEP GROWING.
AND YOU CAN'T DROP ME WITHOUT CRUSHING HALF THE CITY.
I'M NOT JUST TOUGHER LIKE THIS. I'M SMARTER.

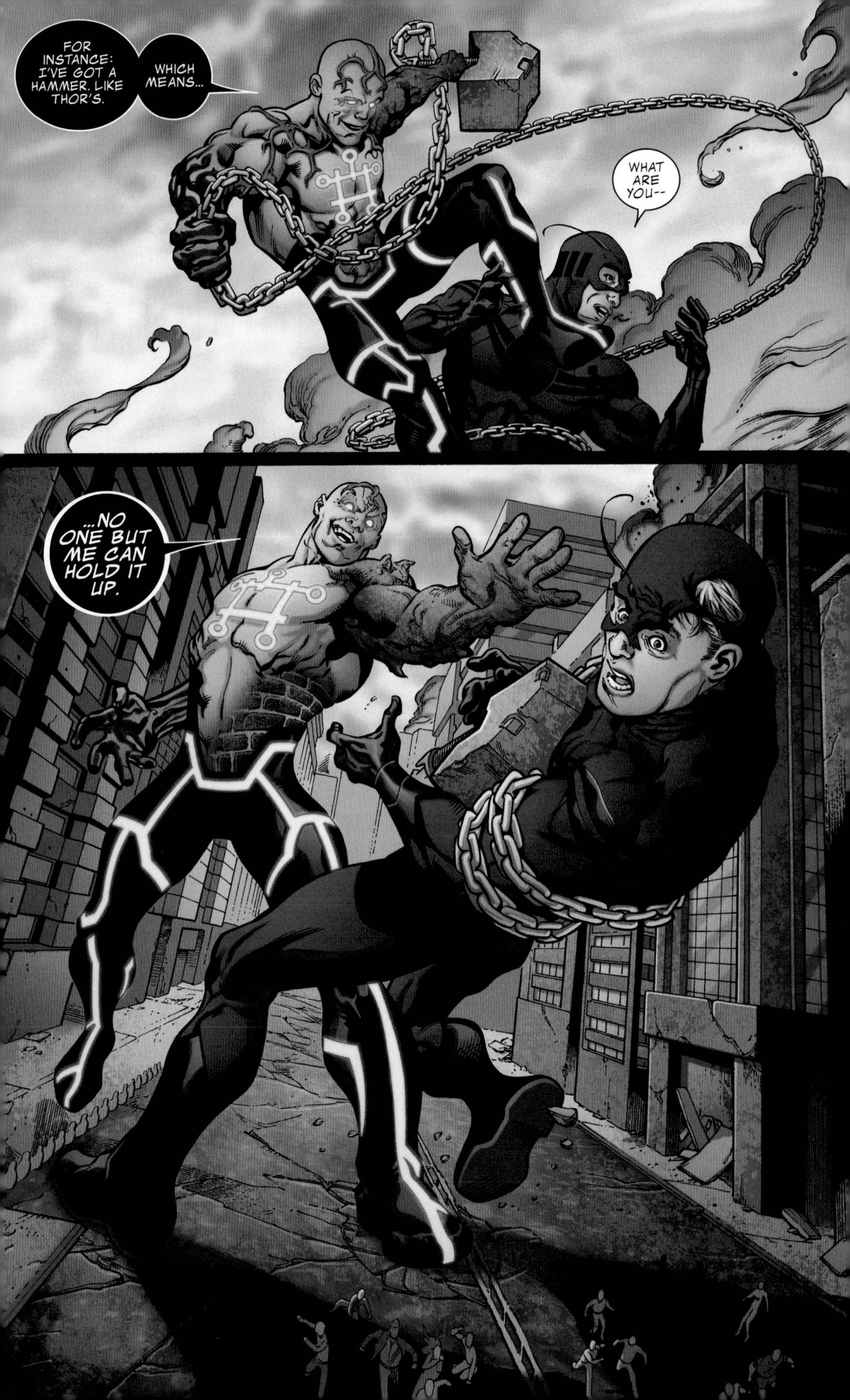
FOR INSTANCE: I'VE GOT A HAMMER. LIKE THOR'S.
WHICH MEANS...
WHAT ARE YOU--
...NO ONE BUT ME CAN HOLD IT UP.

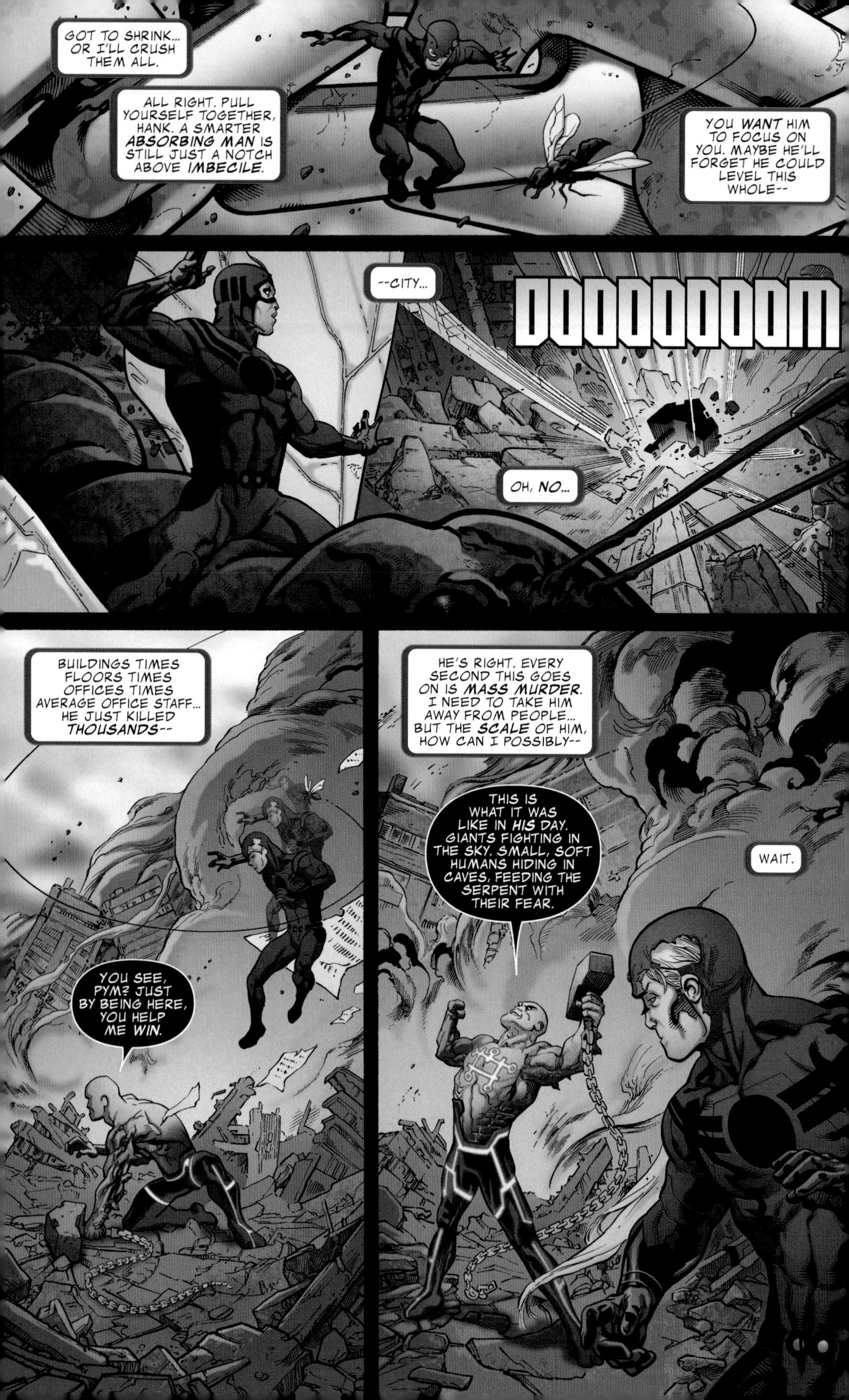
GOT TO SHRINK... OR I'LL CRUSH THEM ALL.
ALL RIGHT. PULL YOURSELF TOGETHER, HANK. A SMARTER ABSORBING MAN IS STILL JUST A NOTCH ABOVE IMBECILE.
YOU WANT HIM TO FOCUS ON YOU. MAYBE HE'LL FORGET HE COULD LEVEL THIS WHOLE--
--CITY...
DOOOOOOOOM
OH, NO...
BUILDINGS TIMES FLOORS TIMES OFFICES TIMES AVERAGE OFFICE STAFF... HE JUST KILLED THOUSANDS--
YOU SEE, PYM? JUST BY BEING HERE, YOU HELP ME WIN.
HE'S RIGHT. EVERY SECOND THIS GOES ON IS MASS MURDER. I NEED TO TAKE HIM AWAY FROM PEOPLE... BUT THE SCALE OF HIM, HOW CAN I POSSIBLY--
THIS IS WHAT IT WAS LIKE IN HIS DAY. GIANTS FIGHTING IN THE SKY. SMALL, SOFT HUMANS HIDING IN CAVES, FEEDING THE SERPENT WITH THEIR FEAR.
WAIT.

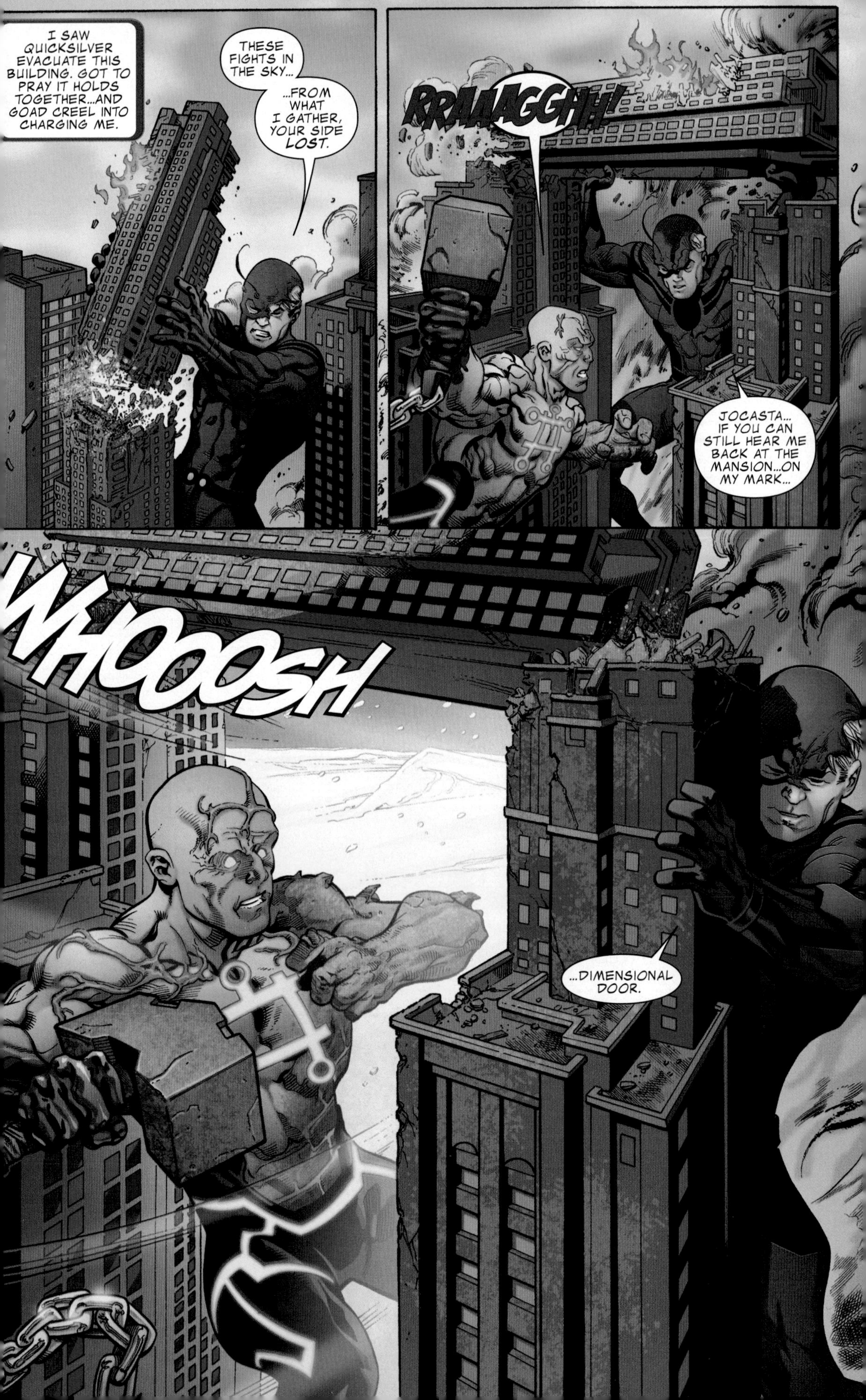
I SAW QUICKSILVER EVACUATE THIS BUILDING. GOT TO PRAY IT HOLDS TOGETHER...AND GOAD CREEL INTO CHARGING ME.
THESE FIGHTS IN THE SKY...
...FROM WHAT I GATHER, YOUR SIDE LOST.
RRAAAGGHH!
JOCASTA... IF YOU CAN STILL HEAR ME BACK AT THE MANSION...ON MY MARK...
WHOOOSH
...DIMENSIONAL DOOR.

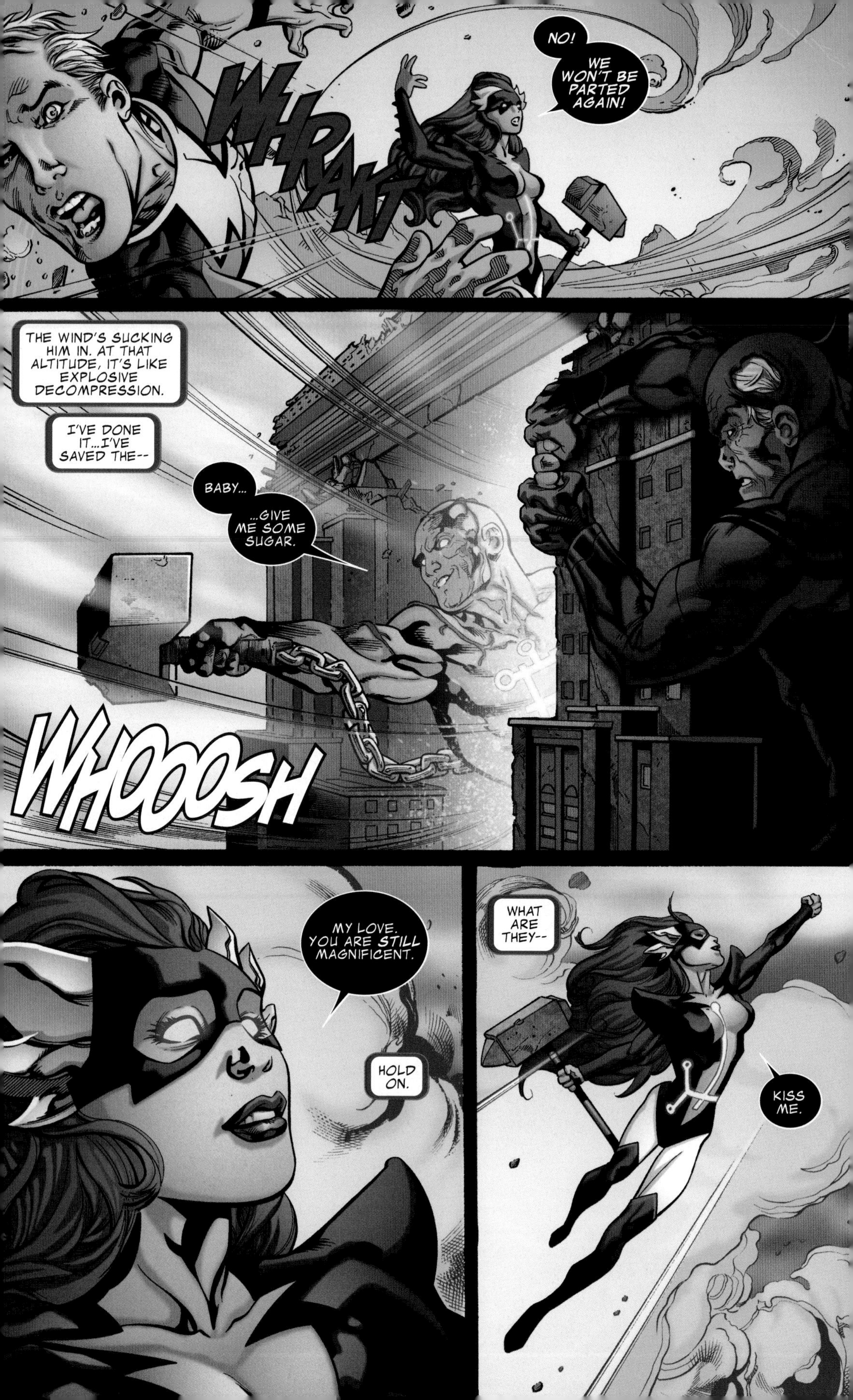
WHRAKT
NO!
WE WON'T BE PARTED AGAIN!
THE WIND'S SUCKING HIM IN. AT THAT ALTITUDE, IT'S LIKE EXPLOSIVE DECOMPRESSION.
I'VE DONE IT...I'VE SAVED THE--
BABY...
...GIVE ME SOME SUGAR.
WHOOOSH
MY LOVE. YOU ARE STILL MAGNIFICENT.
HOLD ON.
WHAT ARE THEY--
KISS ME.

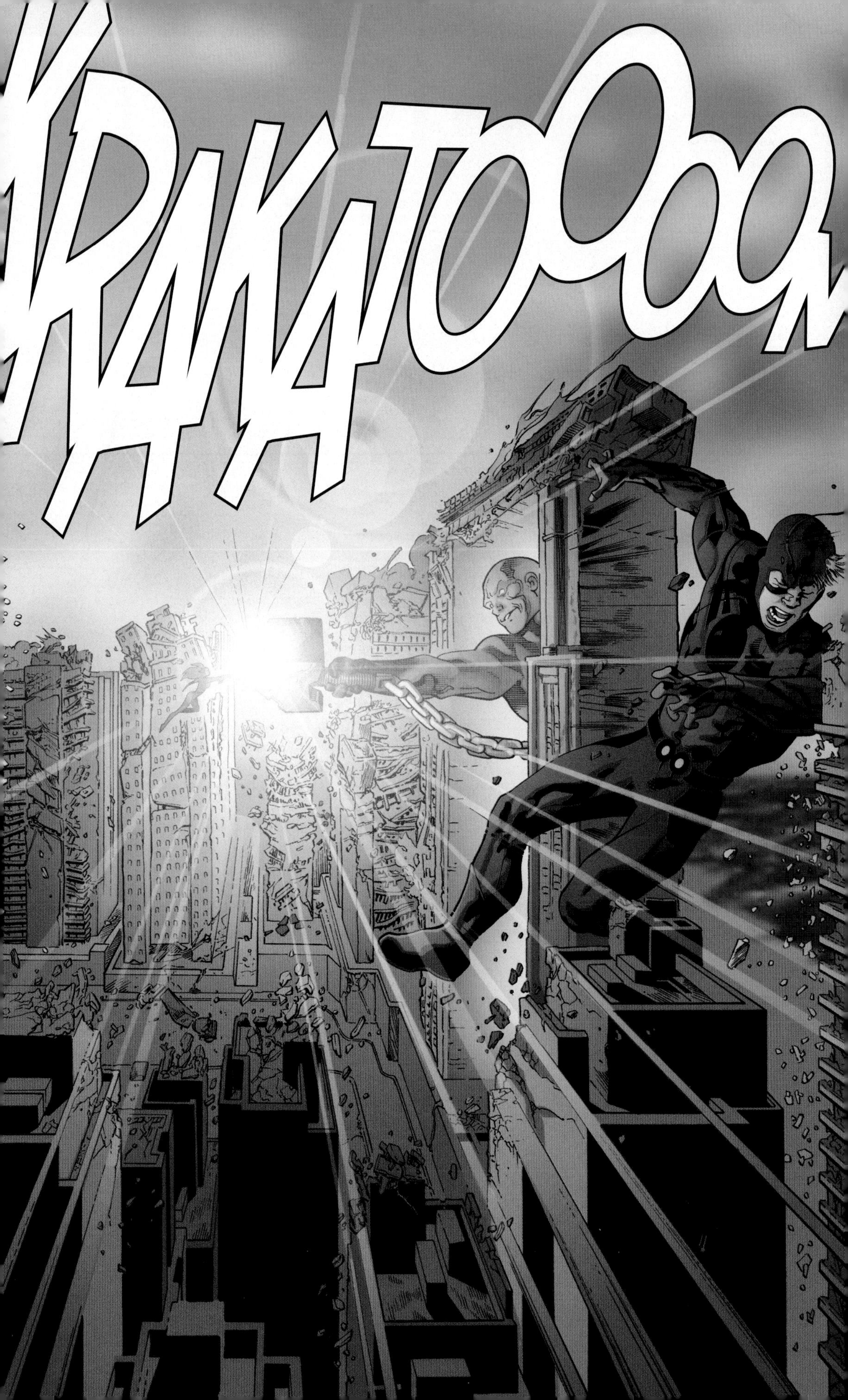
KRAKATOOOOM

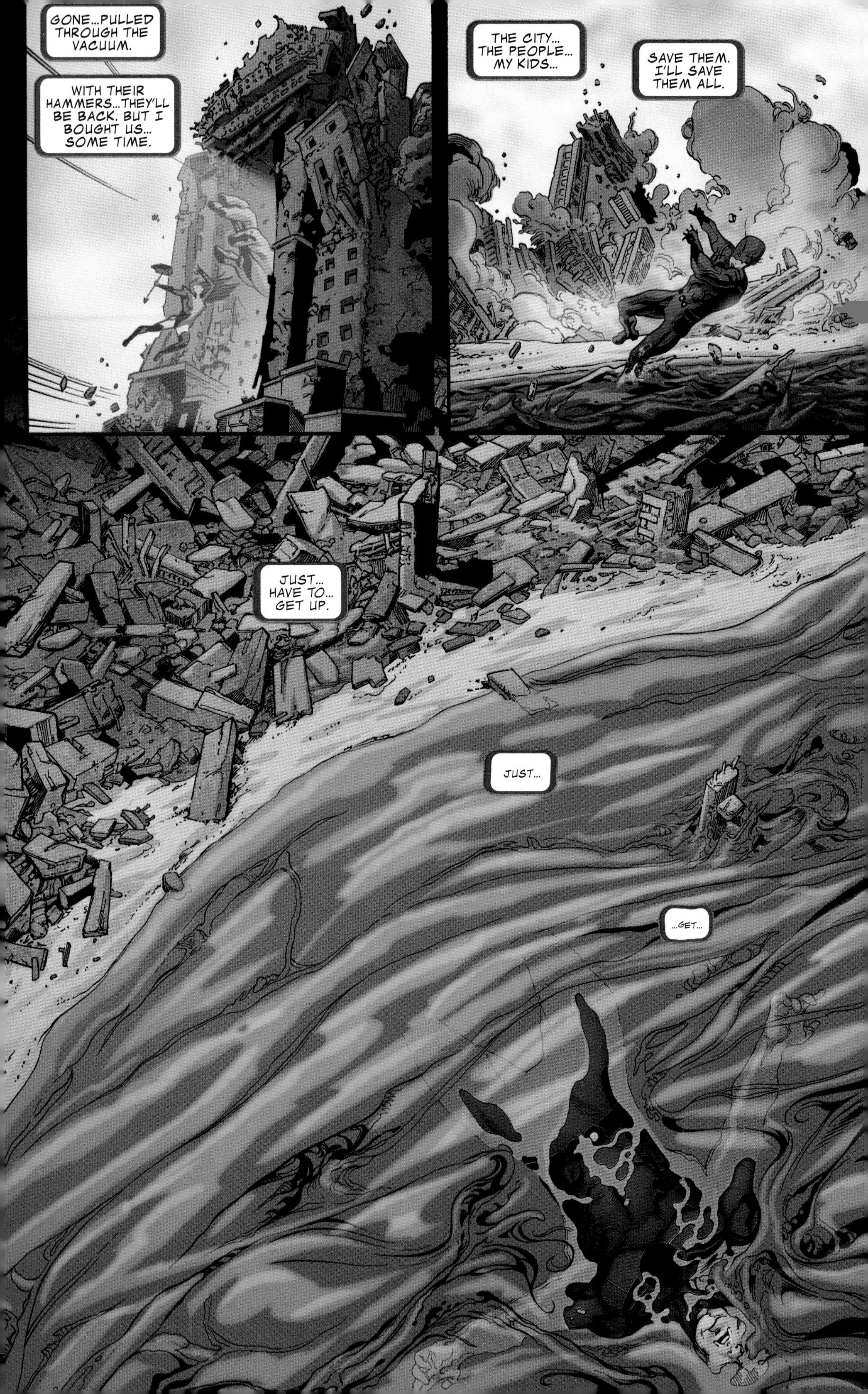
GONE...PULLED THROUGH THE VACUUM.
WITH THEIR HAMMERS...THEY'LL BE BACK. BUT I BOUGHT US... SOME TIME.
THE CITY... THE PEOPLE... MY KIDS...
SAVE THEM. I'LL SAVE THEM ALL.
JUST... HAVE TO... GET UP.
JUST...
...GET...

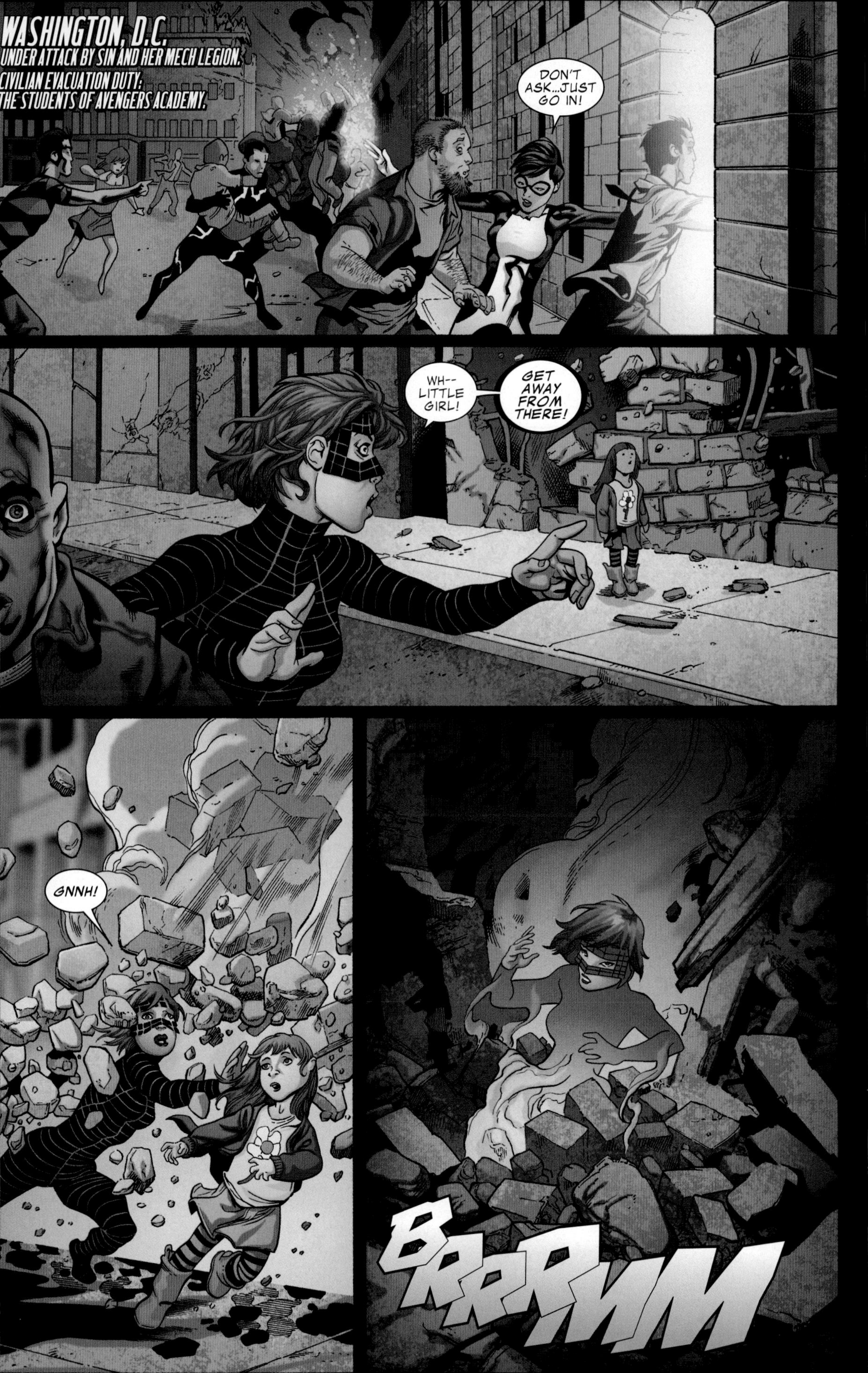
WASHINGTON, D.C.
UNDER ATTACK BY SIN AND HER MECH LEGION.
CIVILIAN EVACUATION DUTY: THE STUDENTS OF AVENGERS ACADEMY.
DON'T ASK...JUST GO IN!
WH-- LITTLE GIRL!
GET AWAY FROM THERE!
GNNH!
BRRRMM

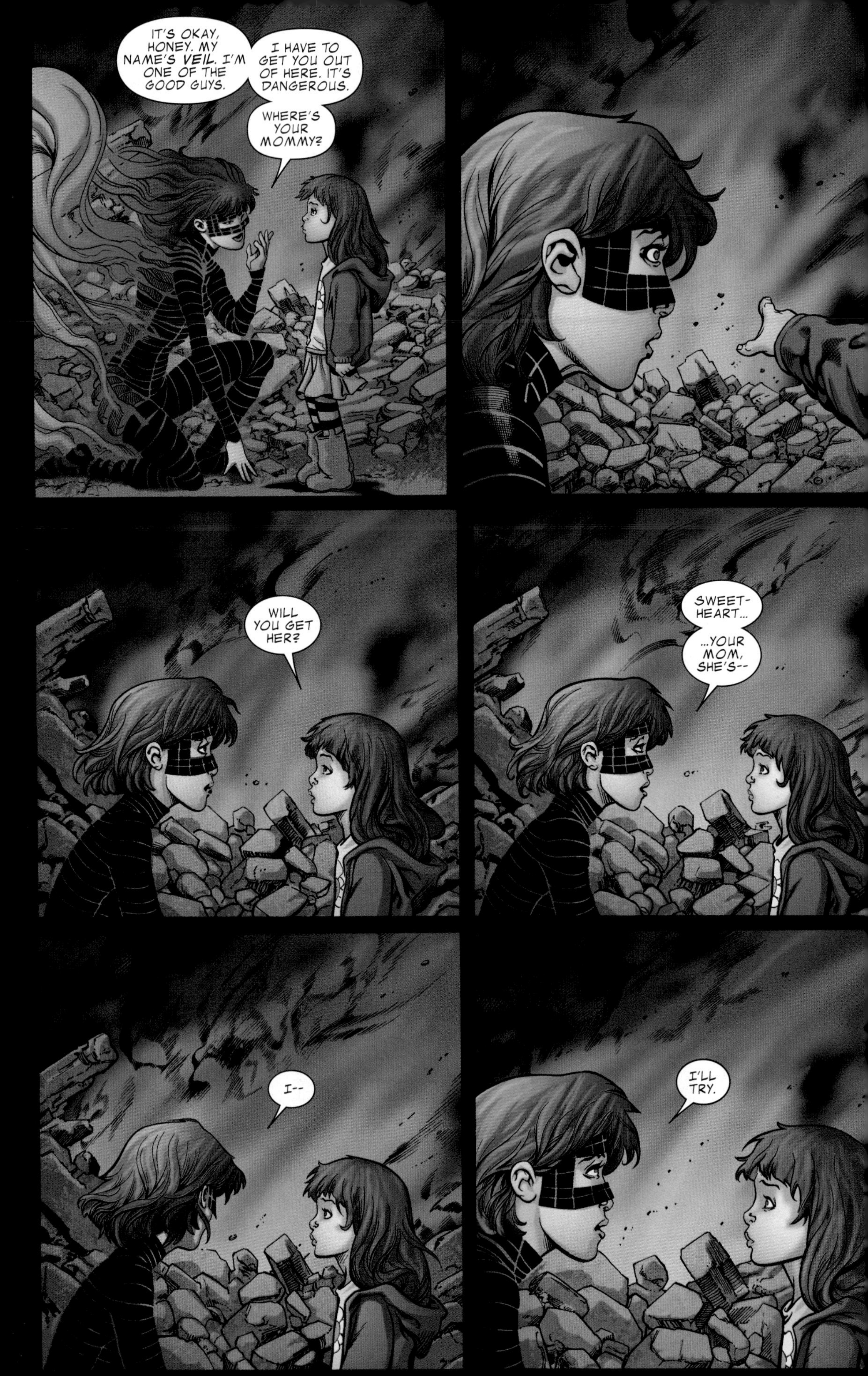
IT'S OKAY, HONEY. MY NAME'S VEIL. I'M ONE OF THE GOOD GUYS.
I HAVE TO GET YOU OUT OF HERE. IT'S DANGEROUS.
WHERE'S YOUR MOMMY?
WILL YOU GET HER?
SWEET-HEART...
...YOUR MOM, SHE'S--
I--
I'LL TRY.

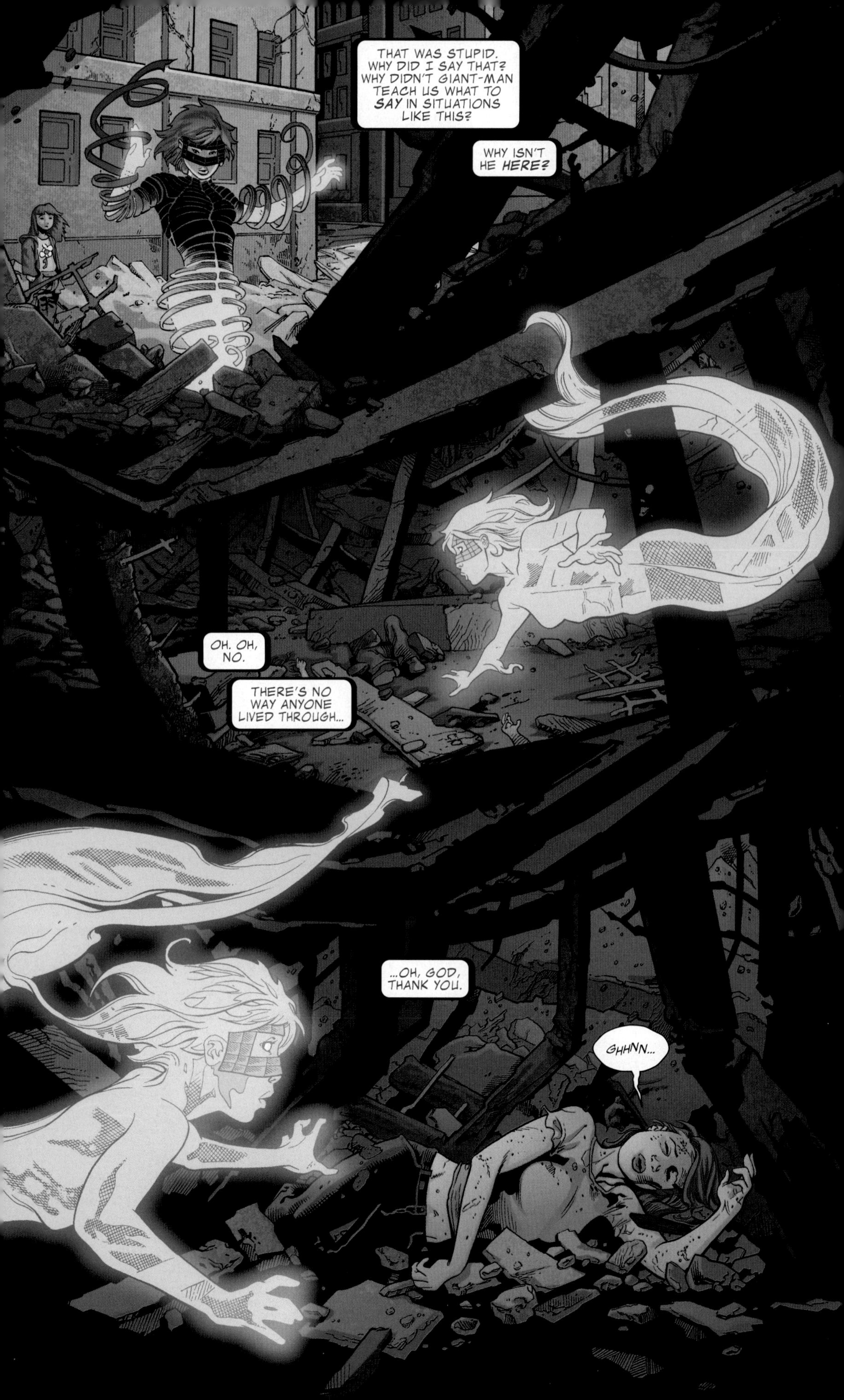
THAT WAS STUPID. WHY DID I SAY THAT? WHY DIDN'T GIANT-MAN TEACH US WHAT TO SAY IN SITUATIONS LIKE THIS?
WHY ISN'T HE HERE?
OH. OH, NO.
THERE'S NO WAY ANYONE LIVED THROUGH...
...OH, GOD, THANK YOU.
GHHNN...

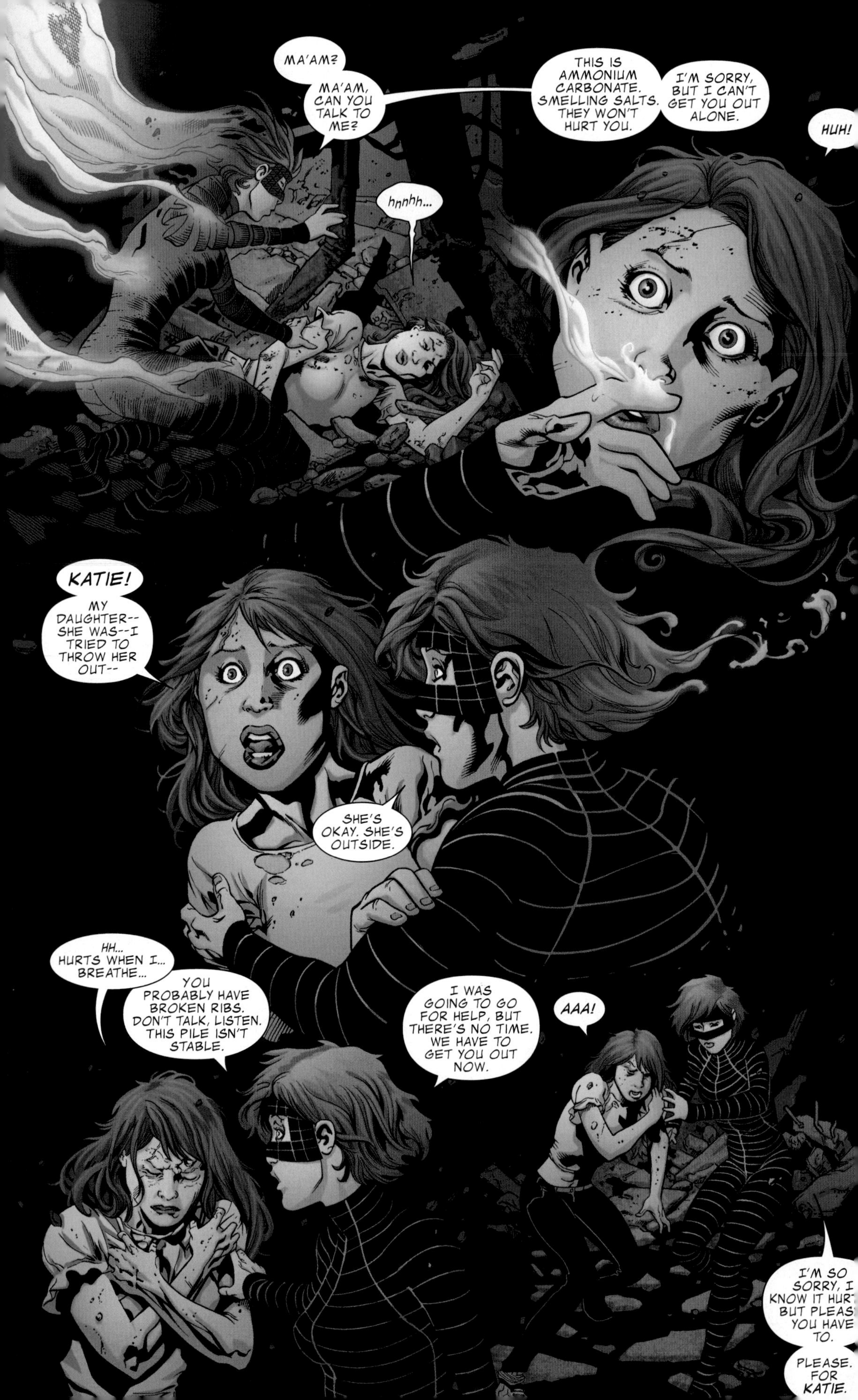
MA'AM?
MA'AM, CAN YOU TALK TO ME?
THIS IS AMMONIUM CARBONATE. SMELLING SALTS. THEY WON'T HURT YOU.
I'M SORRY, BUT I CAN'T GET YOU OUT ALONE.
hnnhh...
HUH!
KATIE!
MY DAUGHTER-- SHE WAS--I TRIED TO THROW HER OUT--
SHE'S OKAY. SHE'S OUTSIDE.
HH... HURTS WHEN I... BREATHE...
YOU PROBABLY HAVE BROKEN RIBS. DON'T TALK, LISTEN. THIS PILE ISN'T STABLE.
I WAS GOING TO GO FOR HELP, BUT THERE'S NO TIME. WE HAVE TO GET YOU OUT NOW.
AAA!
I'M SO SORRY, I KNOW IT HURT BUT PLEAS YOU HAVE TO.
PLEASE. FOR KATIE.

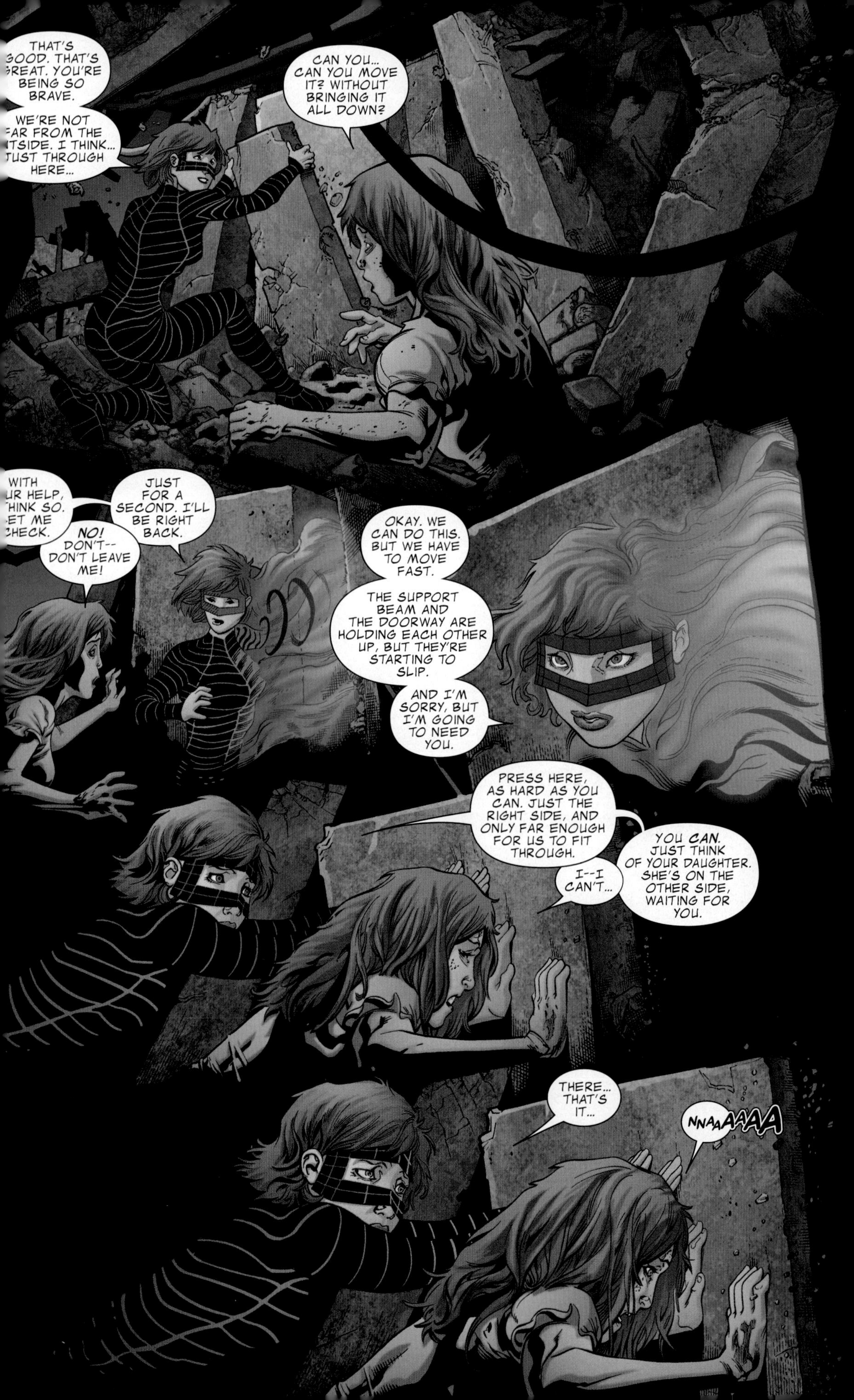
THAT'S GOOD. THAT'S GREAT. YOU'RE BEING SO BRAVE.
WE'RE NOT FAR FROM THE TSIDE. I THINK... JUST THROUGH HERE...
CAN YOU... CAN YOU MOVE IT? WITHOUT BRINGING IT ALL DOWN?
WITH R HELP, THINK SO. ET ME CHECK.
JUST FOR A SECOND. I'LL BE RIGHT BACK.
NO! DON'T-- DON'T LEAVE ME!
OKAY. WE CAN DO THIS. BUT WE HAVE TO MOVE FAST.
THE SUPPORT BEAM AND THE DOORWAY ARE HOLDING EACH OTHER UP, BUT THEY'RE STARTING TO SLIP.
AND I'M SORRY, BUT I'M GOING TO NEED YOU.
PRESS HERE, AS HARD AS YOU CAN. JUST THE RIGHT SIDE, AND ONLY FAR ENOUGH FOR US TO FIT THROUGH.
I--I CAN'T...
YOU CAN. JUST THINK OF YOUR DAUGHTER. SHE'S ON THE OTHER SIDE, WAITING FOR YOU.
THERE... THAT'S IT...
NNAAAAAA

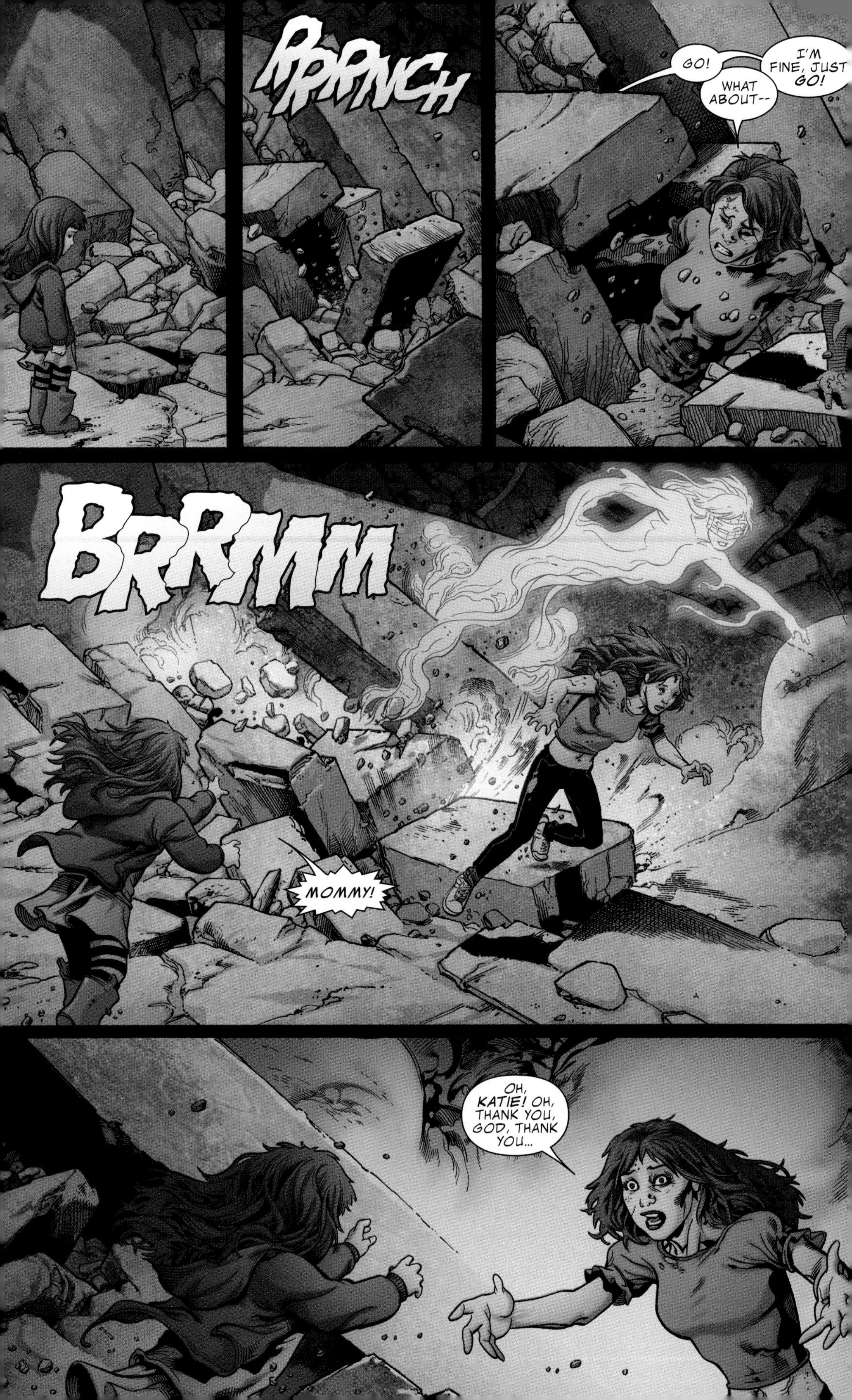
RRRRNCH
GO!
WHAT ABOUT--
I'M FINE, JUST GO!
BRRMM
MOMMY!
OH, KATIE! OH, THANK YOU, GOD, THANK YOU...

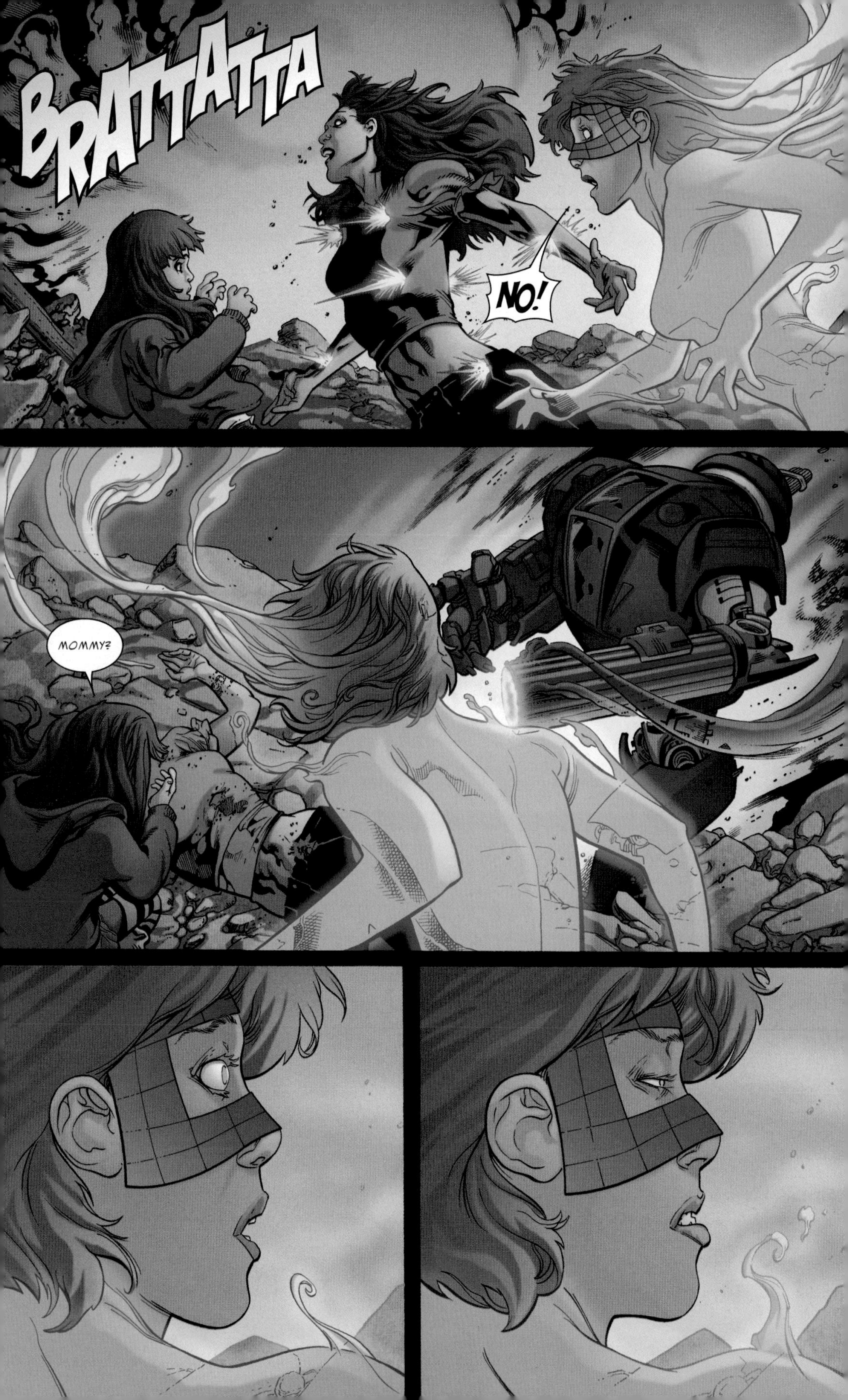
BRATTATTA
NO!
MOMMY?

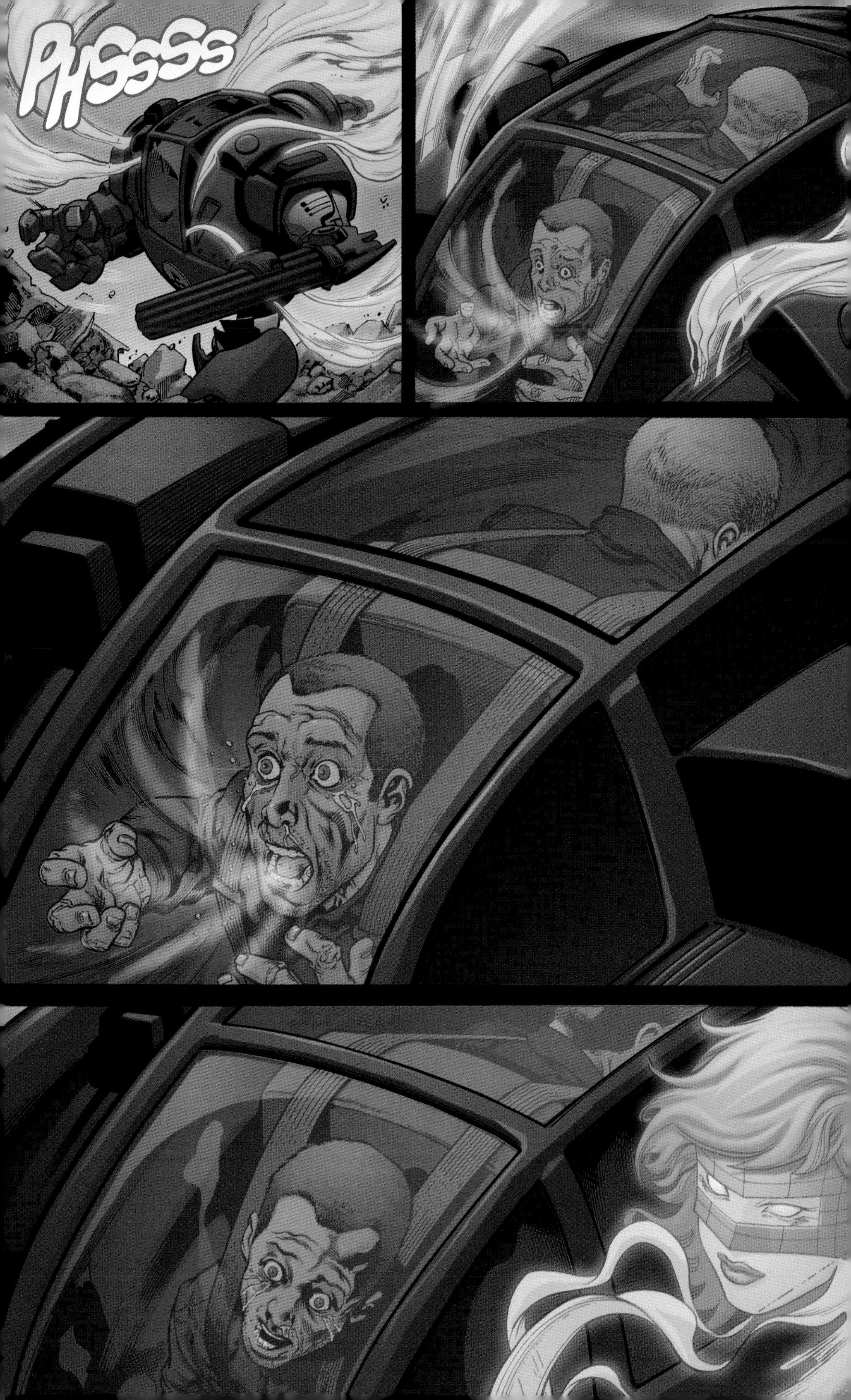
PHSSSS

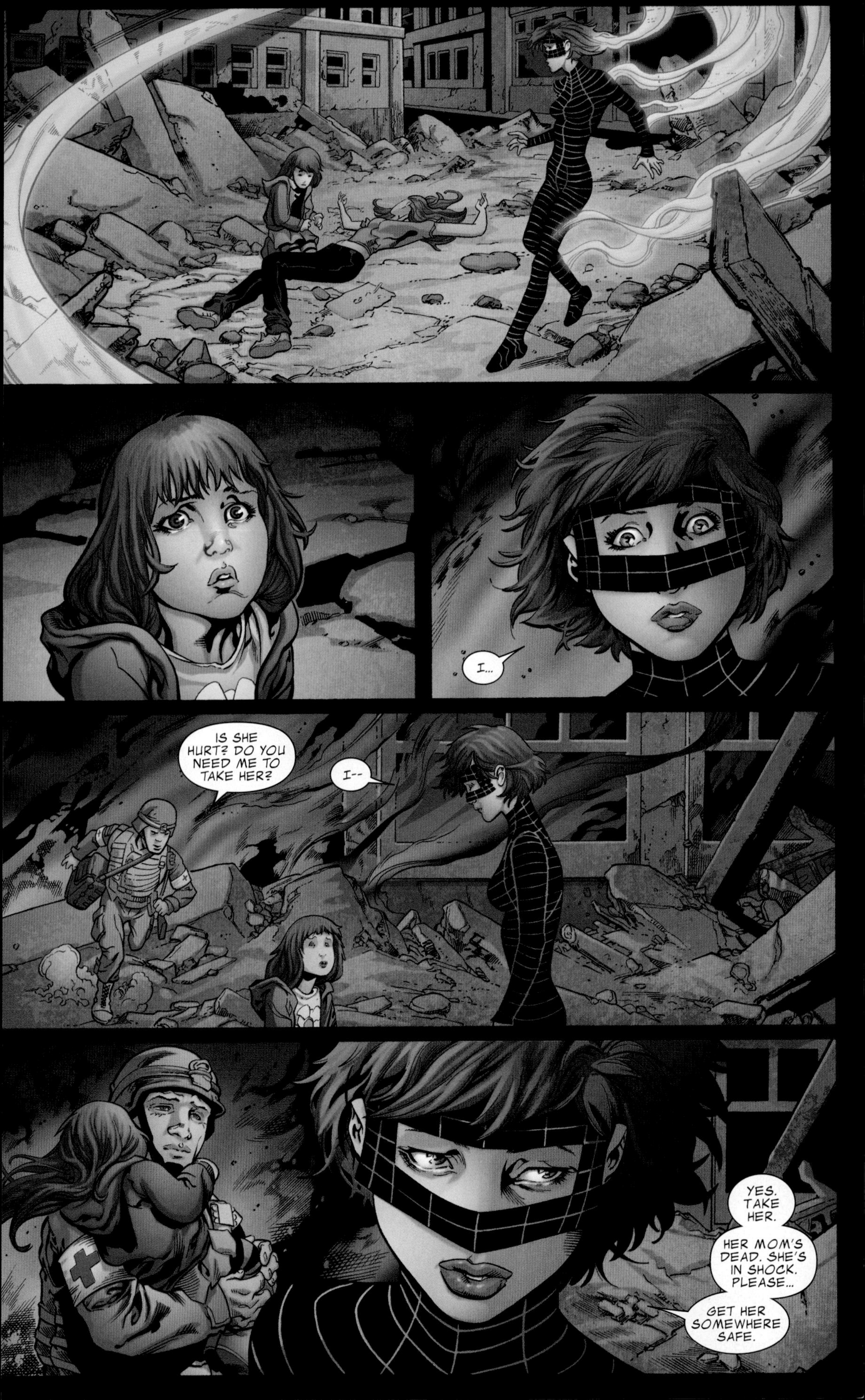
I...
IS SHE HURT? DO YOU NEED ME TO TAKE HER?
I--
YES. TAKE HER.
HER MOM'S DEAD. SHE'S IN SHOCK. PLEASE...
GET HER SOMEWHERE SAFE.

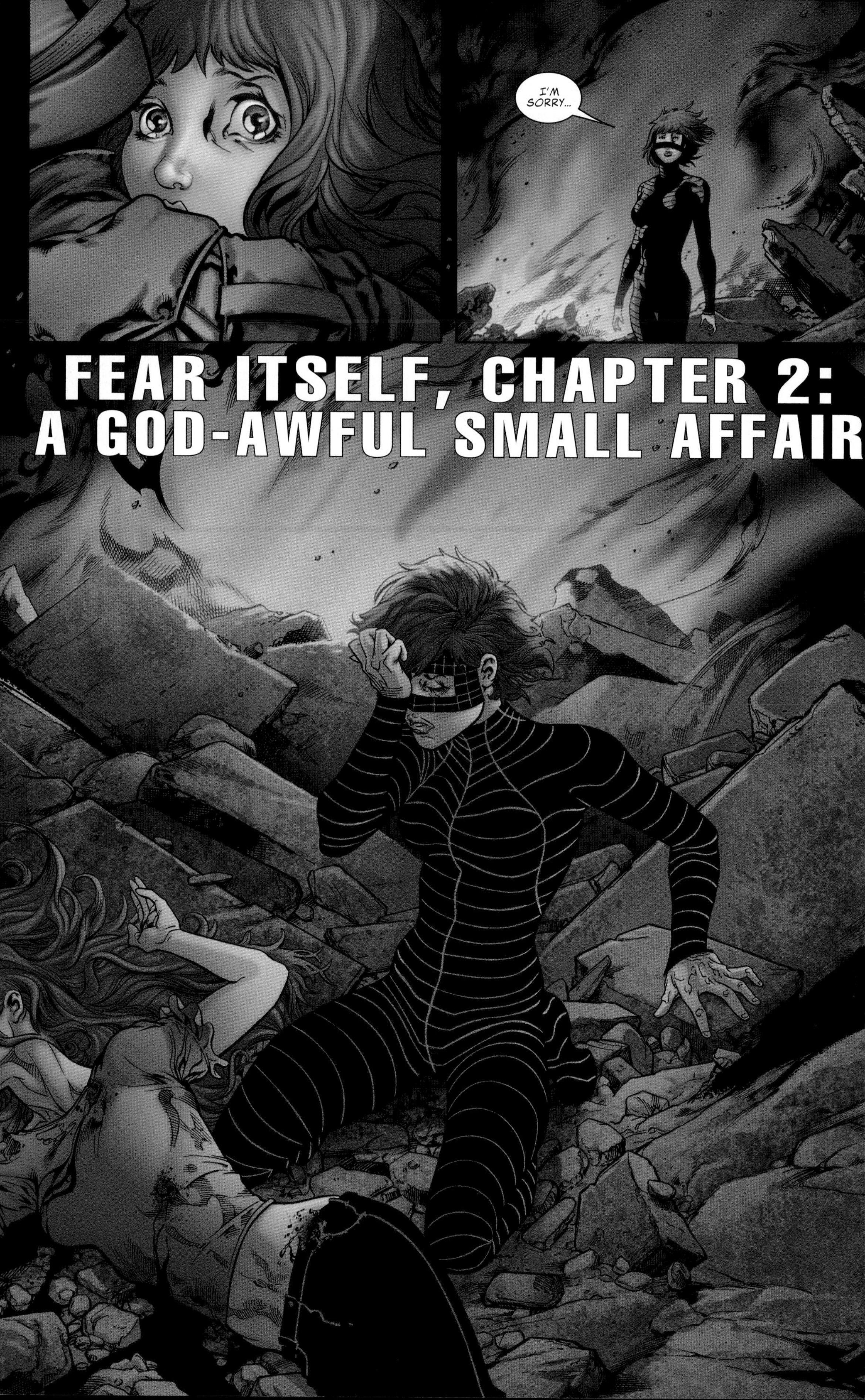
I'M SORRY...
FEAR ITSELF, CHAPTER 2:
A GOD-AWFUL SMALL AFFAIR

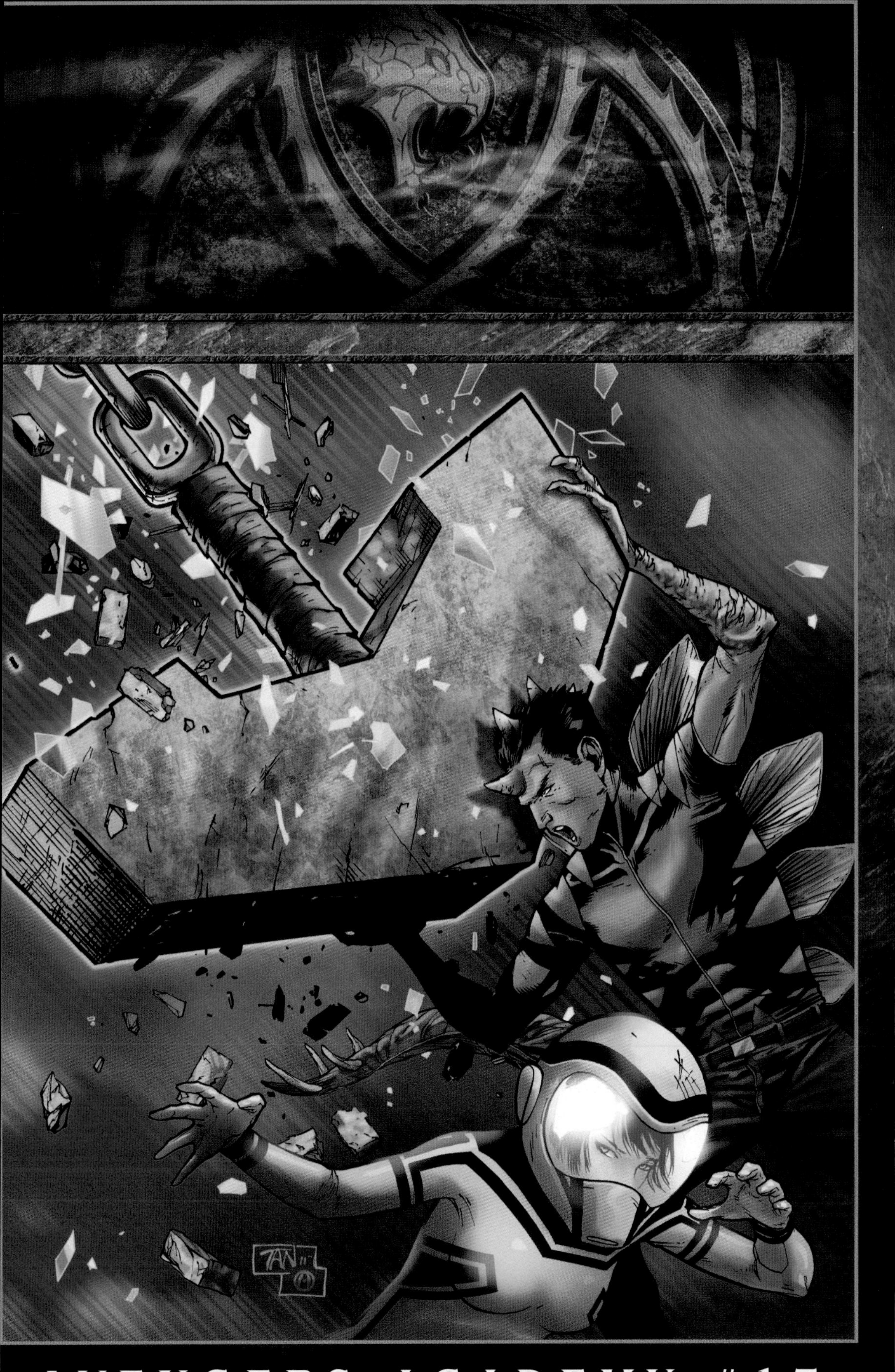

AVENGERS ACADEMY #17

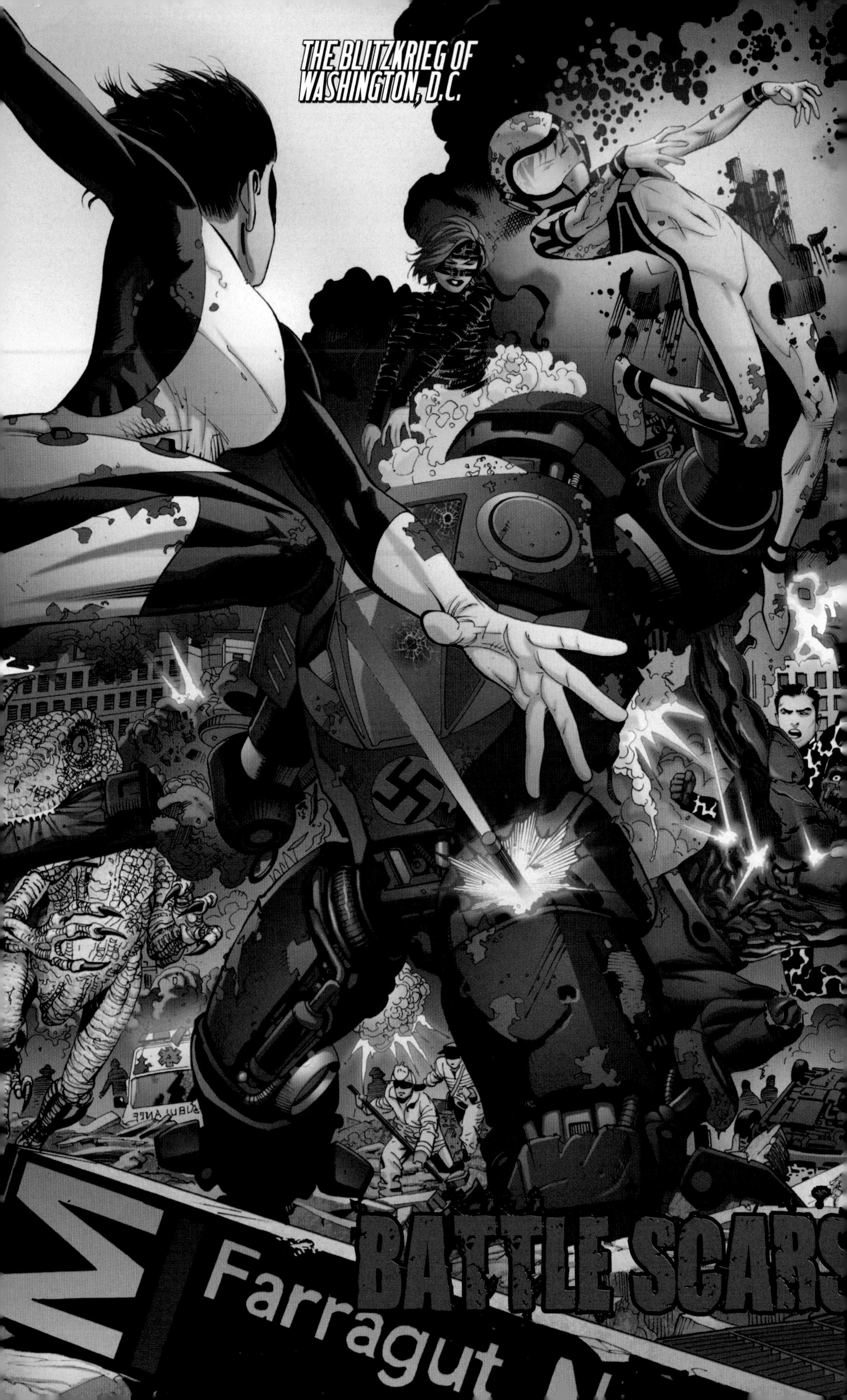
THE BLITZKRIEG OF WASHINGTON, D.C.
BATTLE SCARS
Farragut

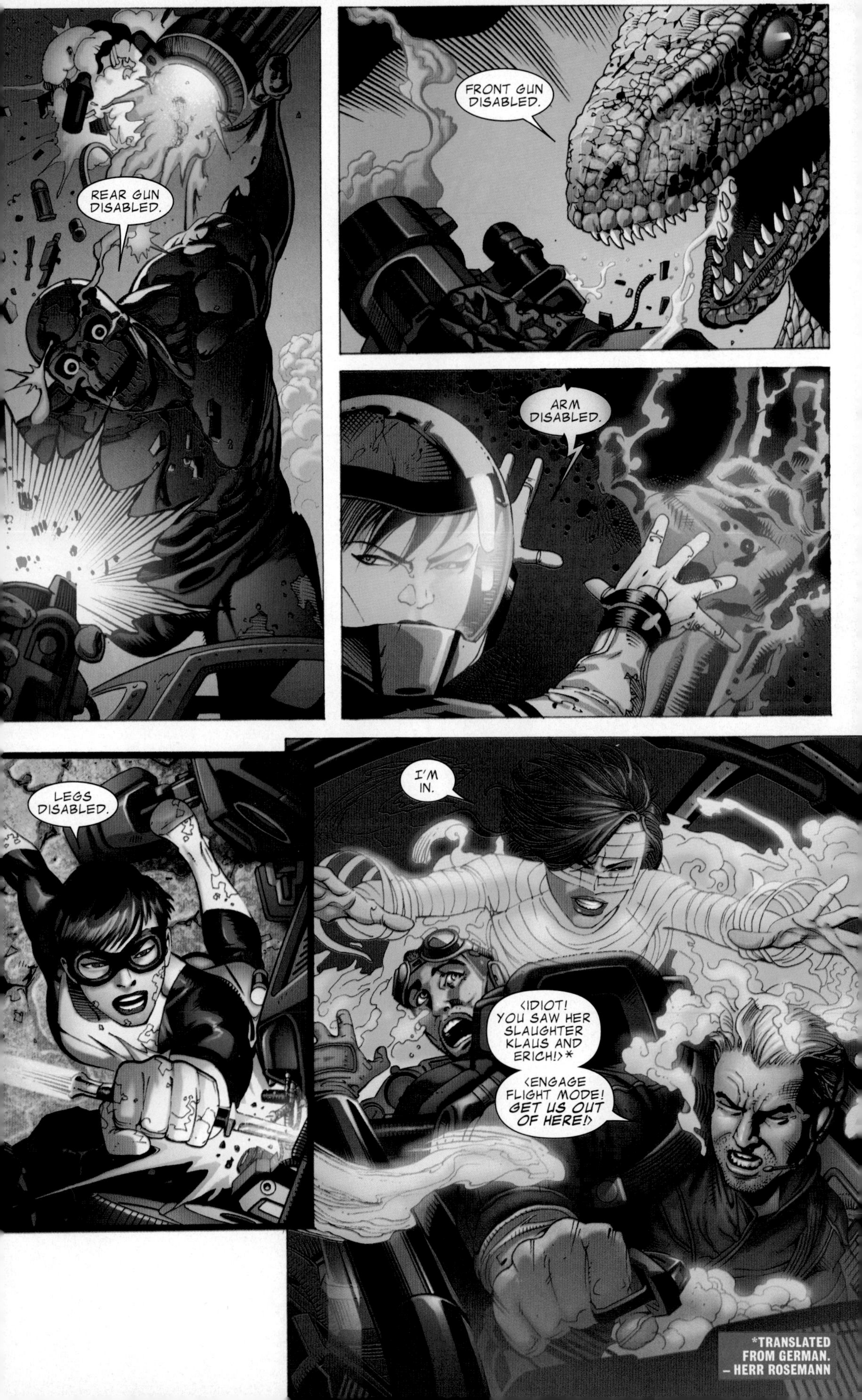
REAR GUN DISABLED.
FRONT GUN DISABLED.
ARM DISABLED.
LEGS DISABLED.
I'M IN.
<IDIOT! YOU SAW HER SLAUGHTER KLAUS AND ERICH!>*
<ENGAGE FLIGHT MODE! GET US OUT OF HERE!>
*TRANSLATED FROM GERMAN. – HERR ROSEMANN

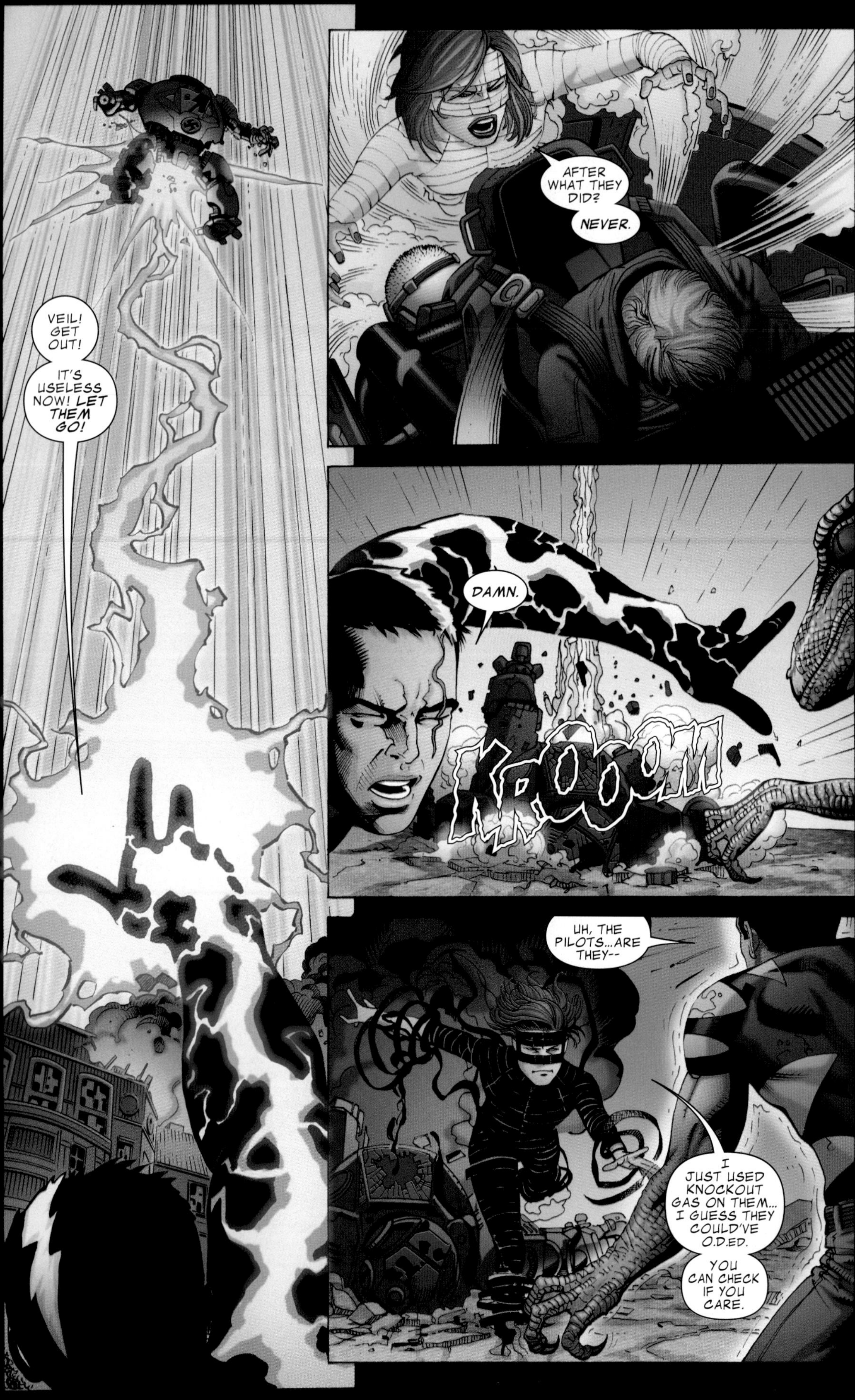

VEIL! GET OUT!
IT'S USELESS NOW! LET THEM GO!
AFTER WHAT THEY DID?
NEVER.
DAMN.
KROOOOM
UH, THE PILOTS...ARE THEY--
I JUST USED KNOCKOUT GAS ON THEM... I GUESS THEY COULD'VE O.D.ED.
YOU CAN CHECK IF YOU CARE.

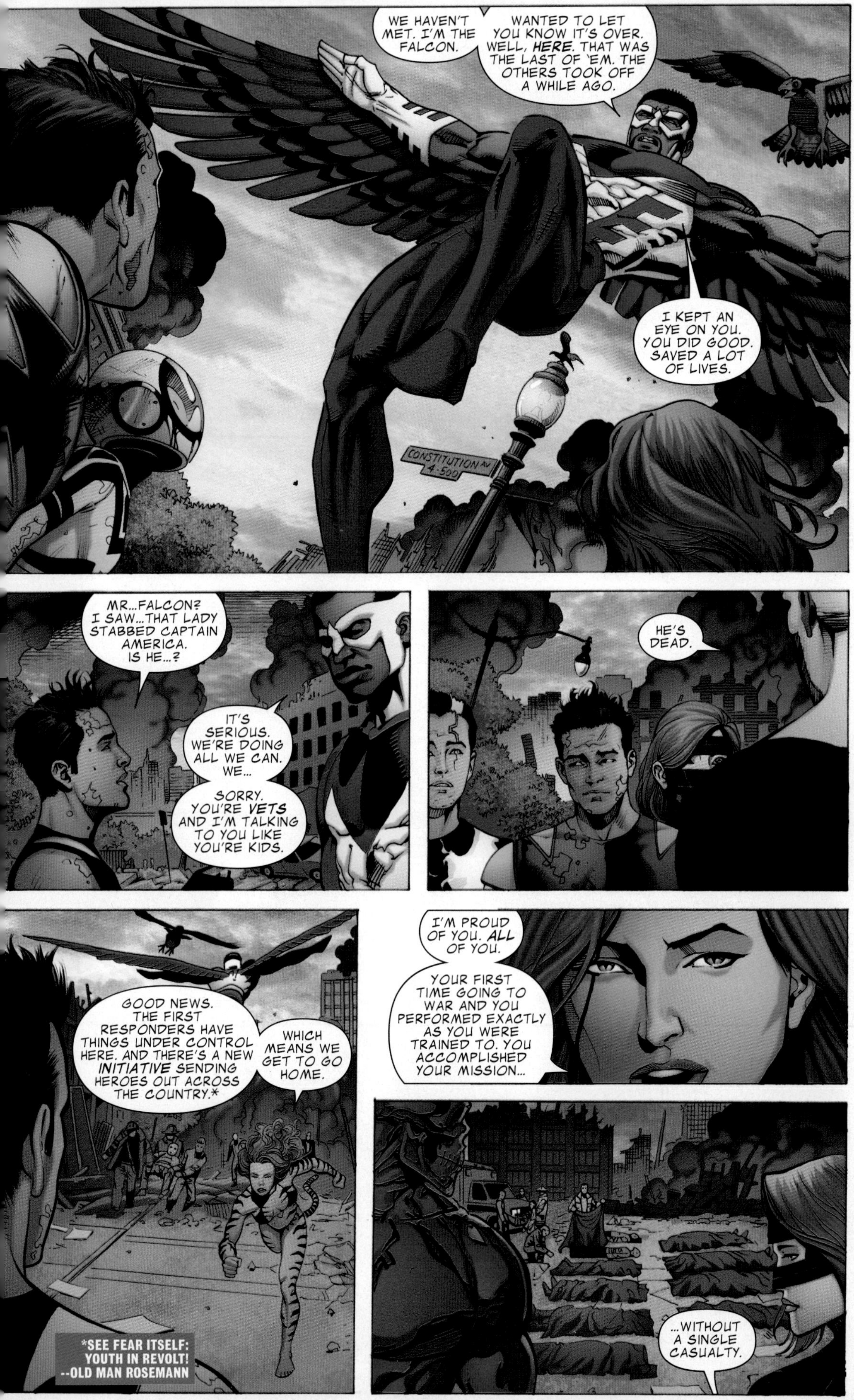
WE HAVEN'T MET. I'M THE FALCON.
WANTED TO LET YOU KNOW IT'S OVER. WELL, HERE. THAT WAS THE LAST OF 'EM. THE OTHERS TOOK OFF A WHILE AGO.
I KEPT AN EYE ON YOU. YOU DID GOOD. SAVED A LOT OF LIVES.
CONSTITUTION AV
4-500
MR...FALCON? I SAW...THAT LADY STABBED CAPTAIN AMERICA. IS HE...?
IT'S SERIOUS. WE'RE DOING ALL WE CAN. WE...
SORRY. YOU'RE VETS AND I'M TALKING TO YOU LIKE YOU'RE KIDS.
HE'S DEAD.
GOOD NEWS. THE FIRST RESPONDERS HAVE THINGS UNDER CONTROL HERE. AND THERE'S A NEW INITIATIVE SENDING HEROES OUT ACROSS THE COUNTRY.*
WHICH MEANS WE GET TO GO HOME.
*SEE FEAR ITSELF: YOUTH IN REVOLT! --OLD MAN ROSEMANN
I'M PROUD OF YOU. ALL OF YOU.
YOUR FIRST TIME GOING TO WAR AND YOU PERFORMED EXACTLY AS YOU WERE TRAINED TO. YOU ACCOMPLISHED YOUR MISSION...
...WITHOUT A SINGLE CASUALTY.

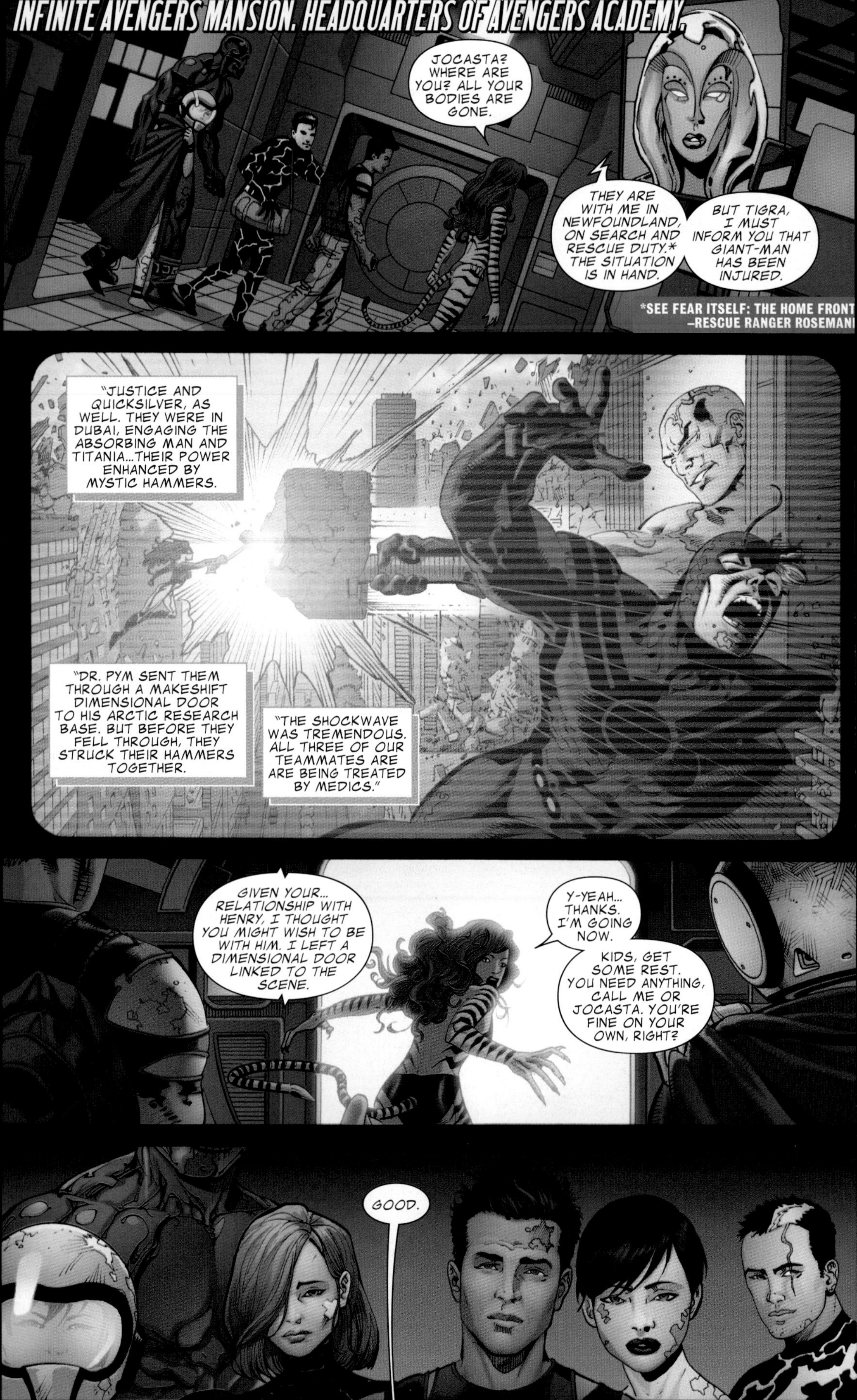
INFINITE AVENGERS MANSION. HEADQUARTERS OF AVENGERS ACADEMY.
JOCASTA? WHERE ARE YOU? ALL YOUR BODIES ARE GONE.
THEY ARE WITH ME IN NEWFOUNDLAND, ON SEARCH AND RESCUE DUTY.* THE SITUATION IS IN HAND.
BUT TIGRA, I MUST INFORM YOU THAT GIANT-MAN HAS BEEN INJURED.
*SEE FEAR ITSELF: THE HOME FRONT –RESCUE RANGER ROSEMAN
"JUSTICE AND QUICKSILVER, AS WELL. THEY WERE IN DUBAI, ENGAGING THE ABSORBING MAN AND TITANIA...THEIR POWER ENHANCED BY MYSTIC HAMMERS.
"DR. PYM SENT THEM THROUGH A MAKESHIFT DIMENSIONAL DOOR TO HIS ARCTIC RESEARCH BASE. BUT BEFORE THEY FELL THROUGH, THEY STRUCK THEIR HAMMERS TOGETHER.
"THE SHOCKWAVE WAS TREMENDOUS. ALL THREE OF OUR TEAMMATES ARE ARE BEING TREATED BY MEDICS."
GIVEN YOUR... RELATIONSHIP WITH HENRY, I THOUGHT YOU MIGHT WISH TO BE WITH HIM. I LEFT A DIMENSIONAL DOOR LINKED TO THE SCENE.
Y-YEAH... THANKS. I'M GOING NOW.
KIDS, GET SOME REST. YOU NEED ANYTHING, CALL ME OR JOCASTA. YOU'RE FINE ON YOUR OWN, RIGHT?
GOOD.

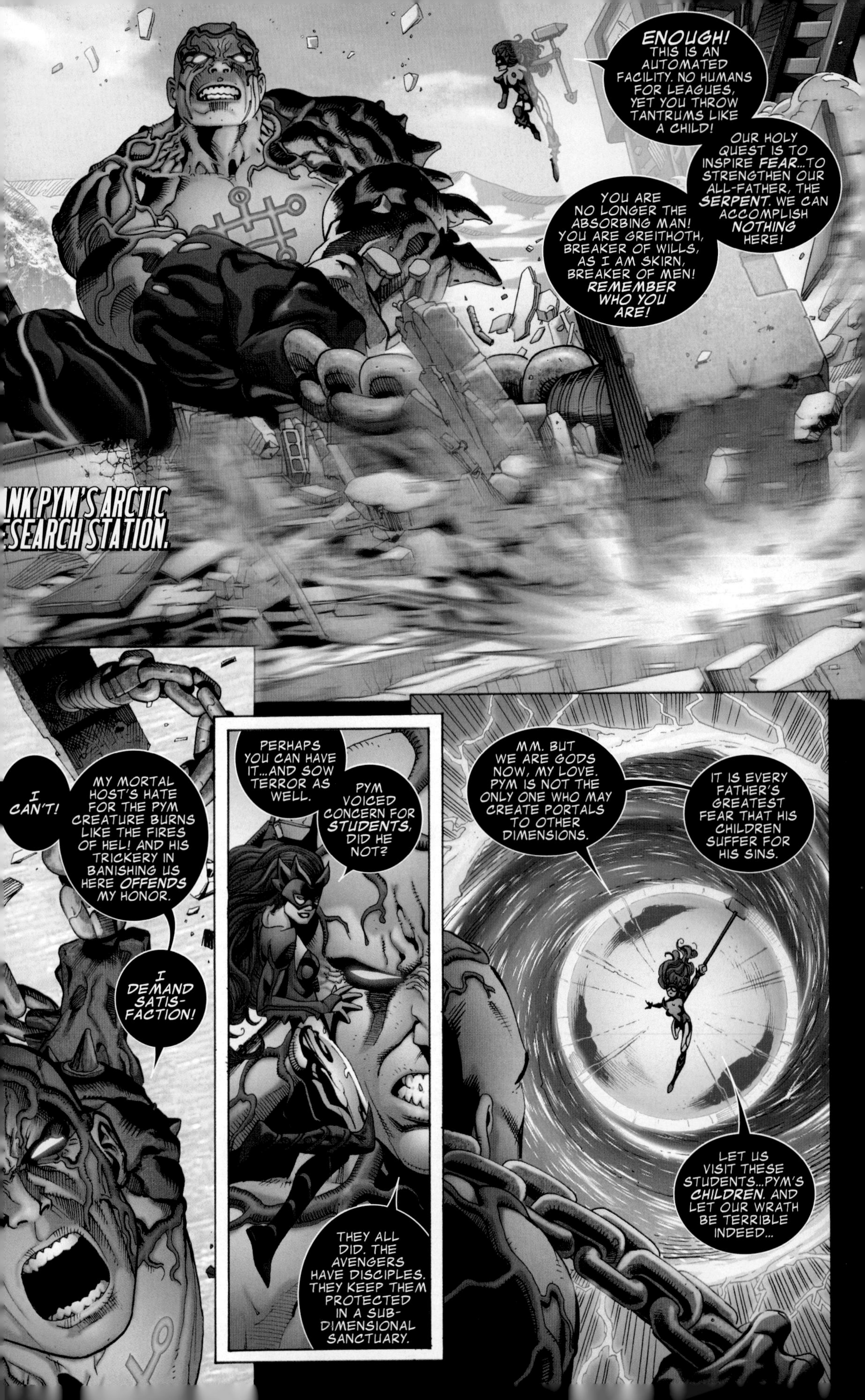
NK PYM'S ARCTIC
ESEARCH STATION.
ENOUGH! THIS IS AN AUTOMATED FACILITY. NO HUMANS FOR LEAGUES, YET YOU THROW TANTRUMS LIKE A CHILD!
OUR HOLY QUEST IS TO INSPIRE FEAR...TO STRENGTHEN OUR ALL-FATHER, THE SERPENT. WE CAN ACCOMPLISH NOTHING HERE!
YOU ARE NO LONGER THE ABSORBING MAN! YOU ARE GREITHOTH, BREAKER OF WILLS, AS I AM SKIRN, BREAKER OF MEN! REMEMBER WHO YOU ARE!
I CAN'T!
MY MORTAL HOST'S HATE FOR THE PYM CREATURE BURNS LIKE THE FIRES OF HEL! AND HIS TRICKERY IN BANISHING US HERE OFFENDS MY HONOR.
I DEMAND SATIS-FACTION!
PERHAPS YOU CAN HAVE IT...AND SOW TERROR AS WELL.
PYM VOICED CONCERN FOR STUDENTS, DID HE NOT?
THEY ALL DID. THE AVENGERS HAVE DISCIPLES. THEY KEEP THEM PROTECTED IN A SUB-DIMENSIONAL SANCTUARY.
MM. BUT WE ARE GODS NOW, MY LOVE. PYM IS NOT THE ONLY ONE WHO MAY CREATE PORTALS TO OTHER DIMENSIONS.
IT IS EVERY FATHER'S GREATEST FEAR THAT HIS CHILDREN SUFFER FOR HIS SINS.
LET US VISIT THESE STUDENTS...PYM'S CHILDREN. AND LET OUR WRATH BE TERRIBLE INDEED...

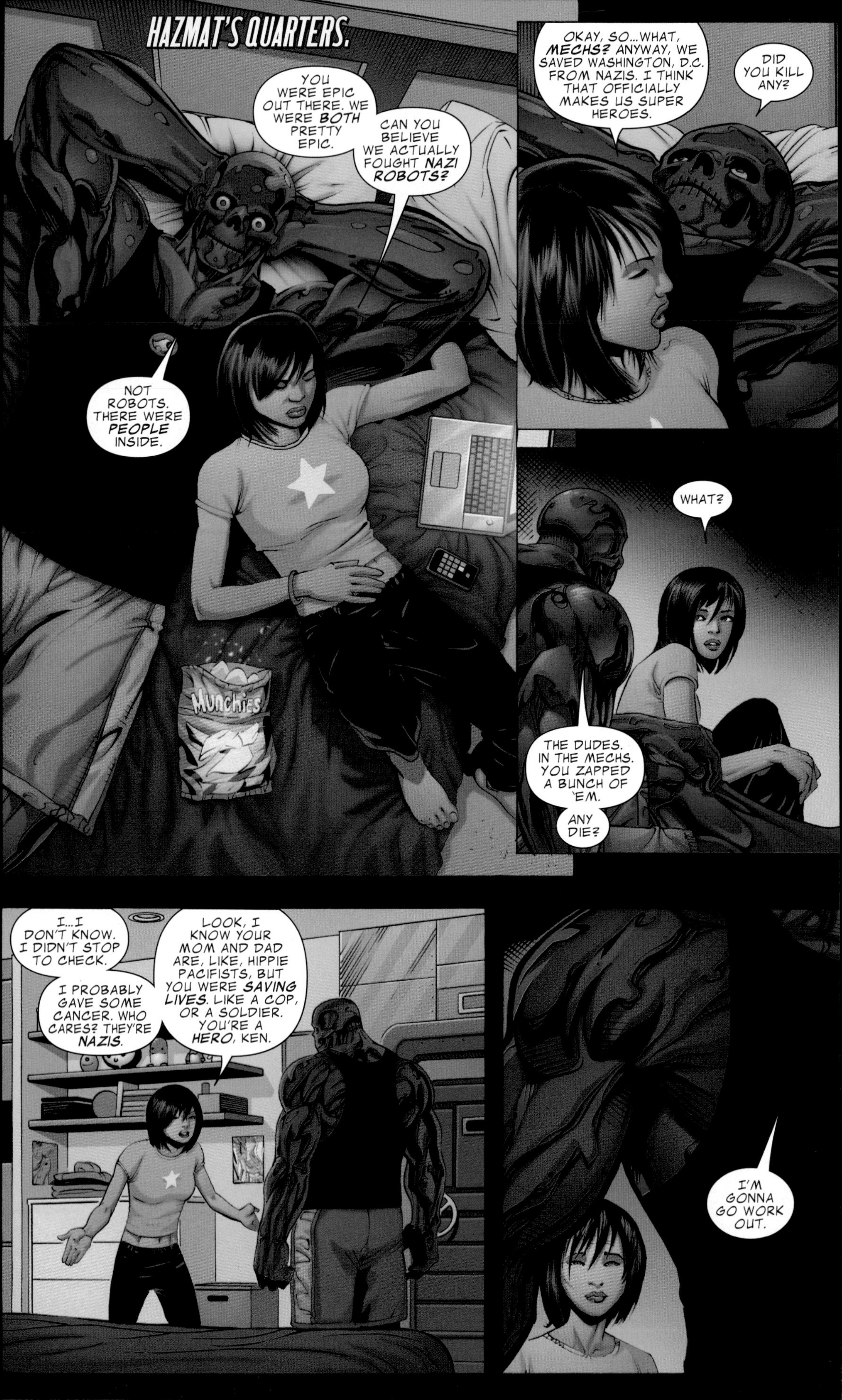
HAZMAT'S QUARTERS.
YOU WERE EPIC OUT THERE. WE WERE BOTH PRETTY EPIC.
CAN YOU BELIEVE WE ACTUALLY FOUGHT NAZI ROBOTS?
NOT ROBOTS. THERE WERE PEOPLE INSIDE.
OKAY, SO...WHAT, MECHS? ANYWAY, WE SAVED WASHINGTON, D.C. FROM NAZIS. I THINK THAT OFFICIALLY MAKES US SUPER HEROES.
DID YOU KILL ANY?
WHAT?
THE DUDES. IN THE MECHS. YOU ZAPPED A BUNCH OF 'EM.
ANY DIE?
I...I DON'T KNOW. I DIDN'T STOP TO CHECK.
I PROBABLY GAVE SOME CANCER. WHO CARES? THEY'RE NAZIS.
LOOK, I KNOW YOUR MOM AND DAD ARE, LIKE, HIPPIE PACIFISTS, BUT YOU WERE SAVING LIVES. LIKE A COP, OR A SOLDIER. YOU'RE A HERO, KEN.
I'M GONNA GO WORK OUT.

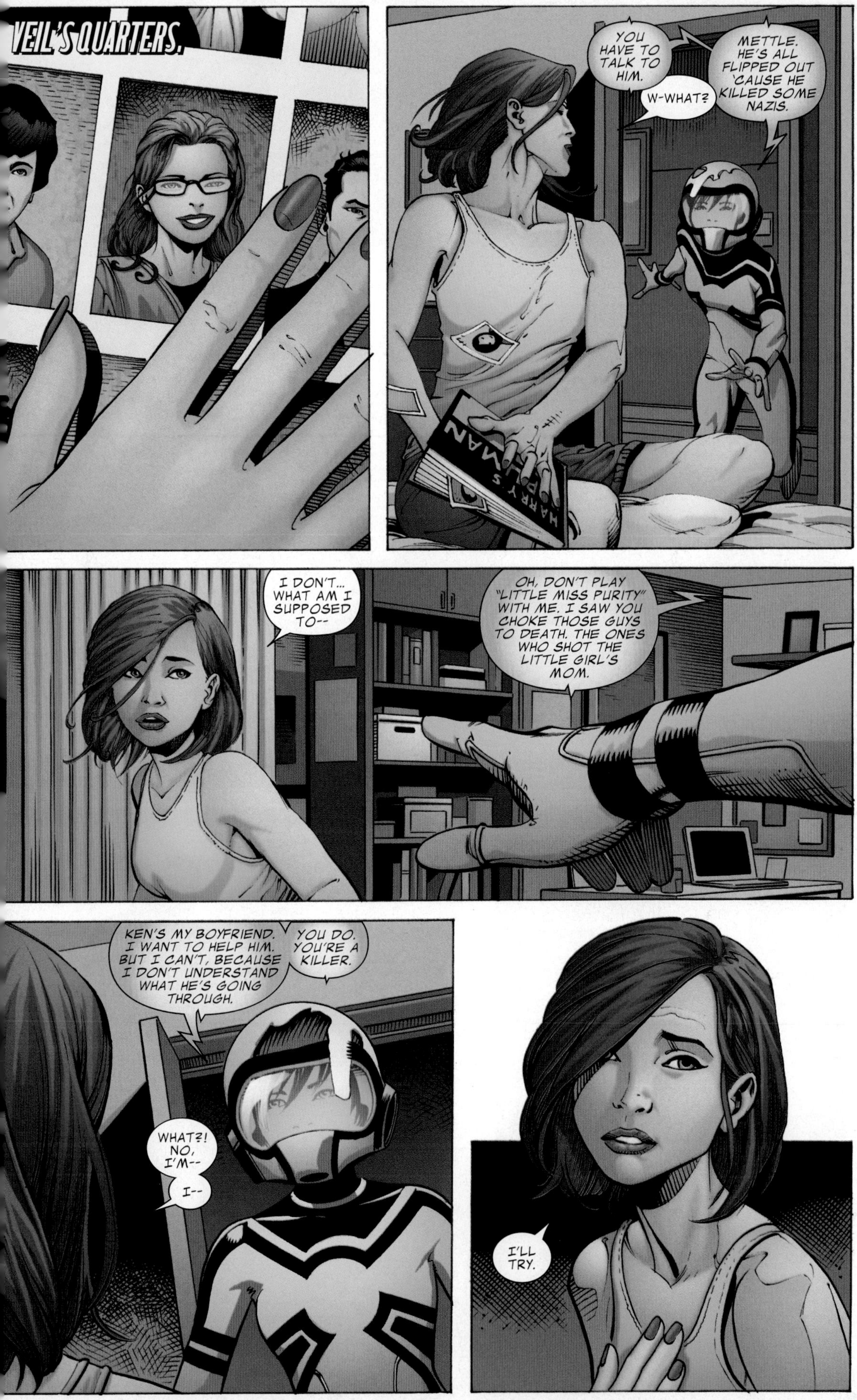
VEIL'S QUARTERS.
YOU HAVE TO TALK TO HIM.
W-WHAT?
METTLE. HE'S ALL FLIPPED OUT 'CAUSE HE KILLED SOME NAZIS.
HARRY'S MAN
I DON'T... WHAT AM I SUPPOSED TO--
OH, DON'T PLAY "LITTLE MISS PURITY" WITH ME. I SAW YOU CHOKE THOSE GUYS TO DEATH. THE ONES WHO SHOT THE LITTLE GIRL'S MOM.
KEN'S MY BOYFRIEND. I WANT TO HELP HIM. BUT I CAN'T, BECAUSE I DON'T UNDERSTAND WHAT HE'S GOING THROUGH.
YOU DO. YOU'RE A KILLER.
WHAT?! NO, I'M--
I--
I'LL TRY.

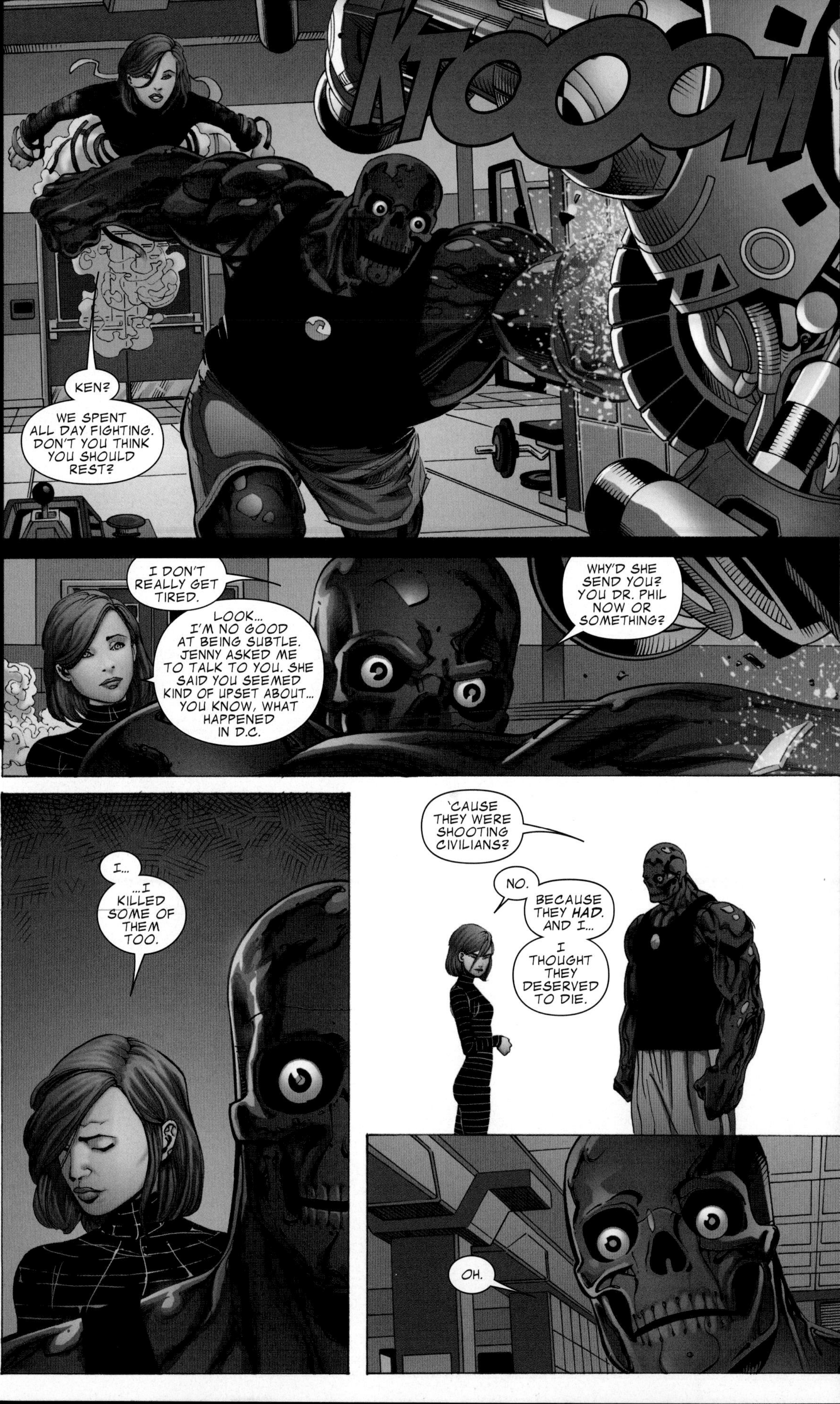
KTOOOM
KEN?
WE SPENT ALL DAY FIGHTING. DON'T YOU THINK YOU SHOULD REST?
I DON'T REALLY GET TIRED.
WHY'D SHE SEND YOU? YOU DR. PHIL NOW OR SOMETHING?
LOOK... I'M NO GOOD AT BEING SUBTLE. JENNY ASKED ME TO TALK TO YOU. SHE SAID YOU SEEMED KIND OF UPSET ABOUT... YOU KNOW, WHAT HAPPENED IN D.C.
I...
...I KILLED SOME OF THEM TOO.
'CAUSE THEY WERE SHOOTING CIVILIANS?
NO.
BECAUSE THEY HAD. AND I...
I THOUGHT THEY DESERVED TO DIE.
OH.

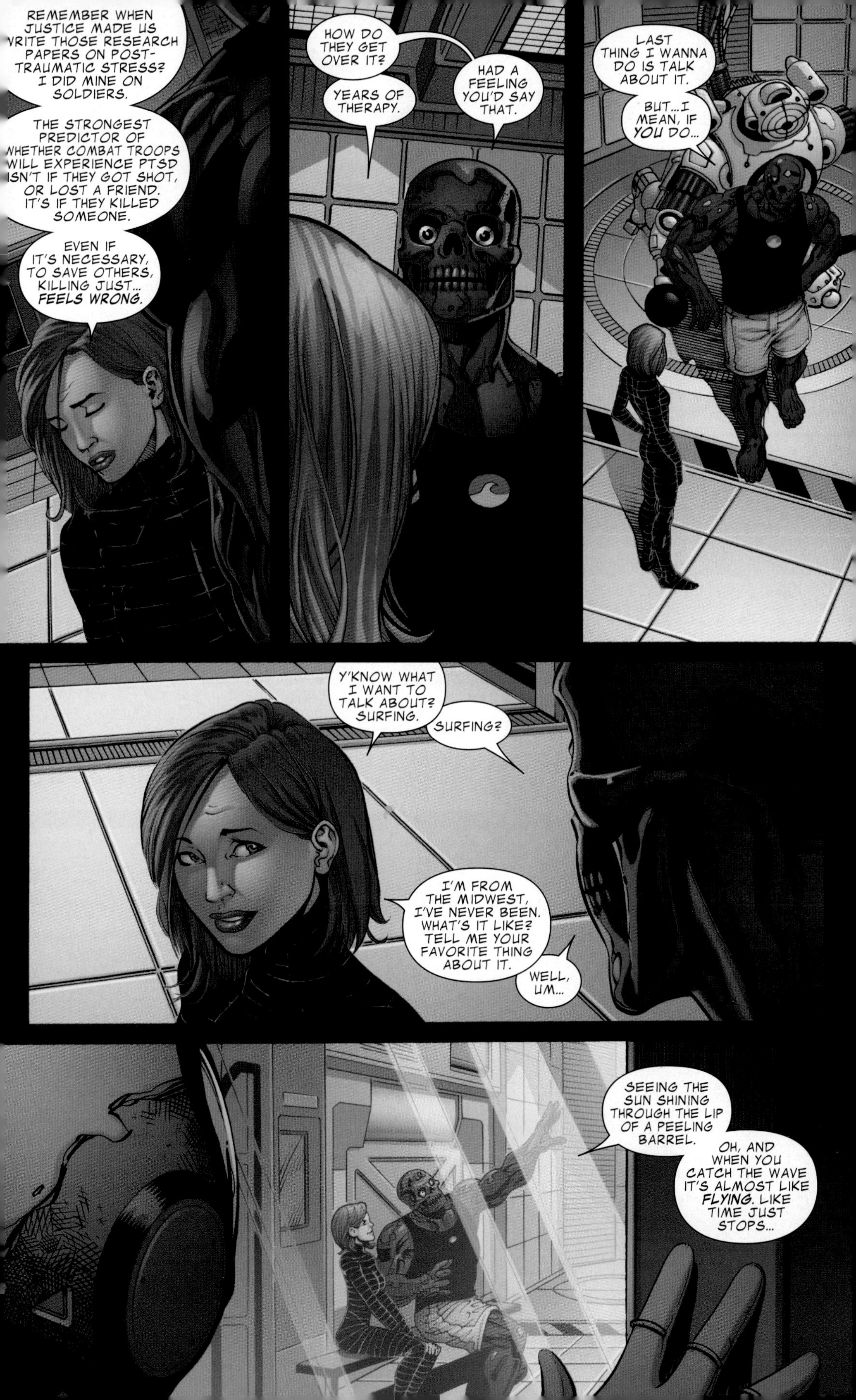
REMEMBER WHEN JUSTICE MADE US WRITE THOSE RESEARCH PAPERS ON POST-TRAUMATIC STRESS? I DID MINE ON SOLDIERS.
THE STRONGEST PREDICTOR OF WHETHER COMBAT TROOPS WILL EXPERIENCE PTSD ISN'T IF THEY GOT SHOT, OR LOST A FRIEND. IT'S IF THEY KILLED SOMEONE.
EVEN IF IT'S NECESSARY, TO SAVE OTHERS, KILLING JUST... FEELS WRONG.
HOW DO THEY GET OVER IT?
YEARS OF THERAPY.
HAD A FEELING YOU'D SAY THAT.
LAST THING I WANNA DO IS TALK ABOUT IT.
BUT...I MEAN, IF YOU DO...
Y'KNOW WHAT I WANT TO TALK ABOUT? SURFING.
SURFING?
I'M FROM THE MIDWEST, I'VE NEVER BEEN. WHAT'S IT LIKE? TELL ME YOUR FAVORITE THING ABOUT IT.
WELL, UM...
SEEING THE SUN SHINING THROUGH THE LIP OF A PEELING BARREL.
OH, AND WHEN YOU CATCH THE WAVE IT'S ALMOST LIKE FLYING. LIKE TIME JUST STOPS...

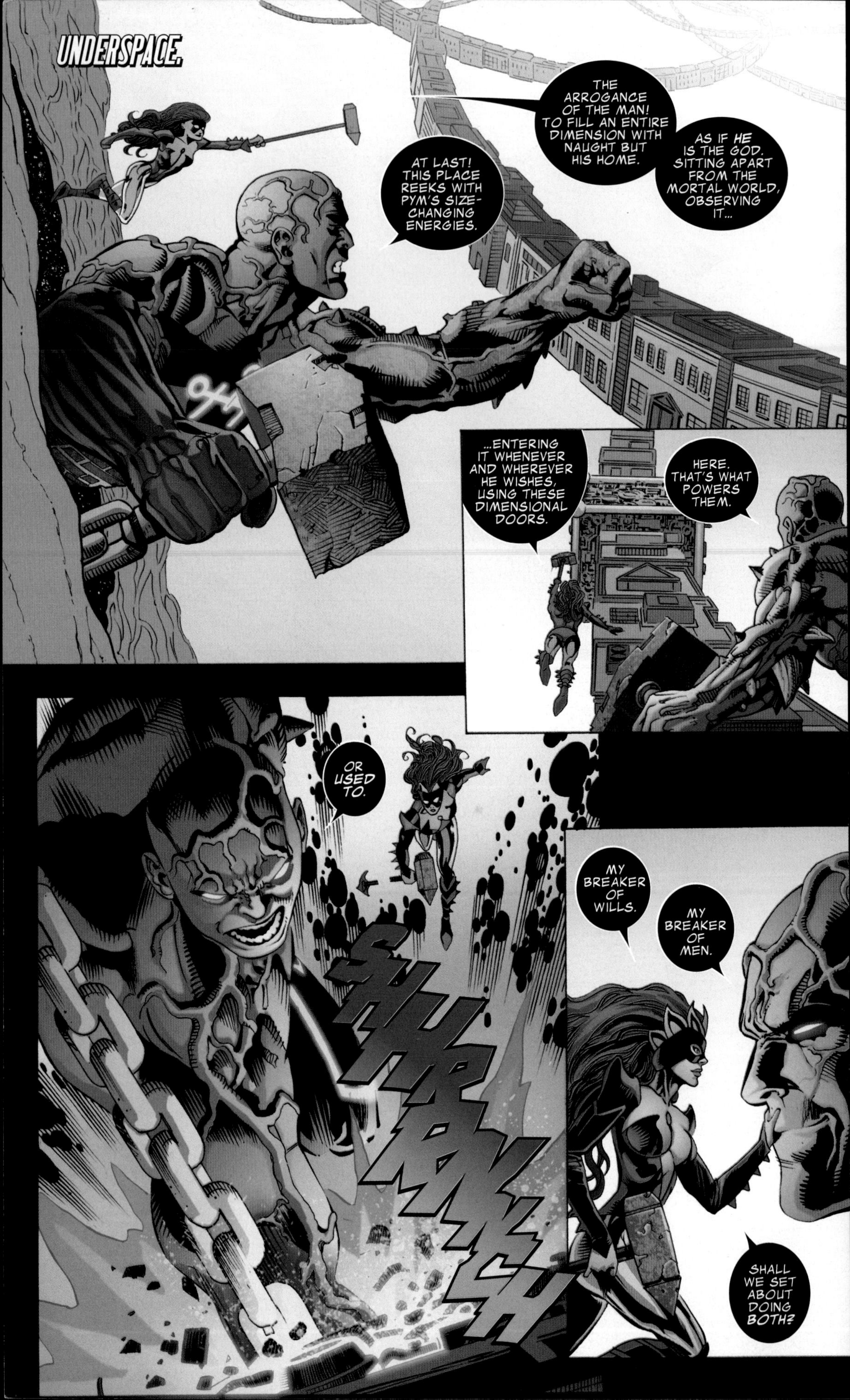
UNDERSPACE.
AT LAST! THIS PLACE REEKS WITH PYM'S SIZE-CHANGING ENERGIES.
THE ARROGANCE OF THE MAN! TO FILL AN ENTIRE DIMENSION WITH NAUGHT BUT HIS HOME.
AS IF HE IS THE GOD. SITTING APART FROM THE MORTAL WORLD, OBSERVING IT...
...ENTERING IT WHENEVER AND WHEREVER HE WISHES, USING THESE DIMENSIONAL DOORS.
HERE. THAT'S WHAT POWERS THEM.
OR USED TO.
SHHRAKKSH
MY BREAKER OF WILLS.
MY BREAKER OF MEN.
SHALL WE SET ABOUT DOING BOTH?

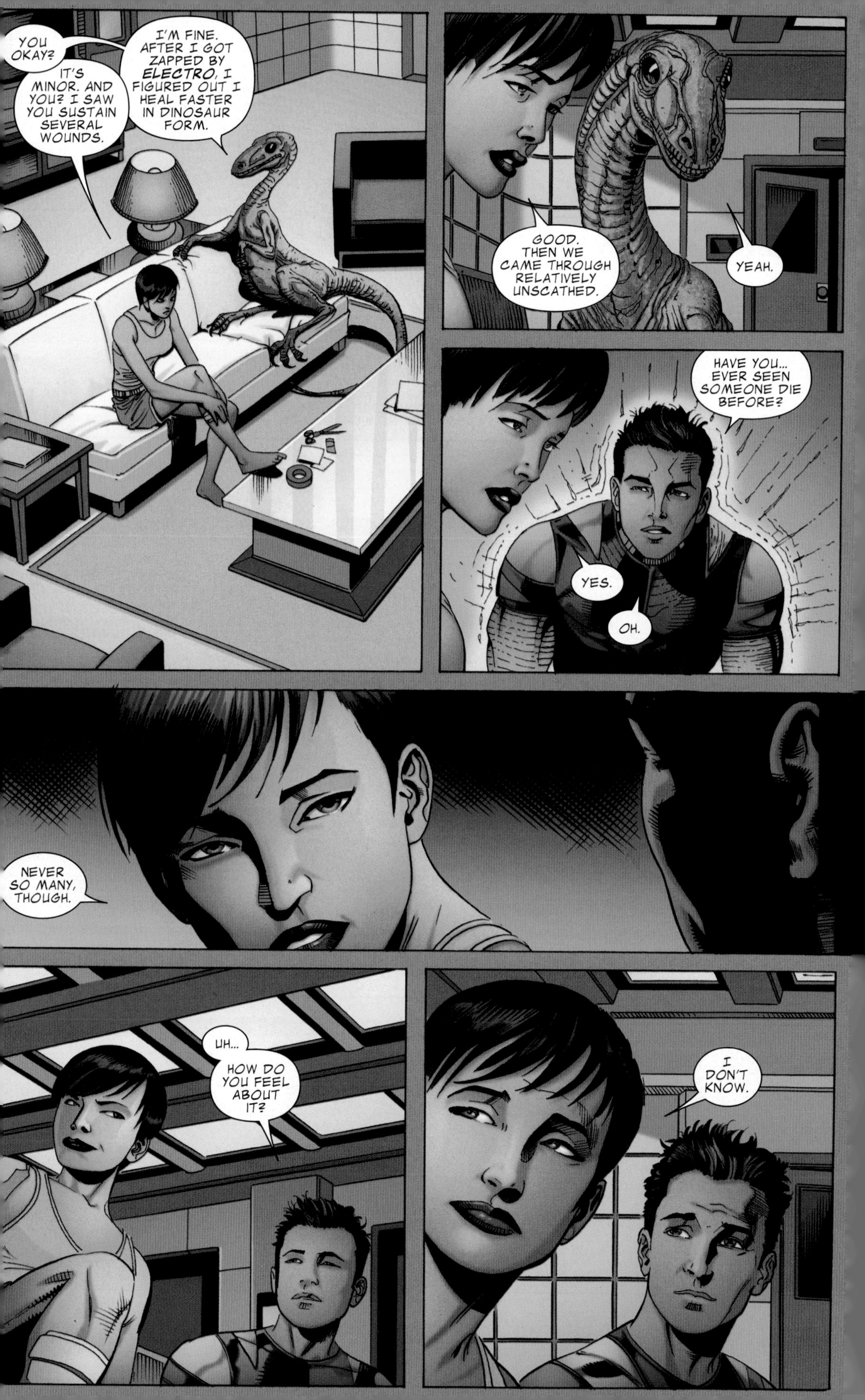
YOU OKAY?
I'M FINE. AFTER I GOT ZAPPED BY ELECTRO, I FIGURED OUT I HEAL FASTER IN DINOSAUR FORM.
IT'S MINOR. AND YOU? I SAW YOU SUSTAIN SEVERAL WOUNDS.
GOOD. THEN WE CAME THROUGH RELATIVELY UNSCATHED.
YEAH.
HAVE YOU... EVER SEEN SOMEONE DIE BEFORE?
YES.
OH.
NEVER SO MANY, THOUGH.
UH...
HOW DO YOU FEEL ABOUT IT?
I DON'T KNOW.

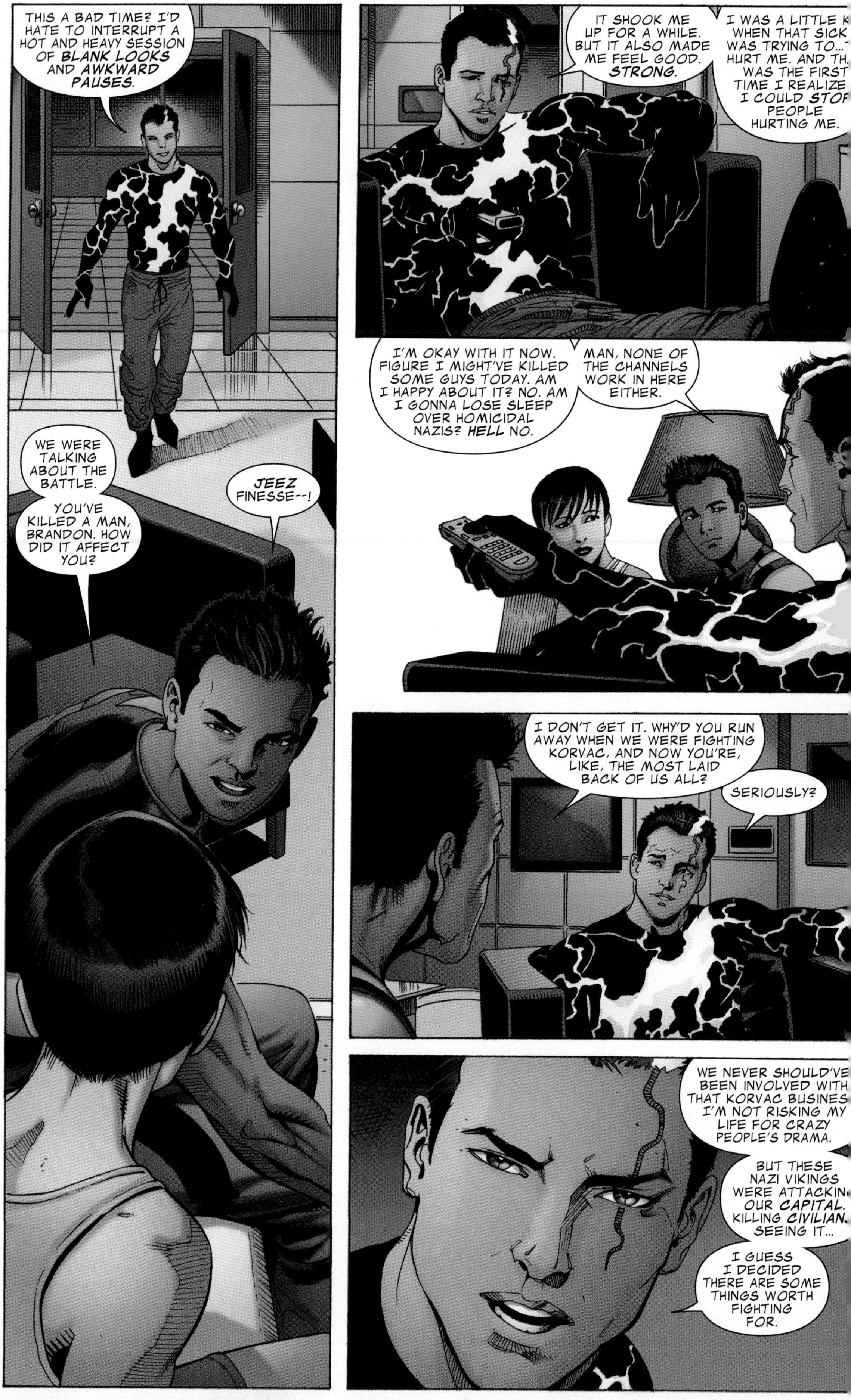

THIS A BAD TIME? I'D HATE TO INTERRUPT A HOT AND HEAVY SESSION OF BLANK LOOKS AND AWKWARD PAUSES.
WE WERE TALKING ABOUT THE BATTLE.
YOU'VE KILLED A MAN, BRANDON. HOW DID IT AFFECT YOU?
JEEZ FINESSE--!
IT SHOOK ME UP FOR A WHILE. BUT IT ALSO MADE ME FEEL GOOD. STRONG.
I WAS A LITTLE K WHEN THAT SICK WAS TRYING TO... HURT ME. AND TH WAS THE FIRST TIME I REALIZE I COULD STOP PEOPLE HURTING ME.
I'M OKAY WITH IT NOW. FIGURE I MIGHT'VE KILLED SOME GUYS TODAY. AM I HAPPY ABOUT IT? NO. AM I GONNA LOSE SLEEP OVER HOMICIDAL NAZIS? HELL NO.
MAN, NONE OF THE CHANNELS WORK IN HERE EITHER.
I DON'T GET IT. WHY'D YOU RUN AWAY WHEN WE WERE FIGHTING KORVAC, AND NOW YOU'RE, LIKE, THE MOST LAID BACK OF US ALL?
SERIOUSLY?
WE NEVER SHOULD'VE BEEN INVOLVED WITH THAT KORVAC BUSINES I'M NOT RISKING MY LIFE FOR CRAZY PEOPLE'S DRAMA.
BUT THESE NAZI VIKINGS WERE ATTACKIN OUR CAPITAL, KILLING CIVILIAN SEEING IT...
I GUESS I DECIDED THERE ARE SOME THINGS WORTH FIGHTING FOR.

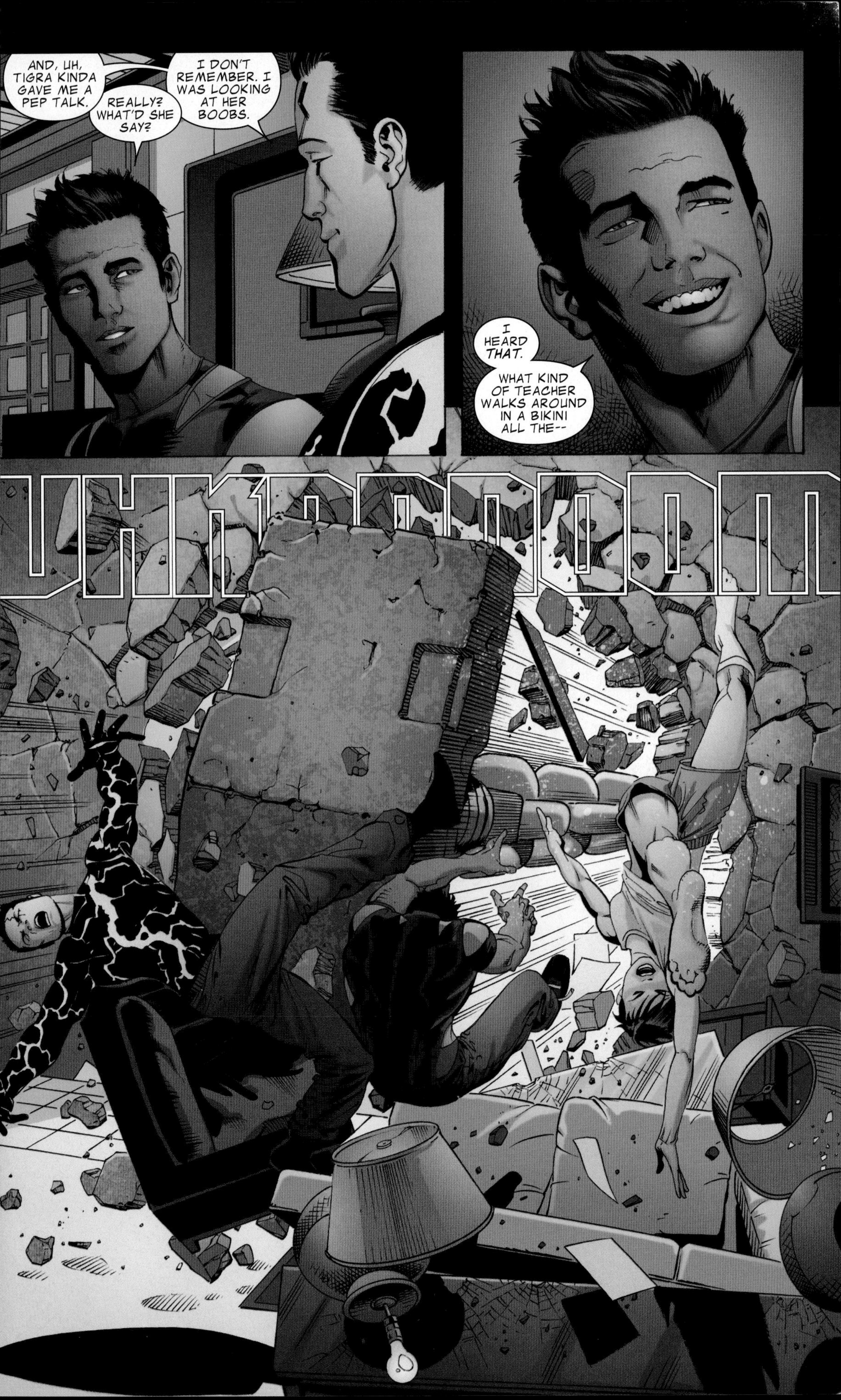
AND, UH, TIGRA KINDA GAVE ME A PEP TALK.
REALLY? WHAT'D SHE SAY?
I DON'T REMEMBER. I WAS LOOKING AT HER BOOBS.
I HEARD *THAT.*
WHAT KIND OF TEACHER WALKS AROUND IN A BIKINI ALL THE--

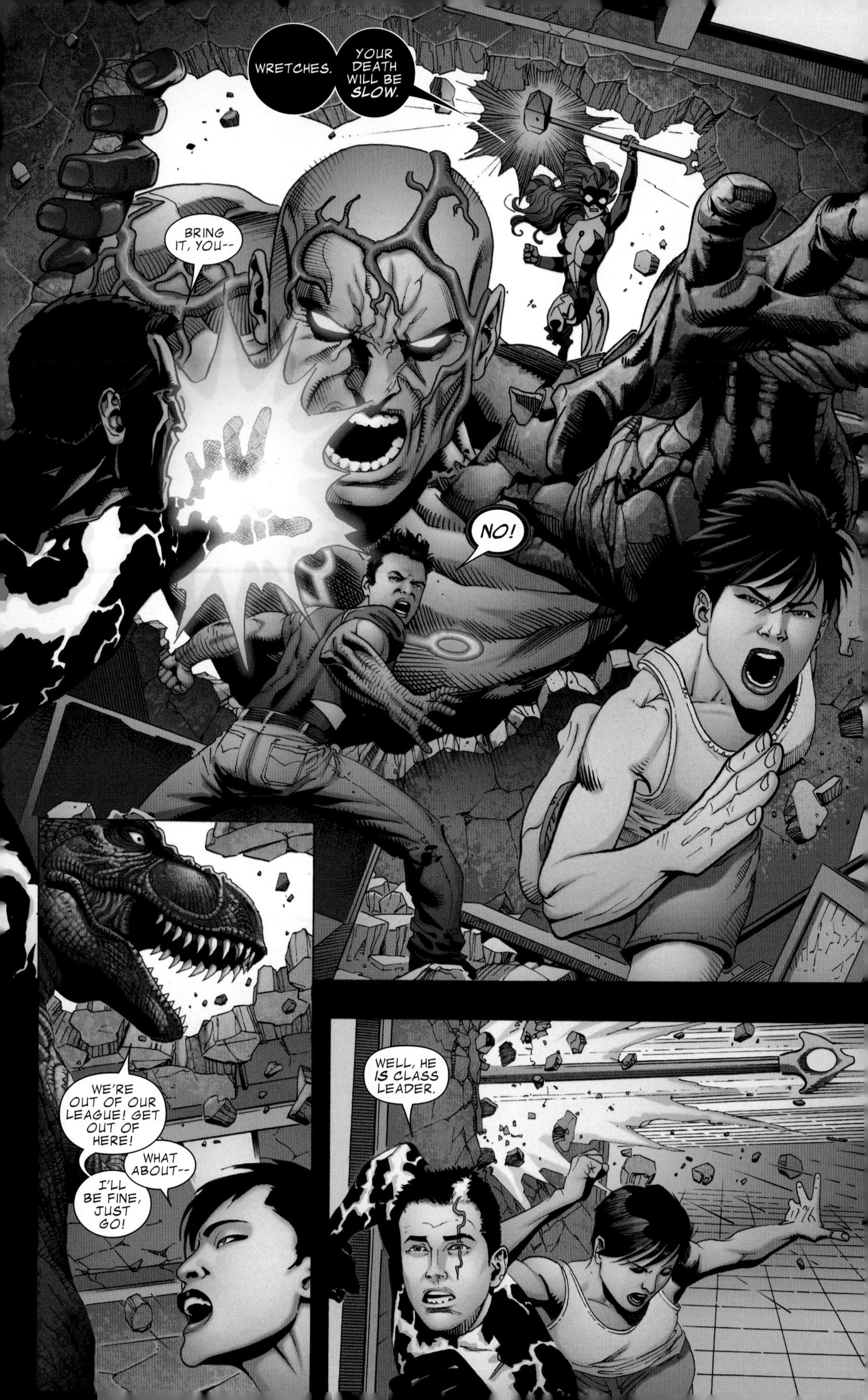
WRETCHES.
YOUR DEATH WILL BE SLOW.
BRING IT, YOU--
NO!
WE'RE OUT OF OUR LEAGUE! GET OUT OF HERE!
WHAT ABOUT--
I'LL BE FINE, JUST GO!
WELL, HE IS CLASS LEADER.

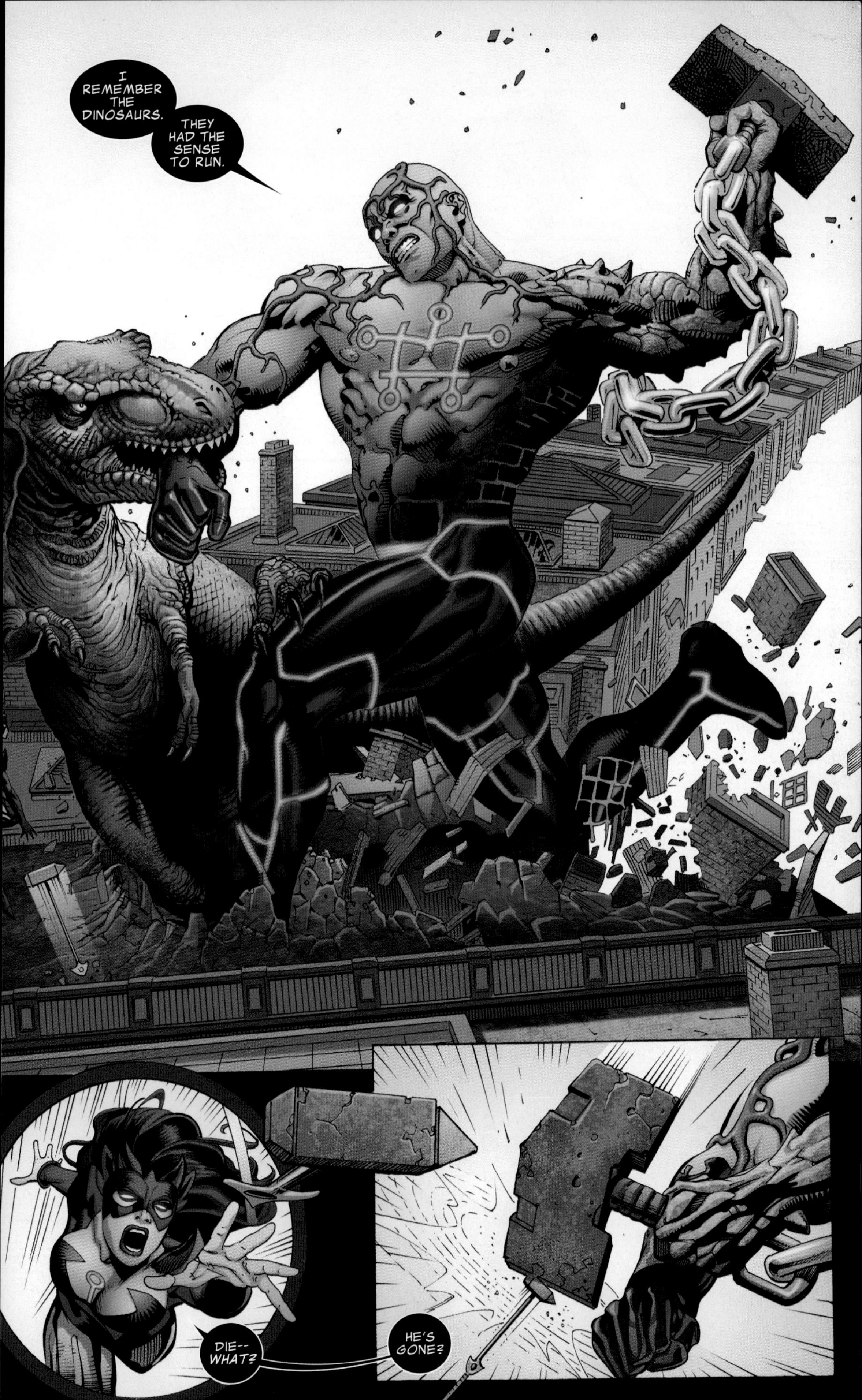
I REMEMBER THE DINOSAURS.
THEY HAD THE SENSE TO RUN.
DIE-- WHAT?
HE'S GONE?

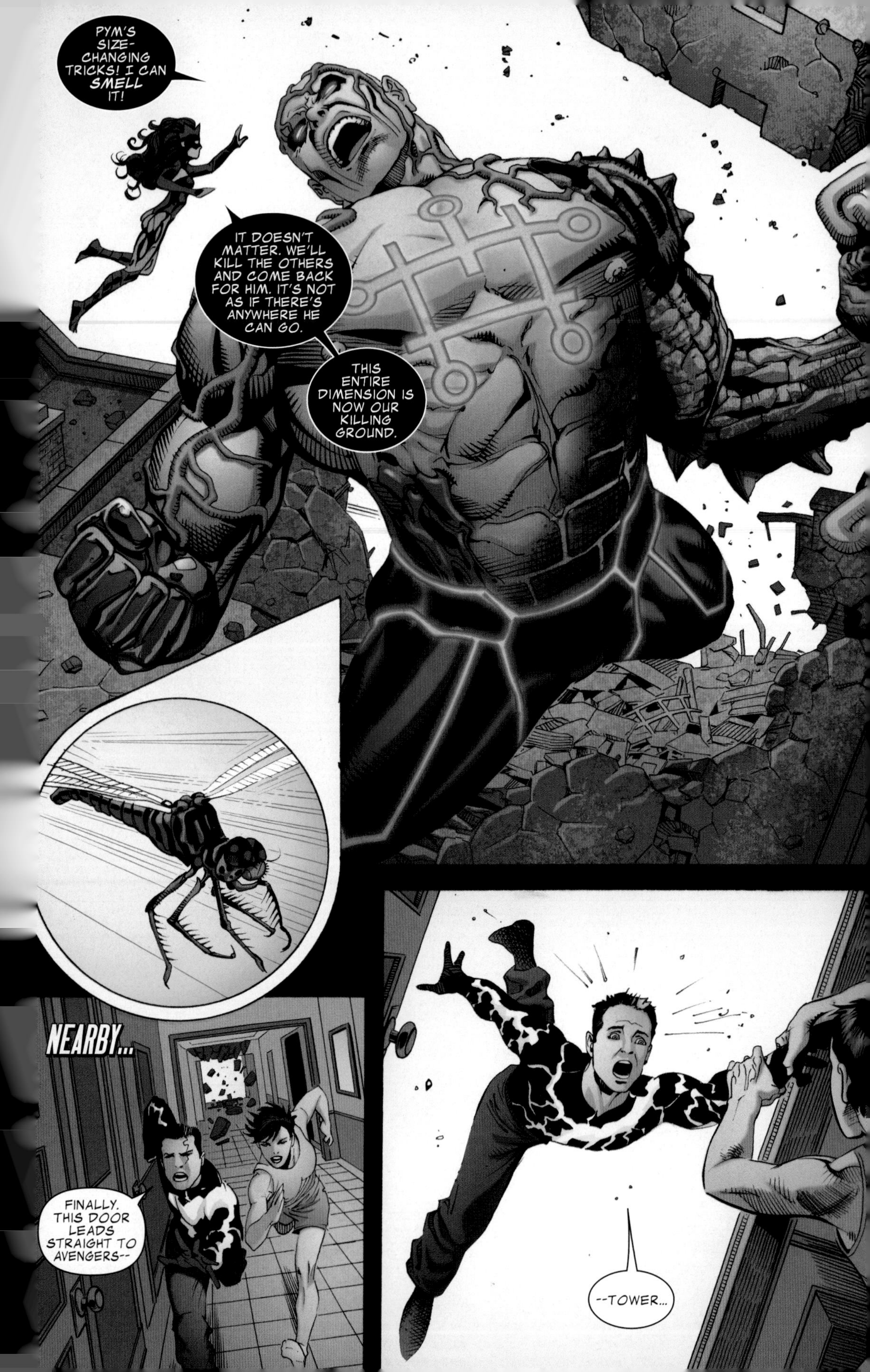
PYM'S SIZE-CHANGING TRICKS! I CAN SMELL IT!
IT DOESN'T MATTER. WE'LL KILL THE OTHERS AND COME BACK FOR HIM. IT'S NOT AS IF THERE'S ANYWHERE HE CAN GO.
THIS ENTIRE DIMENSION IS NOW OUR KILLING GROUND.
NEARBY...
FINALLY. THIS DOOR LEADS STRAIGHT TO AVENGERS--
--TOWER...

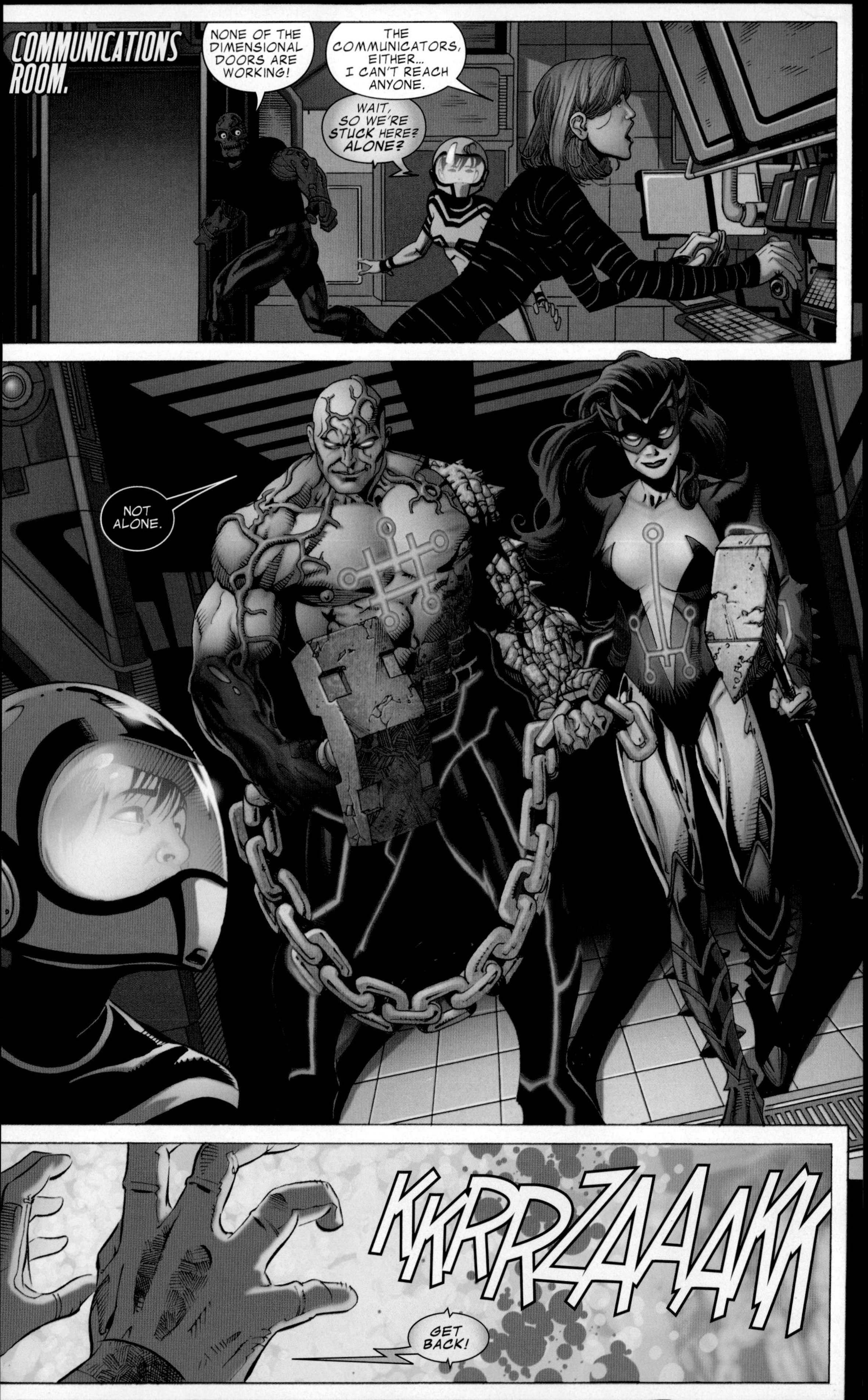
COMMUNICATIONS ROOM.
NONE OF THE DIMENSIONAL DOORS ARE WORKING!
THE COMMUNICATORS, EITHER... I CAN'T REACH ANYONE.
WAIT, SO WE'RE STUCK HERE? ALONE?
NOT ALONE.
KKRRZAAAM
GET BACK!

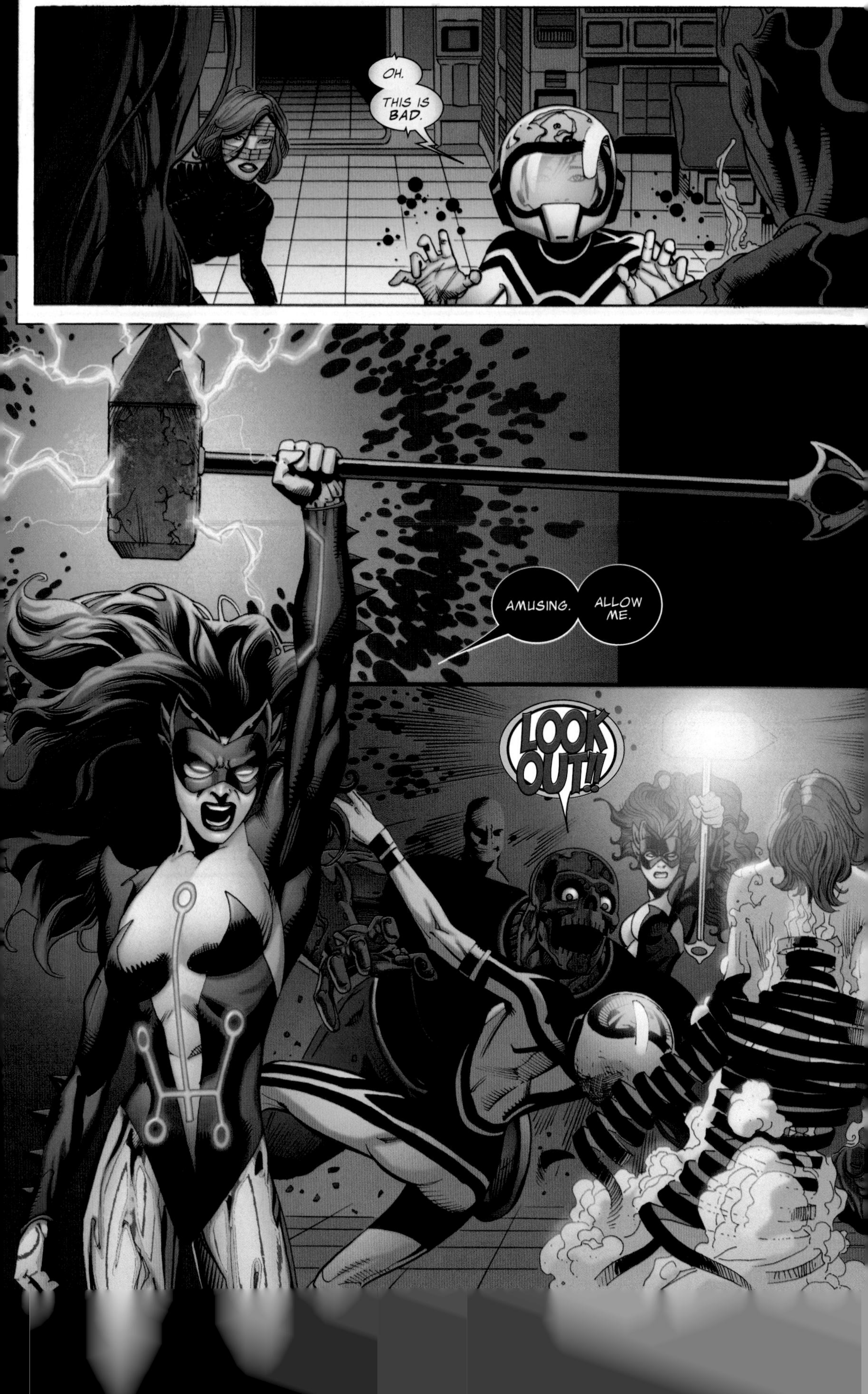
OH.
THIS IS BAD.
AMUSING.
ALLOW ME.
LOOK OUT!!

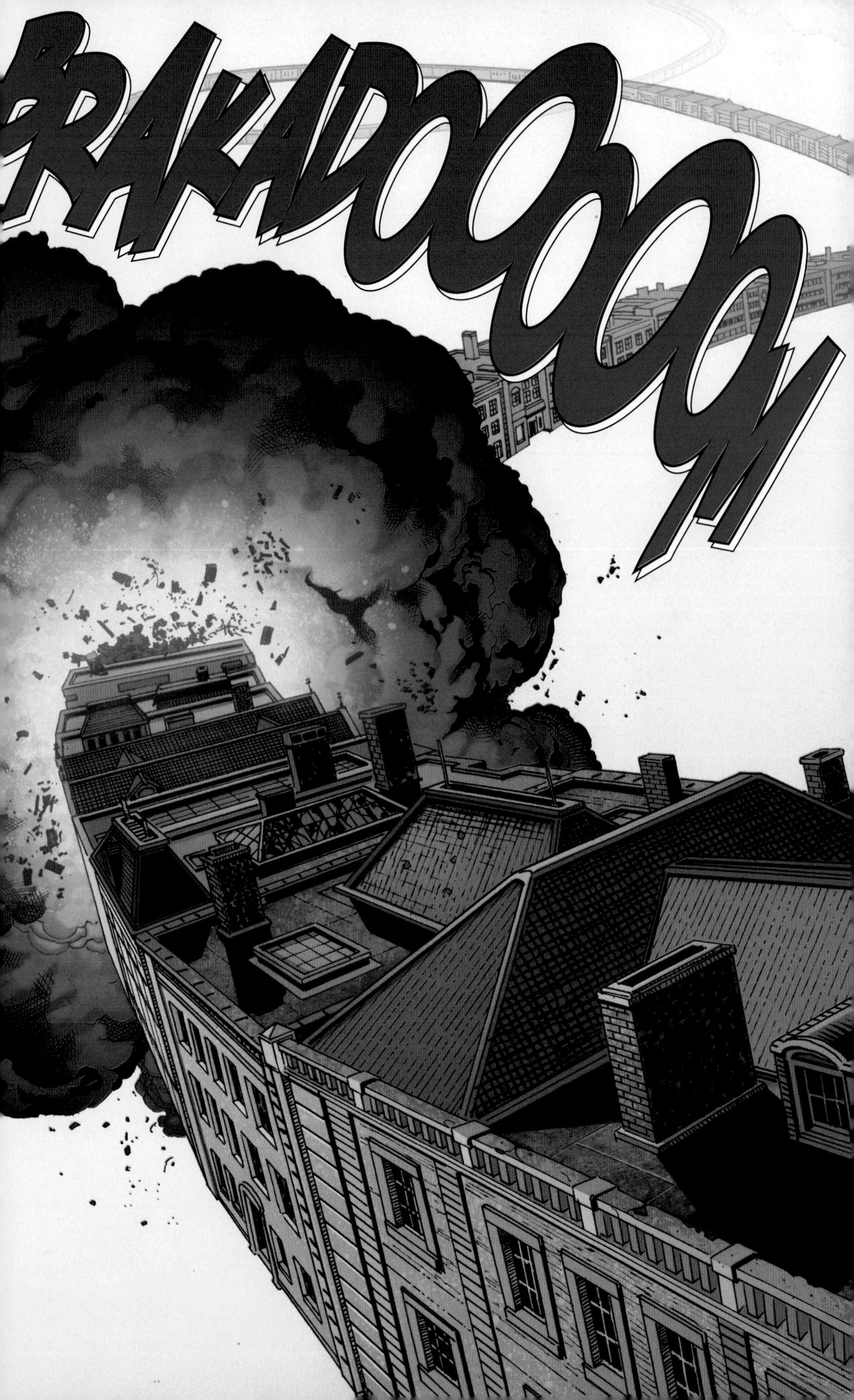
BRAKADOOOOM

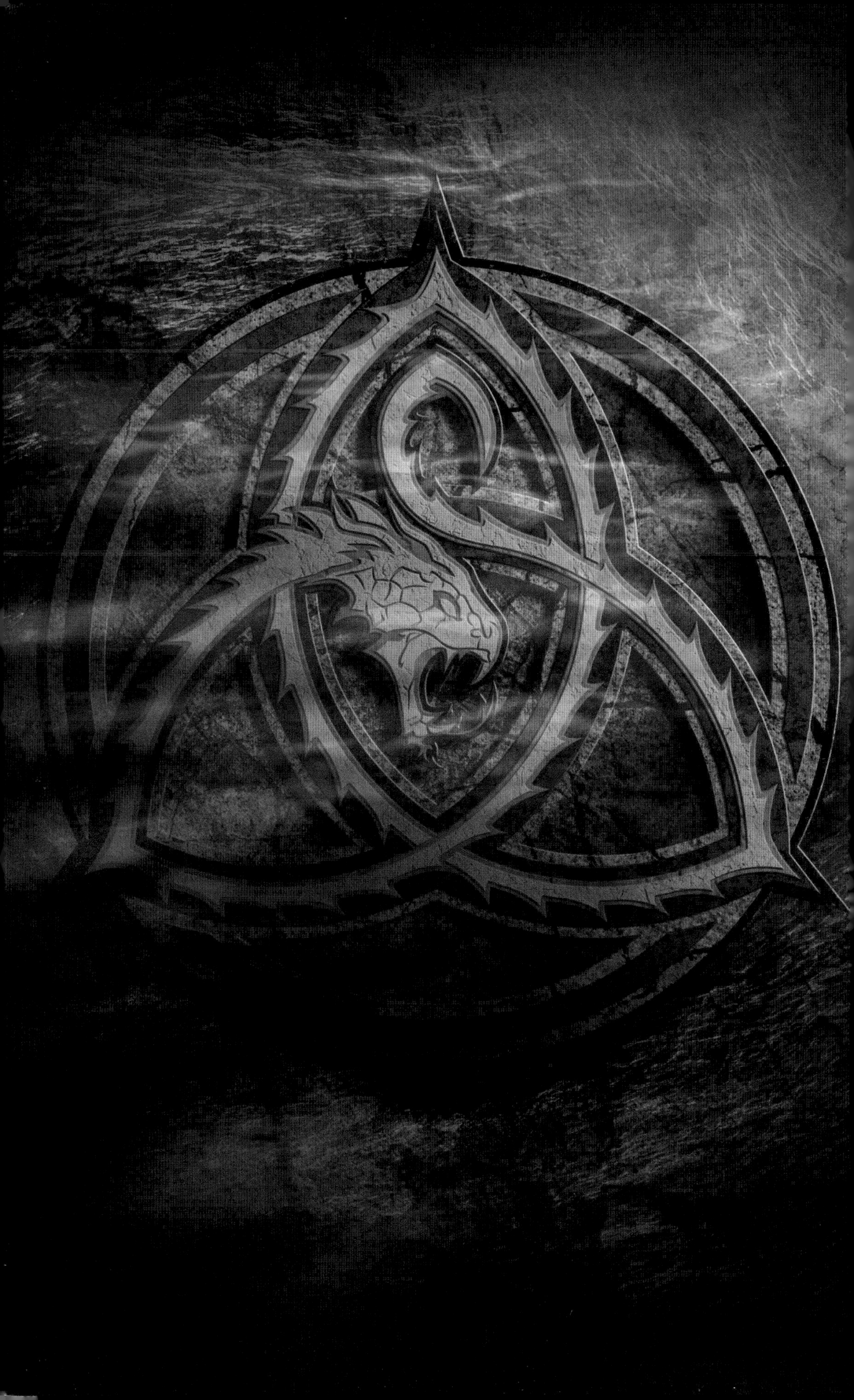

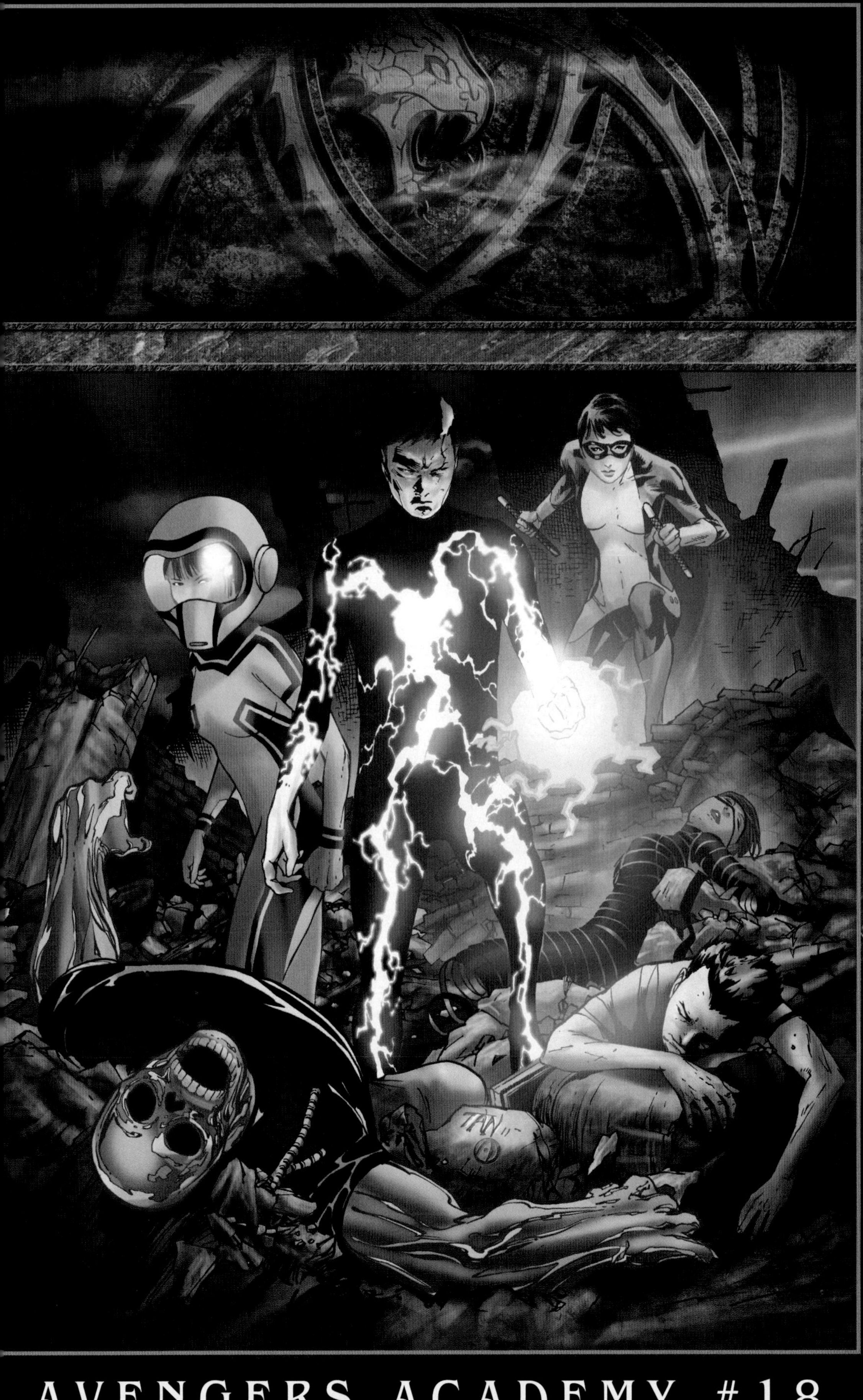

AVENGERS ACADEMY #18

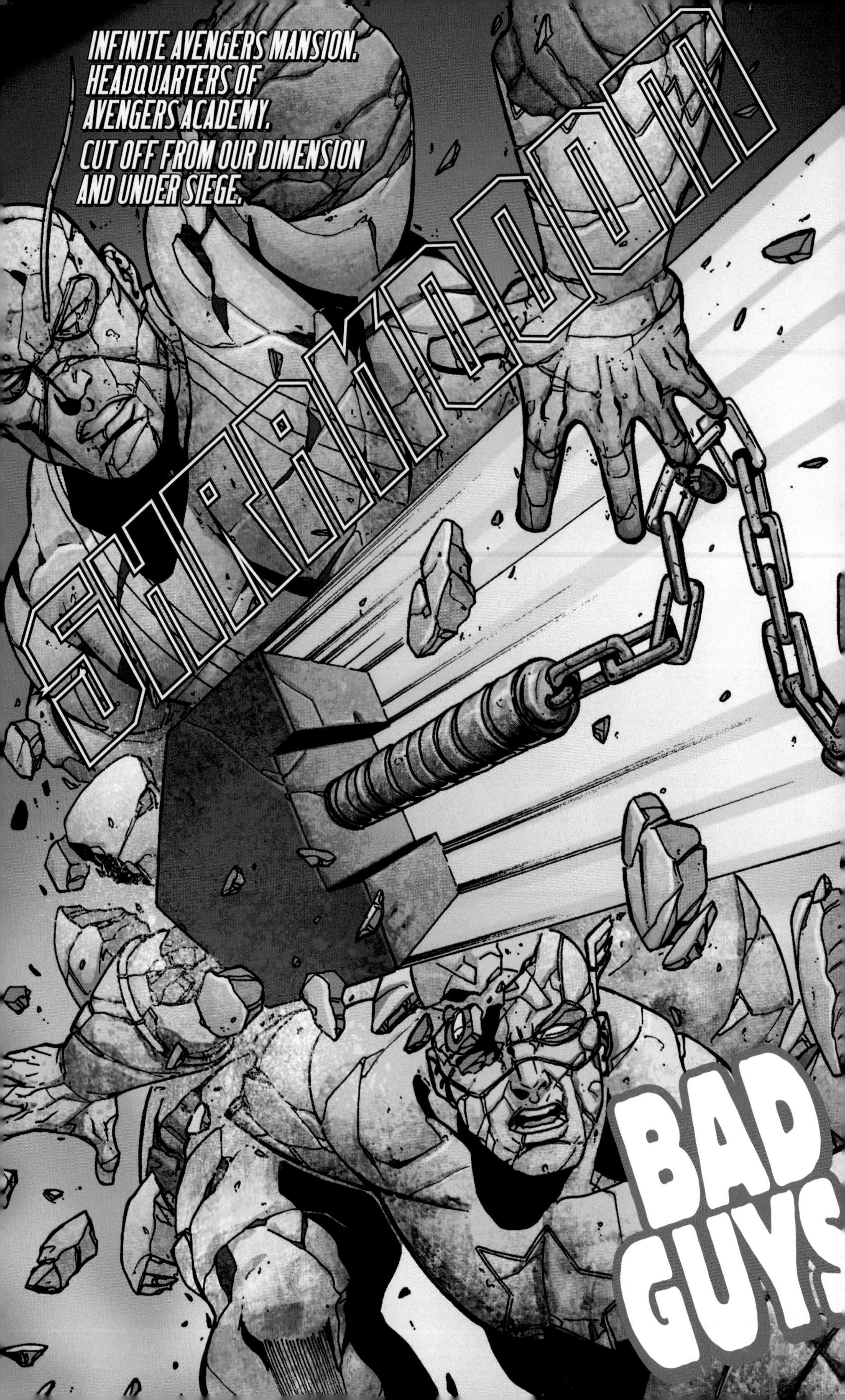
INFINITE AVENGERS MANSION.
HEADQUARTERS OF
AVENGERS ACADEMY.
CUT OFF FROM OUR DIMENSION
AND UNDER SIEGE.
BAD
GUYS

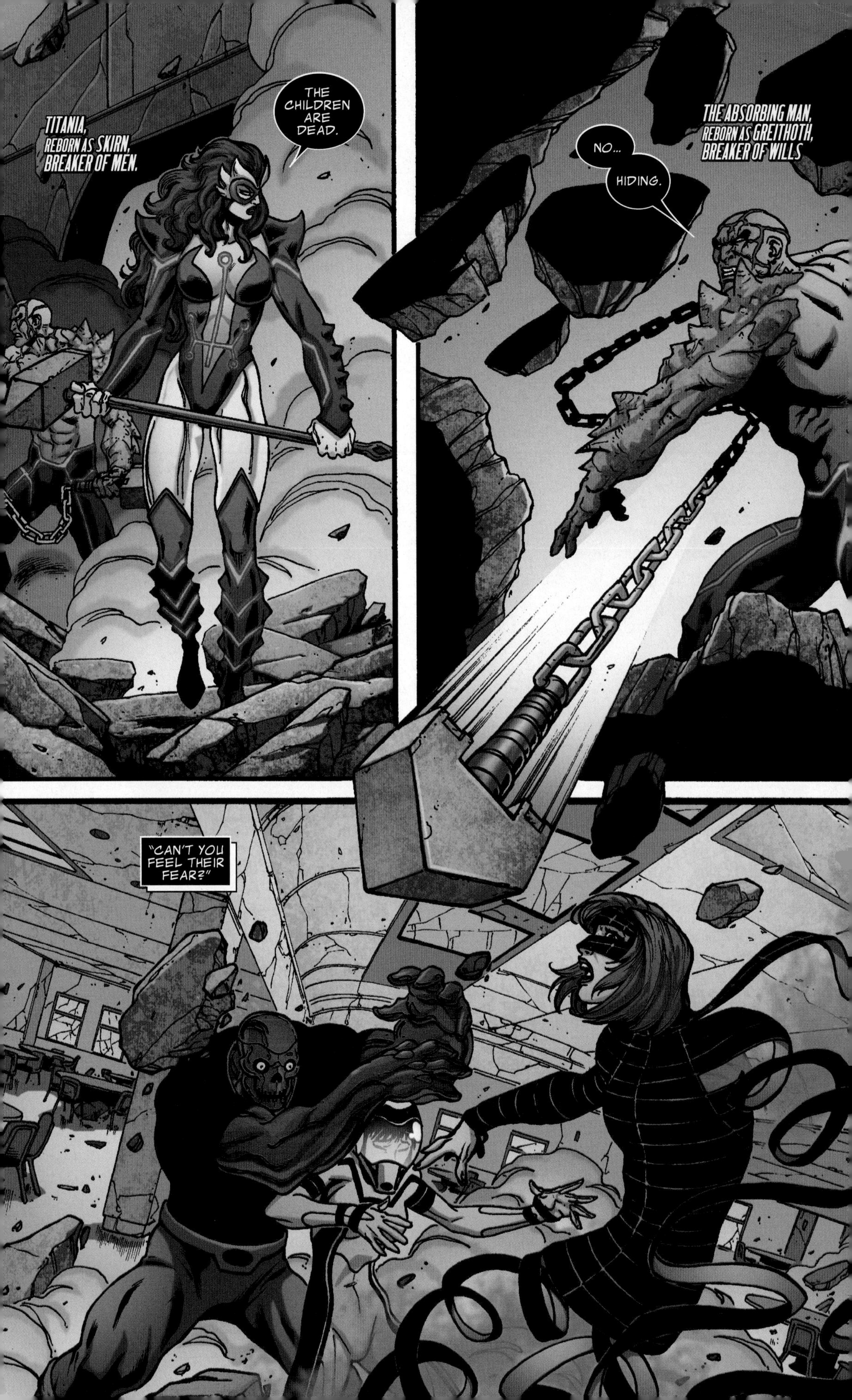
TITANIA, REBORN AS SKIRN, BREAKER OF MEN.
THE CHILDREN ARE DEAD.
THE ABSORBING MAN, REBORN AS GREITHOTH, BREAKER OF WILLS
NO...
HIDING.
"CAN'T YOU FEEL THEIR FEAR?"

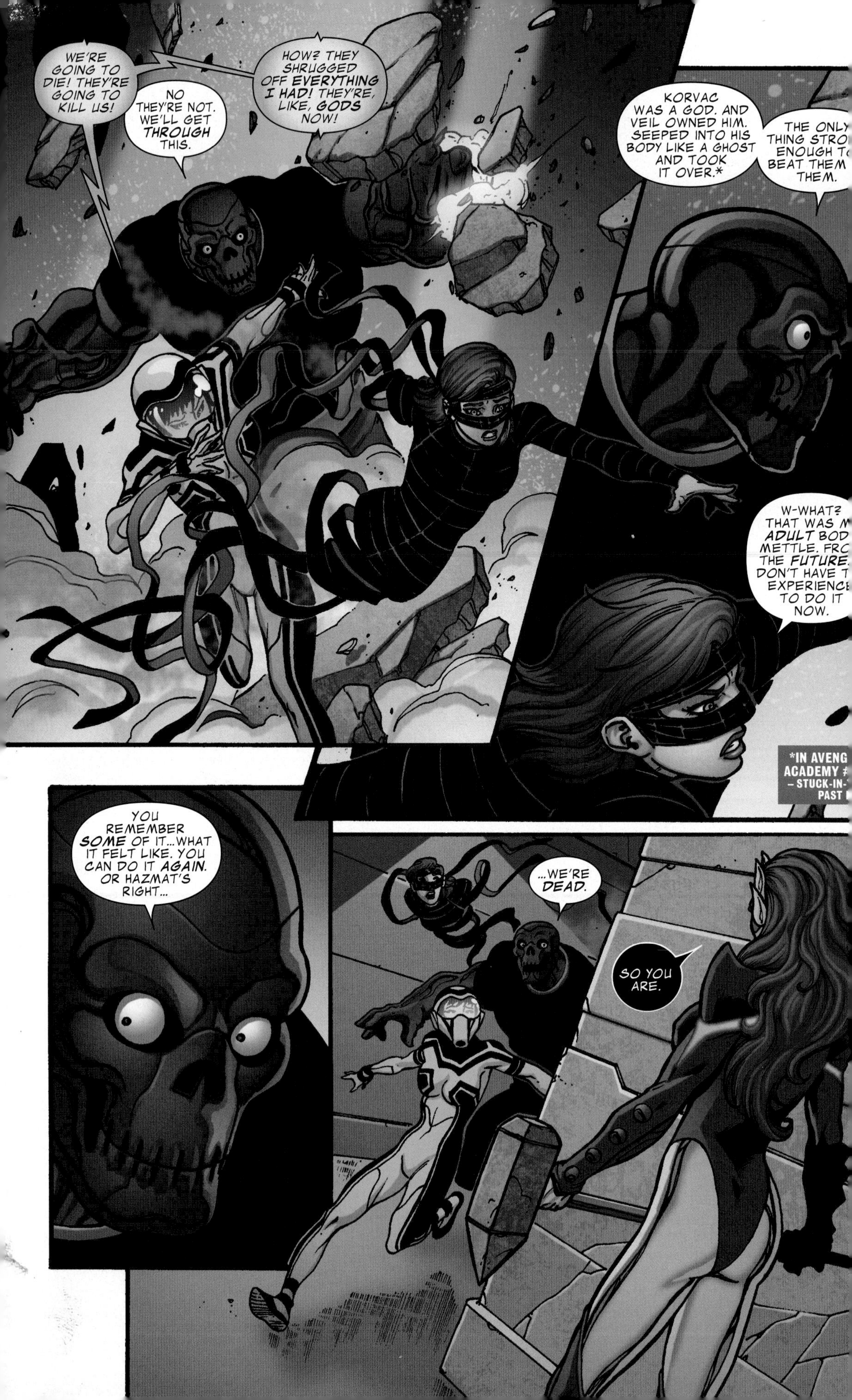

WE'RE GOING TO DIE! THEY'RE GOING TO KILL US!
HOW? THEY SHRUGGED OFF EVERYTHING I HAD! THEY'RE, LIKE, GODS NOW!
NO THEY'RE NOT. WE'LL GET THROUGH THIS.
KORVAC WAS A GOD. AND VEIL OWNED HIM. SEEPED INTO HIS BODY LIKE A GHOST AND TOOK IT OVER.*
W-WHAT? THAT WAS M ADULT BOD METTLE. FRO THE FUTURE. DON'T HAVE T EXPERIENCE TO DO IT NOW.
*IN AVENG ACADEMY # – STUCK-IN- PAST
YOU REMEMBER SOME OF IT... WHAT IT FELT LIKE. YOU CAN DO IT AGAIN. OR HAZMAT'S RIGHT...
...WE'RE DEAD.
SO YOU ARE.

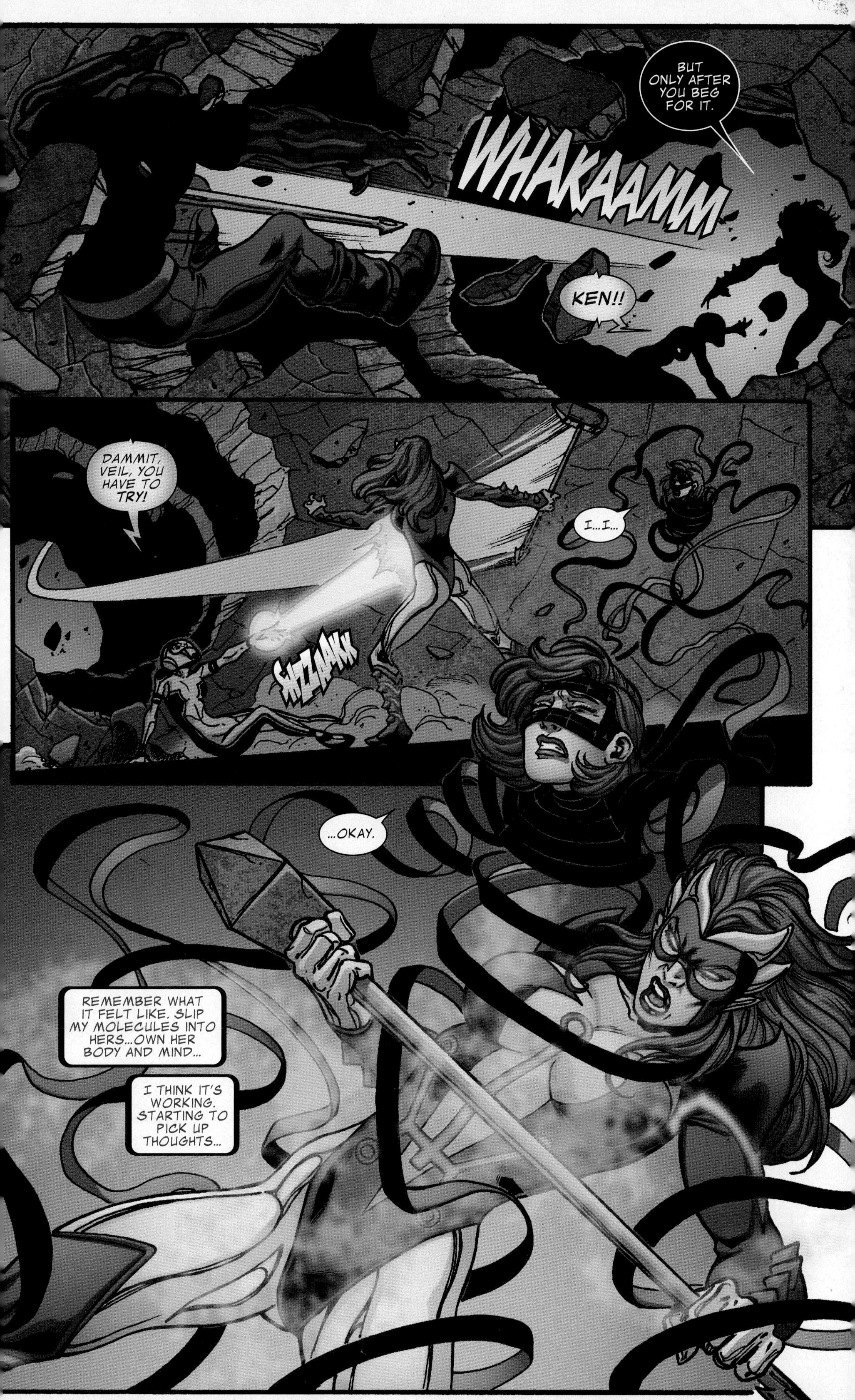
BUT ONLY AFTER YOU BEG FOR IT.
WHAKAAMM
KEN!!
DAMMIT, VEIL, YOU HAVE TO TRY!
I... I...
SHZZAAKK
...OKAY.
REMEMBER WHAT IT FELT LIKE. SLIP MY MOLECULES INTO HERS...OWN HER BODY AND MIND...
I THINK IT'S WORKING. STARTING TO PICK UP THOUGHTS...

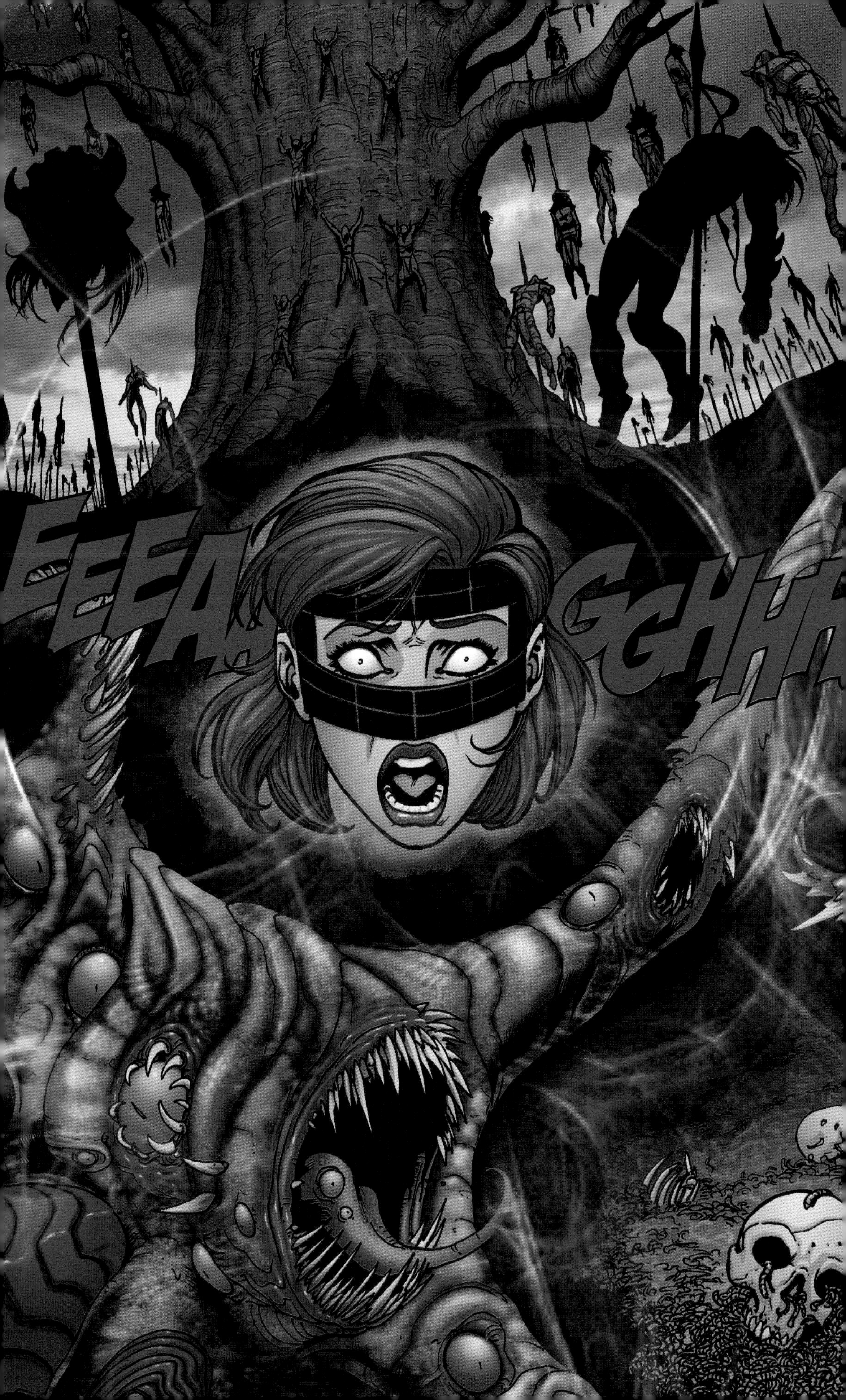
EEEA
GGHH

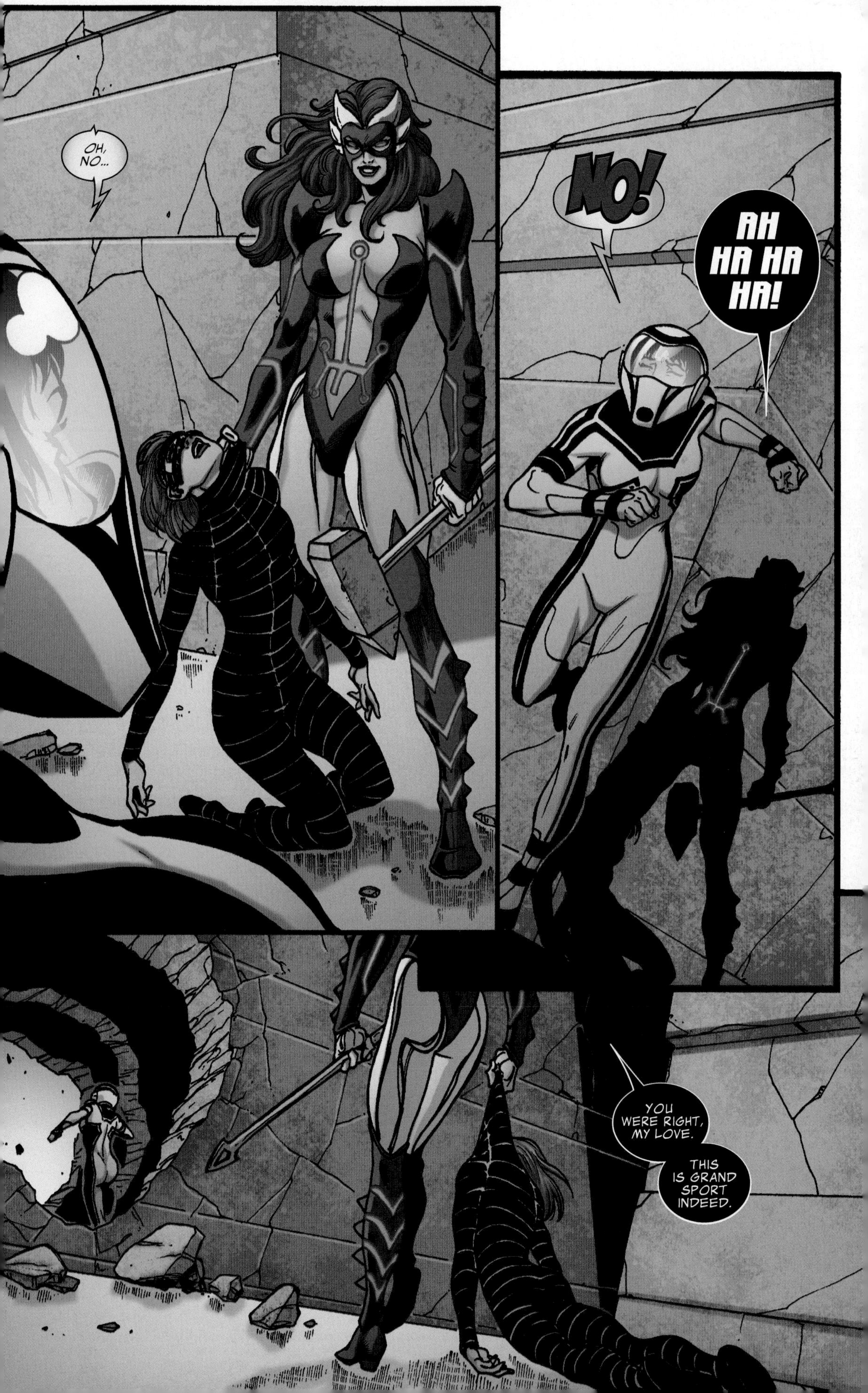
OH, NO...
NO!
AH HA HA HA!
YOU WERE RIGHT, MY LOVE.
THIS IS GRAND SPORT INDEED.

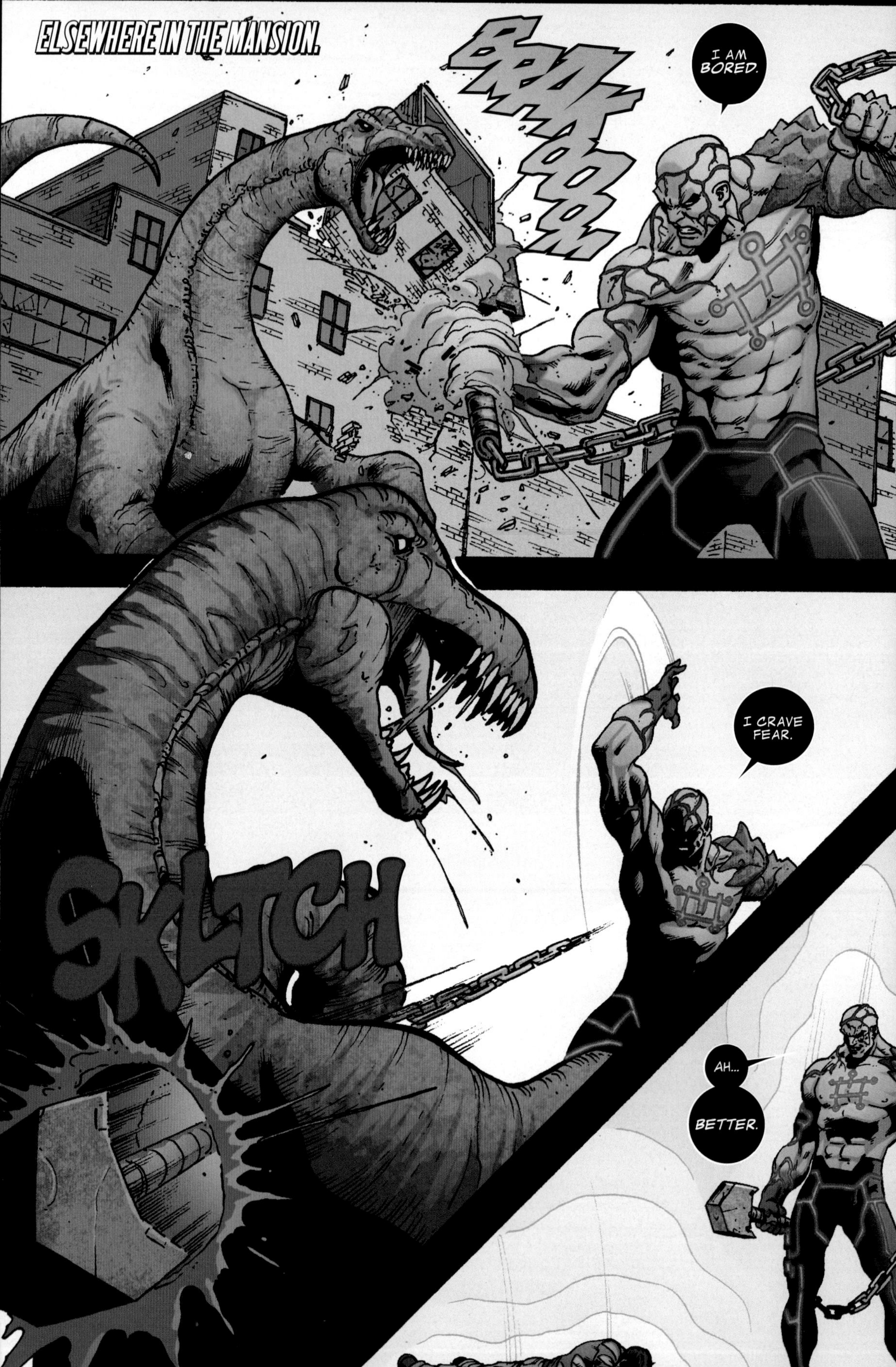
ELSEWHERE IN THE MANSION.
BRAKOOOM
I AM BORED.
I CRAVE FEAR.
SKLTCH
AH...
BETTER.

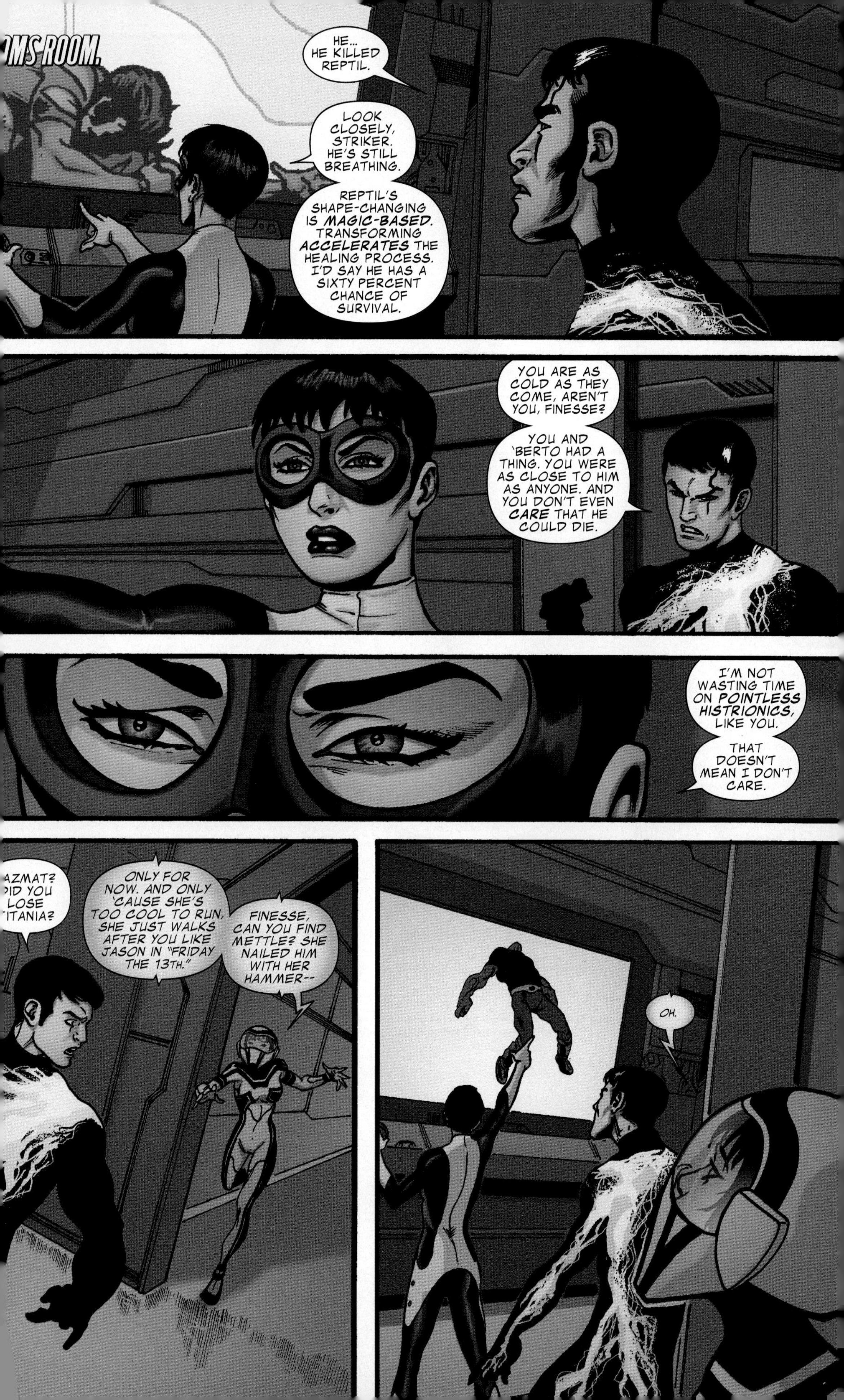
...OMS ROOM.
HE... HE KILLED REPTIL.
LOOK CLOSELY, STRIKER. HE'S STILL BREATHING.
REPTIL'S SHAPE-CHANGING IS MAGIC-BASED. TRANSFORMING ACCELERATES THE HEALING PROCESS. I'D SAY HE HAS A SIXTY PERCENT CHANCE OF SURVIVAL.
YOU ARE AS COLD AS THEY COME, AREN'T YOU, FINESSE?
'BERTO HAD A THING. YOU WERE AS CLOSE TO HIM AS ANYONE. AND YOU DON'T EVEN CARE THAT HE COULD DIE.
I'M NOT WASTING TIME ON POINTLESS HISTRIONICS, LIKE YOU.
THAT DOESN'T MEAN I DON'T CARE.
...AZMAT? ...ID YOU LOSE ...ITANIA?
ONLY FOR NOW. AND ONLY 'CAUSE SHE'S TOO COOL TO RUN, SHE JUST WALKS AFTER YOU LIKE JASON IN "FRIDAY THE 13TH."
FINESSE, CAN YOU FIND METTLE? SHE NAILED HIM WITH HER HAMMER--
OH.

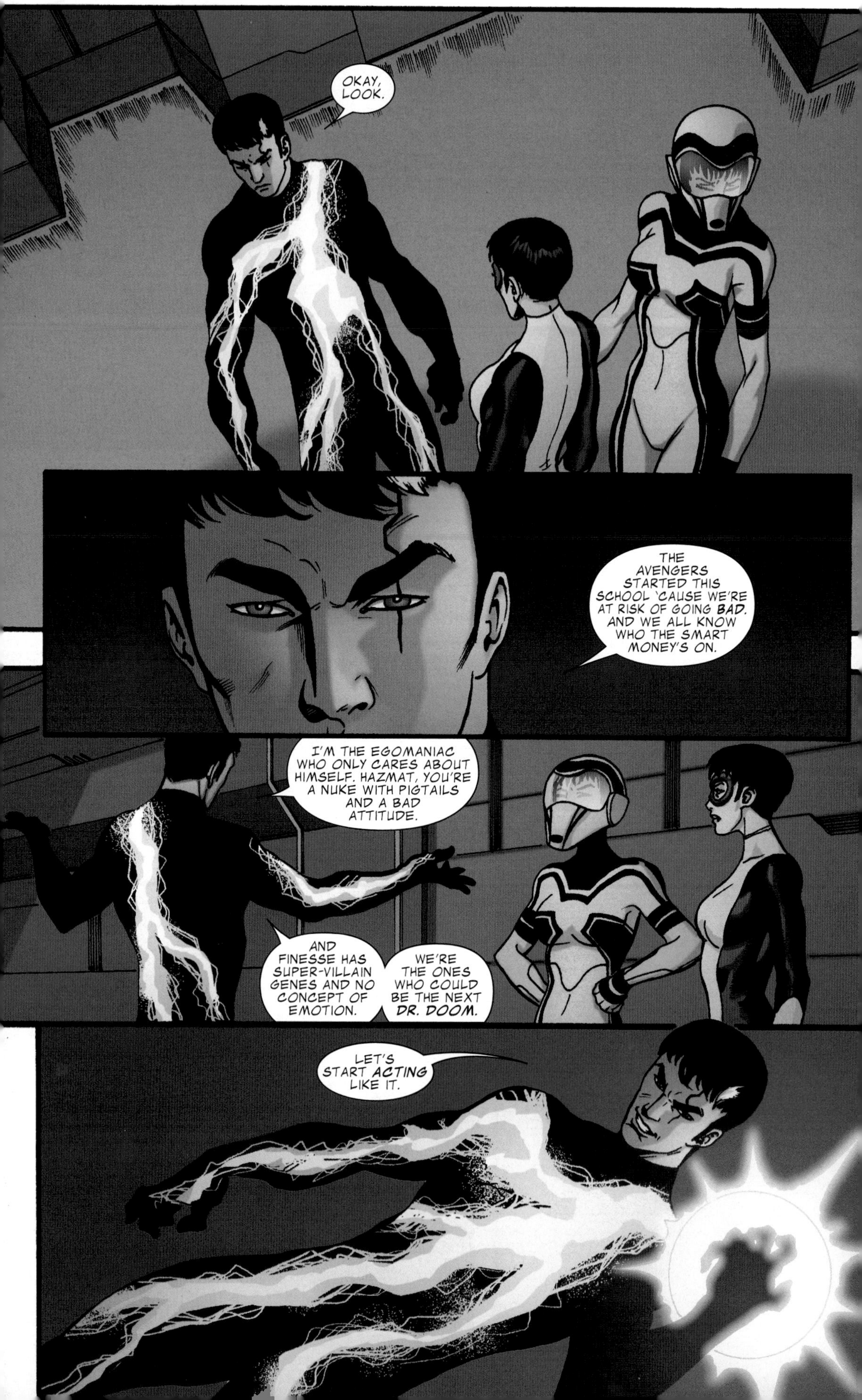
OKAY, LOOK.
THE AVENGERS STARTED THIS SCHOOL 'CAUSE WE'RE AT RISK OF GOING BAD. AND WE ALL KNOW WHO THE SMART MONEY'S ON.
I'M THE EGOMANIAC WHO ONLY CARES ABOUT HIMSELF. HAZMAT, YOU'RE A NUKE WITH PIGTAILS AND A BAD ATTITUDE.
AND FINESSE HAS SUPER-VILLAIN GENES AND NO CONCEPT OF EMOTION.
WE'RE THE ONES WHO COULD BE THE NEXT DR. DOOM.
LET'S START ACTING LIKE IT.

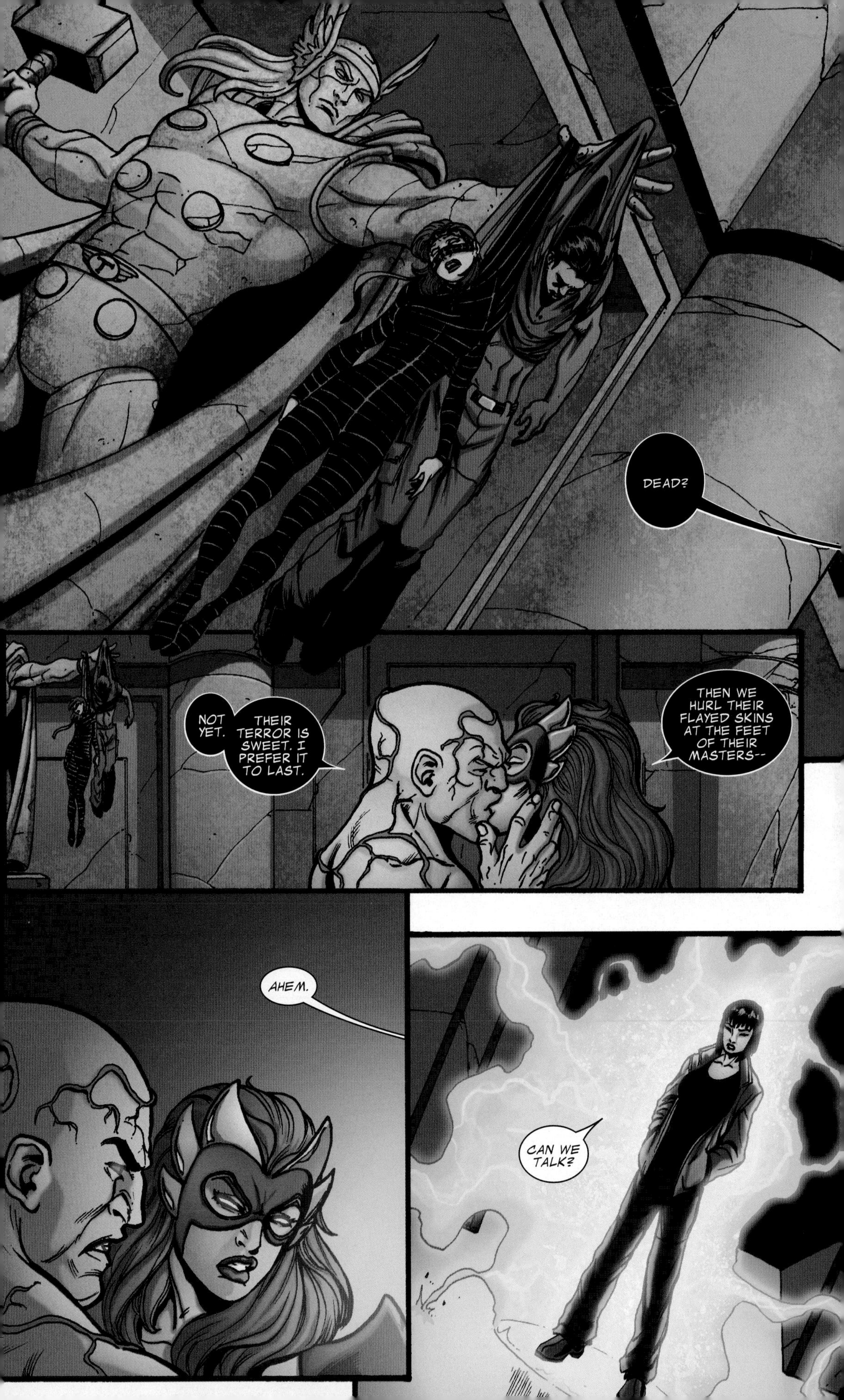
DEAD?
NOT YET.
THEIR TERROR IS SWEET. I PREFER IT TO LAST.
THEN WE HURL THEIR FLAYED SKINS AT THE FEET OF THEIR MASTERS--
AHEM.
CAN WE TALK?

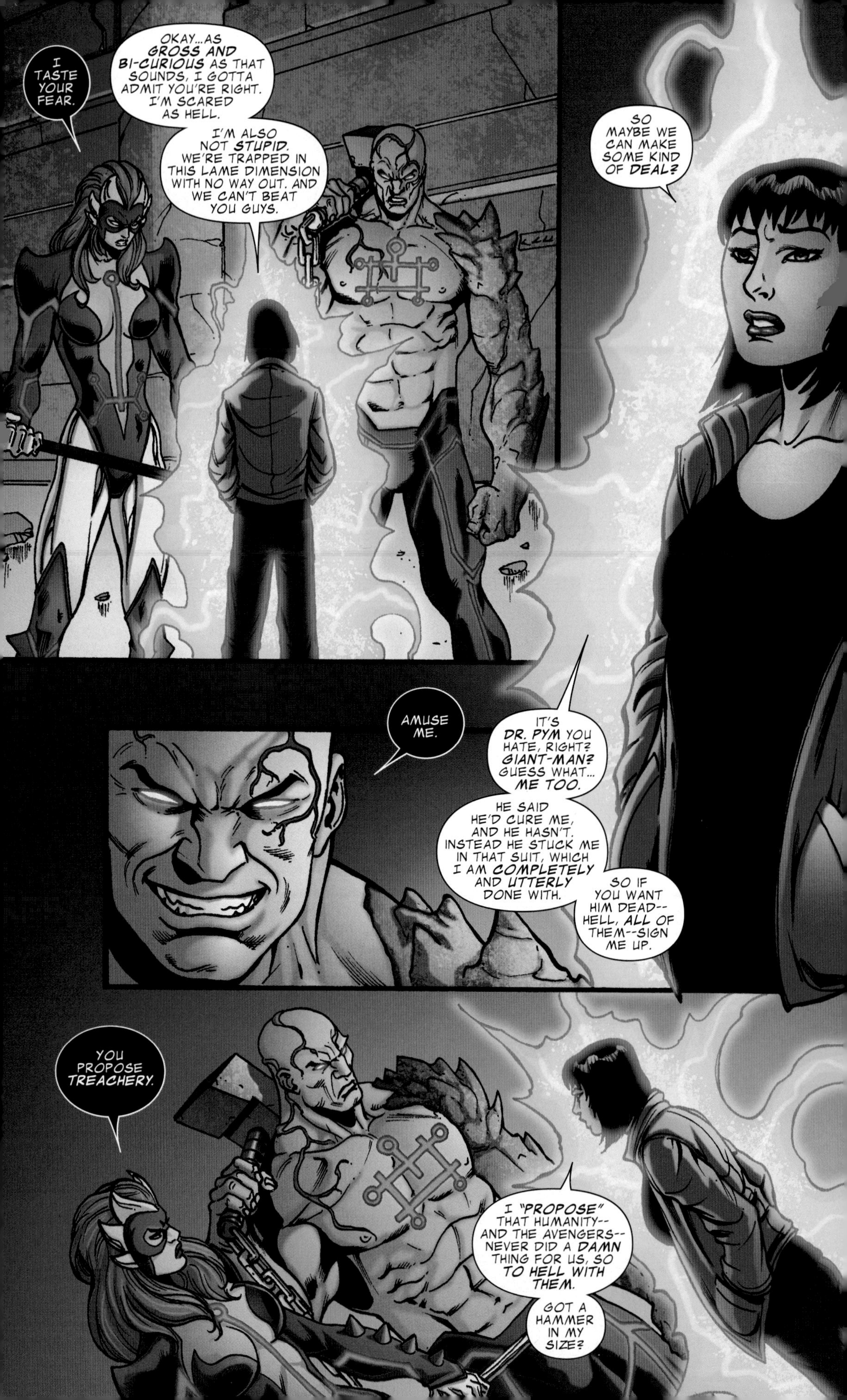
I TASTE YOUR FEAR.
OKAY...AS GROSS AND BI-CURIOUS AS THAT SOUNDS, I GOTTA ADMIT YOU'RE RIGHT. I'M SCARED AS HELL.
I'M ALSO NOT STUPID. WE'RE TRAPPED IN THIS LAME DIMENSION WITH NO WAY OUT. AND WE CAN'T BEAT YOU GUYS.
SO MAYBE WE CAN MAKE SOME KIND OF DEAL?
AMUSE ME.
IT'S DR. PYM YOU HATE, RIGHT? GIANT-MAN? GUESS WHAT... ME TOO.
HE SAID HE'D CURE ME, AND HE HASN'T. INSTEAD HE STUCK ME IN THAT SUIT, WHICH I AM COMPLETELY AND UTTERLY DONE WITH.
SO IF YOU WANT HIM DEAD--HELL, ALL OF THEM--SIGN ME UP.
YOU PROPOSE TREACHERY.
I "PROPOSE" THAT HUMANITY--AND THE AVENGERS--NEVER DID A DAMN THING FOR US, SO TO HELL WITH THEM.
GOT A HAMMER IN MY SIZE?

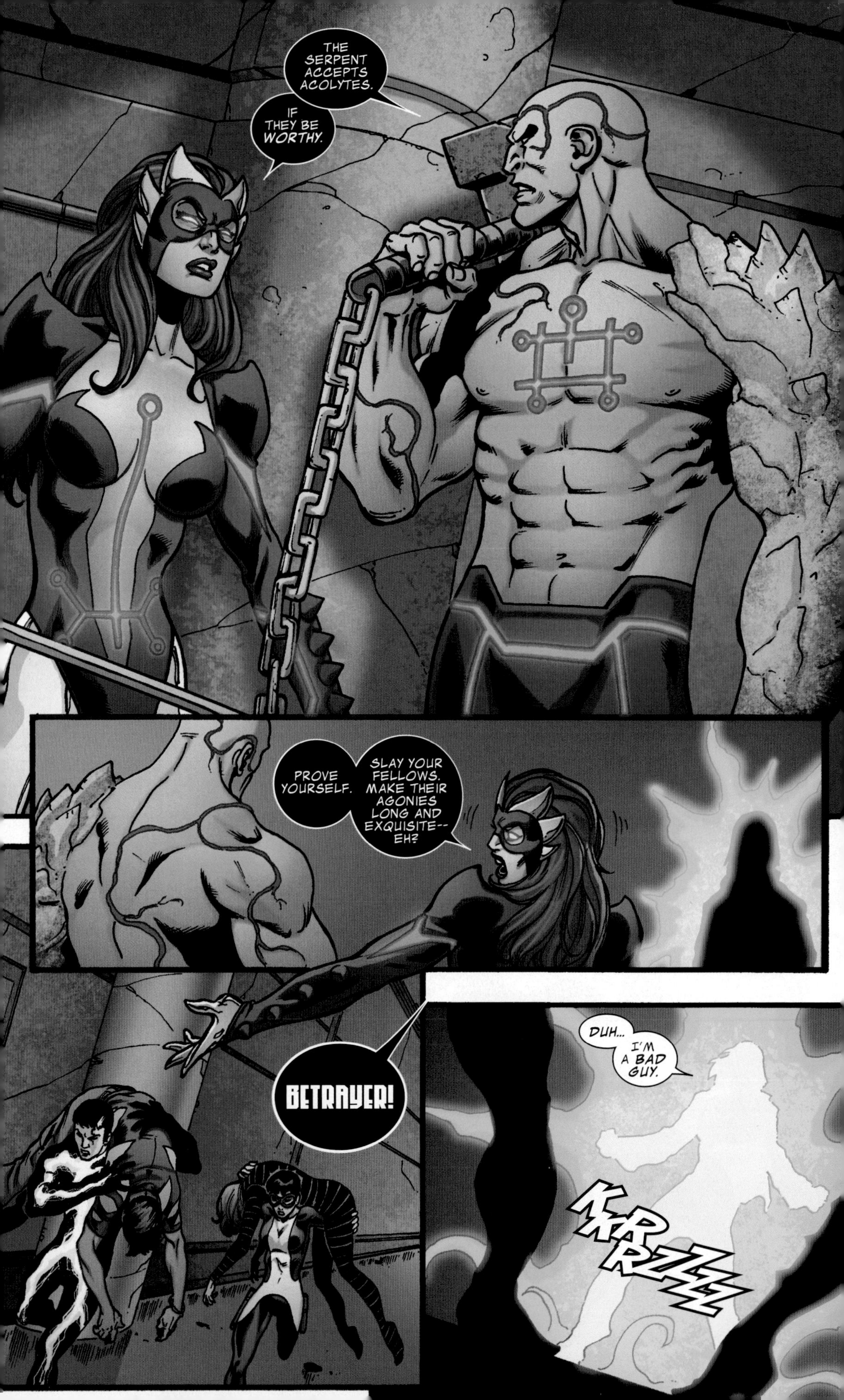
THE SERPENT ACCEPTS ACOLYTES.
IF THEY BE WORTHY.
PROVE YOURSELF.
SLAY YOUR FELLOWS. MAKE THEIR AGONIES LONG AND EXQUISITE-- EH?
BETRAYER!
DUH... I'M A BAD GUY.
KKRRZZZZZ

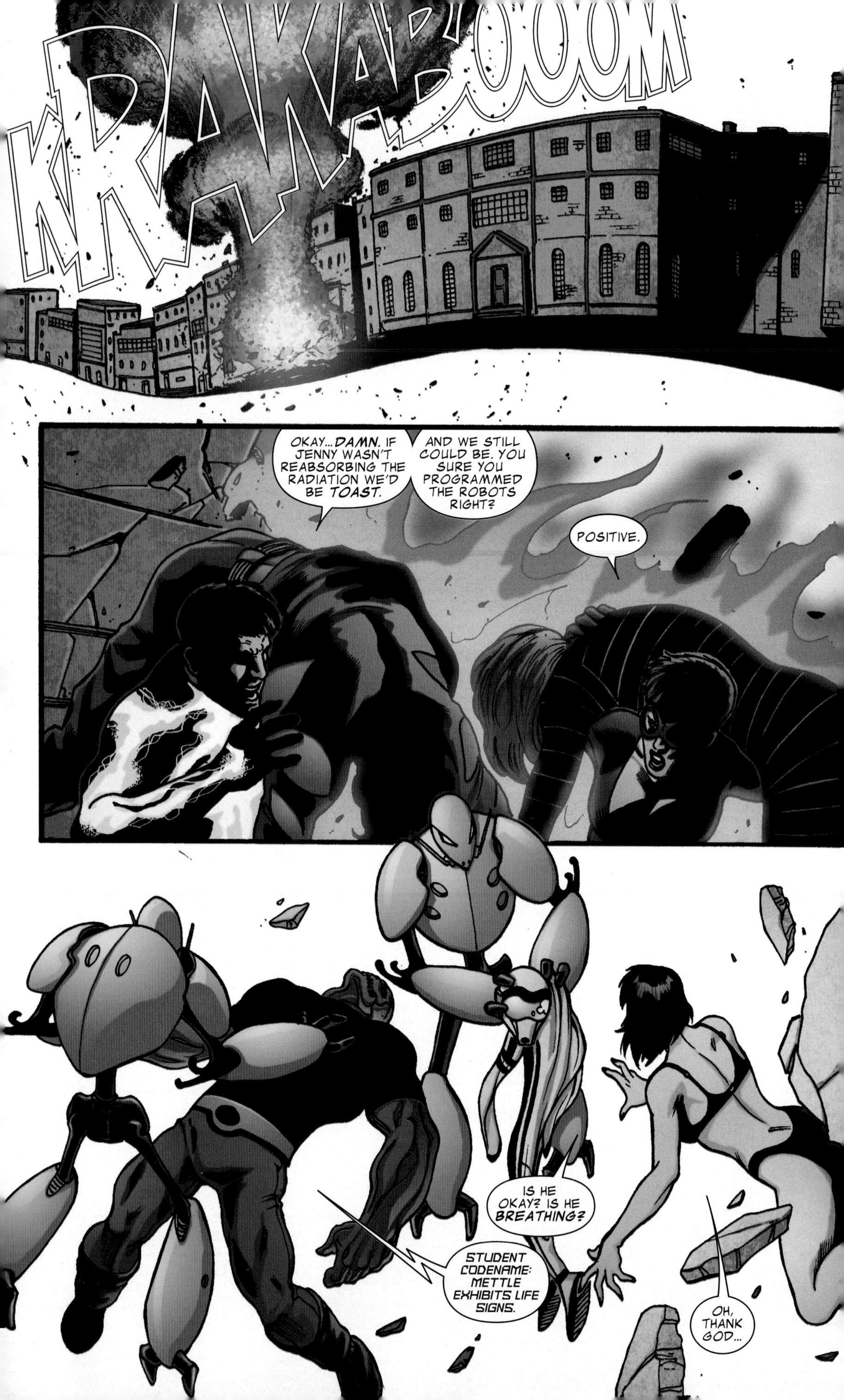
KRAKABOOOM
OKAY...DAMN. IF JENNY WASN'T REABSORBING THE RADIATION WE'D BE TOAST.
AND WE STILL COULD BE. YOU SURE YOU PROGRAMMED THE ROBOTS RIGHT?
POSITIVE.
IS HE OKAY? IS HE BREATHING?
STUDENT CODENAME: METTLE EXHIBITS LIFE SIGNS.
OH, THANK GOD...

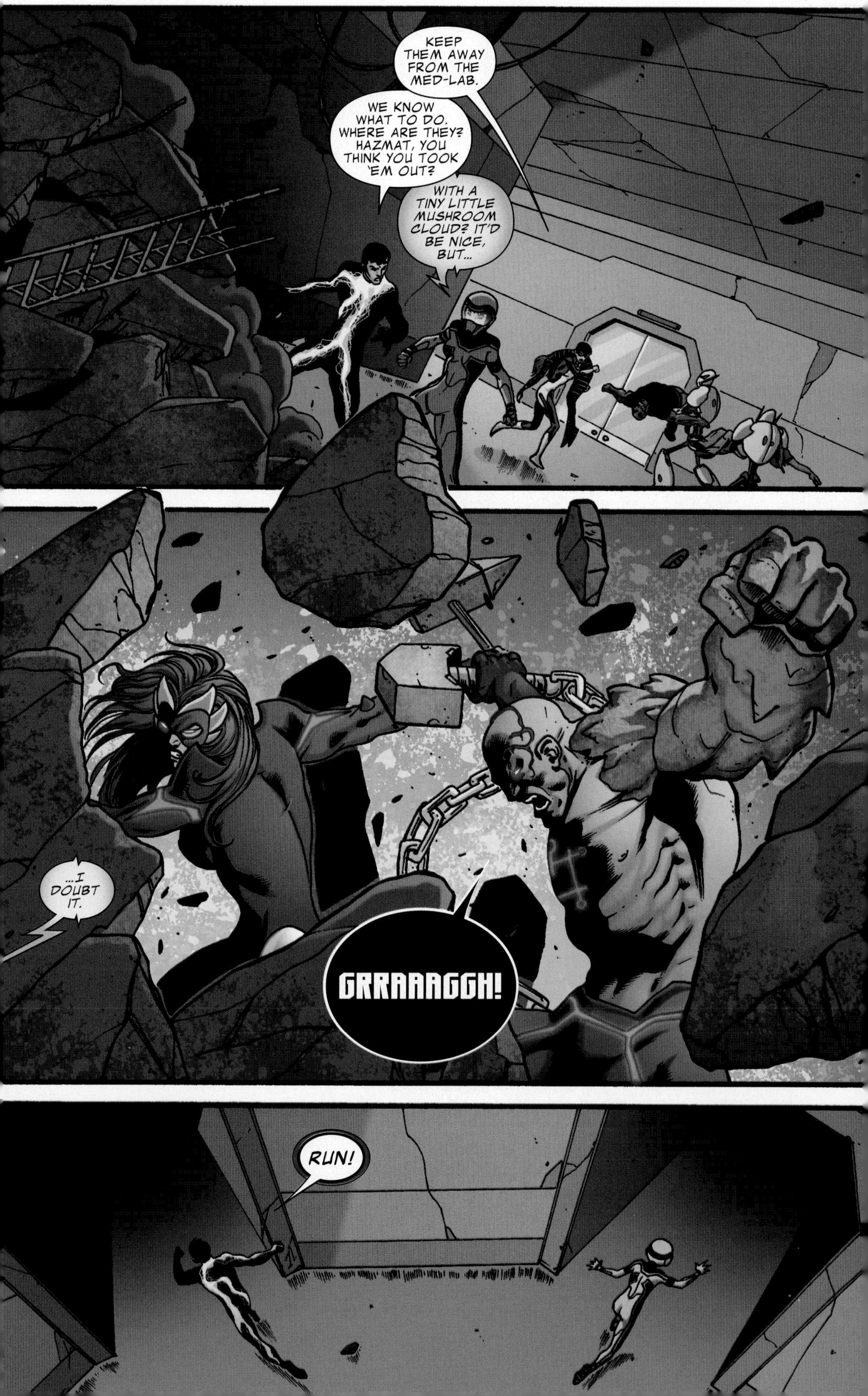

KEEP THEM AWAY FROM THE MED-LAB.
WE KNOW WHAT TO DO. WHERE ARE THEY? HAZMAT, YOU THINK YOU TOOK 'EM OUT?
WITH A TINY LITTLE MUSHROOM CLOUD? IT'D BE NICE, BUT...
...I DOUBT IT.
GRRAAAGGH!
RUN!

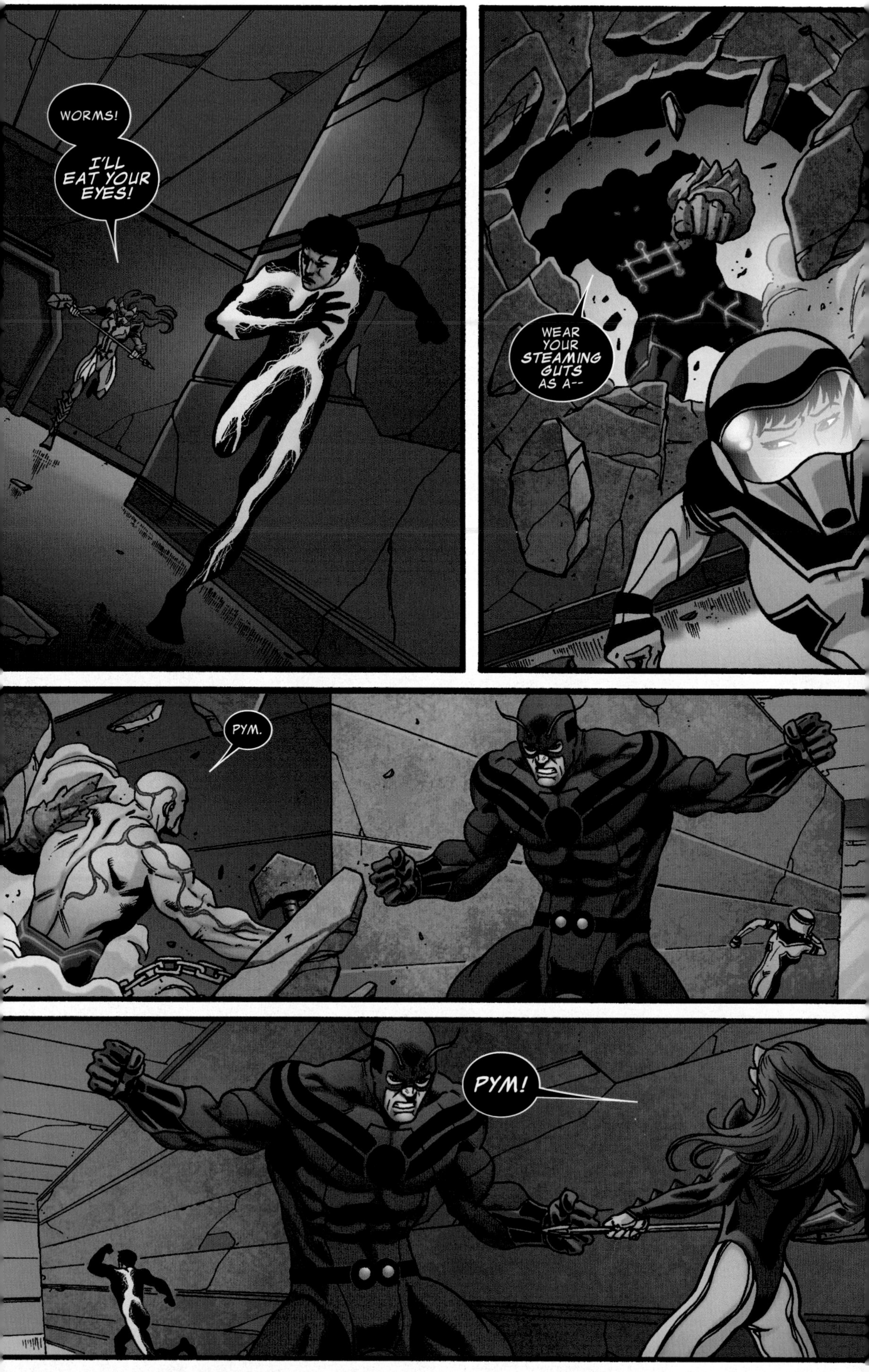
WORMS!
I'LL EAT YOUR EYES!
WEAR YOUR STEAMING GUTS AS A--
PYM.
PYM!

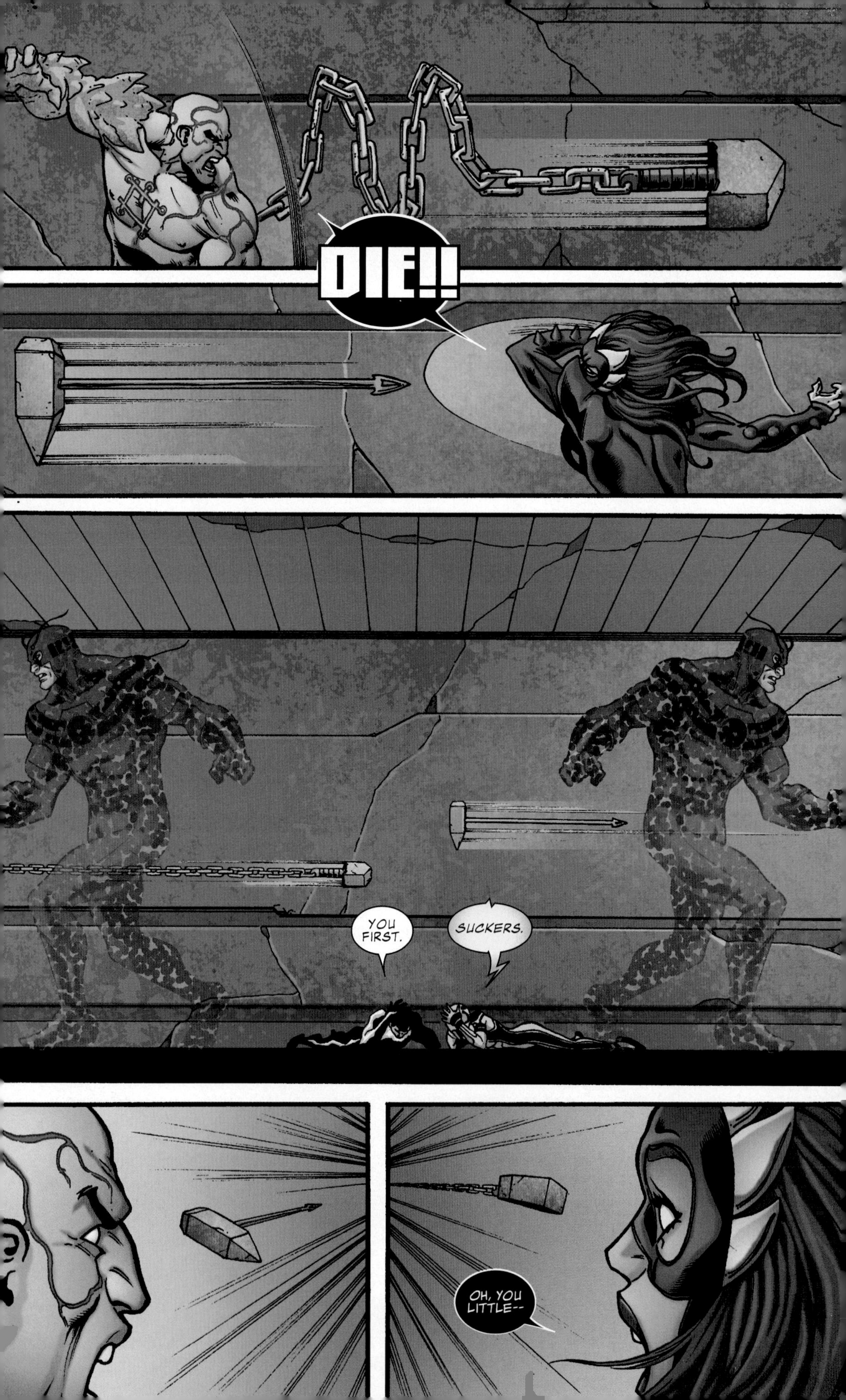
DIE!!
YOU FIRST.
SUCKERS.
OH, YOU LITTLE--

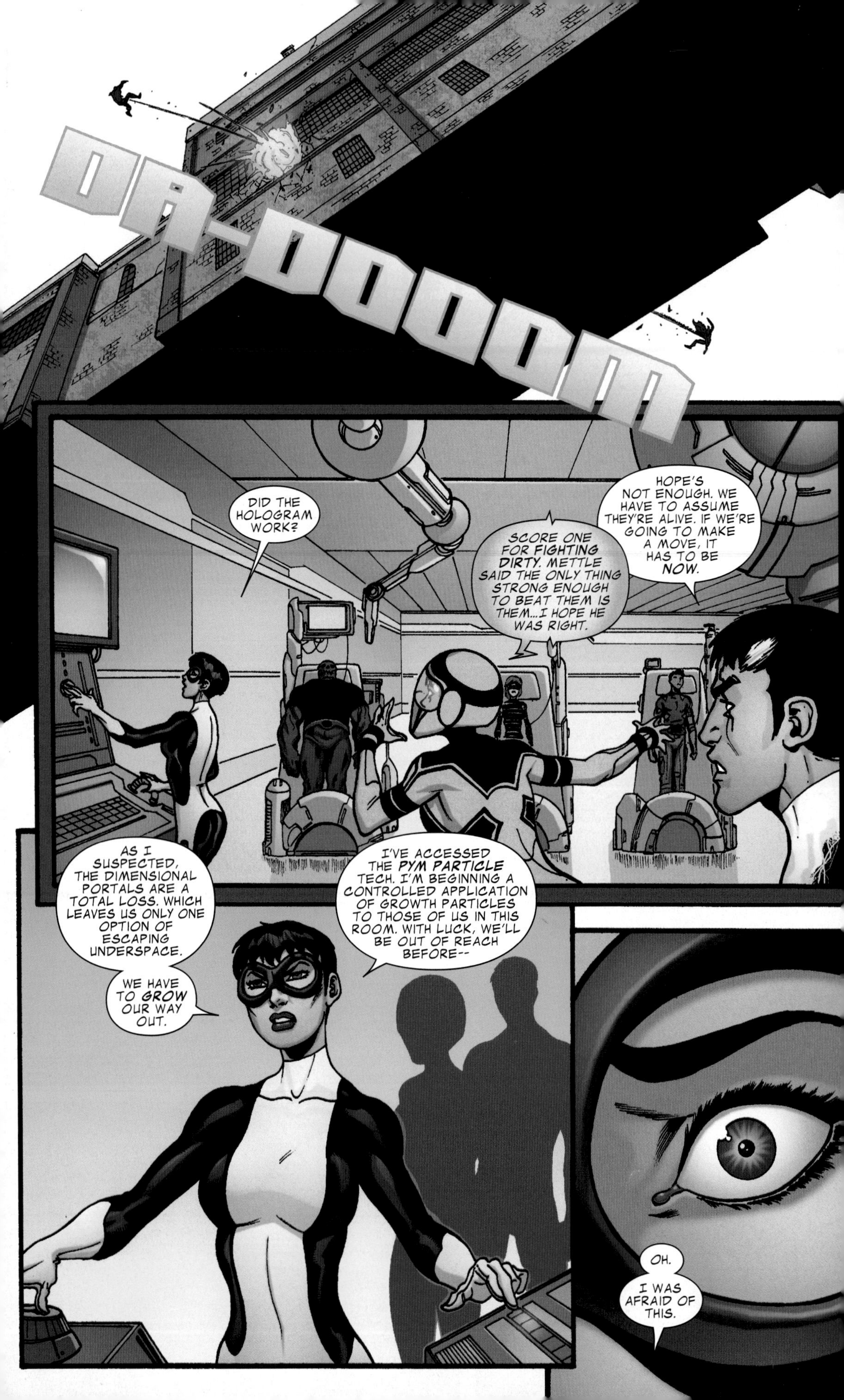
DA-DOOOM
DID THE HOLOGRAM WORK?
SCORE ONE FOR FIGHTING DIRTY. METTLE SAID THE ONLY THING STRONG ENOUGH TO BEAT THEM IS THEM...I HOPE HE WAS RIGHT.
HOPE'S NOT ENOUGH. WE HAVE TO ASSUME THEY'RE ALIVE. IF WE'RE GOING TO MAKE A MOVE, IT HAS TO BE NOW.
AS I SUSPECTED, THE DIMENSIONAL PORTALS ARE A TOTAL LOSS. WHICH LEAVES US ONLY ONE OPTION OF ESCAPING UNDERSPACE.
WE HAVE TO GROW OUR WAY OUT.
I'VE ACCESSED THE PYM PARTICLE TECH. I'M BEGINNING A CONTROLLED APPLICATION OF GROWTH PARTICLES TO THOSE OF US IN THIS ROOM. WITH LUCK, WE'LL BE OUT OF REACH BEFORE--
OH.
I WAS AFRAID OF THIS.

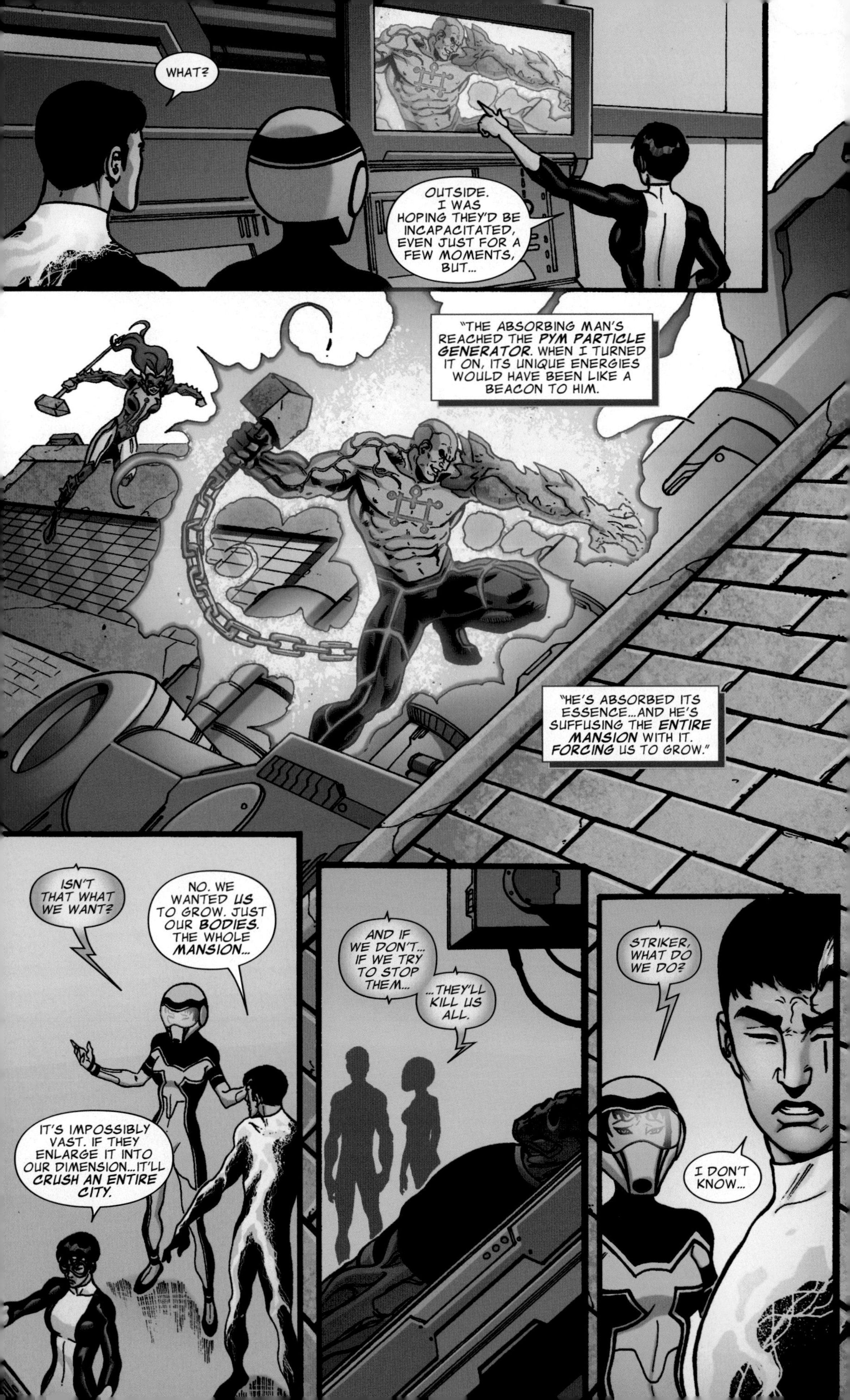
WHAT?
OUTSIDE. I WAS HOPING THEY'D BE INCAPACITATED, EVEN JUST FOR A FEW MOMENTS, BUT...
"THE ABSORBING MAN'S REACHED THE PYM PARTICLE GENERATOR. WHEN I TURNED IT ON, ITS UNIQUE ENERGIES WOULD HAVE BEEN LIKE A BEACON TO HIM.
"HE'S ABSORBED ITS ESSENCE...AND HE'S SUFFUSING THE ENTIRE MANSION WITH IT. FORCING US TO GROW."
ISN'T THAT WHAT WE WANT?
NO. WE WANTED US TO GROW. JUST OUR BODIES. THE WHOLE MANSION...
IT'S IMPOSSIBLY VAST. IF THEY ENLARGE IT INTO OUR DIMENSION...IT'LL CRUSH AN ENTIRE CITY.
AND IF WE DON'T... IF WE TRY TO STOP THEM...
...THEY'LL KILL US ALL.
STRIKER, WHAT DO WE DO?
I DON'T KNOW...

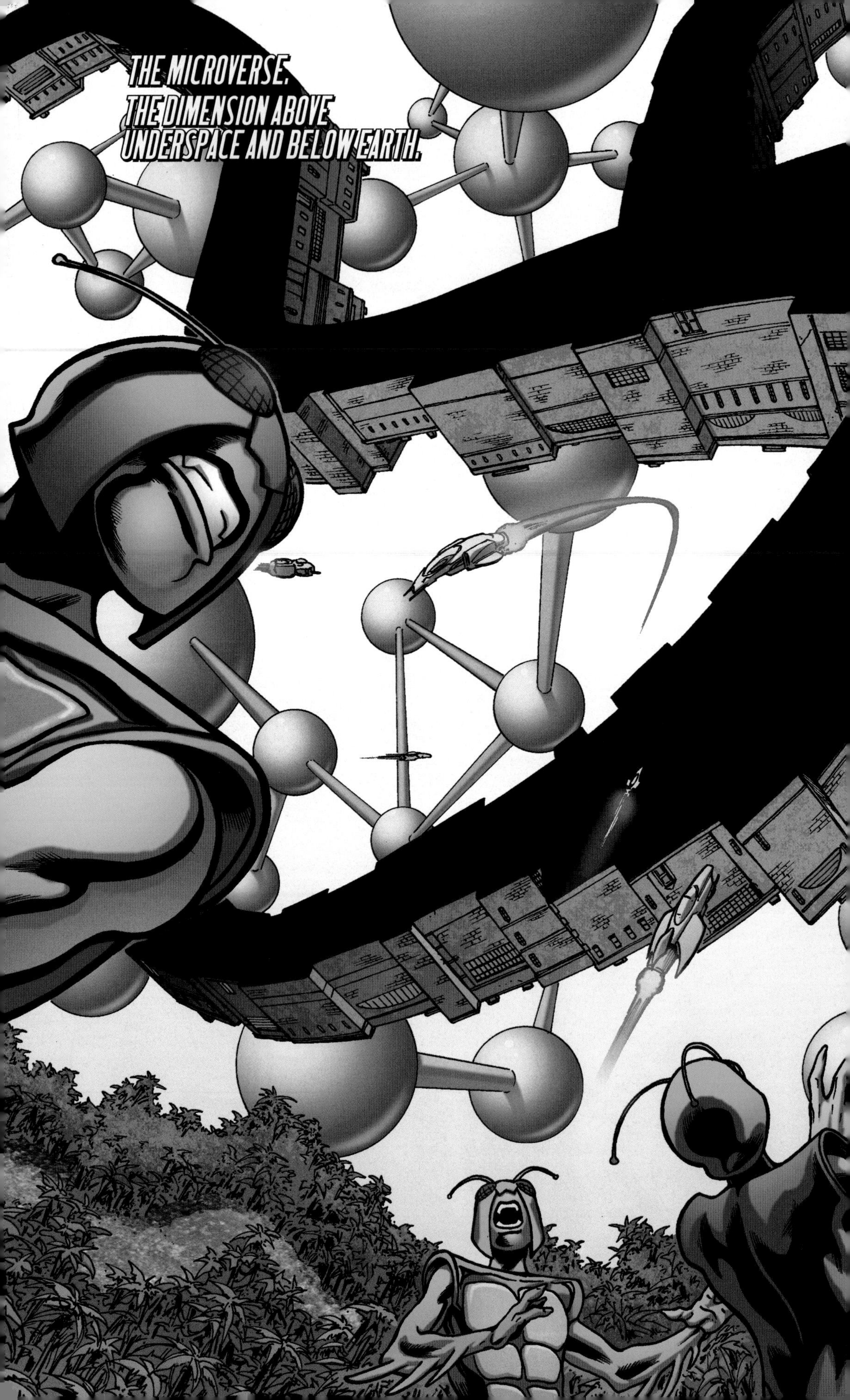
THE MICROVERSE.
THE DIMENSION ABOVE UNDERSPACE AND BELOW EARTH.

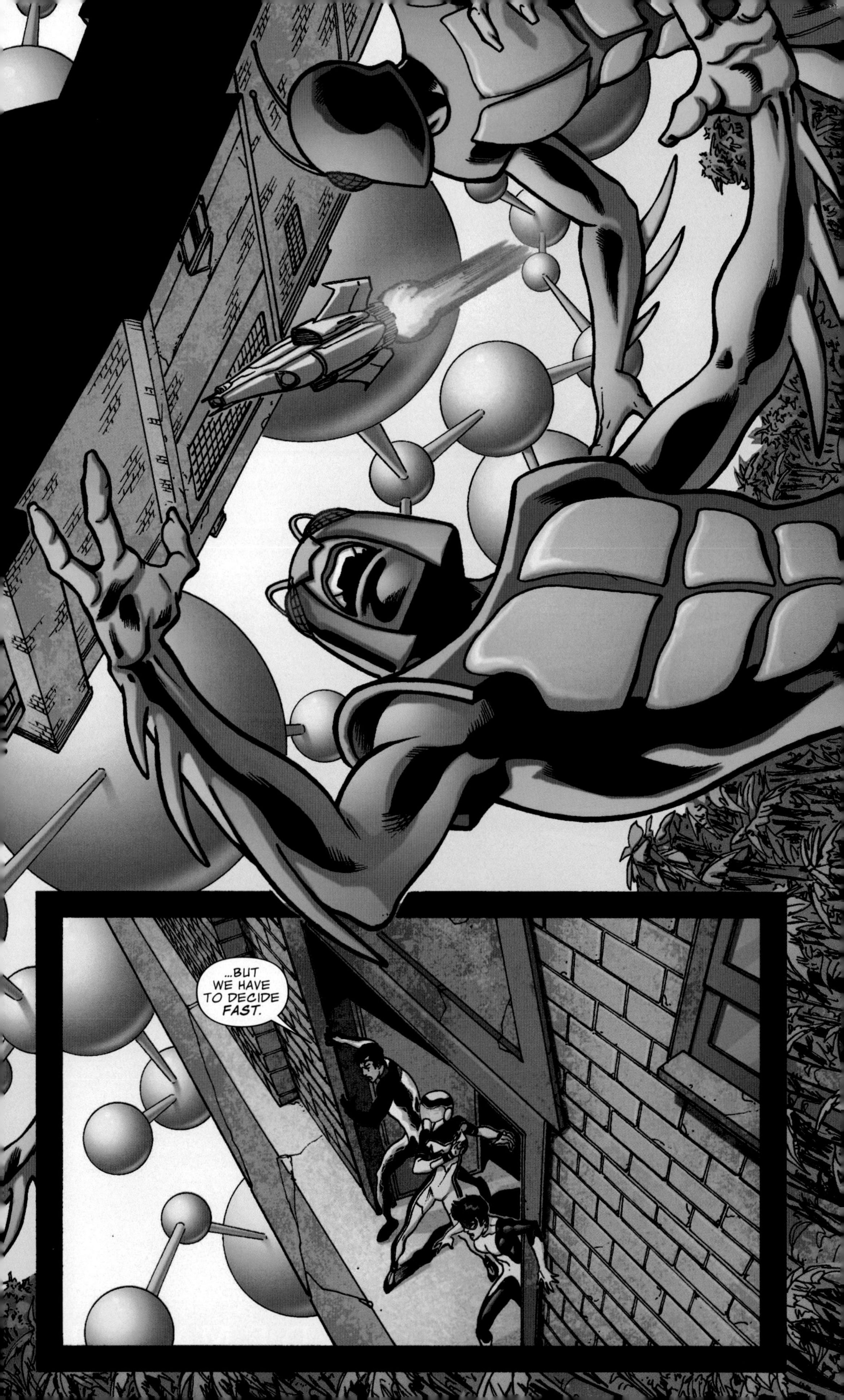
...BUT WE HAVE TO DECIDE FAST.

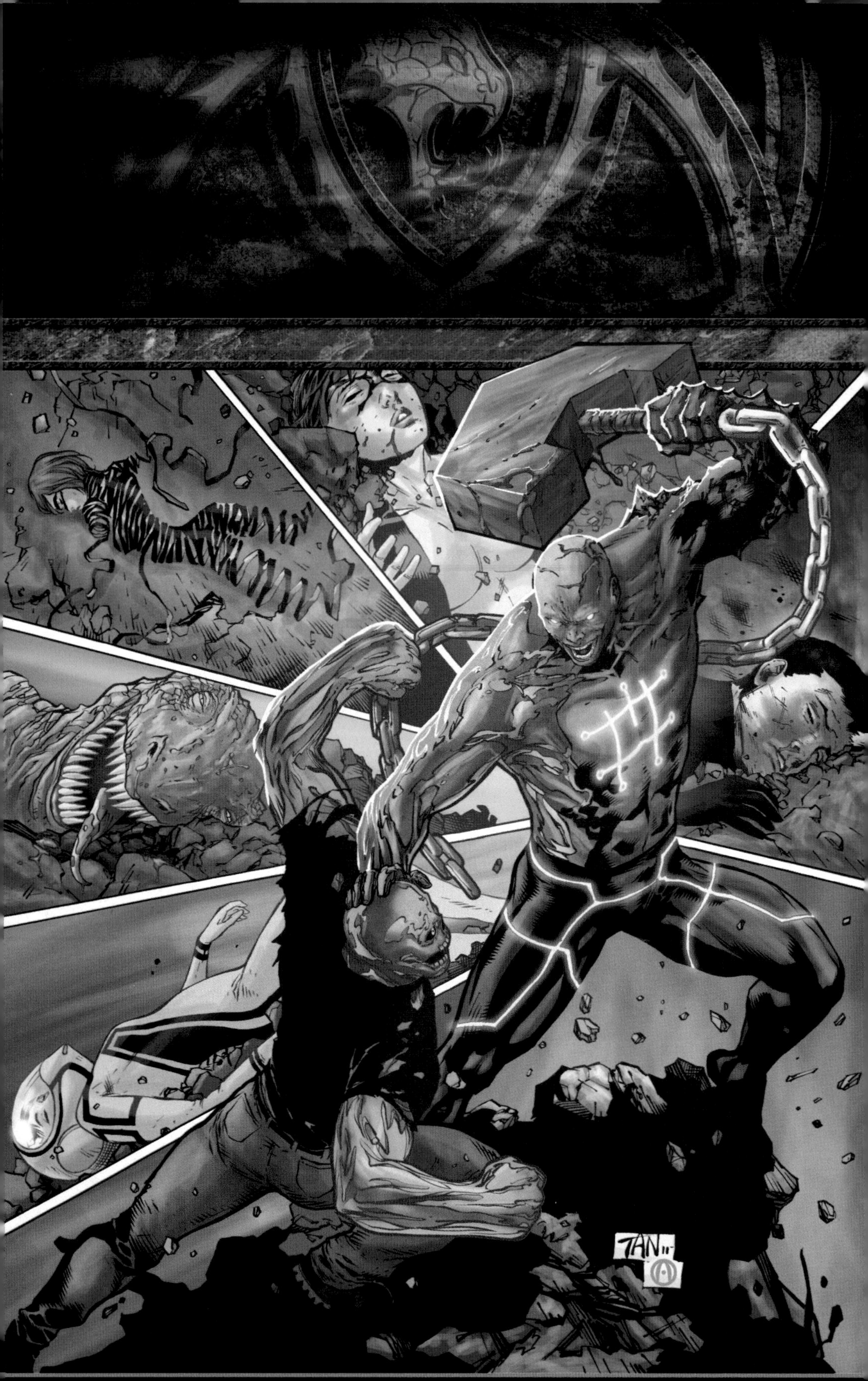

AVENGERS ACADEMY #19

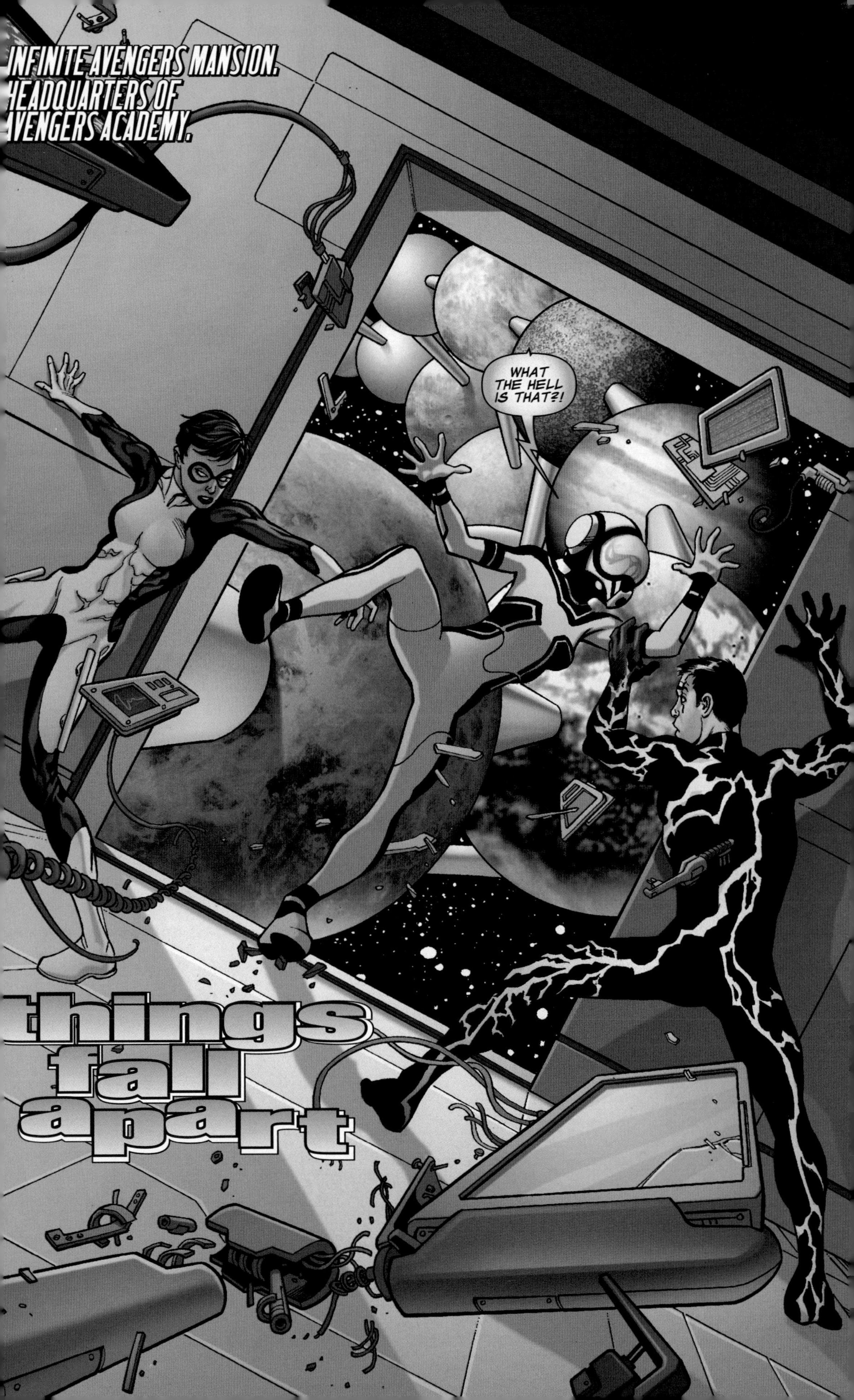
INFINITE AVENGERS MANSION. HEADQUARTERS OF AVENGERS ACADEMY.
WHAT THE HELL IS THAT?!
things fall apart

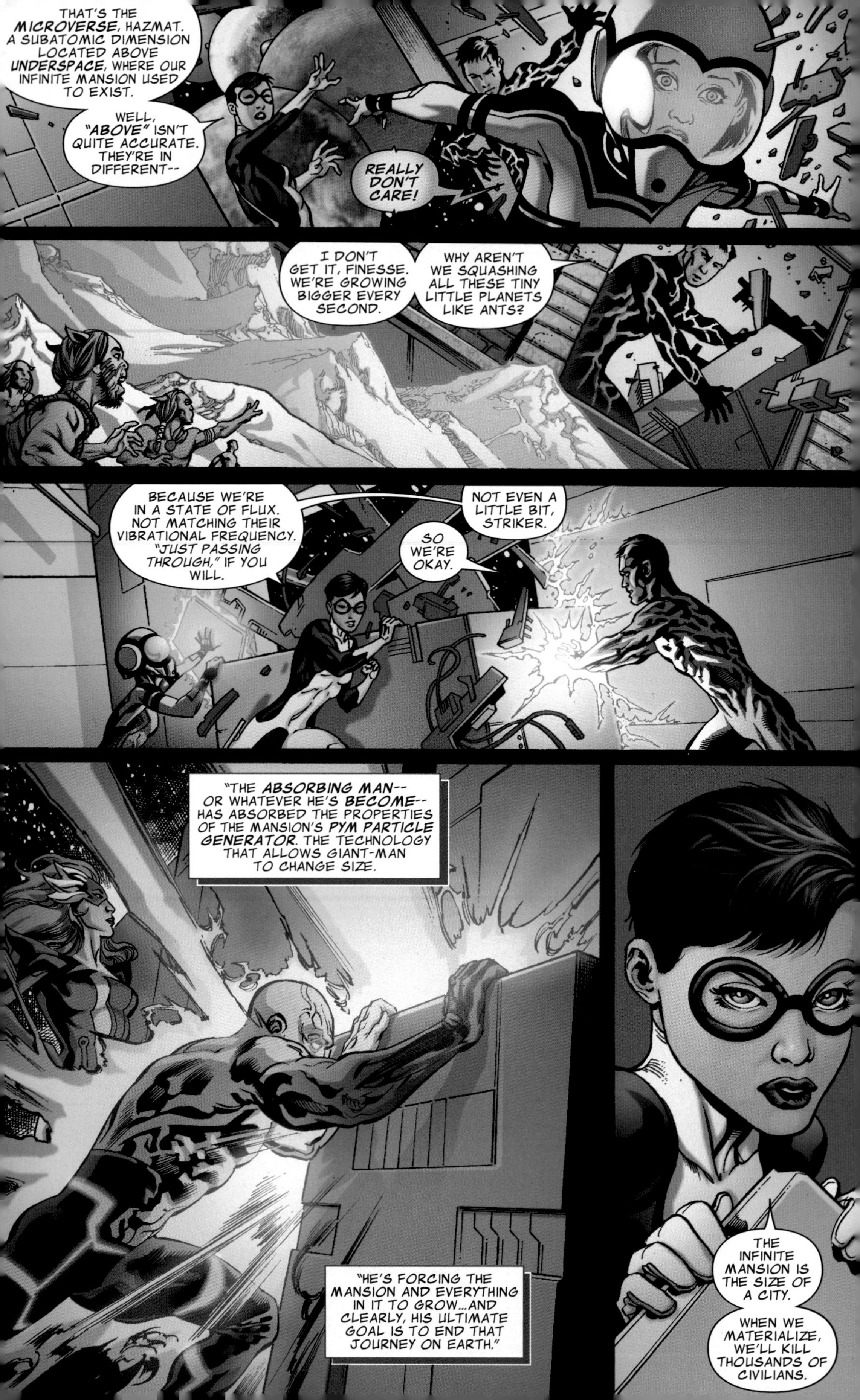

THAT'S THE MICROVERSE, HAZMAT. A SUBATOMIC DIMENSION LOCATED ABOVE UNDERSPACE, WHERE OUR INFINITE MANSION USED TO EXIST.
WELL, "ABOVE" ISN'T QUITE ACCURATE. THEY'RE IN DIFFERENT--
REALLY DON'T CARE!
I DON'T GET IT, FINESSE. WE'RE GROWING BIGGER EVERY SECOND.
WHY AREN'T WE SQUASHING ALL THESE TINY LITTLE PLANETS LIKE ANTS?
BECAUSE WE'RE IN A STATE OF FLUX. NOT MATCHING THEIR VIBRATIONAL FREQUENCY. "JUST PASSING THROUGH," IF YOU WILL.
SO WE'RE OKAY.
NOT EVEN A LITTLE BIT, STRIKER.
"THE ABSORBING MAN-- OR WHATEVER HE'S BECOME-- HAS ABSORBED THE PROPERTIES OF THE MANSION'S PYM PARTICLE GENERATOR. THE TECHNOLOGY THAT ALLOWS GIANT-MAN TO CHANGE SIZE.
"HE'S FORCING THE MANSION AND EVERYTHING IN IT TO GROW...AND CLEARLY, HIS ULTIMATE GOAL IS TO END THAT JOURNEY ON EARTH."
THE INFINITE MANSION IS THE SIZE OF A CITY.
WHEN WE MATERIALIZE, WE'LL KILL THOUSANDS OF CIVILIANS.

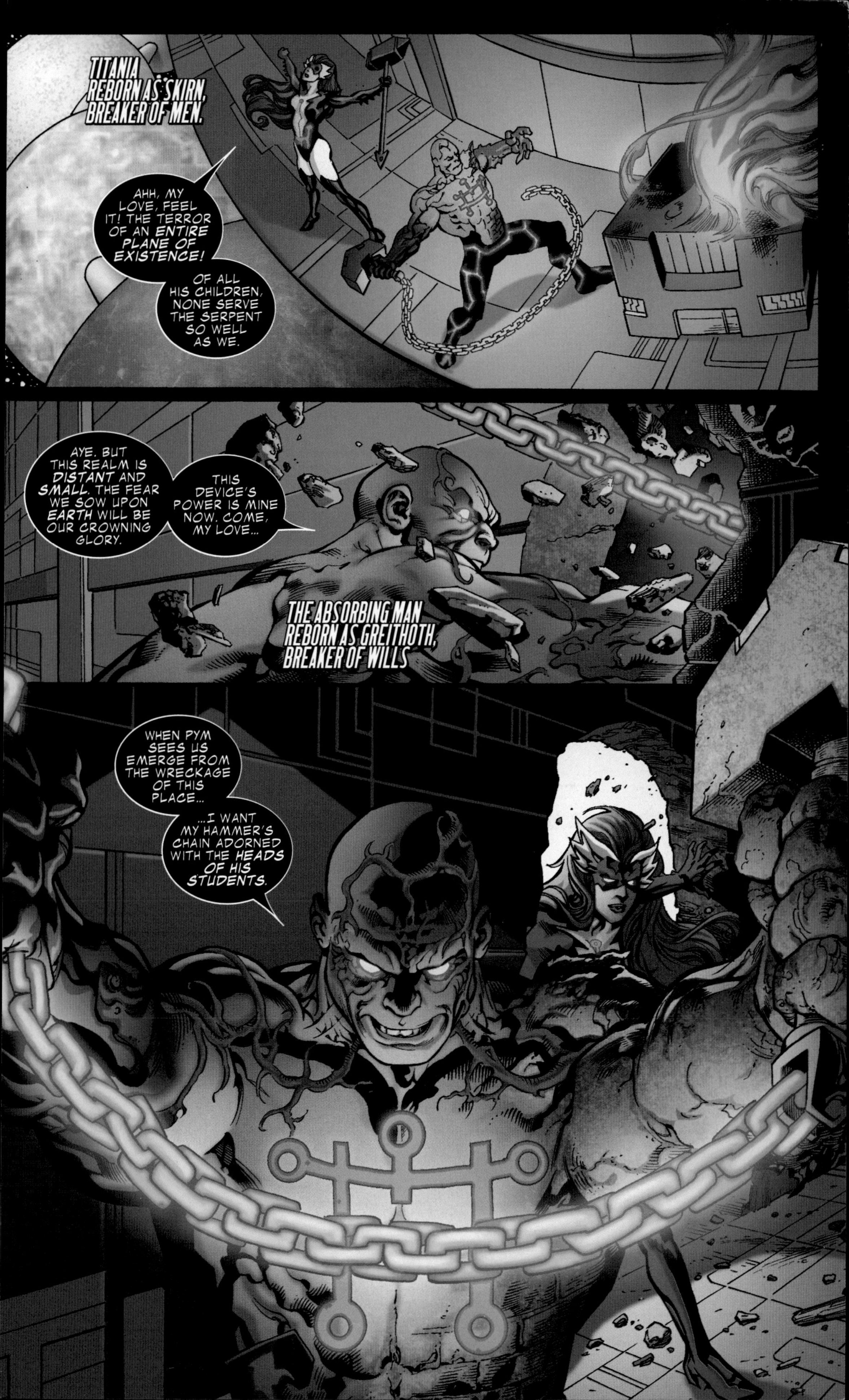
TITANIA REBORN AS SKIRN, BREAKER OF MEN.
AHH, MY LOVE, FEEL IT! THE TERROR OF AN ENTIRE PLANE OF EXISTENCE!
OF ALL HIS CHILDREN, NONE SERVE THE SERPENT SO WELL AS WE.
AYE. BUT THIS REALM IS DISTANT AND SMALL. THE FEAR WE SOW UPON EARTH WILL BE OUR CROWNING GLORY.
THIS DEVICE'S POWER IS MINE NOW. COME, MY LOVE...
THE ABSORBING MAN REBORN AS GREITHOTH, BREAKER OF WILLS
WHEN PYM SEES US EMERGE FROM THE WRECKAGE OF THIS PLACE...
...I WANT MY HAMMER'S CHAIN ADORNED WITH THE HEADS OF HIS STUDENTS.

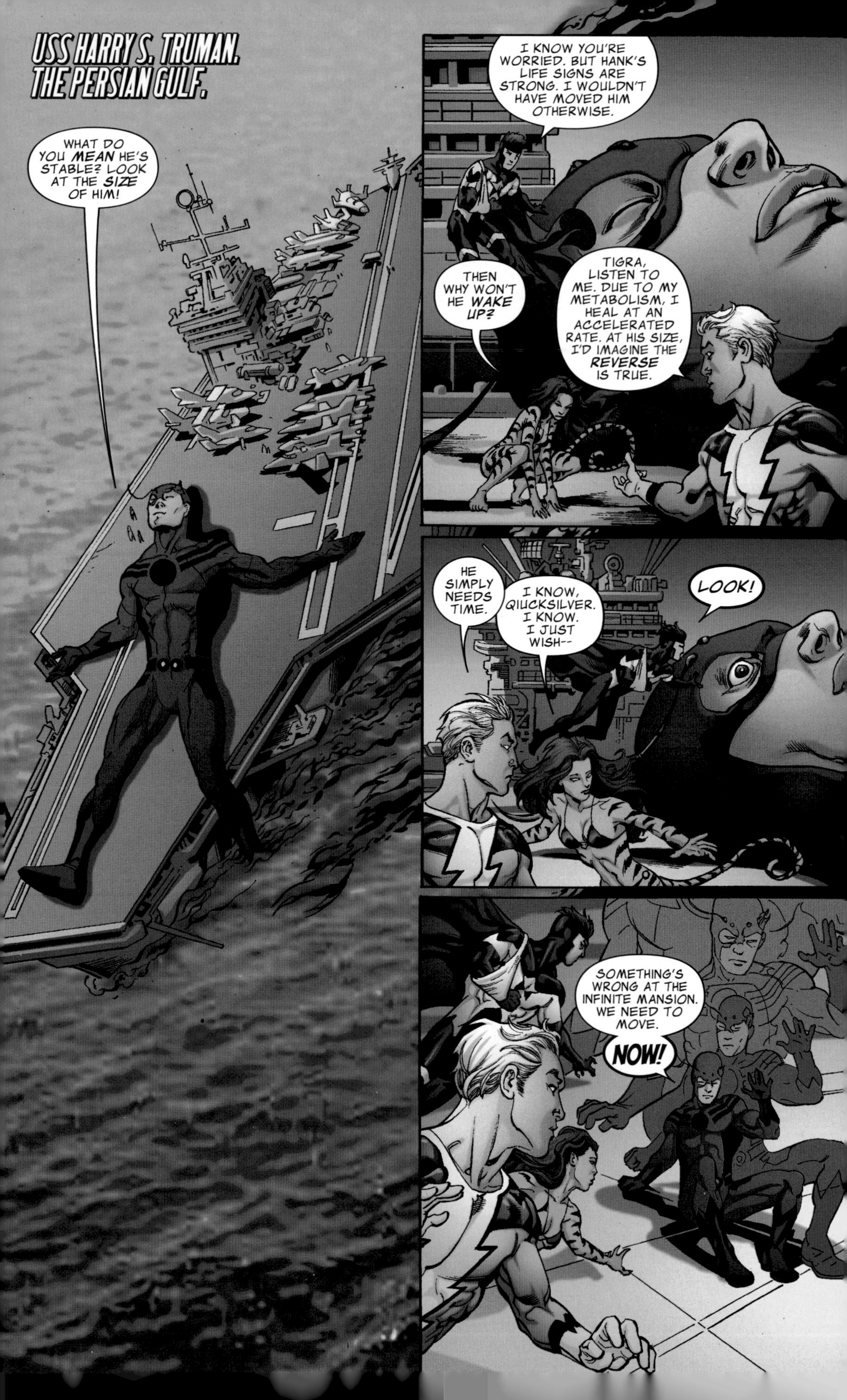
USS HARRY S. TRUMAN. THE PERSIAN GULF.
WHAT DO YOU MEAN HE'S STABLE? LOOK AT THE SIZE OF HIM!
I KNOW YOU'RE WORRIED. BUT HANK'S LIFE SIGNS ARE STRONG. I WOULDN'T HAVE MOVED HIM OTHERWISE.
THEN WHY WON'T HE WAKE UP?
TIGRA, LISTEN TO ME. DUE TO MY METABOLISM, I HEAL AT AN ACCELERATED RATE. AT HIS SIZE, I'D IMAGINE THE REVERSE IS TRUE.
HE SIMPLY NEEDS TIME.
I KNOW, QIUCKSILVER. I KNOW. I JUST WISH--
LOOK!
SOMETHING'S WRONG AT THE INFINITE MANSION. WE NEED TO MOVE.
NOW!

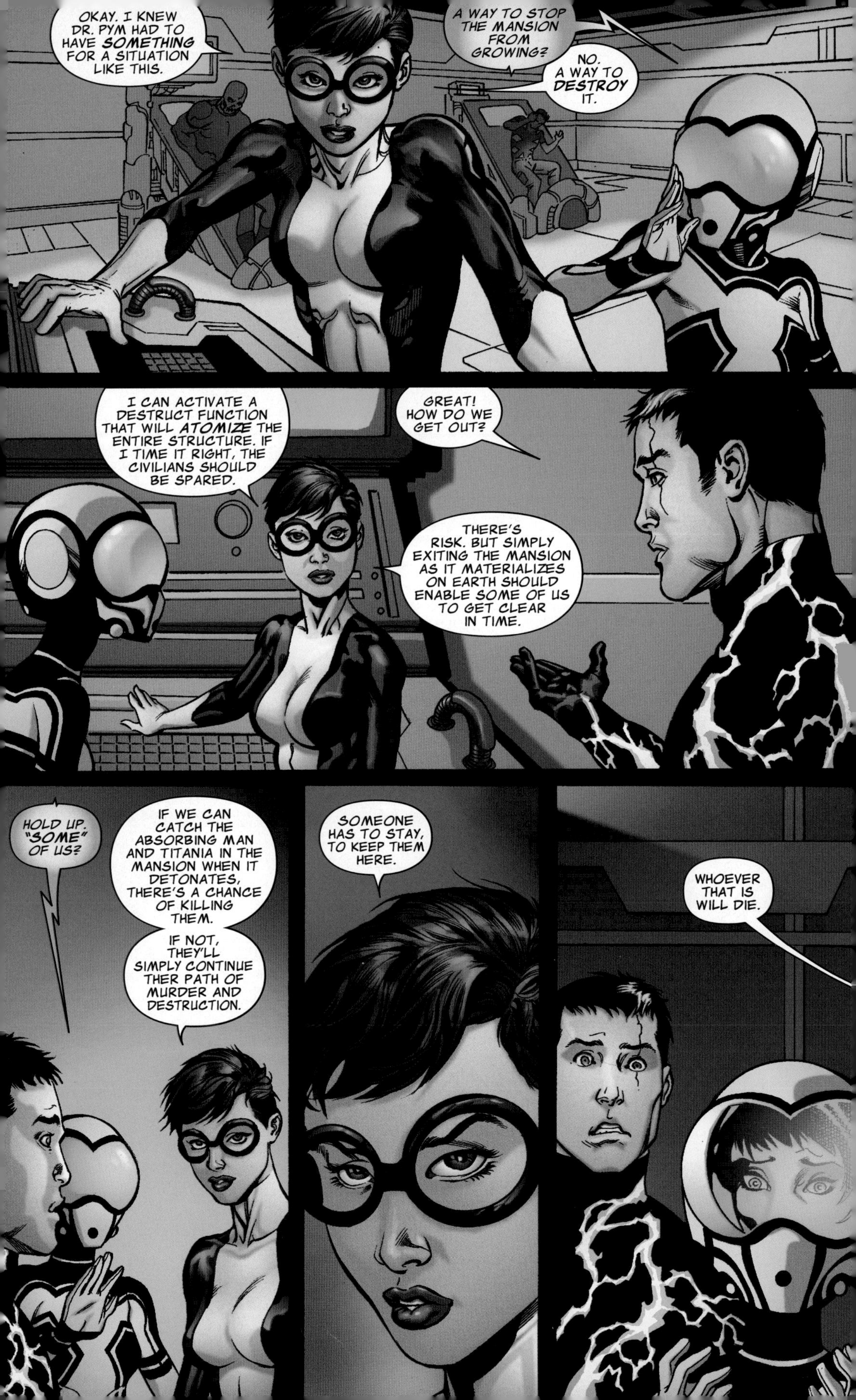
OKAY. I KNEW DR. PYM HAD TO HAVE SOMETHING FOR A SITUATION LIKE THIS.
A WAY TO STOP THE MANSION FROM GROWING?
NO. A WAY TO DESTROY IT.
I CAN ACTIVATE A DESTRUCT FUNCTION THAT WILL ATOMIZE THE ENTIRE STRUCTURE. IF I TIME IT RIGHT, THE CIVILIANS SHOULD BE SPARED.
GREAT! HOW DO WE GET OUT?
THERE'S RISK. BUT SIMPLY EXITING THE MANSION AS IT MATERIALIZES ON EARTH SHOULD ENABLE SOME OF US TO GET CLEAR IN TIME.
HOLD UP. "SOME" OF US?
IF WE CAN CATCH THE ABSORBING MAN AND TITANIA IN THE MANSION WHEN IT DETONATES, THERE'S A CHANCE OF KILLING THEM.
IF NOT, THEY'LL SIMPLY CONTINUE THER PATH OF MURDER AND DESTRUCTION.
SOMEONE HAS TO STAY, TO KEEP THEM HERE.
WHOEVER THAT IS WILL DIE.

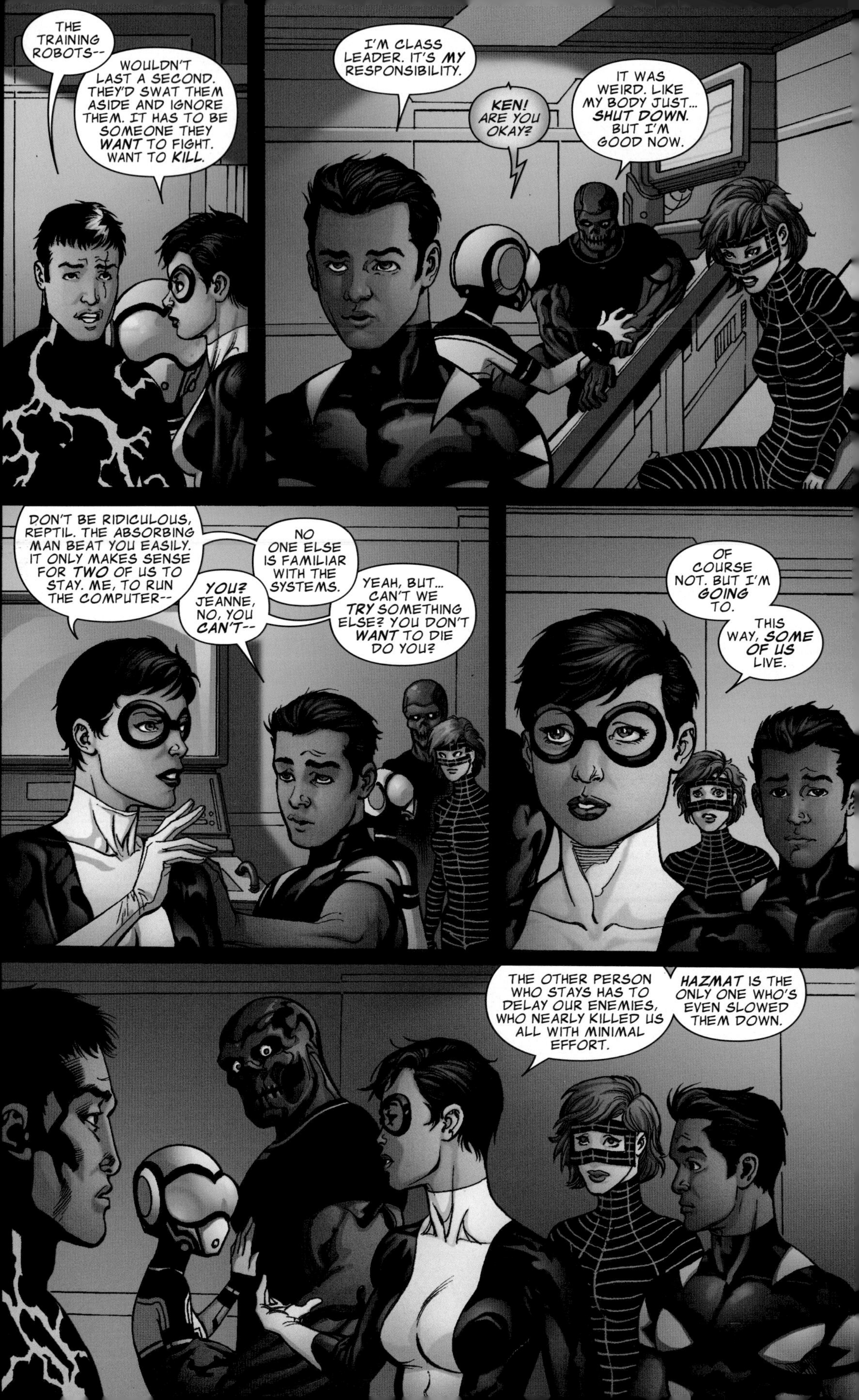
THE TRAINING ROBOTS--
WOULDN'T LAST A SECOND. THEY'D SWAT THEM ASIDE AND IGNORE THEM. IT HAS TO BE SOMEONE THEY WANT TO FIGHT. WANT TO KILL.
I'M CLASS LEADER. IT'S MY RESPONSIBILITY.
KEN! ARE YOU OKAY?
IT WAS WEIRD. LIKE MY BODY JUST... SHUT DOWN. BUT I'M GOOD NOW.
DON'T BE RIDICULOUS, REPTIL. THE ABSORBING MAN BEAT YOU EASILY. IT ONLY MAKES SENSE FOR TWO OF US TO STAY. ME, TO RUN THE COMPUTER--
NO ONE ELSE IS FAMILIAR WITH THE SYSTEMS.
YOU? JEANNE, NO, YOU CAN'T--
YEAH, BUT... CAN'T WE TRY SOMETHING ELSE? YOU DON'T WANT TO DIE DO YOU?
OF COURSE NOT. BUT I'M GOING TO.
THIS WAY, SOME OF US LIVE.
THE OTHER PERSON WHO STAYS HAS TO DELAY OUR ENEMIES, WHO NEARLY KILLED US ALL WITH MINIMAL EFFORT.
HAZMAT IS THE ONLY ONE WHO'S EVEN SLOWED THEM DOWN.

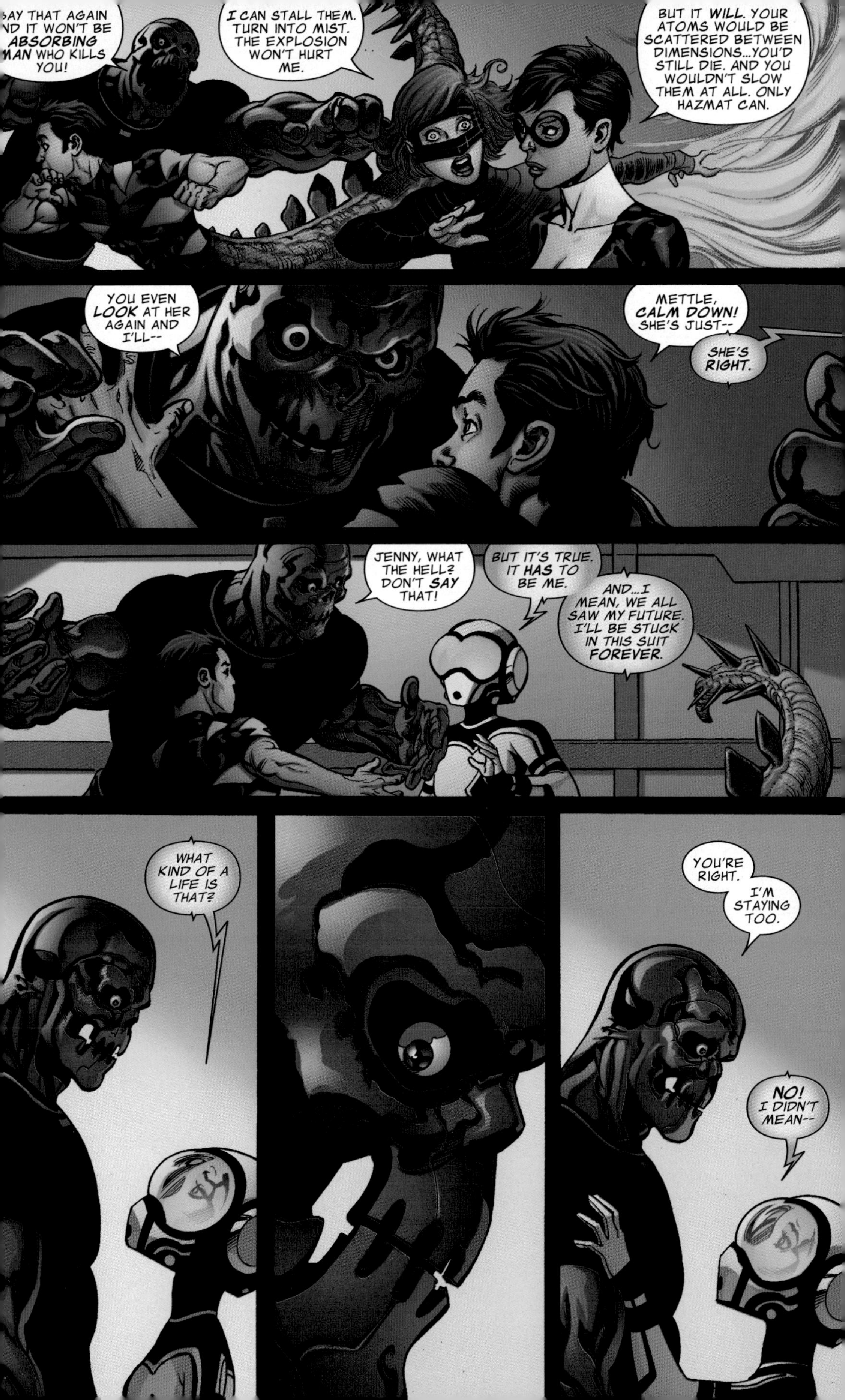
SAY THAT AGAIN AND IT WON'T BE ABSORBING MAN WHO KILLS YOU!
I CAN STALL THEM. TURN INTO MIST. THE EXPLOSION WON'T HURT ME.
BUT IT WILL. YOUR ATOMS WOULD BE SCATTERED BETWEEN DIMENSIONS...YOU'D STILL DIE. AND YOU WOULDN'T SLOW THEM AT ALL. ONLY HAZMAT CAN.
YOU EVEN LOOK AT HER AGAIN AND I'LL--
METTLE, CALM DOWN! SHE'S JUST--
SHE'S RIGHT.
JENNY, WHAT THE HELL? DON'T SAY THAT!
BUT IT'S TRUE. IT HAS TO BE ME.
AND...I MEAN, WE ALL SAW MY FUTURE. I'LL BE STUCK IN THIS SUIT FOREVER.
WHAT KIND OF A LIFE IS THAT?
YOU'RE RIGHT.
I'M STAYING TOO.
NO! I DIDN'T MEAN--

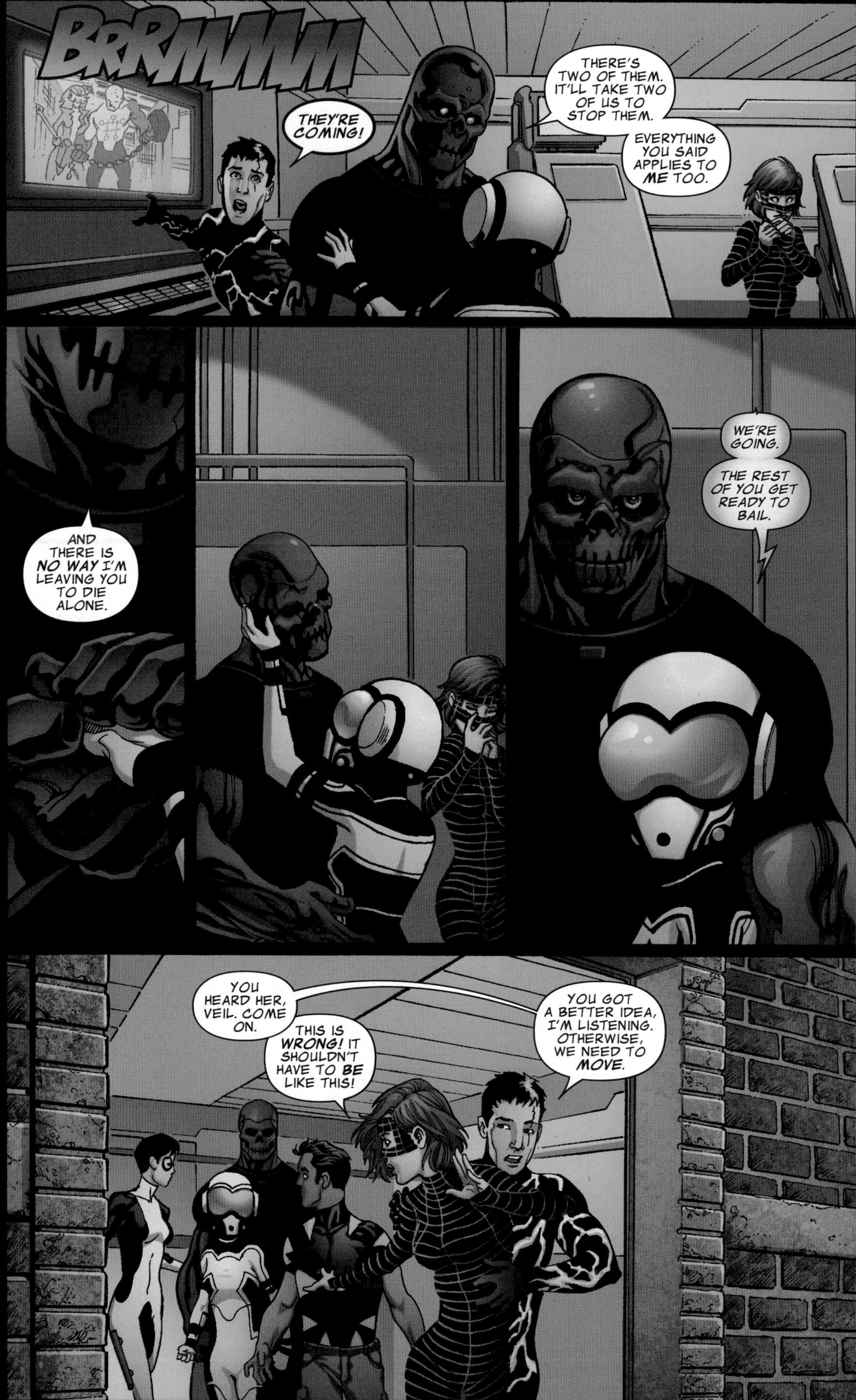
BRRMMMM
THEY'RE COMING!
THERE'S TWO OF THEM. IT'LL TAKE TWO OF US TO STOP THEM.
EVERYTHING YOU SAID APPLIES TO ME TOO.
AND THERE IS NO WAY I'M LEAVING YOU TO DIE ALONE.
WE'RE GOING.
THE REST OF YOU GET READY TO BAIL.
YOU HEARD HER, VEIL. COME ON.
THIS IS WRONG! IT SHOULDN'T HAVE TO BE LIKE THIS!
YOU GOT A BETTER IDEA, I'M LISTENING. OTHERWISE, WE NEED TO MOVE.

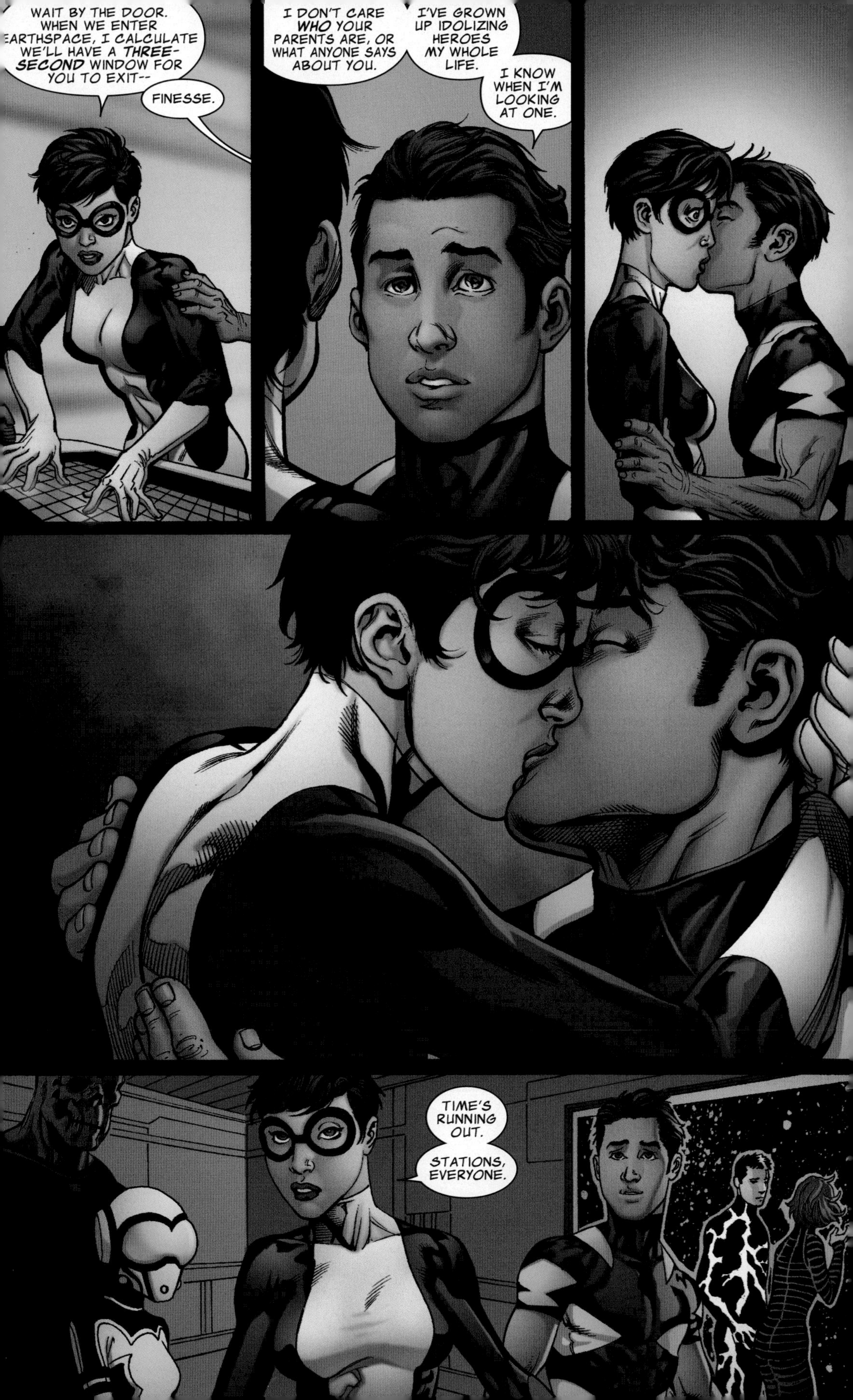
WAIT BY THE DOOR. WHEN WE ENTER EARTHSPACE, I CALCULATE WE'LL HAVE A THREE-SECOND WINDOW FOR YOU TO EXIT--
FINESSE.
I DON'T CARE WHO YOUR PARENTS ARE, OR WHAT ANYONE SAYS ABOUT YOU.
I'VE GROWN UP IDOLIZING HEROES MY WHOLE LIFE.
I KNOW WHEN I'M LOOKING AT ONE.
TIME'S RUNNING OUT.
STATIONS, EVERYONE.

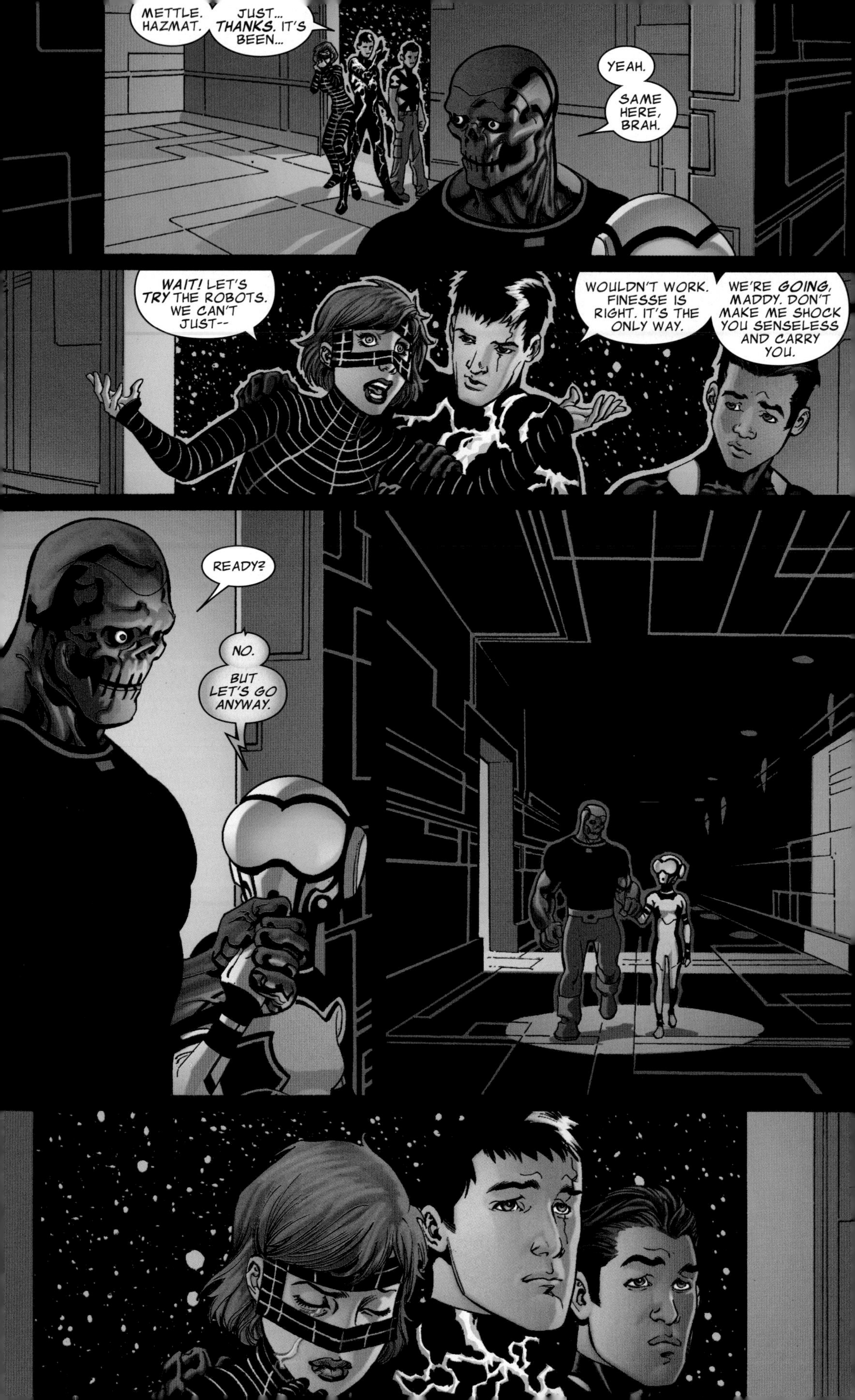
METTLE. HAZMAT.
JUST... THANKS. IT'S BEEN...
YEAH.
SAME HERE, BRAH.
WAIT! LET'S TRY THE ROBOTS. WE CAN'T JUST--
WOULDN'T WORK. FINESSE IS RIGHT. IT'S THE ONLY WAY.
WE'RE GOING, MADDY. DON'T MAKE ME SHOCK YOU SENSELESS AND CARRY YOU.
READY?
NO.
BUT LET'S GO ANYWAY.

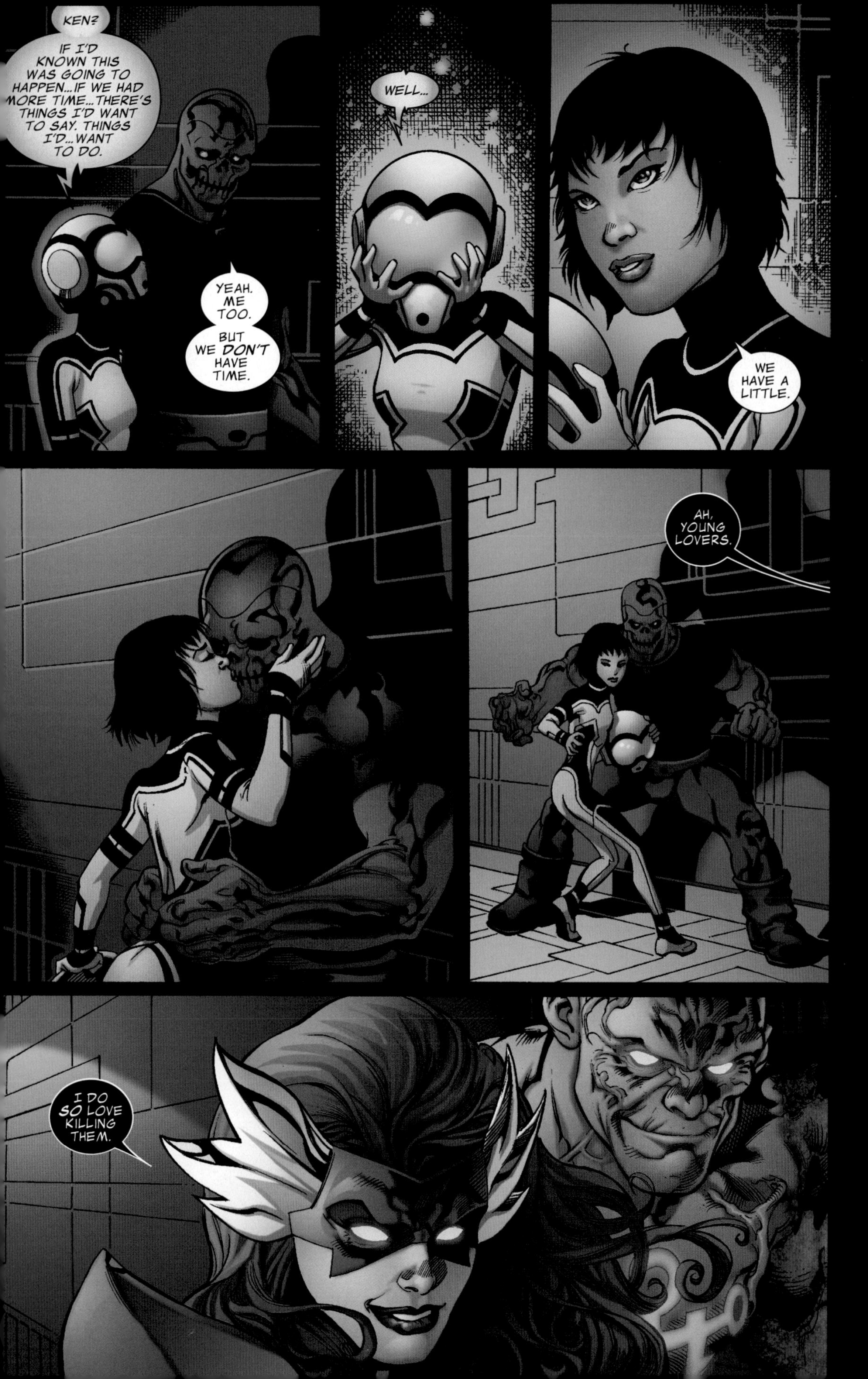
KEN?
IF I'D KNOWN THIS WAS GOING TO HAPPEN...IF WE HAD MORE TIME...THERE'S THINGS I'D WANT TO SAY. THINGS I'D...WANT TO DO.
YEAH. ME TOO.
BUT WE DON'T HAVE TIME.
WELL...
WE HAVE A LITTLE.
AH, YOUNG LOVERS.
I DO SO LOVE KILLING THEM.

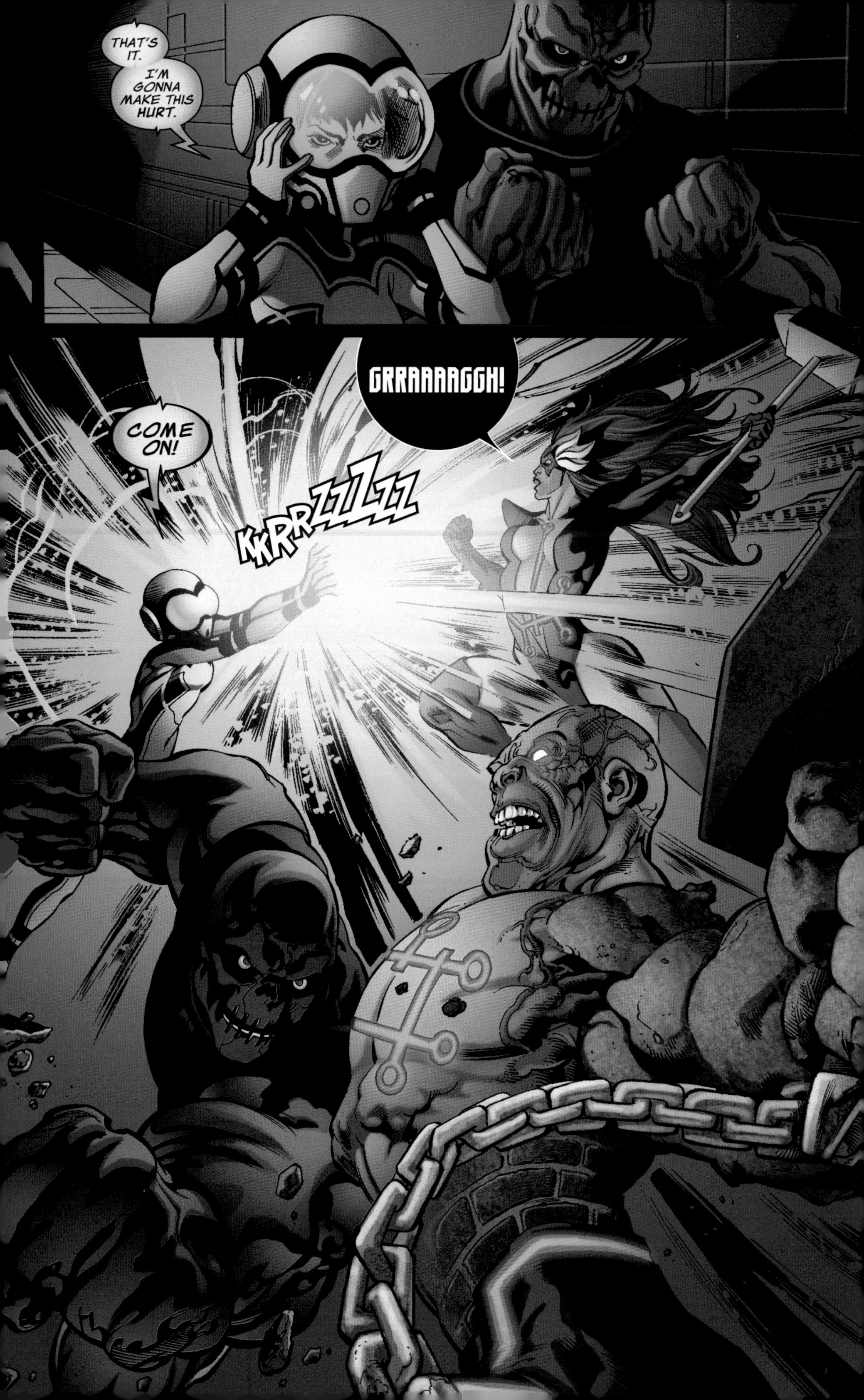
THAT'S IT.
I'M GONNA MAKE THIS HURT.
COME ON!
GRRAAAAAGGH!
KKRRZZZZZZ

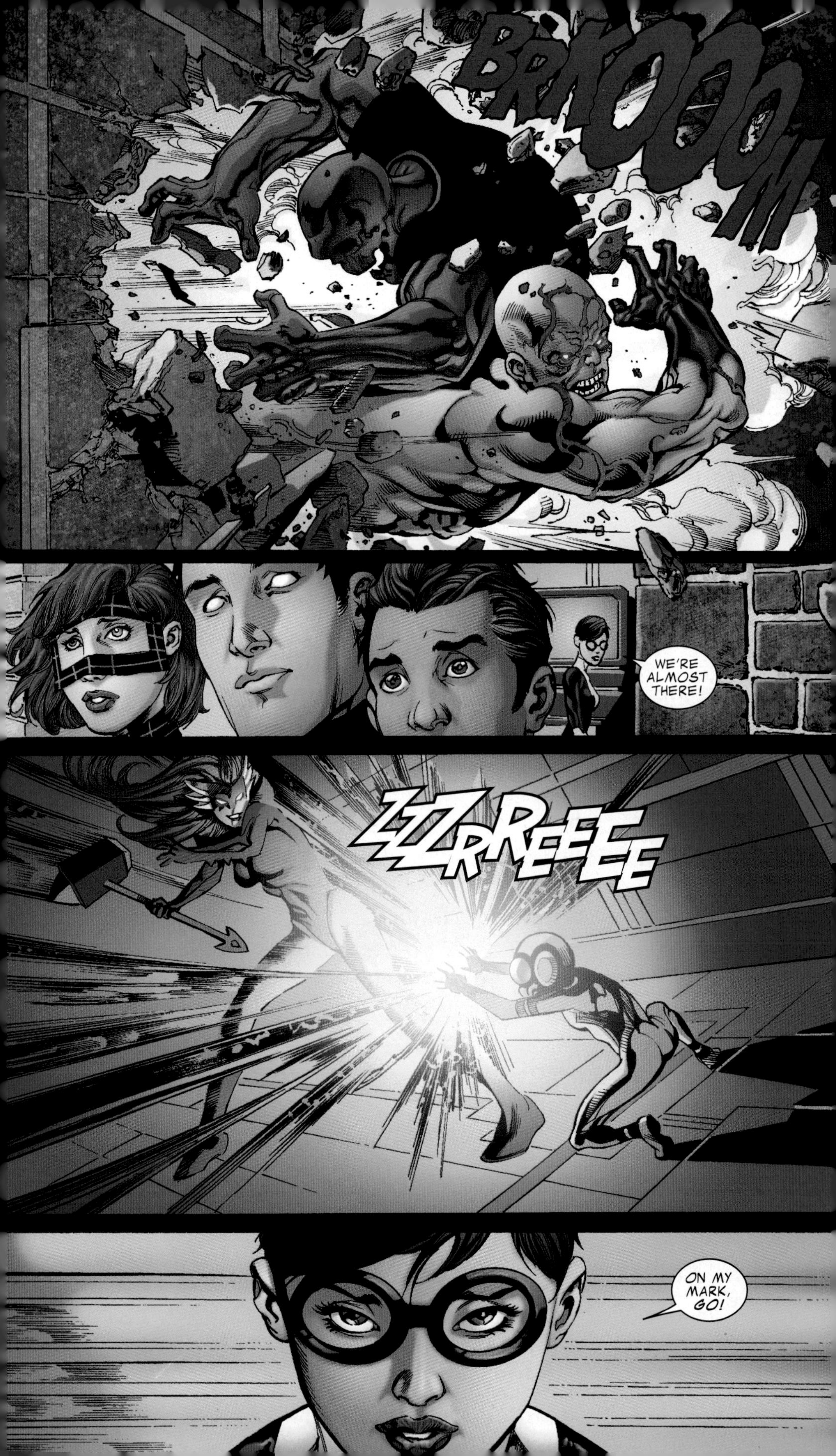
BRKOOOM
WE'RE ALMOST THERE!
ZZZRREEEE
ON MY MARK, GO!

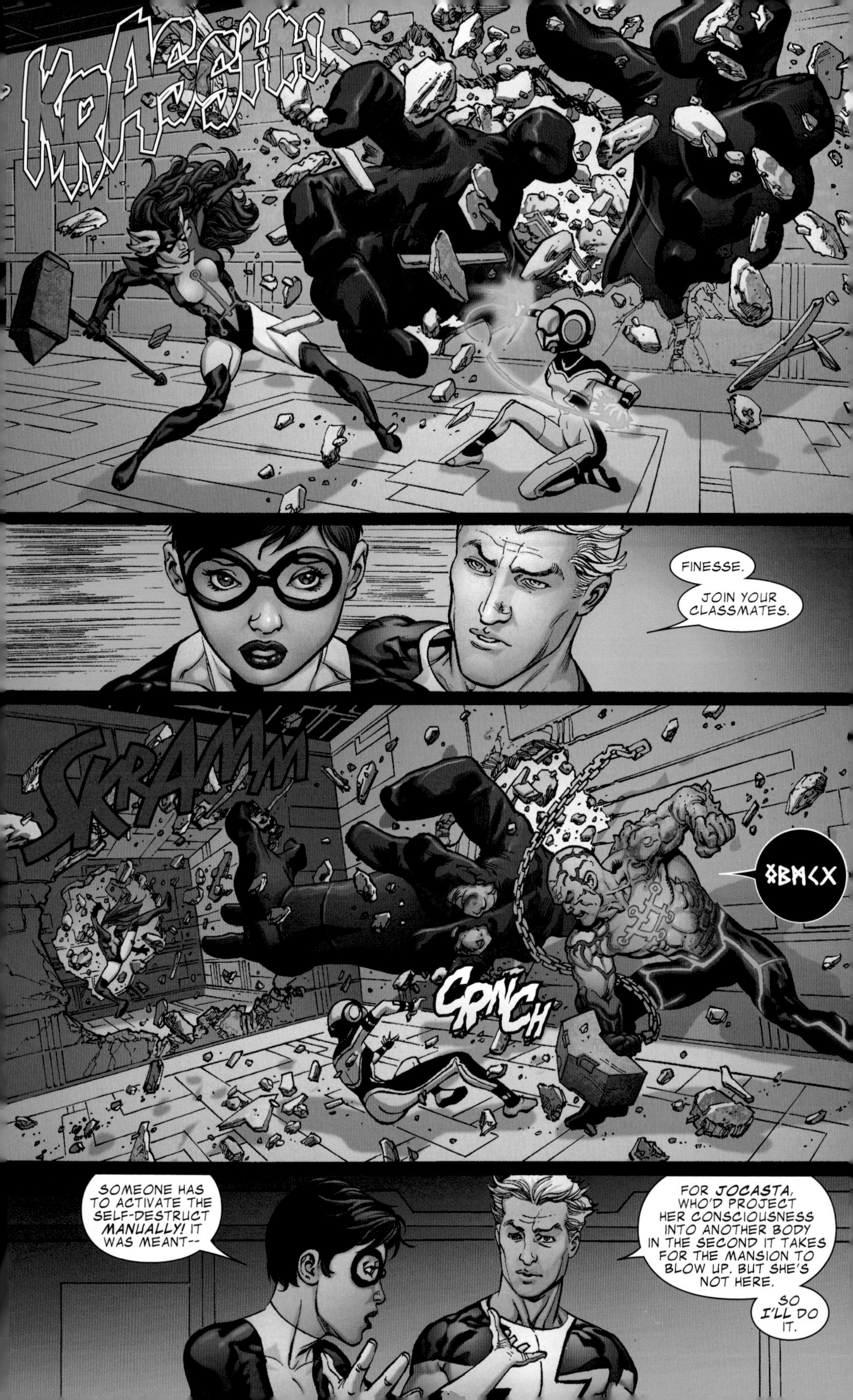
FINESSE.
JOIN YOUR CLASSMATES.
CRNCH
SOMEONE HAS TO ACTIVATE THE SELF-DESTRUCT *MANUALLY!* IT WAS MEANT--
FOR *JOCASTA,* WHO'D PROJECT HER CONSCIOUSNESS INTO ANOTHER BODY IN THE SECOND IT TAKES FOR THE MANSION TO BLOW UP. BUT SHE'S NOT HERE.
SO *I'LL* DO IT.

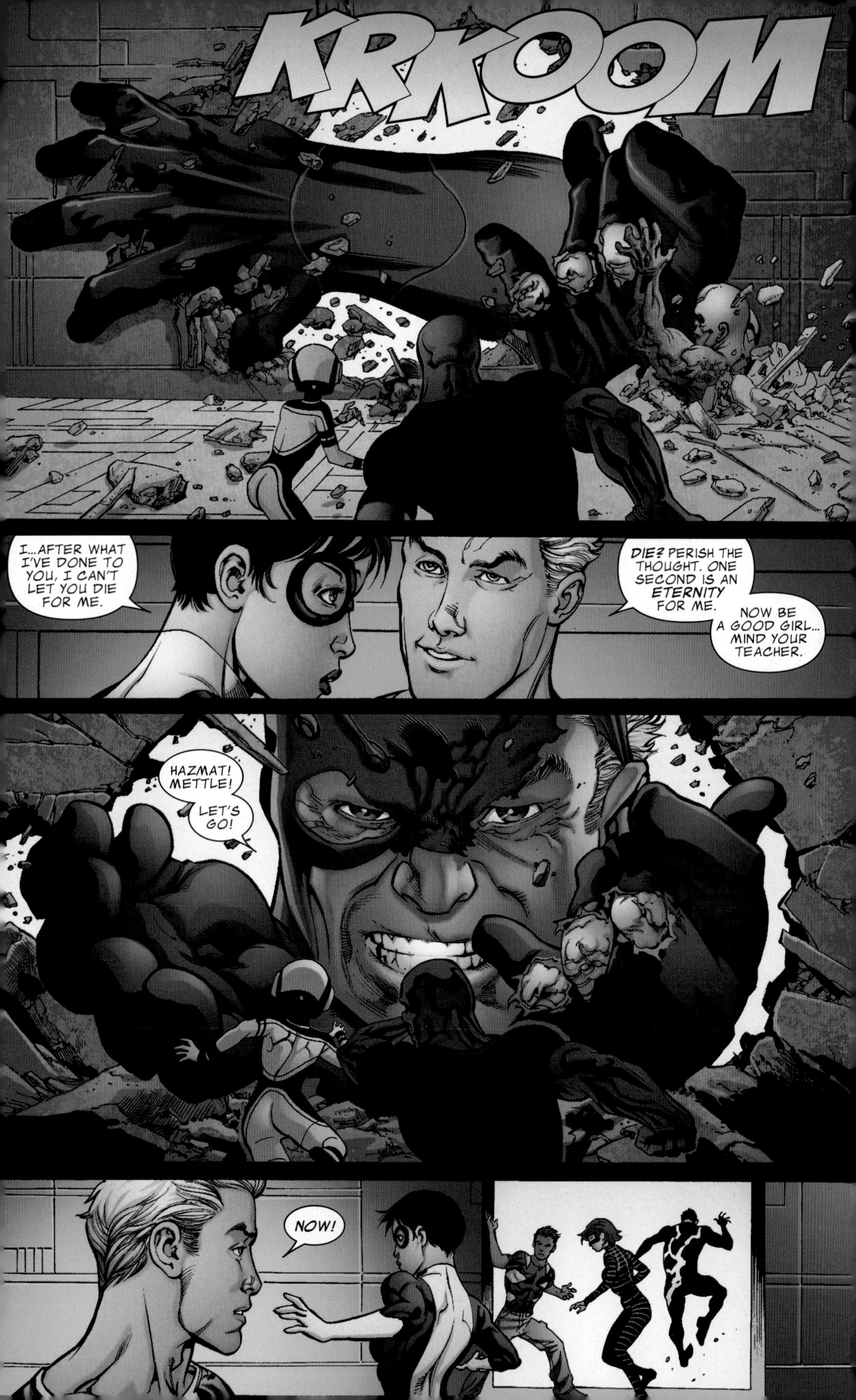
KRKOOM
I...AFTER WHAT I'VE DONE TO YOU, I CAN'T LET YOU DIE FOR ME.
DIE? PERISH THE THOUGHT. ONE SECOND IS AN ETERNITY FOR ME.
NOW BE A GOOD GIRL... MIND YOUR TEACHER.
HAZMAT! METTLE!
LET'S GO!
NOW!

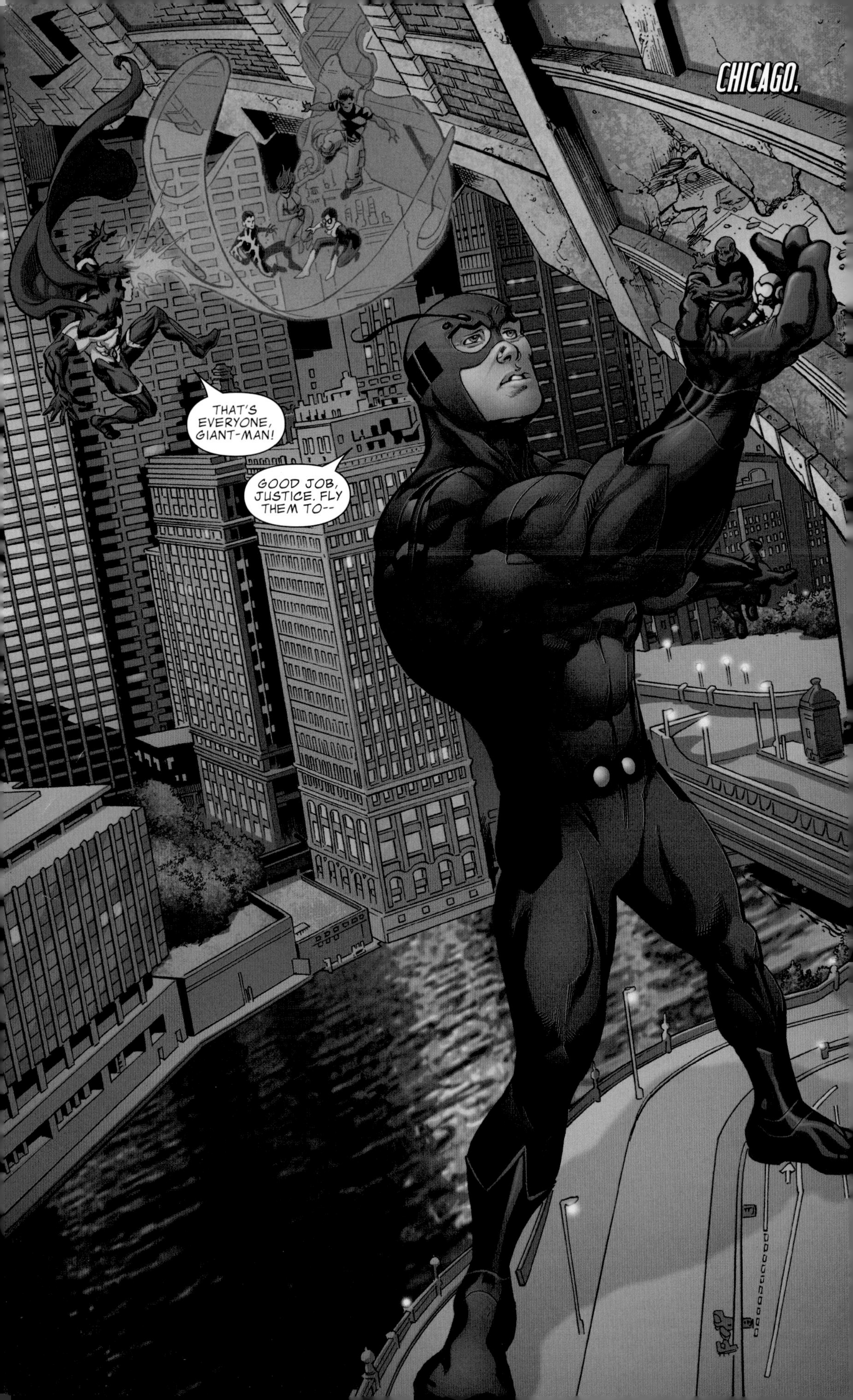
CHICAGO.
THAT'S EVERYONE, GIANT-MAN!
GOOD JOB, JUSTICE. FLY THEM TO--

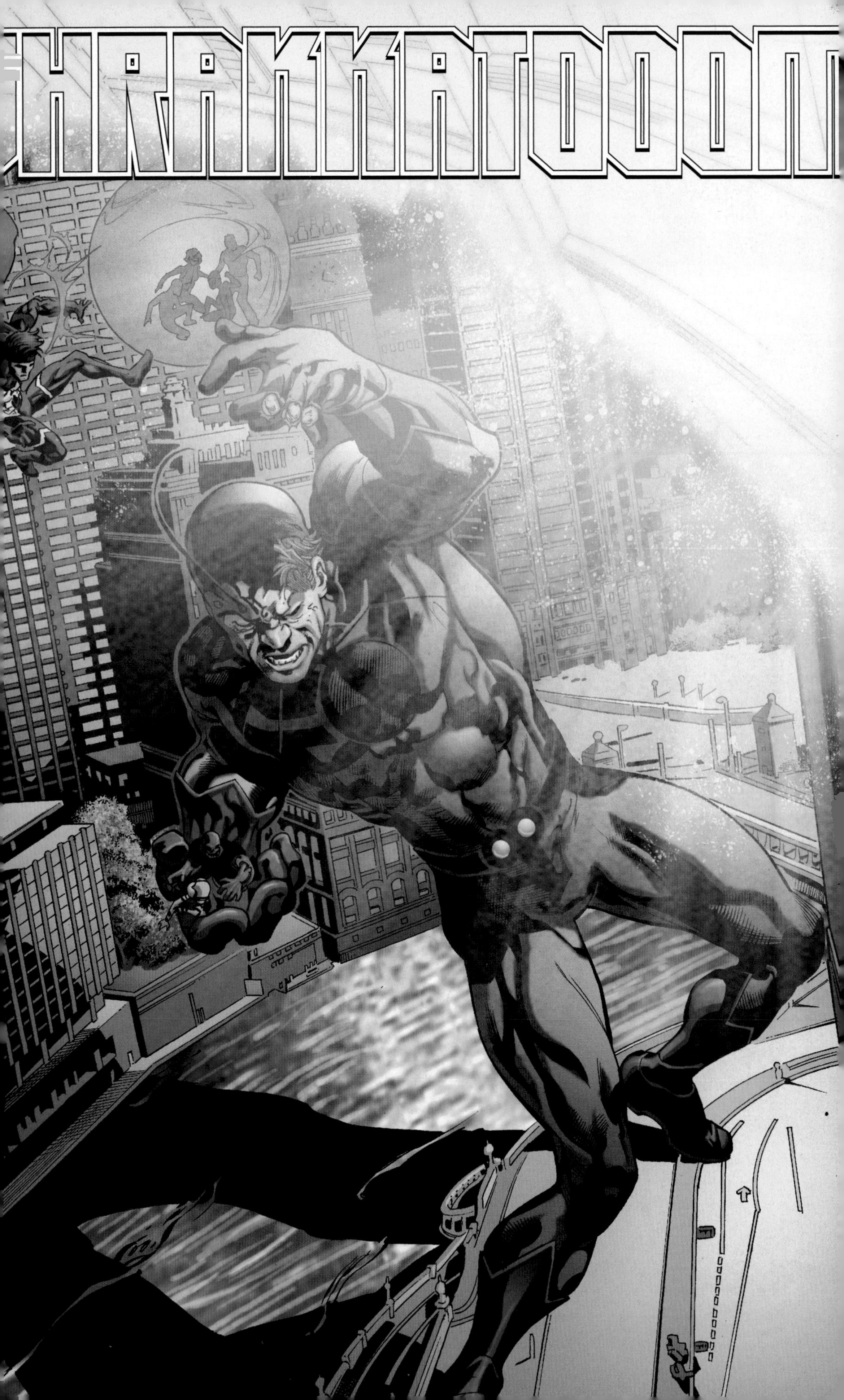
HRAKKATOOOM

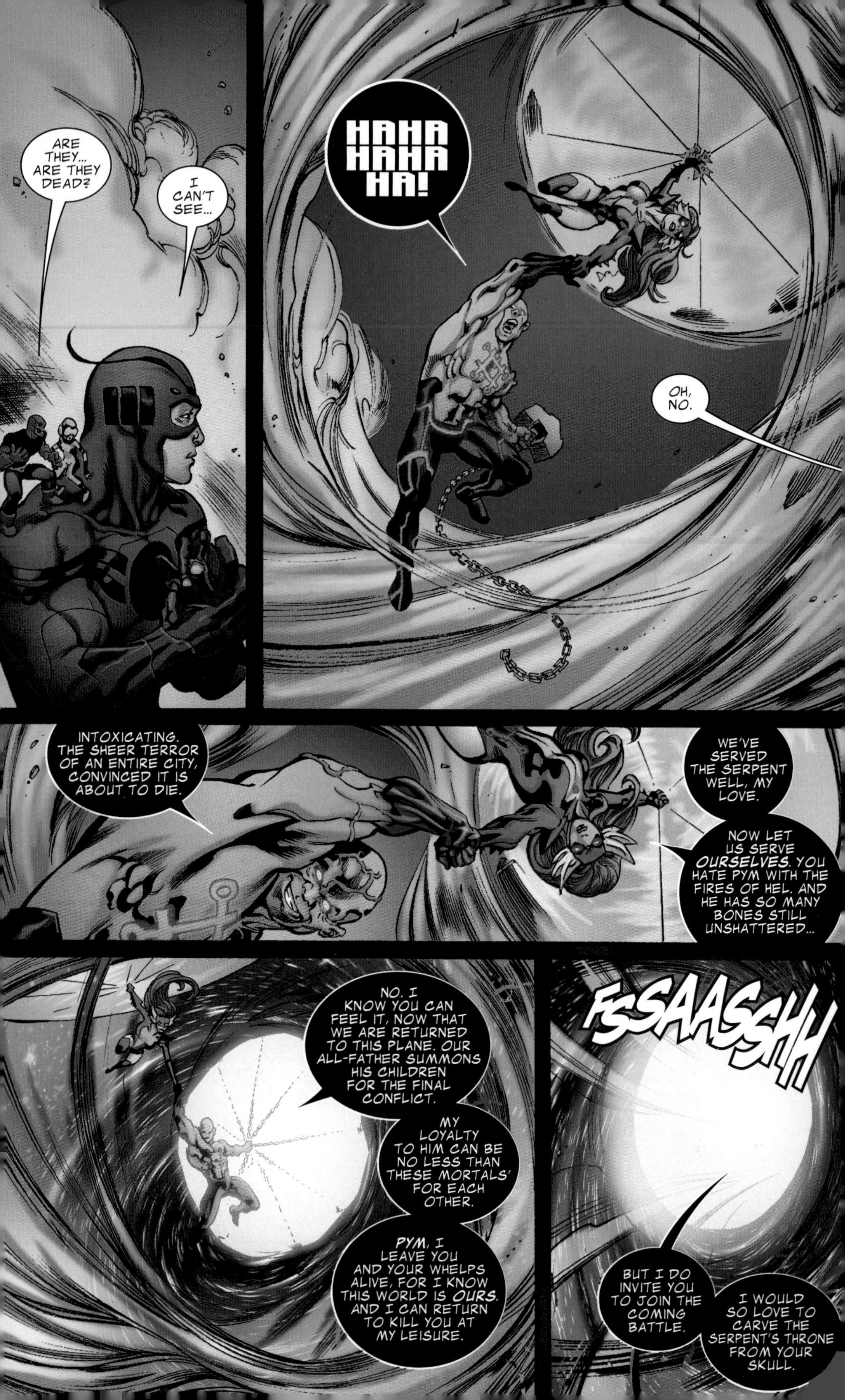
ARE THEY... ARE THEY DEAD?
I CAN'T SEE...
HAHA HAHA HA!
OH, NO.
INTOXICATING. THE SHEER TERROR OF AN ENTIRE CITY, CONVINCED IT IS ABOUT TO DIE.
WE'VE SERVED THE SERPENT WELL, MY LOVE.
NOW LET US SERVE OURSELVES. YOU HATE PYM WITH THE FIRES OF HEL. AND HE HAS SO MANY BONES STILL UNSHATTERED...
NO. I KNOW YOU CAN FEEL IT, NOW THAT WE ARE RETURNED TO THIS PLANE. OUR ALL-FATHER SUMMONS HIS CHILDREN FOR THE FINAL CONFLICT.
MY LOYALTY TO HIM CAN BE NO LESS THAN THESE MORTALS' FOR EACH OTHER.
PYM, I LEAVE YOU AND YOUR WHELPS ALIVE, FOR I KNOW THIS WORLD IS OURS. AND I CAN RETURN TO KILL YOU AT MY LEISURE.
FSSAASSHH
BUT I DO INVITE YOU TO JOIN THE COMING BATTLE.
I WOULD SO LOVE TO CARVE THE SERPENT'S THRONE FROM YOUR SKULL.

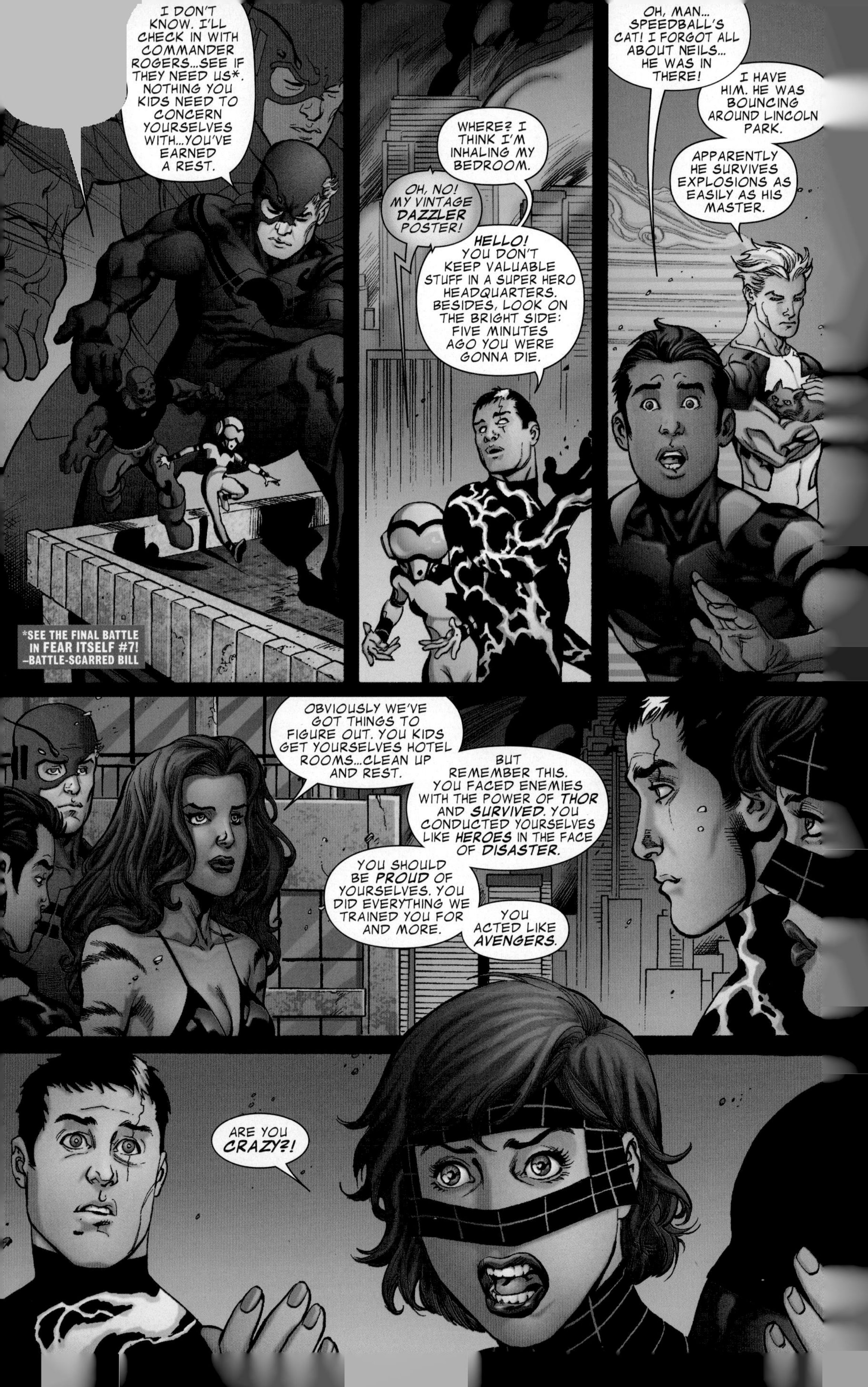
I DON'T KNOW. I'LL CHECK IN WITH COMMANDER ROGERS...SEE IF THEY NEED US*. NOTHING YOU KIDS NEED TO CONCERN YOURSELVES WITH...YOU'VE EARNED A REST.
*SEE THE FINAL BATTLE IN FEAR ITSELF #7! –BATTLE-SCARRED BILL
WHERE? I THINK I'M INHALING MY BEDROOM.
OH, NO! MY VINTAGE DAZZLER POSTER!
HELLO! YOU DON'T KEEP VALUABLE STUFF IN A SUPER HERO HEADQUARTERS. BESIDES, LOOK ON THE BRIGHT SIDE: FIVE MINUTES AGO YOU WERE GONNA DIE.
OH, MAN... SPEEDBALL'S CAT! I FORGOT ALL ABOUT NEILS... HE WAS IN THERE!
I HAVE HIM. HE WAS BOUNCING AROUND LINCOLN PARK.
APPARENTLY HE SURVIVES EXPLOSIONS AS EASILY AS HIS MASTER.
OBVIOUSLY WE'VE GOT THINGS TO FIGURE OUT. YOU KIDS GET YOURSELVES HOTEL ROOMS...CLEAN UP AND REST.
BUT REMEMBER THIS. YOU FACED ENEMIES WITH THE POWER OF THOR AND SURVIVED. YOU CONDUCTED YOURSELVES LIKE HEROES IN THE FACE OF DISASTER.
YOU SHOULD BE PROUD OF YOURSELVES. YOU DID EVERYTHING WE TRAINED YOU FOR AND MORE.
YOU ACTED LIKE AVENGERS.
ARE YOU CRAZY?!

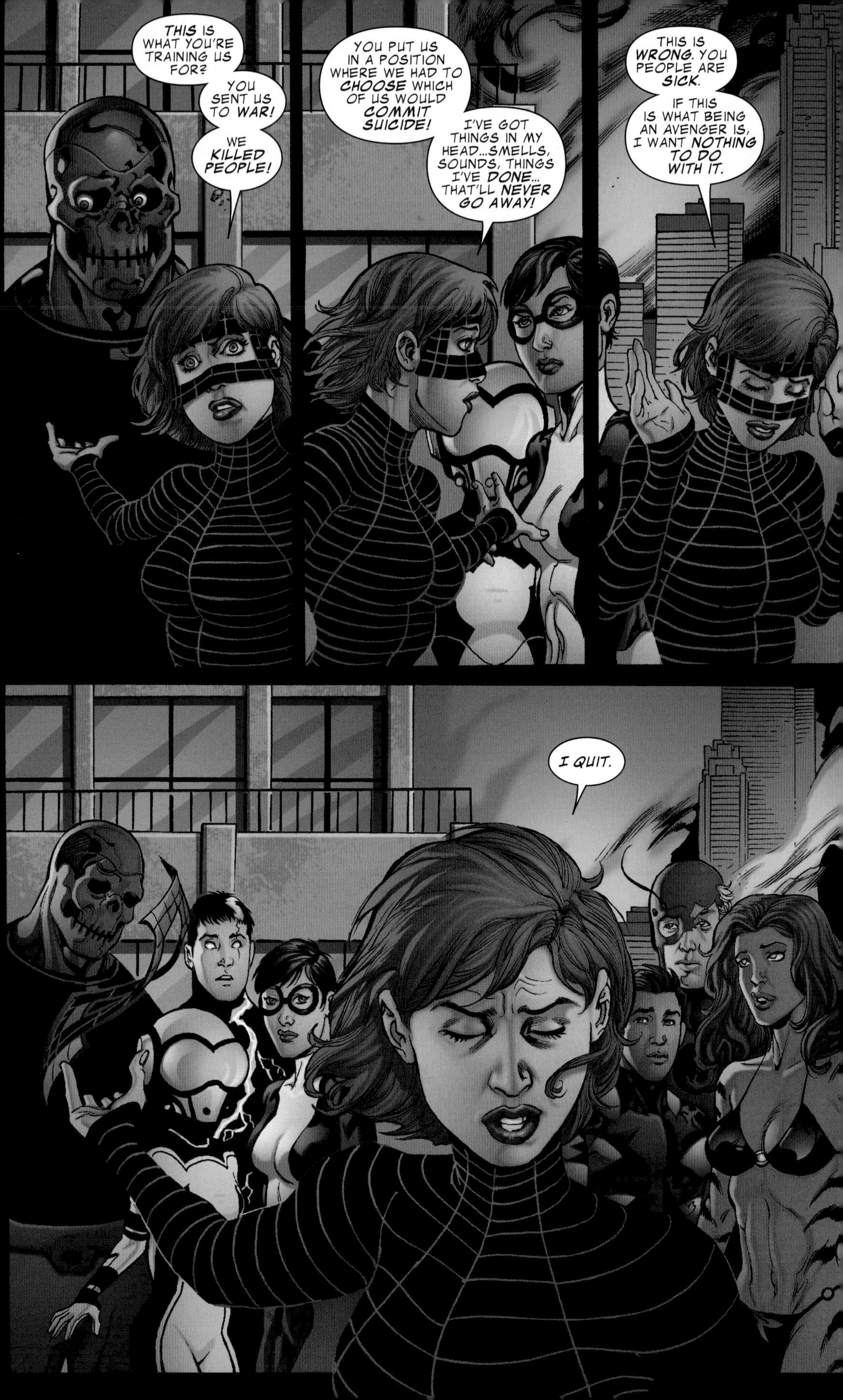
THIS IS WHAT YOU'RE TRAINING US FOR?
YOU SENT US TO WAR!
WE KILLED PEOPLE!
YOU PUT US IN A POSITION WHERE WE HAD TO CHOOSE WHICH OF US WOULD COMMIT SUICIDE!
I'VE GOT THINGS IN MY HEAD...SMELLS, SOUNDS, THINGS I'VE DONE... THAT'LL NEVER GO AWAY!
THIS IS WRONG. YOU PEOPLE ARE SICK.
IF THIS IS WHAT BEING AN AVENGER IS, I WANT NOTHING TO DO WITH IT.
I QUIT.

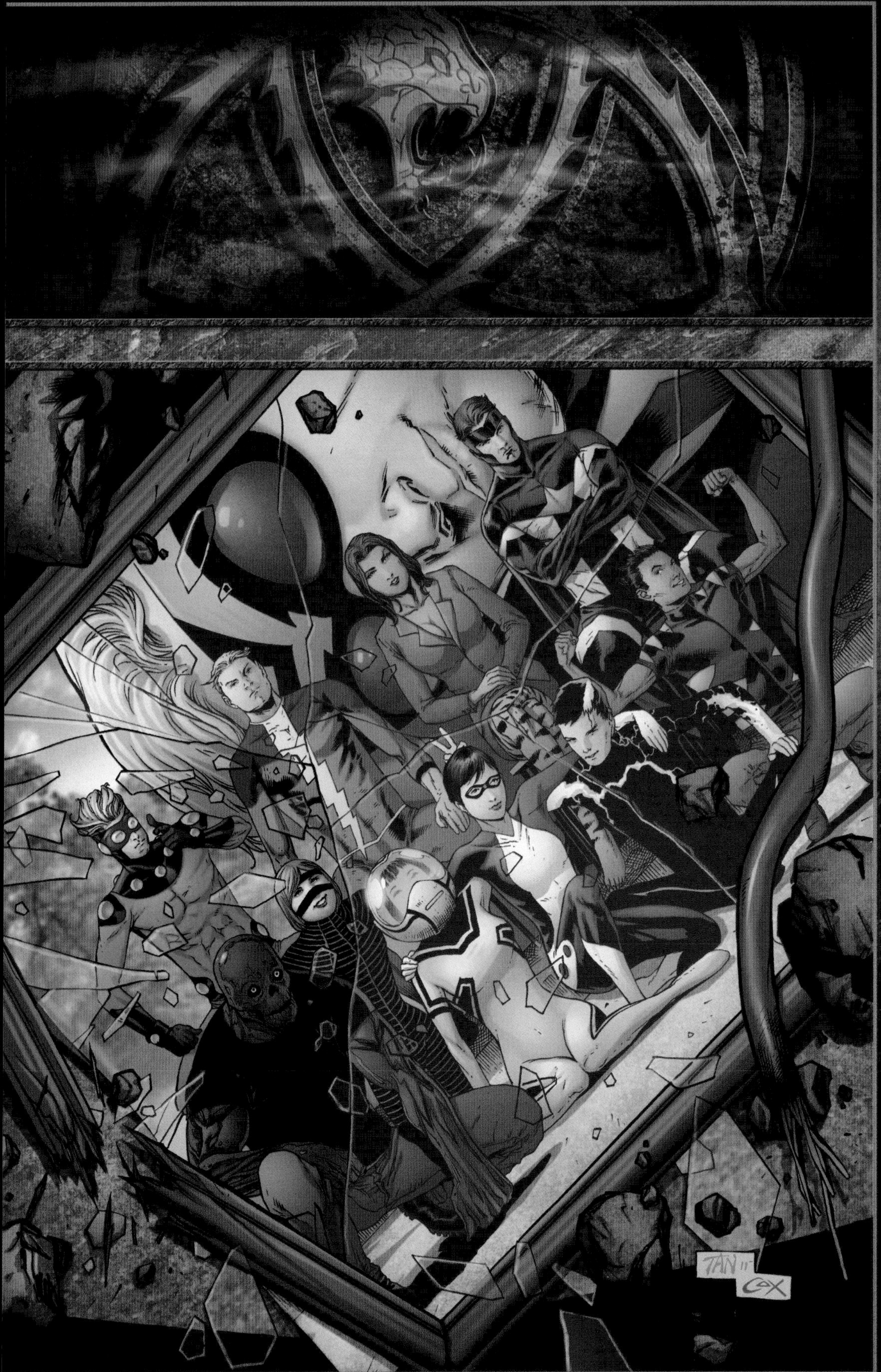
TAN '11
COX

AVENGERS ACADEMY #20

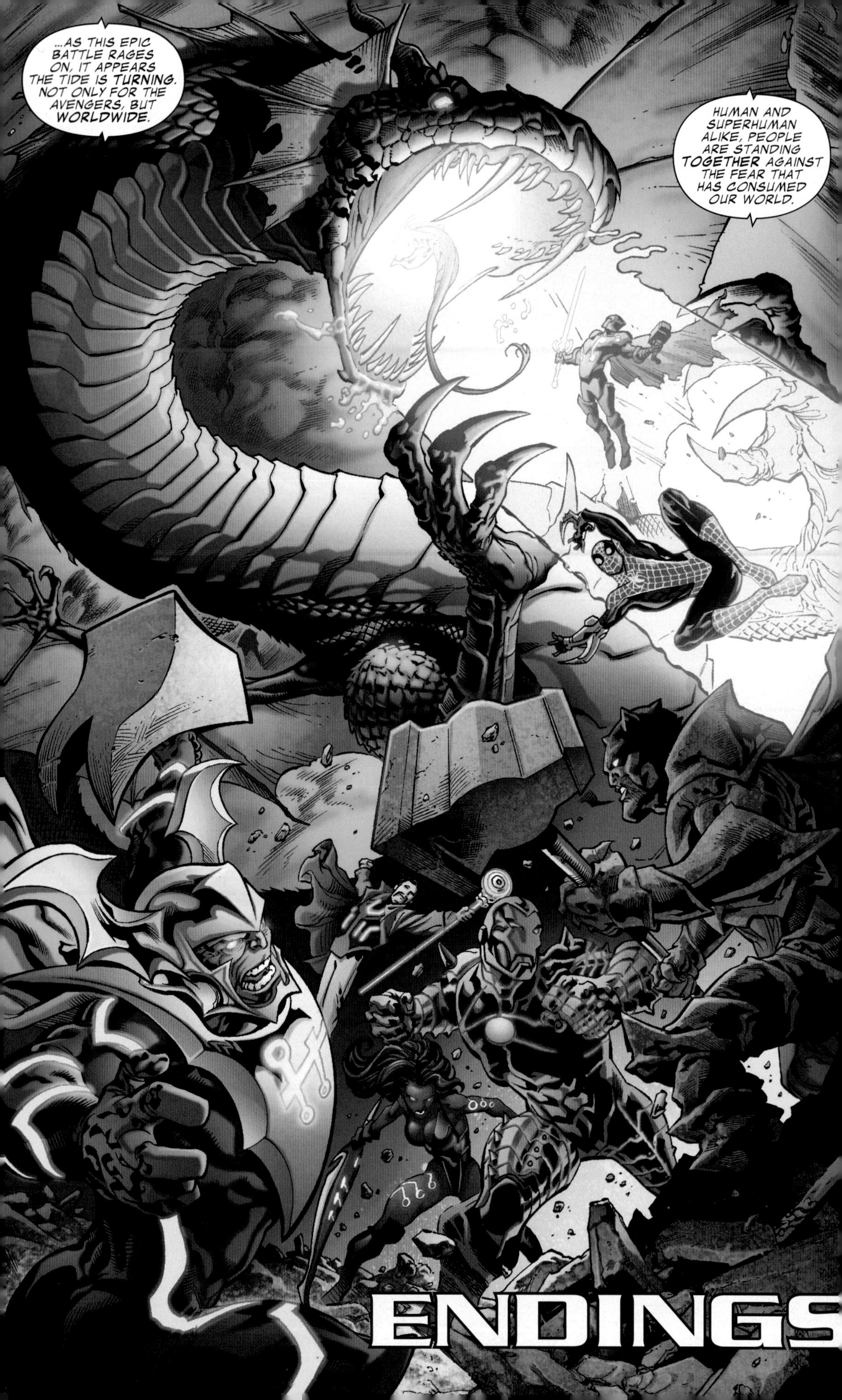
...AS THIS EPIC BATTLE RAGES ON, IT APPEARS THE TIDE IS TURNING. NOT ONLY FOR THE AVENGERS, BUT WORLDWIDE.
HUMAN AND SUPERHUMAN ALIKE, PEOPLE ARE STANDING TOGETHER AGAINST THE FEAR THAT HAS CONSUMED OUR WORLD.
ENDINGS

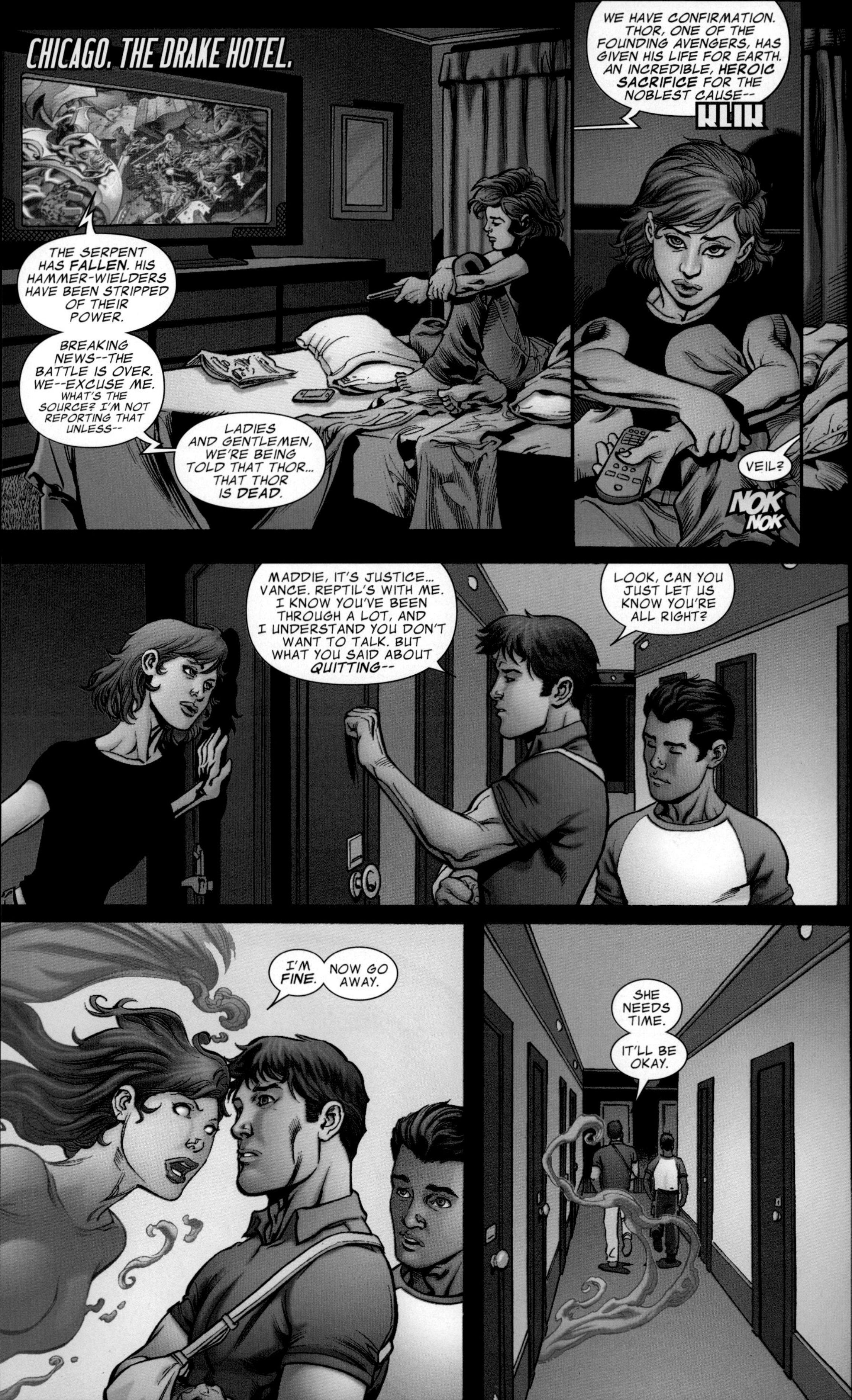
CHICAGO. THE DRAKE HOTEL.
THE SERPENT HAS FALLEN. HIS HAMMER-WIELDERS HAVE BEEN STRIPPED OF THEIR POWER.
BREAKING NEWS--THE BATTLE IS OVER. WE--EXCUSE ME. WHAT'S THE SOURCE? I'M NOT REPORTING THAT UNLESS--
LADIES AND GENTLEMEN, WE'RE BEING TOLD THAT THOR... THAT THOR IS DEAD.
WE HAVE CONFIRMATION. THOR, ONE OF THE FOUNDING AVENGERS, HAS GIVEN HIS LIFE FOR EARTH. AN INCREDIBLE, HEROIC SACRIFICE FOR THE NOBLEST CAUSE--
KLIK
VEIL?
NOK NOK
MADDIE, IT'S JUSTICE... VANCE. REPTIL'S WITH ME. I KNOW YOU'VE BEEN THROUGH A LOT, AND I UNDERSTAND YOU DON'T WANT TO TALK. BUT WHAT YOU SAID ABOUT QUITTING--
LOOK, CAN YOU JUST LET US KNOW YOU'RE ALL RIGHT?
I'M FINE.
NOW GO AWAY.
SHE NEEDS TIME.
IT'LL BE OKAY.

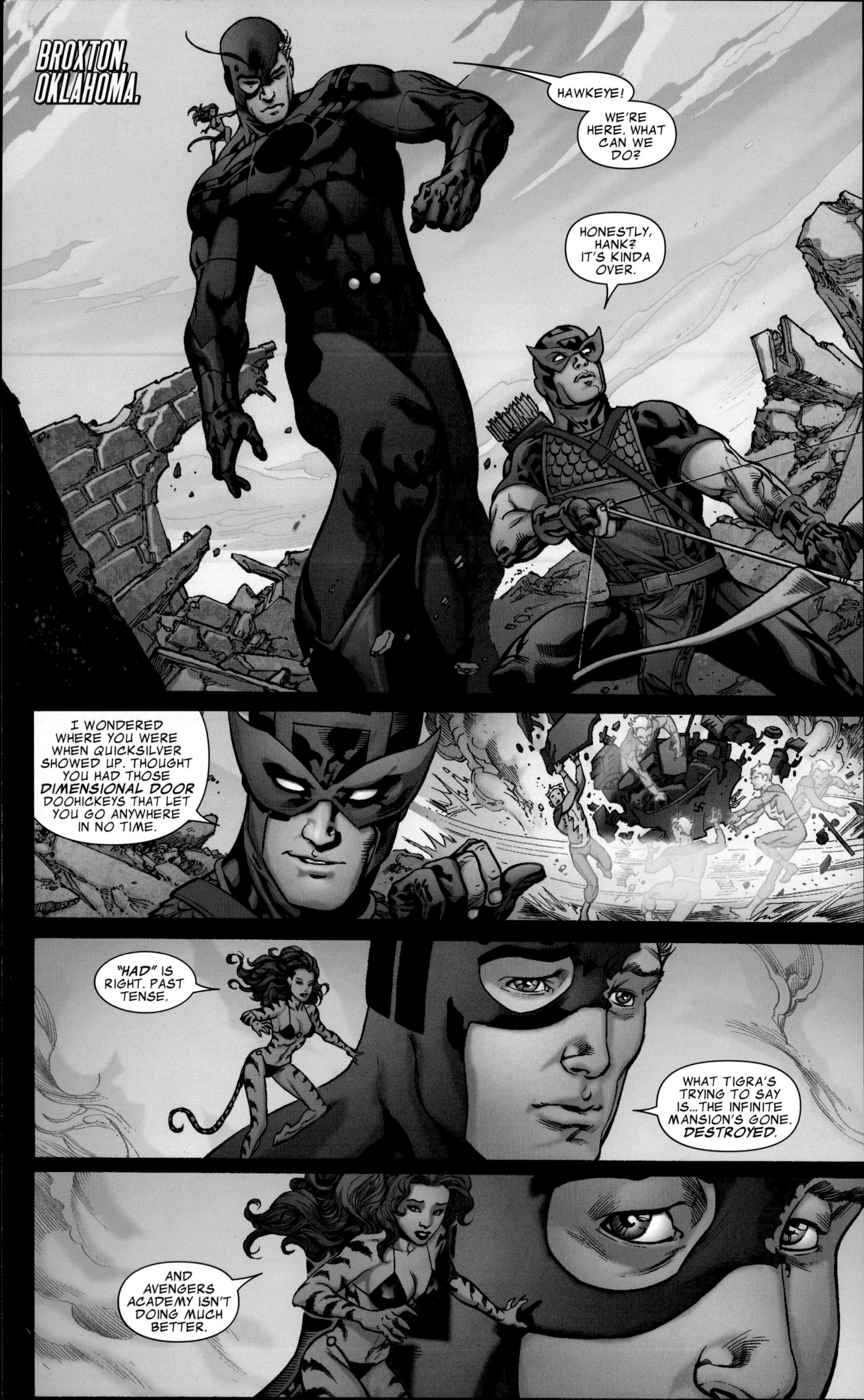
BROXTON, OKLAHOMA.
HAWKEYE!
WE'RE HERE. WHAT CAN WE DO?
HONESTLY, HANK? IT'S KINDA OVER.
I WONDERED WHERE YOU WERE WHEN QUICKSILVER SHOWED UP. THOUGHT YOU HAD THOSE **DIMENSIONAL DOOR** DOOHICKEYS THAT LET YOU GO ANYWHERE IN NO TIME.
"HAD" IS RIGHT. PAST TENSE.
WHAT TIGRA'S TRYING TO SAY IS...THE INFINITE MANSION'S GONE. ***DESTROYED.***
AND AVENGERS ACADEMY ISN'T DOING MUCH BETTER.

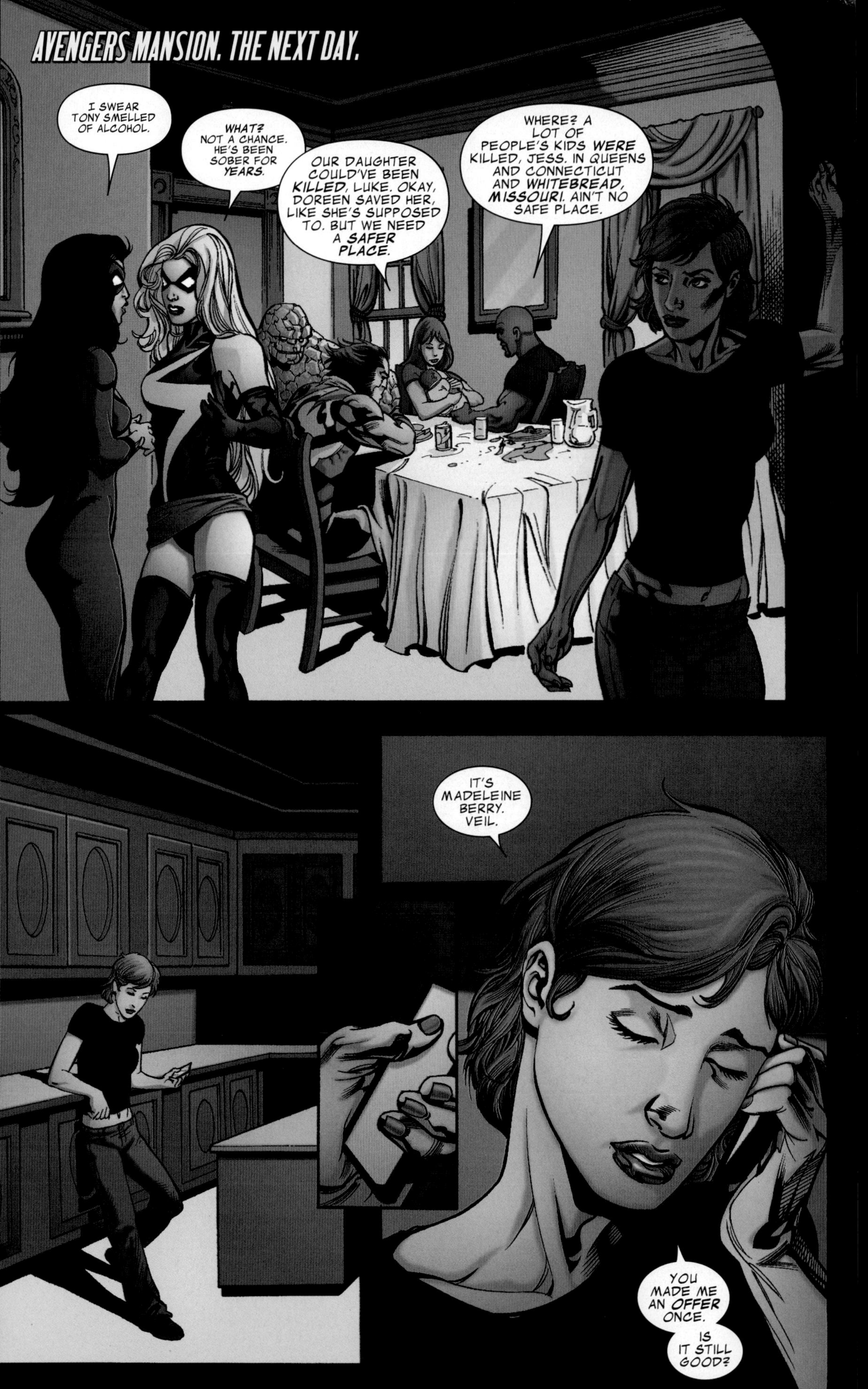
AVENGERS MANSION. THE NEXT DAY.
I SWEAR TONY SMELLED OF ALCOHOL.
WHAT? NOT A CHANCE. HE'S BEEN SOBER FOR YEARS.
OUR DAUGHTER COULD'VE BEEN KILLED, LUKE. OKAY, DOREEN SAVED HER, LIKE SHE'S SUPPOSED TO. BUT WE NEED A SAFER PLACE.
WHERE? A LOT OF PEOPLE'S KIDS WERE KILLED, JESS. IN QUEENS AND CONNECTICUT AND WHITEBREAD, MISSOURI. AIN'T NO SAFE PLACE.
IT'S MADELEINE BERRY. VEIL.
YOU MADE ME AN OFFER ONCE.
IS IT STILL GOOD?

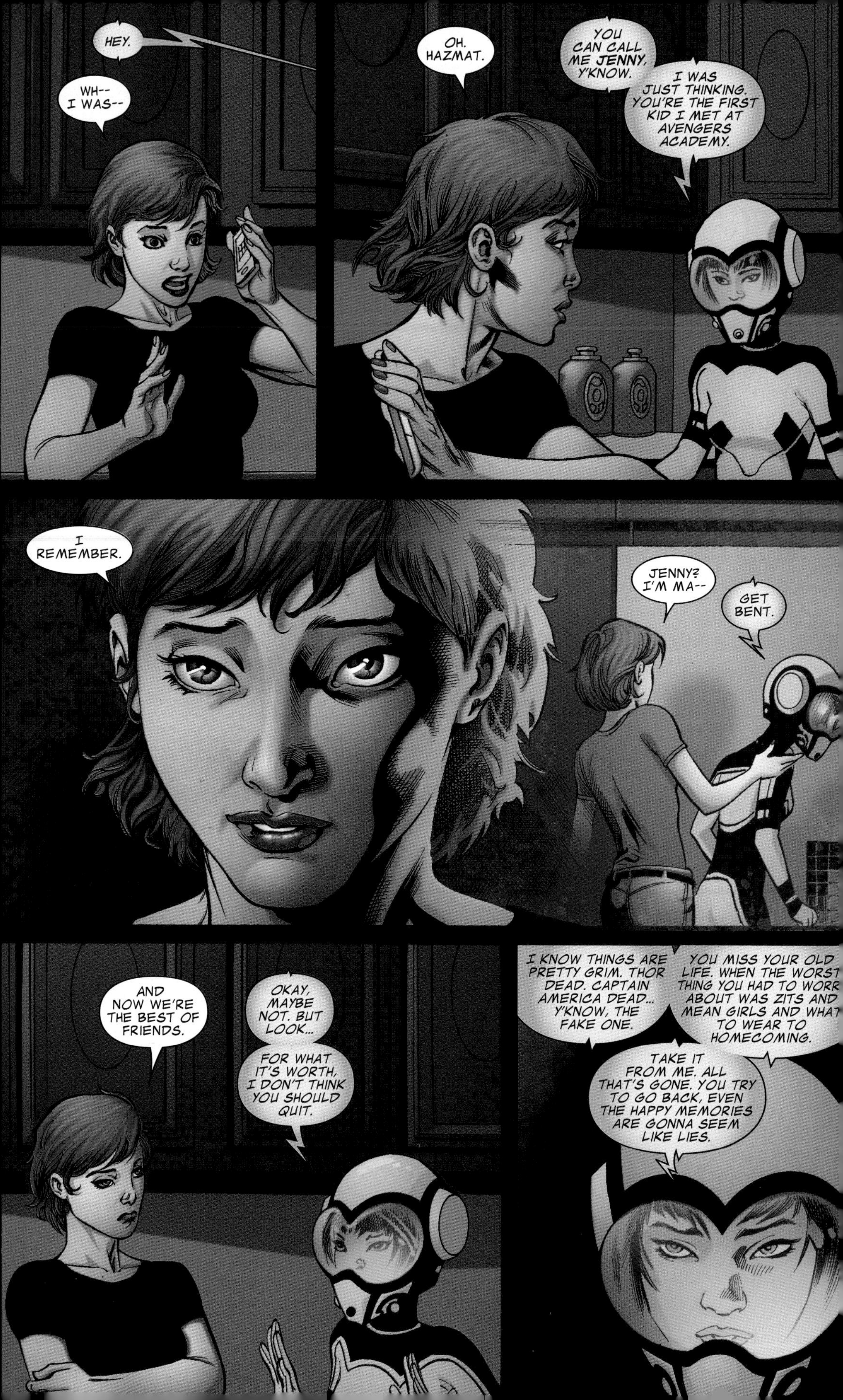

HEY.
WH-- I WAS--
OH. HAZMAT.
YOU CAN CALL ME JENNY, Y'KNOW.
I WAS JUST THINKING. YOU'RE THE FIRST KID I MET AT AVENGERS ACADEMY.
I REMEMBER.
JENNY? I'M MA--
GET BENT.
AND NOW WE'RE THE BEST OF FRIENDS.
OKAY, MAYBE NOT. BUT LOOK...
FOR WHAT IT'S WORTH, I DON'T THINK YOU SHOULD QUIT.
I KNOW THINGS ARE PRETTY GRIM. THOR DEAD. CAPTAIN AMERICA DEAD... Y'KNOW, THE FAKE ONE.
YOU MISS YOUR OLD LIFE. WHEN THE WORST THING YOU HAD TO WORR ABOUT WAS ZITS AND MEAN GIRLS AND WHAT TO WEAR TO HOMECOMING.
TAKE IT FROM ME. ALL THAT'S GONE. YOU TRY TO GO BACK, EVEN THE HAPPY MEMORIES ARE GONNA SEEM LIKE LIES.

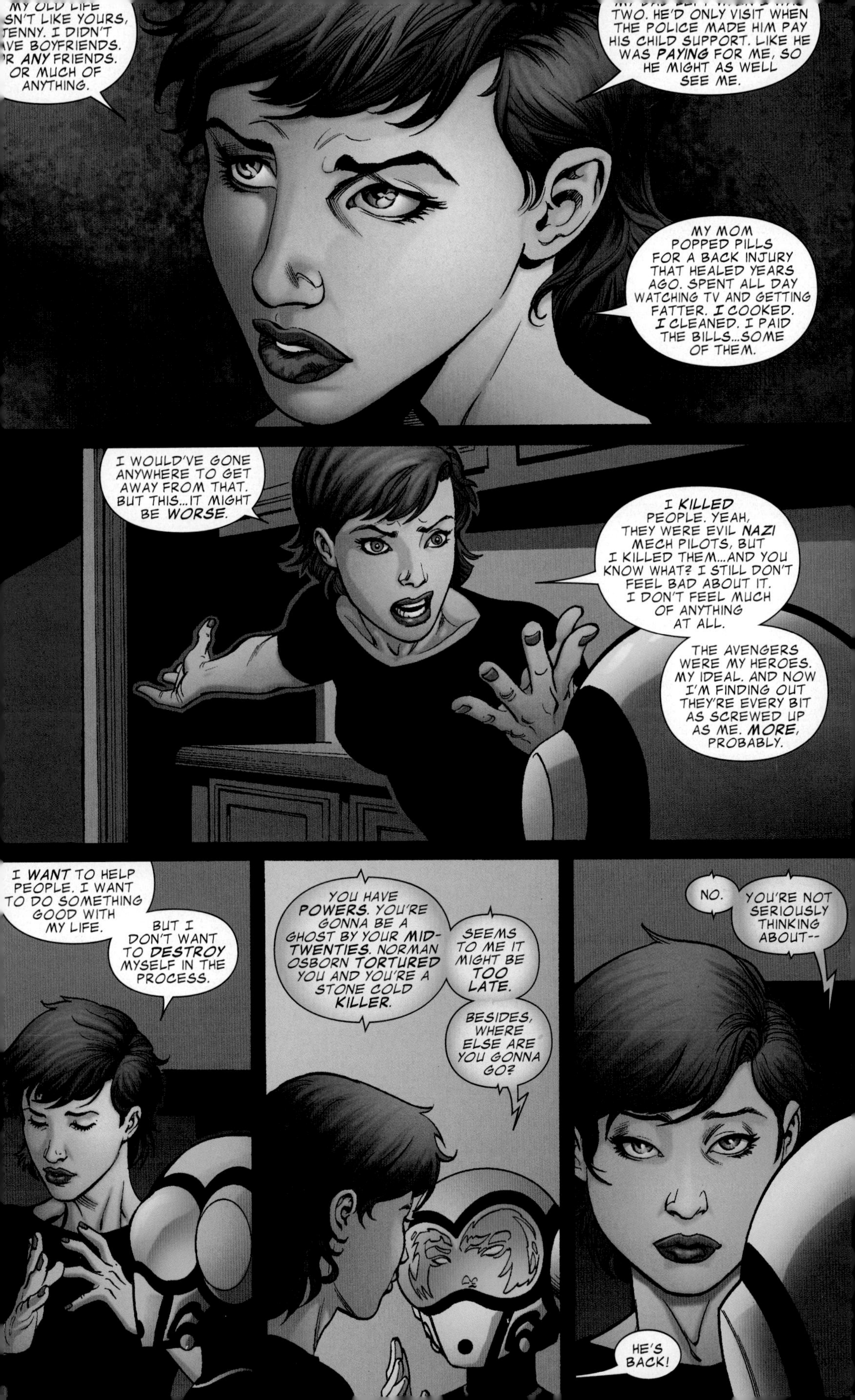

MY OLD LIFE SN'T LIKE YOURS, JENNY. I DIDN'T VE BOYFRIENDS. R ANY FRIENDS. OR MUCH OF ANYTHING.
TWO. HE'D ONLY VISIT WHEN THE POLICE MADE HIM PAY HIS CHILD SUPPORT. LIKE HE WAS PAYING FOR ME, SO HE MIGHT AS WELL SEE ME.
MY MOM POPPED PILLS FOR A BACK INJURY THAT HEALED YEARS AGO. SPENT ALL DAY WATCHING TV AND GETTING FATTER. I COOKED. I CLEANED. I PAID THE BILLS...SOME OF THEM.
I WOULD'VE GONE ANYWHERE TO GET AWAY FROM THAT. BUT THIS...IT MIGHT BE WORSE.
I KILLED PEOPLE. YEAH, THEY WERE EVIL NAZI MECH PILOTS, BUT I KILLED THEM...AND YOU KNOW WHAT? I STILL DON'T FEEL BAD ABOUT IT. I DON'T FEEL MUCH OF ANYTHING AT ALL.
THE AVENGERS WERE MY HEROES. MY IDEAL. AND NOW I'M FINDING OUT THEY'RE EVERY BIT AS SCREWED UP AS ME. MORE, PROBABLY.
I WANT TO HELP PEOPLE. I WANT TO DO SOMETHING GOOD WITH MY LIFE.
BUT I DON'T WANT TO DESTROY MYSELF IN THE PROCESS.
YOU HAVE POWERS. YOU'RE GONNA BE A GHOST BY YOUR MID-TWENTIES. NORMAN OSBORN TORTURED YOU AND YOU'RE A STONE COLD KILLER.
SEEMS TO ME IT MIGHT BE TOO LATE.
BESIDES, WHERE ELSE ARE YOU GONNA GO?
NO.
YOU'RE NOT SERIOUSLY THINKING ABOUT--
HE'S BACK!

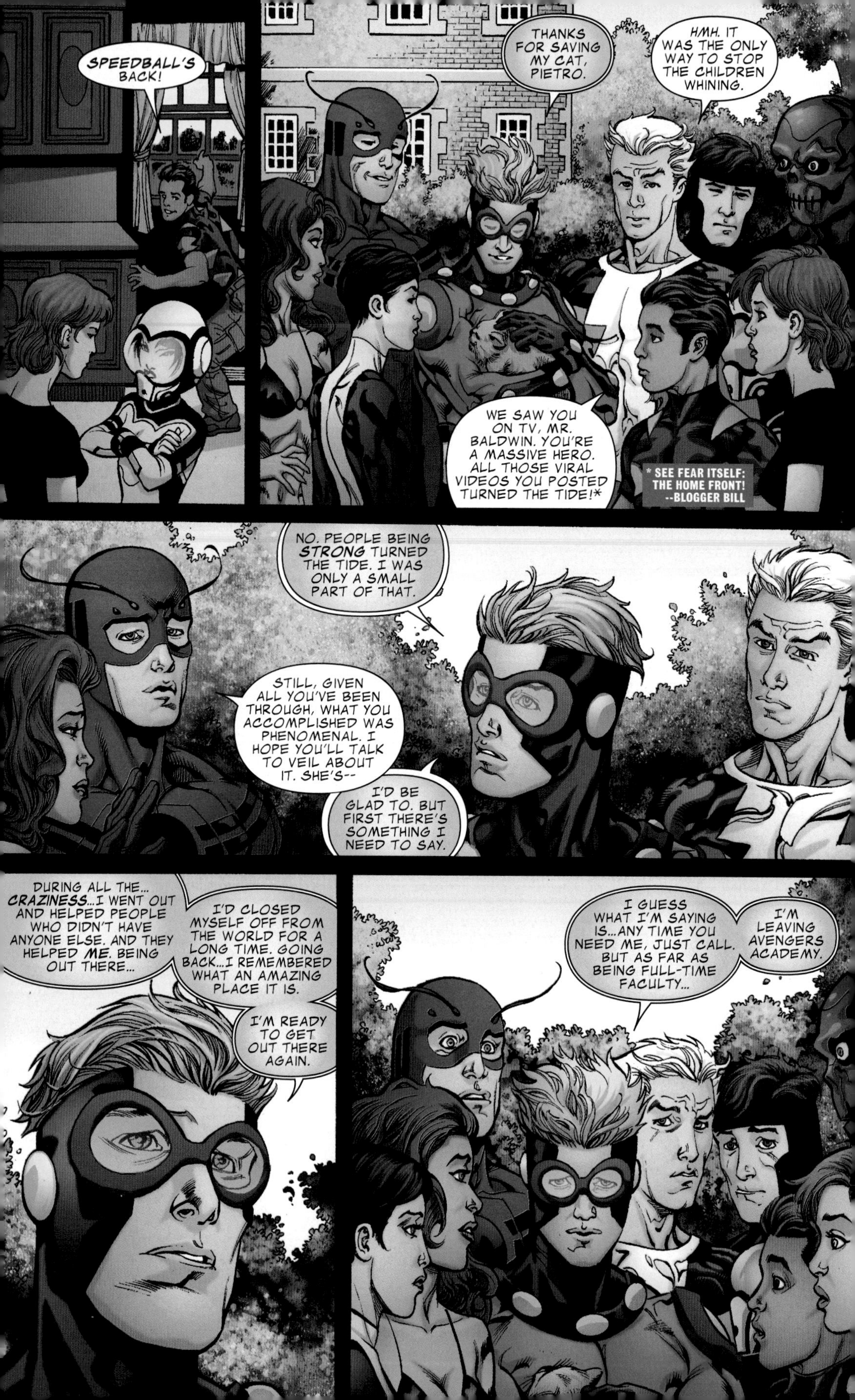
SPEEDBALL'S BACK!
THANKS FOR SAVING MY CAT, PIETRO.
HMH. IT WAS THE ONLY WAY TO STOP THE CHILDREN WHINING.
WE SAW YOU ON TV, MR. BALDWIN. YOU'RE A MASSIVE HERO. ALL THOSE VIRAL VIDEOS YOU POSTED TURNED THE TIDE!*
* SEE FEAR ITSELF: THE HOME FRONT! --BLOGGER BILL
NO. PEOPLE BEING STRONG TURNED THE TIDE. I WAS ONLY A SMALL PART OF THAT.
STILL, GIVEN ALL YOU'VE BEEN THROUGH, WHAT YOU ACCOMPLISHED WAS PHENOMENAL. I HOPE YOU'LL TALK TO VEIL ABOUT IT. SHE'S--
I'D BE GLAD TO. BUT FIRST THERE'S SOMETHING I NEED TO SAY.
DURING ALL THE... CRAZINESS...I WENT OUT AND HELPED PEOPLE WHO DIDN'T HAVE ANYONE ELSE. AND THEY HELPED ME. BEING OUT THERE...
I'D CLOSED MYSELF OFF FROM THE WORLD FOR A LONG TIME. GOING BACK...I REMEMBERED WHAT AN AMAZING PLACE IT IS.
I'M READY TO GET OUT THERE AGAIN.
I GUESS WHAT I'M SAYING IS...ANY TIME YOU NEED ME, JUST CALL. BUT AS FAR AS BEING FULL-TIME FACULTY...
I'M LEAVING AVENGERS ACADEMY.

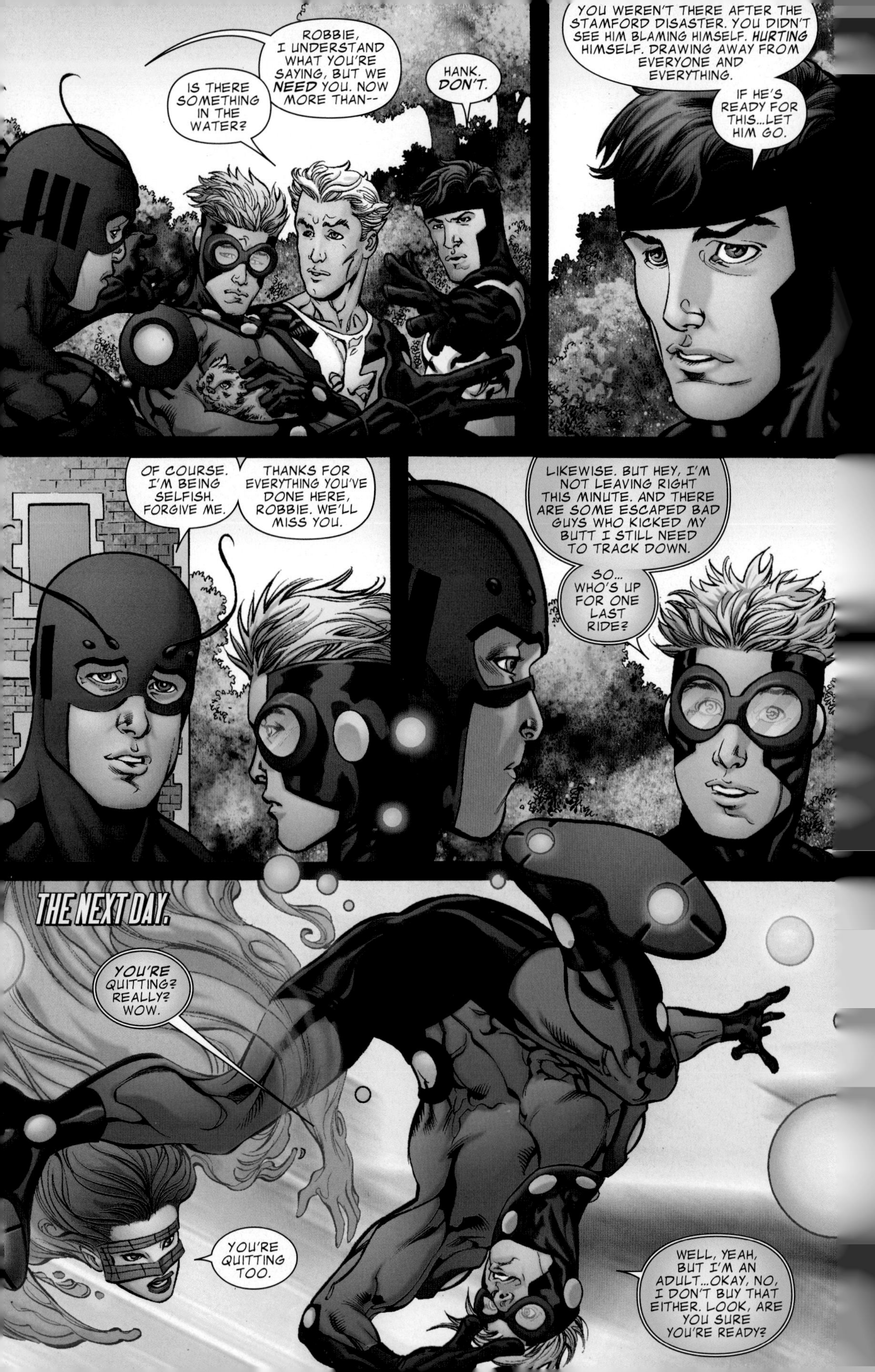
IS THERE SOMETHING IN THE WATER?
ROBBIE, I UNDERSTAND WHAT YOU'RE SAYING, BUT WE NEED YOU. NOW MORE THAN--
HANK. DON'T.
YOU WEREN'T THERE AFTER THE STAMFORD DISASTER. YOU DIDN'T SEE HIM BLAMING HIMSELF. HURTING HIMSELF. DRAWING AWAY FROM EVERYONE AND EVERYTHING.
IF HE'S READY FOR THIS...LET HIM GO.
OF COURSE. I'M BEING SELFISH. FORGIVE ME.
THANKS FOR EVERYTHING YOU'VE DONE HERE, ROBBIE. WE'LL MISS YOU.
LIKEWISE. BUT HEY, I'M NOT LEAVING RIGHT THIS MINUTE. AND THERE ARE SOME ESCAPED BAD GUYS WHO KICKED MY BUTT I STILL NEED TO TRACK DOWN.
SO... WHO'S UP FOR ONE LAST RIDE?
THE NEXT DAY.
YOU'RE QUITTING? REALLY? WOW.
YOU'RE QUITTING TOO.
WELL, YEAH, BUT I'M AN ADULT...OKAY, NO, I DON'T BUY THAT EITHER. LOOK, ARE YOU SURE YOU'RE READY?

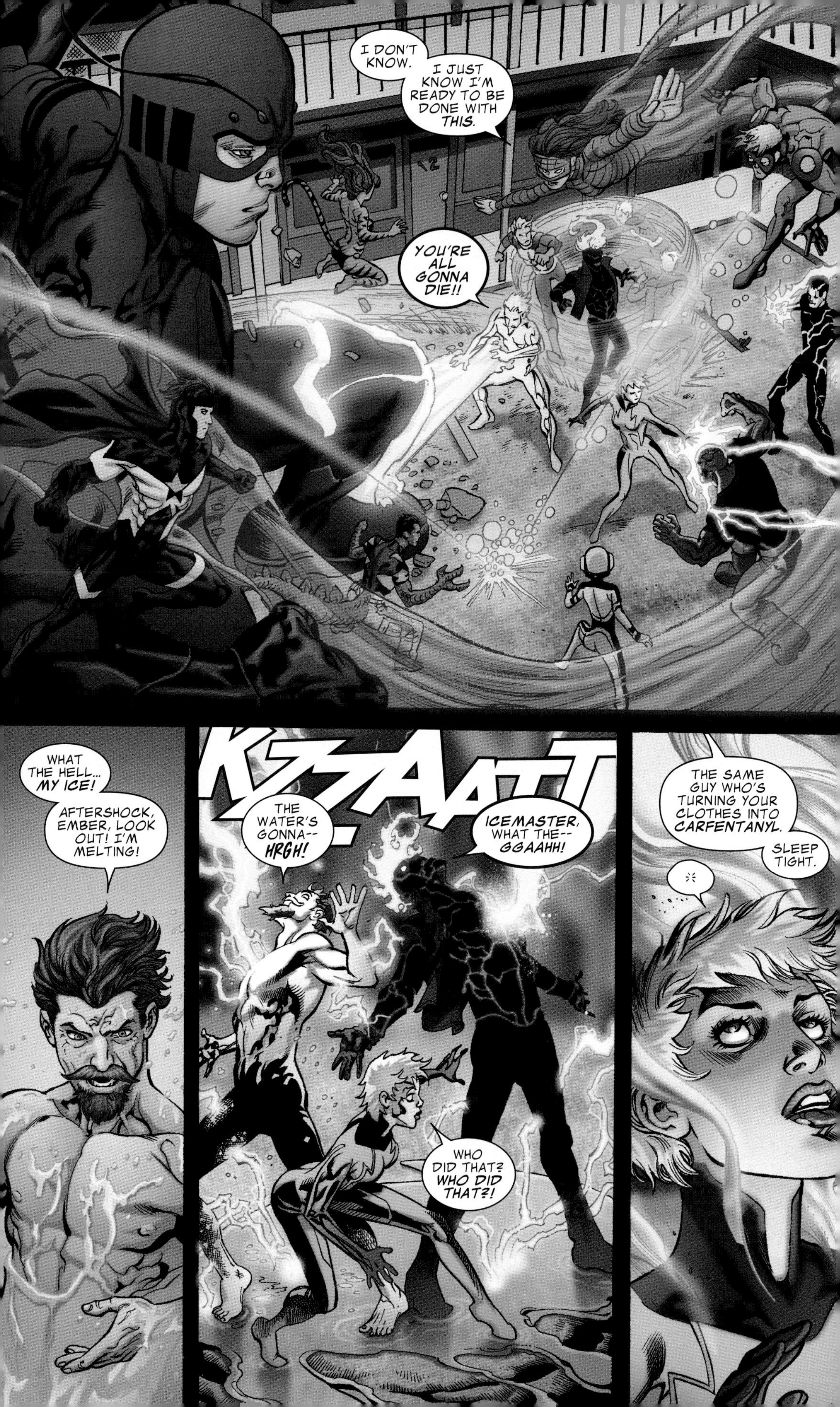
I DON'T KNOW.
I JUST KNOW I'M READY TO BE DONE WITH THIS.
YOU'RE ALL GONNA DIE!!
WHAT THE HELL... MY ICE!
AFTERSHOCK, EMBER, LOOK OUT! I'M MELTING!
KZZAATT
THE WATER'S GONNA-- HRGH!
ICEMASTER, WHAT THE-- GGAAHH!
WHO DID THAT? WHO DID THAT?!
THE SAME GUY WHO'S TURNING YOUR CLOTHES INTO CARFENTANYL.
SLEEP TIGHT.

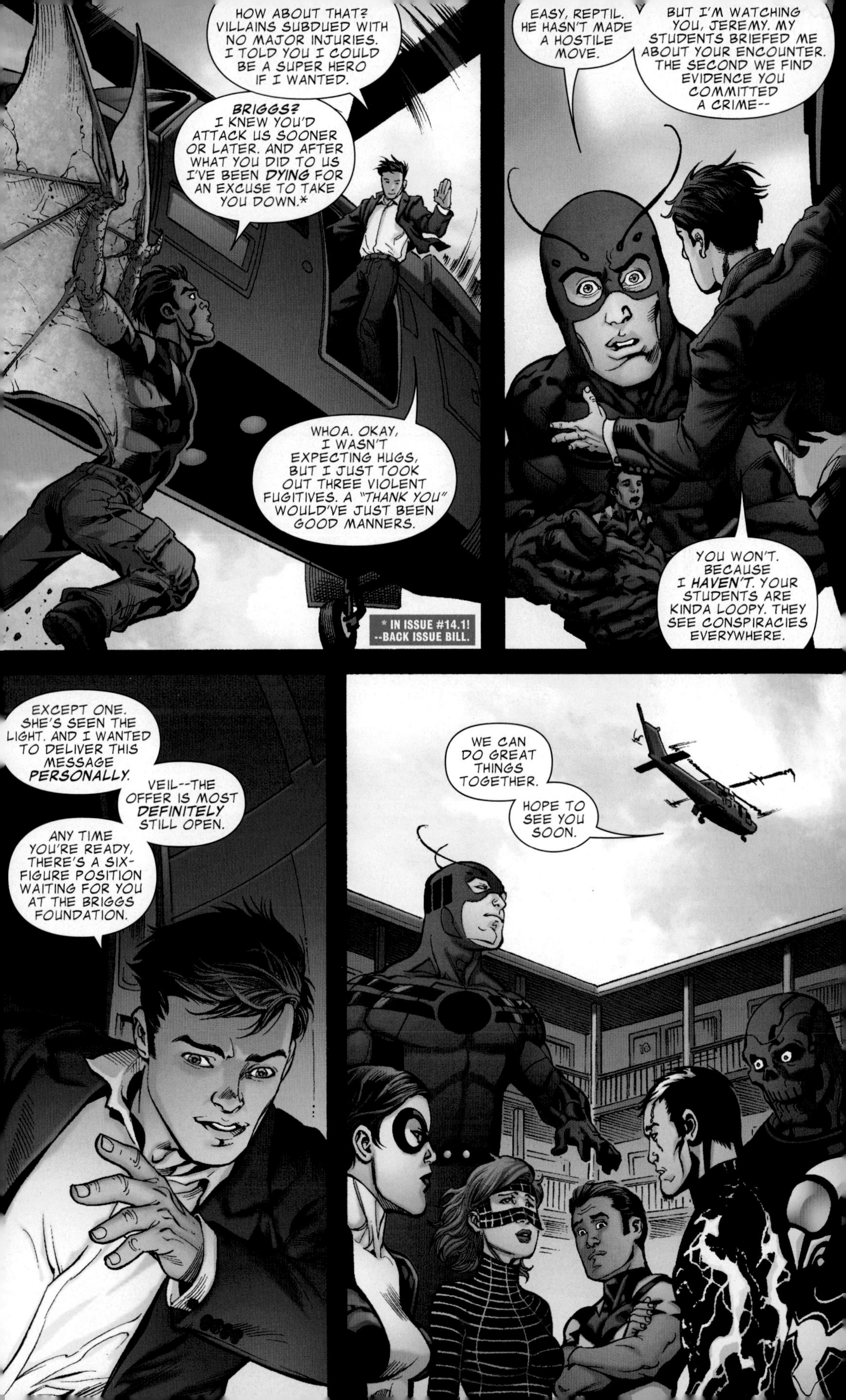
HOW ABOUT THAT? VILLAINS SUBDUED WITH NO MAJOR INJURIES. I TOLD YOU I COULD BE A SUPER HERO IF I WANTED.
BRIGGS? I KNEW YOU'D ATTACK US SOONER OR LATER. AND AFTER WHAT YOU DID TO US I'VE BEEN DYING FOR AN EXCUSE TO TAKE YOU DOWN.*
WHOA. OKAY, I WASN'T EXPECTING HUGS, BUT I JUST TOOK OUT THREE VIOLENT FUGITIVES. A "THANK YOU" WOULD'VE JUST BEEN GOOD MANNERS.
* IN ISSUE #14.1! --BACK ISSUE BILL.
EASY, REPTIL. HE HASN'T MADE A HOSTILE MOVE.
BUT I'M WATCHING YOU, JEREMY. MY STUDENTS BRIEFED ME ABOUT YOUR ENCOUNTER. THE SECOND WE FIND EVIDENCE YOU COMMITTED A CRIME--
YOU WON'T. BECAUSE I HAVEN'T. YOUR STUDENTS ARE KINDA LOOPY. THEY SEE CONSPIRACIES EVERYWHERE.
EXCEPT ONE. SHE'S SEEN THE LIGHT. AND I WANTED TO DELIVER THIS MESSAGE PERSONALLY.
VEIL--THE OFFER IS MOST DEFINITELY STILL OPEN.
ANY TIME YOU'RE READY, THERE'S A SIX-FIGURE POSITION WAITING FOR YOU AT THE BRIGGS FOUNDATION.
WE CAN DO GREAT THINGS TOGETHER.
HOPE TO SEE YOU SOON.

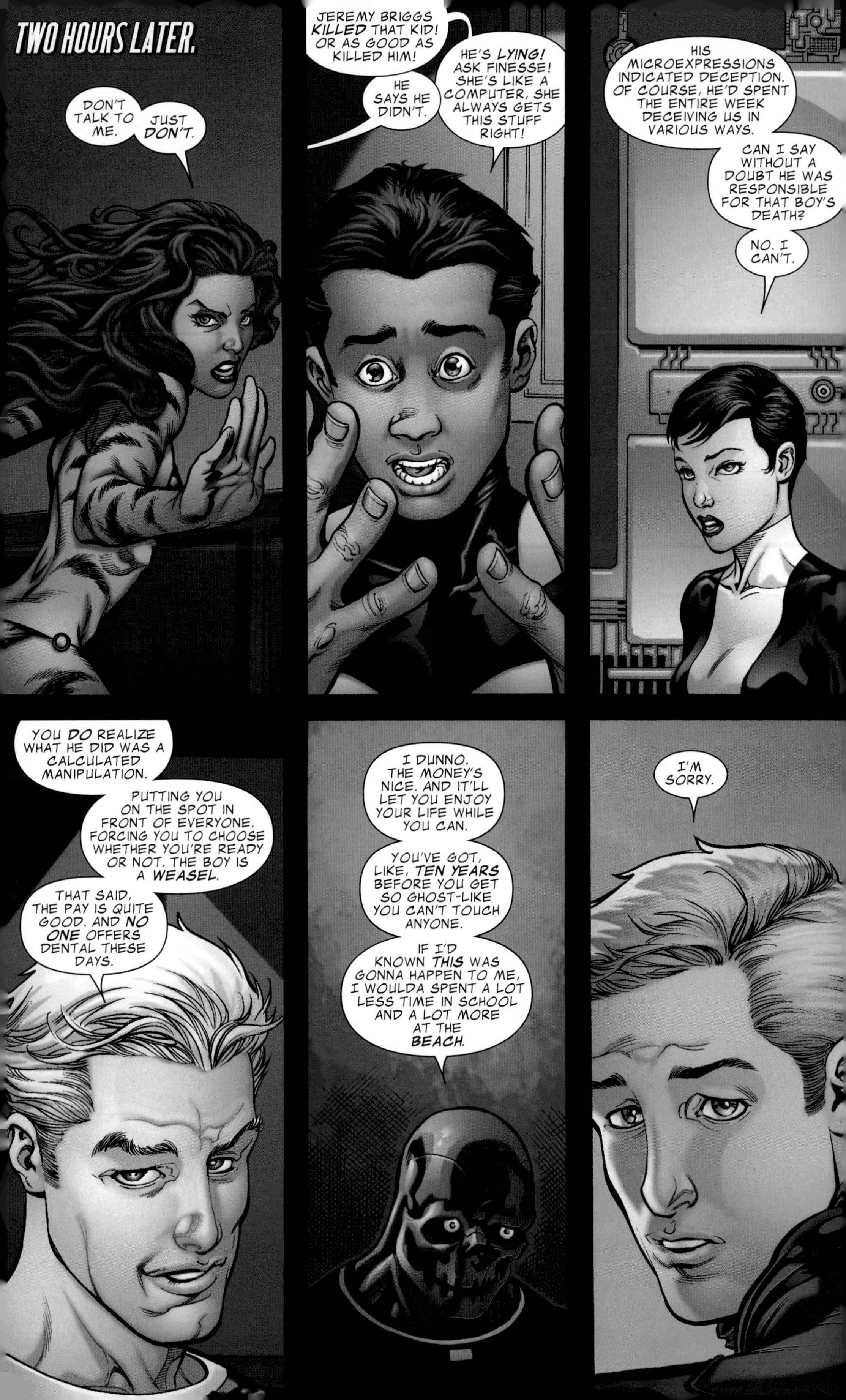
TWO HOURS LATER.
DON'T TALK TO ME.
JUST DON'T.
JEREMY BRIGGS KILLED THAT KID! OR AS GOOD AS KILLED HIM!
HE SAYS HE DIDN'T.
HE'S LYING! ASK FINESSE! SHE'S LIKE A COMPUTER, SHE ALWAYS GETS THIS STUFF RIGHT!
HIS MICROEXPRESSIONS INDICATED DECEPTION. OF COURSE, HE'D SPENT THE ENTIRE WEEK DECEIVING US IN VARIOUS WAYS.
CAN I SAY WITHOUT A DOUBT HE WAS RESPONSIBLE FOR THAT BOY'S DEATH?
NO. I CAN'T.
YOU DO REALIZE WHAT HE DID WAS A CALCULATED MANIPULATION.
PUTTING YOU ON THE SPOT IN FRONT OF EVERYONE. FORCING YOU TO CHOOSE WHETHER YOU'RE READY OR NOT. THE BOY IS A WEASEL.
THAT SAID, THE PAY IS QUITE GOOD. AND NO ONE OFFERS DENTAL THESE DAYS.
I DUNNO. THE MONEY'S NICE. AND IT'LL LET YOU ENJOY YOUR LIFE WHILE YOU CAN.
YOU'VE GOT, LIKE, TEN YEARS BEFORE YOU GET SO GHOST-LIKE YOU CAN'T TOUCH ANYONE.
IF I'D KNOWN THIS WAS GONNA HAPPEN TO ME, I WOULDA SPENT A LOT LESS TIME IN SCHOOL AND A LOT MORE AT THE BEACH.
I'M SORRY.

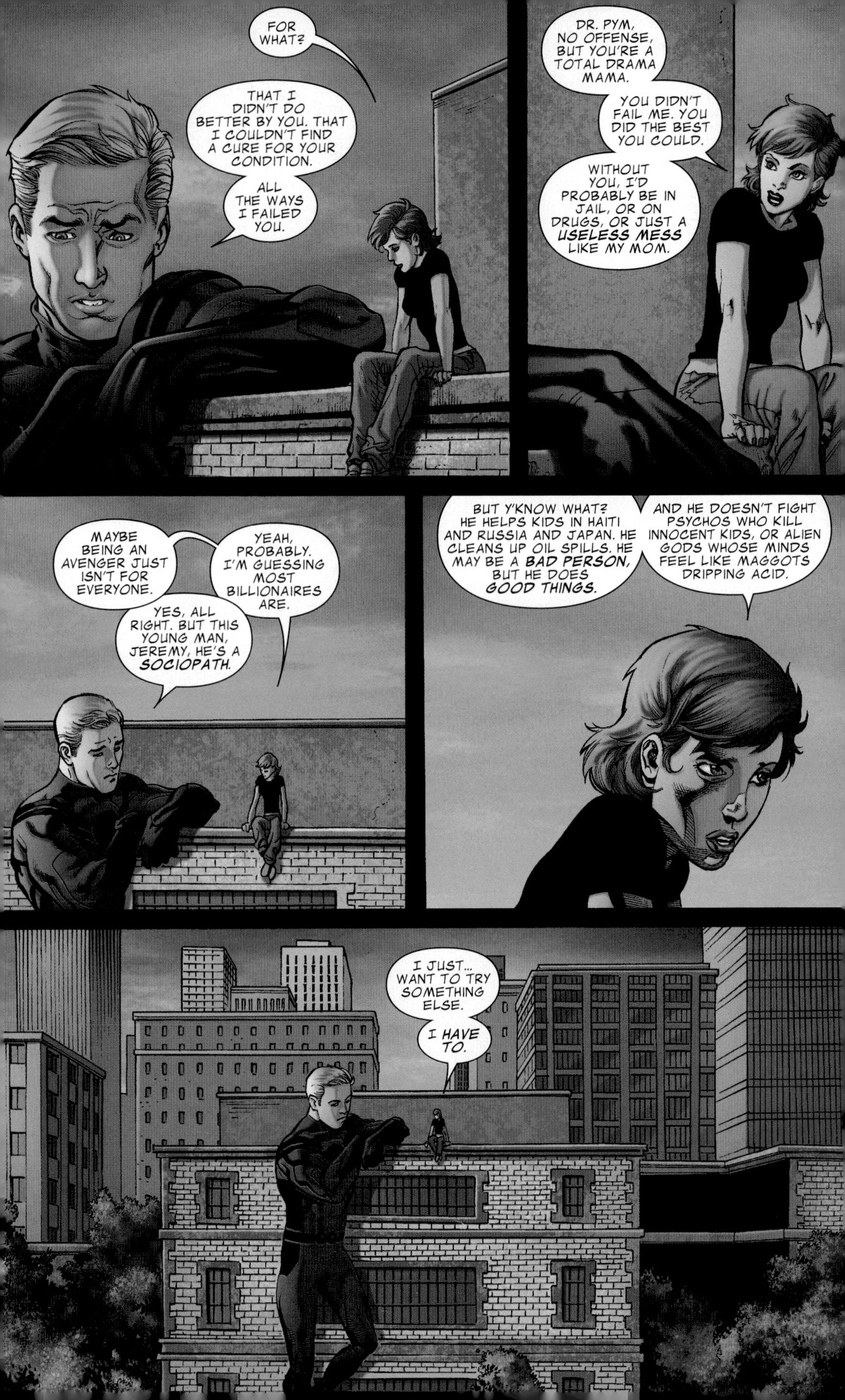
FOR WHAT?
THAT I DIDN'T DO BETTER BY YOU. THAT I COULDN'T FIND A CURE FOR YOUR CONDITION.
ALL THE WAYS I FAILED YOU.
DR. PYM, NO OFFENSE, BUT YOU'RE A TOTAL DRAMA MAMA.
YOU DIDN'T FAIL ME. YOU DID THE BEST YOU COULD.
WITHOUT YOU, I'D PROBABLY BE IN JAIL, OR ON DRUGS, OR JUST A USELESS MESS LIKE MY MOM.
MAYBE BEING AN AVENGER JUST ISN'T FOR EVERYONE.
YEAH, PROBABLY. I'M GUESSING MOST BILLIONAIRES ARE.
YES, ALL RIGHT. BUT THIS YOUNG MAN, JEREMY, HE'S A SOCIOPATH.
BUT Y'KNOW WHAT? HE HELPS KIDS IN HAITI AND RUSSIA AND JAPAN. HE CLEANS UP OIL SPILLS. HE MAY BE A BAD PERSON, BUT HE DOES GOOD THINGS.
AND HE DOESN'T FIGHT PSYCHOS WHO KILL INNOCENT KIDS, OR ALIEN GODS WHOSE MINDS FEEL LIKE MAGGOTS DRIPPING ACID.
I JUST... WANT TO TRY SOMETHING ELSE.
I HAVE TO.

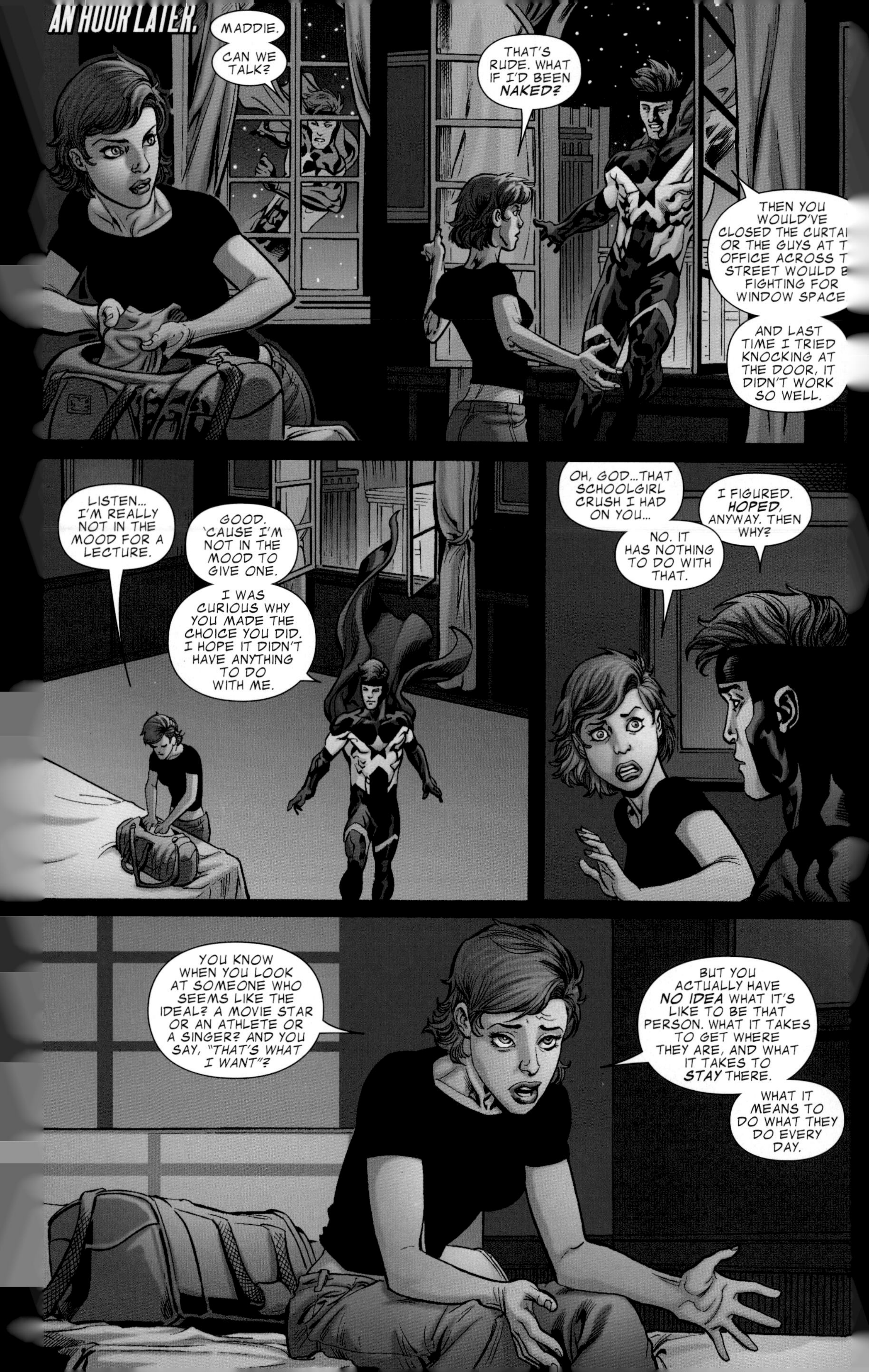
AN HOUR LATER.
MADDIE.
CAN WE TALK?
THAT'S RUDE. WHAT IF I'D BEEN NAKED?
THEN YOU WOULD'VE CLOSED THE CURTAI OR THE GUYS AT T OFFICE ACROSS T STREET WOULD B FIGHTING FOR WINDOW SPACE
AND LAST TIME I TRIED KNOCKING AT THE DOOR, IT DIDN'T WORK SO WELL.
LISTEN... I'M REALLY NOT IN THE MOOD FOR A LECTURE.
GOOD. 'CAUSE I'M NOT IN THE MOOD TO GIVE ONE.
I WAS CURIOUS WHY YOU MADE THE CHOICE YOU DID. I HOPE IT DIDN'T HAVE ANYTHING TO DO WITH ME.
OH, GOD...THAT SCHOOLGIRL CRUSH I HAD ON YOU...
NO. IT HAS NOTHING TO DO WITH THAT.
I FIGURED. HOPED, ANYWAY. THEN WHY?
YOU KNOW WHEN YOU LOOK AT SOMEONE WHO SEEMS LIKE THE IDEAL? A MOVIE STAR OR AN ATHLETE OR A SINGER? AND YOU SAY, "THAT'S WHAT I WANT"?
BUT YOU ACTUALLY HAVE NO IDEA WHAT IT'S LIKE TO BE THAT PERSON. WHAT IT TAKES TO GET WHERE THEY ARE, AND WHAT IT TAKES TO STAY THERE.
WHAT IT MEANS TO DO WHAT THEY DO EVERY DAY.

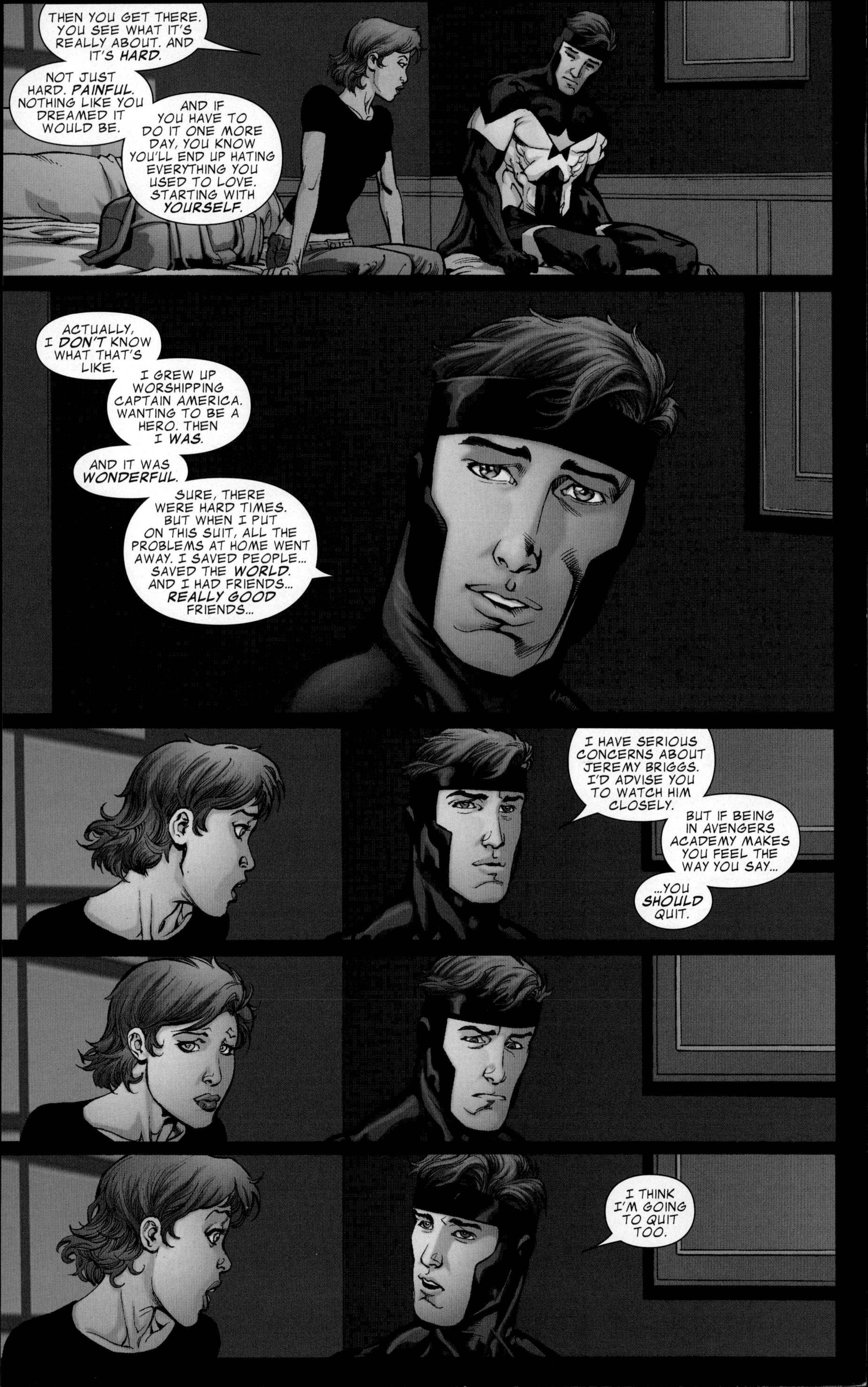
THEN YOU GET THERE. YOU SEE WHAT IT'S REALLY ABOUT. AND IT'S HARD.
NOT JUST HARD. PAINFUL. NOTHING LIKE YOU DREAMED IT WOULD BE.
AND IF YOU HAVE TO DO IT ONE MORE DAY, YOU KNOW YOU'LL END UP HATING EVERYTHING YOU USED TO LOVE. STARTING WITH YOURSELF.
ACTUALLY, I DON'T KNOW WHAT THAT'S LIKE.
I GREW UP WORSHIPPING CAPTAIN AMERICA. WANTING TO BE A HERO. THEN I WAS.
AND IT WAS WONDERFUL.
SURE, THERE WERE HARD TIMES. BUT WHEN I PUT ON THIS SUIT, ALL THE PROBLEMS AT HOME WENT AWAY. I SAVED PEOPLE... SAVED THE WORLD. AND I HAD FRIENDS... REALLY GOOD FRIENDS...
I HAVE SERIOUS CONCERNS ABOUT JEREMY BRIGGS. I'D ADVISE YOU TO WATCH HIM CLOSELY.
BUT IF BEING IN AVENGERS ACADEMY MAKES YOU FEEL THE WAY YOU SAY...
...YOU SHOULD QUIT.
I THINK I'M GOING TO QUIT TOO.

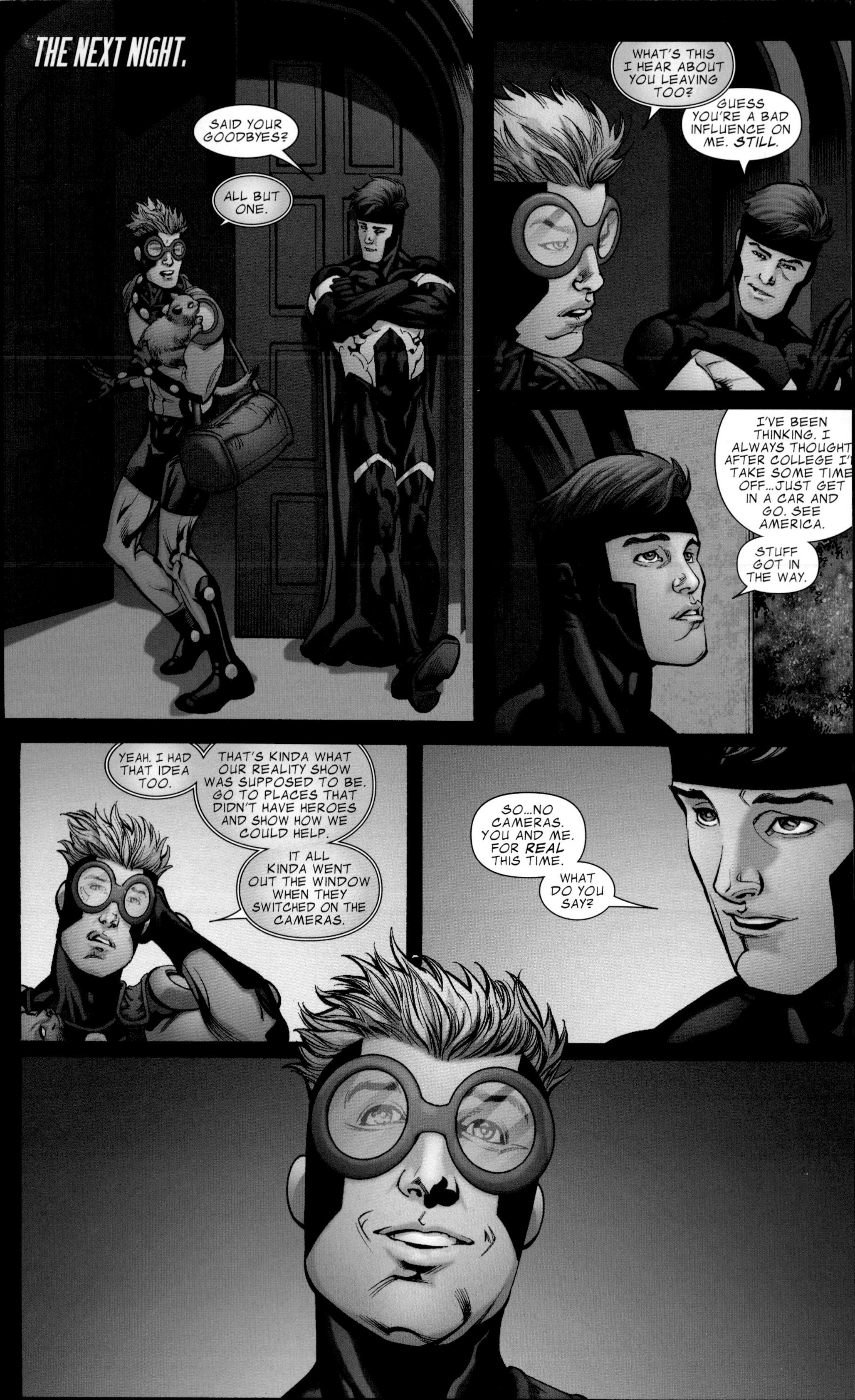
THE NEXT NIGHT.
SAID YOUR GOODBYES?
ALL BUT ONE.
WHAT'S THIS I HEAR ABOUT YOU LEAVING TOO?
GUESS YOU'RE A BAD INFLUENCE ON ME. STILL.
I'VE BEEN THINKING. I ALWAYS THOUGHT AFTER COLLEGE I'D TAKE SOME TIME OFF...JUST GET IN A CAR AND GO. SEE AMERICA.
STUFF GOT IN THE WAY.
YEAH. I HAD THAT IDEA TOO.
THAT'S KINDA WHAT OUR REALITY SHOW WAS SUPPOSED TO BE. GO TO PLACES THAT DIDN'T HAVE HEROES AND SHOW HOW WE COULD HELP.
IT ALL KINDA WENT OUT THE WINDOW WHEN THEY SWITCHED ON THE CAMERAS.
SO...NO CAMERAS. YOU AND ME. FOR REAL THIS TIME.
WHAT DO YOU SAY?

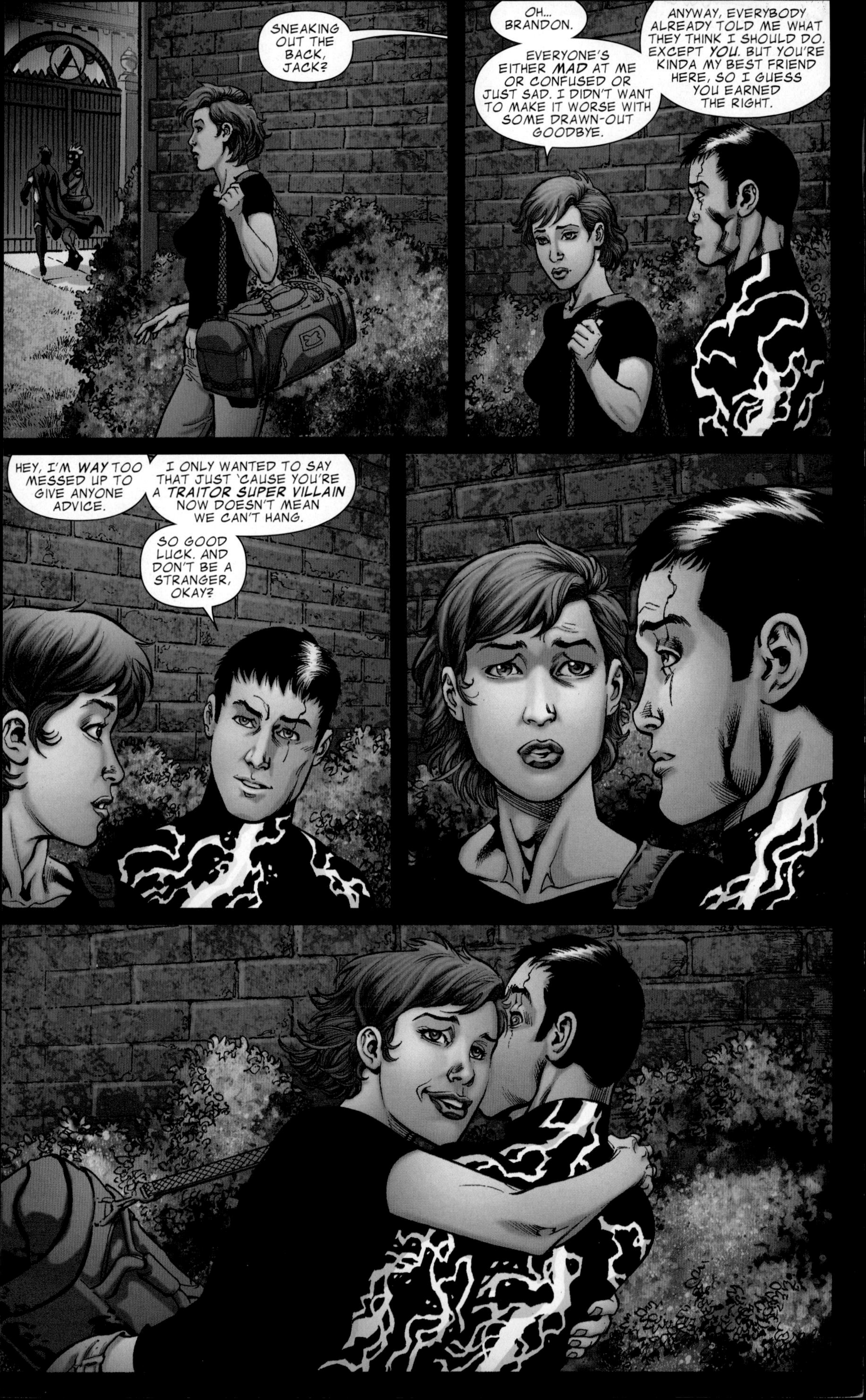
SNEAKING OUT THE BACK, JACK?
OH... BRANDON.
EVERYONE'S EITHER MAD AT ME OR CONFUSED OR JUST SAD. I DIDN'T WANT TO MAKE IT WORSE WITH SOME DRAWN-OUT GOODBYE.
ANYWAY, EVERYBODY ALREADY TOLD ME WHAT THEY THINK I SHOULD DO. EXCEPT YOU. BUT YOU'RE KINDA MY BEST FRIEND HERE, SO I GUESS YOU EARNED THE RIGHT.
HEY, I'M WAY TOO MESSED UP TO GIVE ANYONE ADVICE.
I ONLY WANTED TO SAY THAT JUST 'CAUSE YOU'RE A TRAITOR SUPER VILLAIN NOW DOESN'T MEAN WE CAN'T HANG.
SO GOOD LUCK. AND DON'T BE A STRANGER, OKAY?

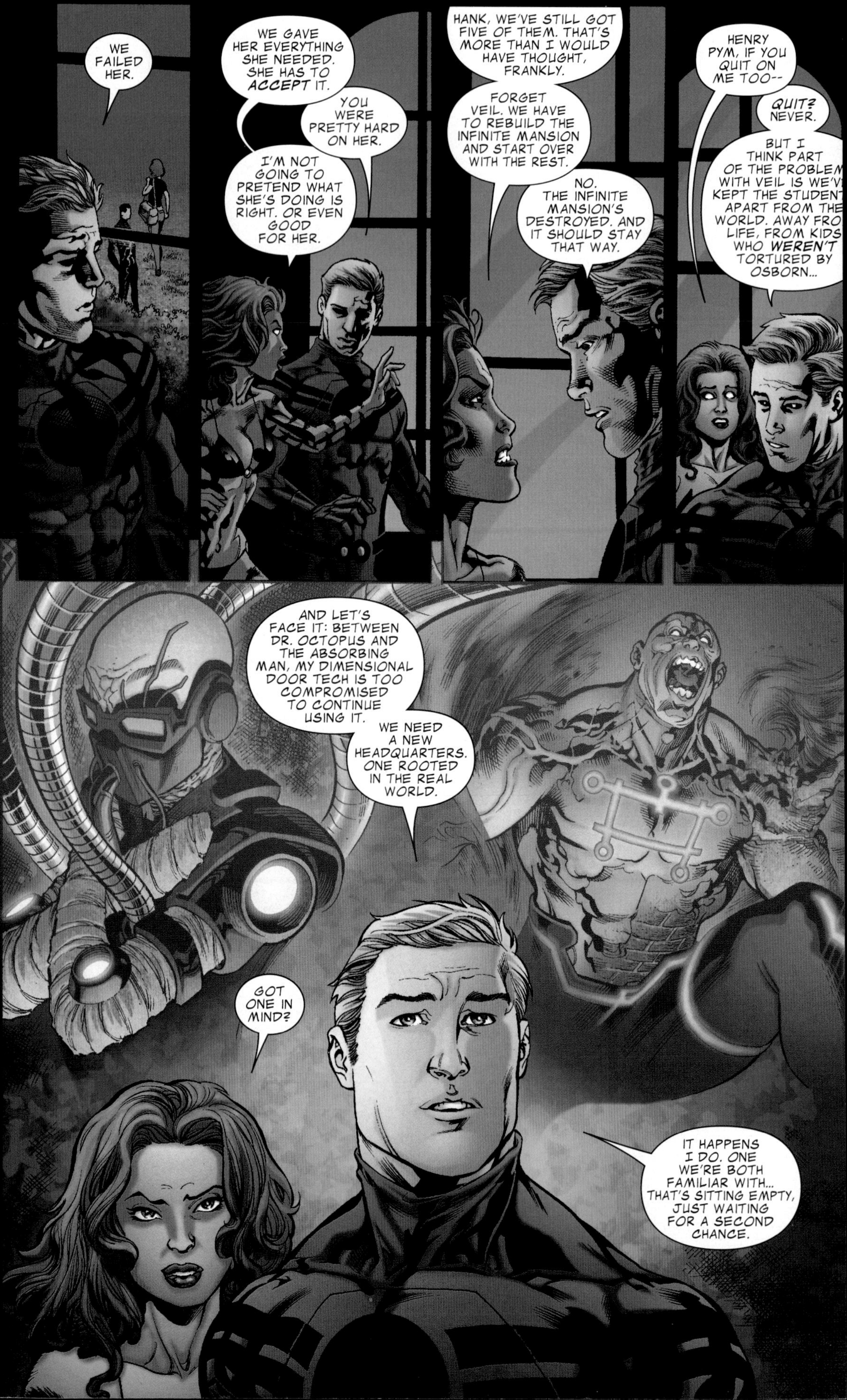
WE FAILED HER.
WE GAVE HER EVERYTHING SHE NEEDED. SHE HAS TO ACCEPT IT.
YOU WERE PRETTY HARD ON HER.
I'M NOT GOING TO PRETEND WHAT SHE'S DOING IS RIGHT. OR EVEN GOOD FOR HER.
HANK, WE'VE STILL GOT FIVE OF THEM. THAT'S MORE THAN I WOULD HAVE THOUGHT, FRANKLY.
FORGET VEIL. WE HAVE TO REBUILD THE INFINITE MANSION AND START OVER WITH THE REST.
NO. THE INFINITE MANSION'S DESTROYED. AND IT SHOULD STAY THAT WAY.
HENRY PYM, IF YOU QUIT ON ME TOO--
QUIT? NEVER.
AND LET'S FACE IT: BETWEEN DR. OCTOPUS AND THE ABSORBING MAN, MY DIMENSIONAL DOOR TECH IS TOO COMPROMISED TO CONTINUE USING IT.
WE NEED A NEW HEADQUARTERS. ONE ROOTED IN THE REAL WORLD.
GOT ONE IN MIND?
IT HAPPENS I DO. ONE WE'RE BOTH FAMILIAR WITH... THAT'S SITTING EMPTY, JUST WAITING FOR A SECOND CHANCE.

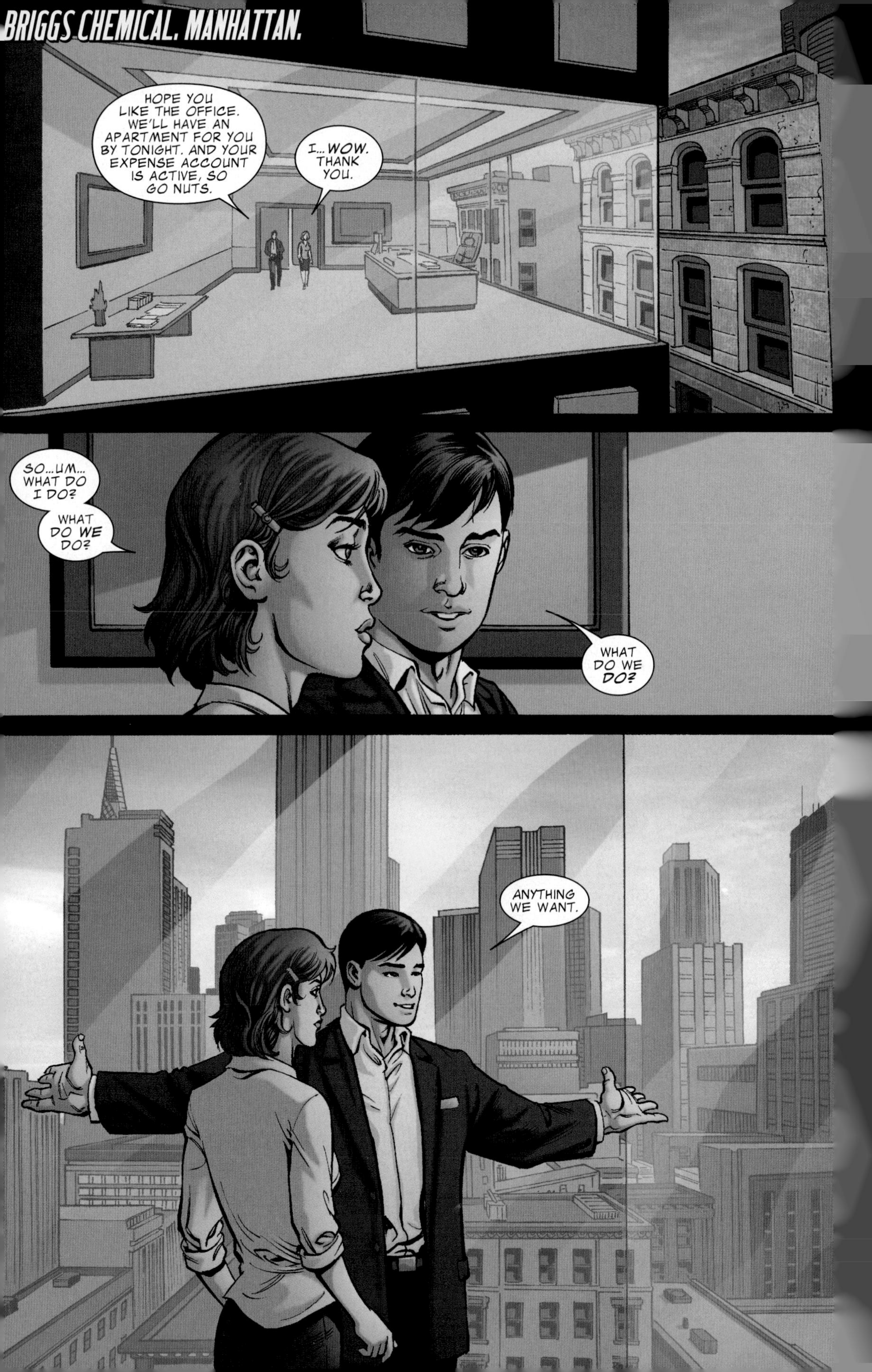
BRIGGS CHEMICAL. MANHATTAN.
HOPE YOU LIKE THE OFFICE. WE'LL HAVE AN APARTMENT FOR YOU BY TONIGHT. AND YOUR EXPENSE ACCOUNT IS ACTIVE, SO GO NUTS.
I...WOW. THANK YOU.
SO...UM... WHAT DO I DO?
WHAT DO WE DO?
WHAT DO WE DO?
ANYTHING WE WANT.

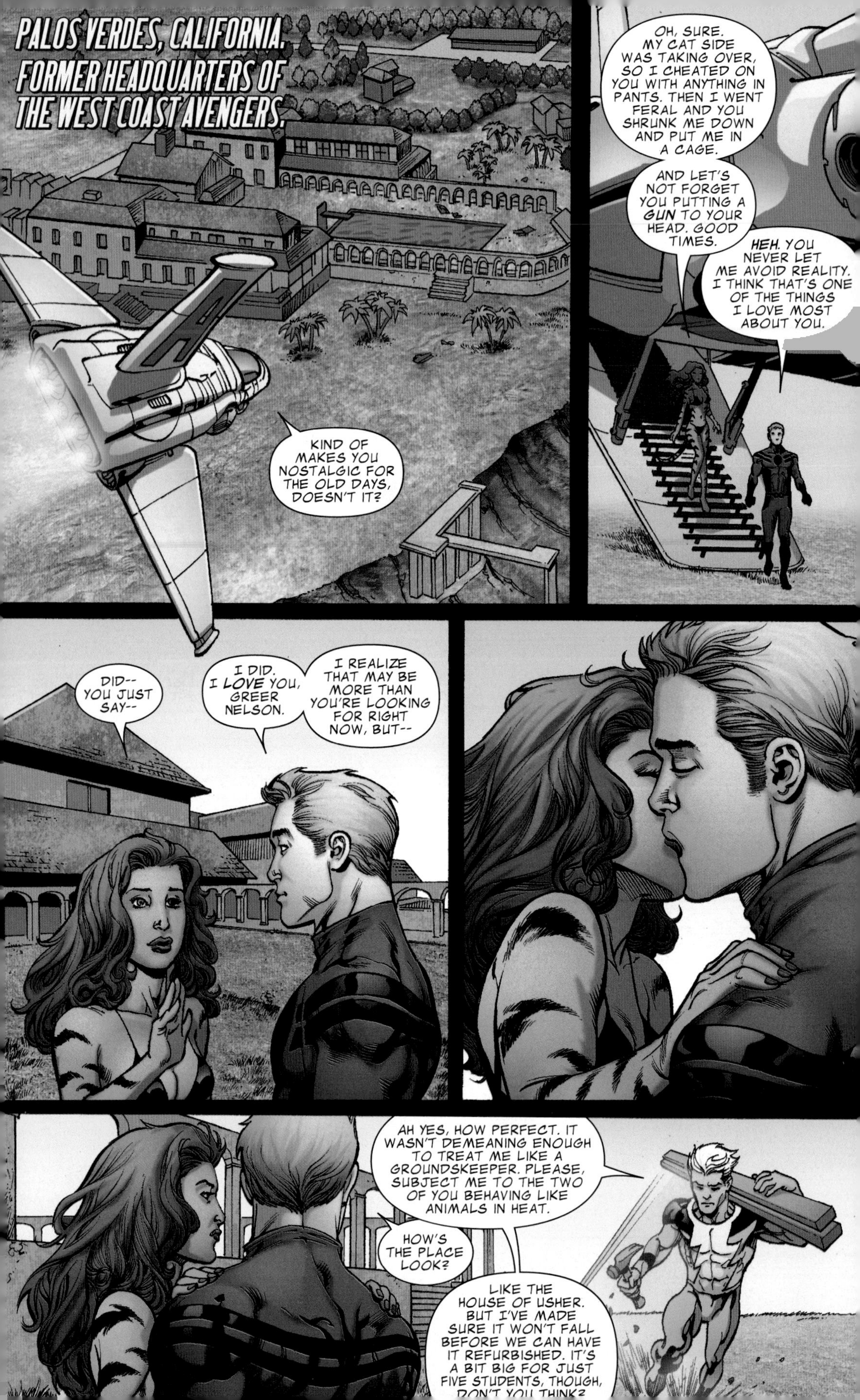
PALOS VERDES, CALIFORNIA. FORMER HEADQUARTERS OF THE WEST COAST AVENGERS.
KIND OF MAKES YOU NOSTALGIC FOR THE OLD DAYS, DOESN'T IT?
OH, SURE. MY CAT SIDE WAS TAKING OVER, SO I CHEATED ON YOU WITH ANYTHING IN PANTS. THEN I WENT FERAL AND YOU SHRUNK ME DOWN AND PUT ME IN A CAGE.
AND LET'S NOT FORGET YOU PUTTING A GUN TO YOUR HEAD. GOOD TIMES.
HEH. YOU NEVER LET ME AVOID REALITY. I THINK THAT'S ONE OF THE THINGS I LOVE MOST ABOUT YOU.
DID-- YOU JUST SAY--
I DID. I LOVE YOU, GREER NELSON.
I REALIZE THAT MAY BE MORE THAN YOU'RE LOOKING FOR RIGHT NOW, BUT--
AH YES, HOW PERFECT. IT WASN'T DEMEANING ENOUGH TO TREAT ME LIKE A GROUNDSKEEPER. PLEASE, SUBJECT ME TO THE TWO OF YOU BEHAVING LIKE ANIMALS IN HEAT.
HOW'S THE PLACE LOOK?
LIKE THE HOUSE OF USHER. BUT I'VE MADE SURE IT WON'T FALL BEFORE WE CAN HAVE IT REFURBISHED. IT'S A BIT BIG FOR JUST FIVE STUDENTS, THOUGH, DON'T YOU THINK?

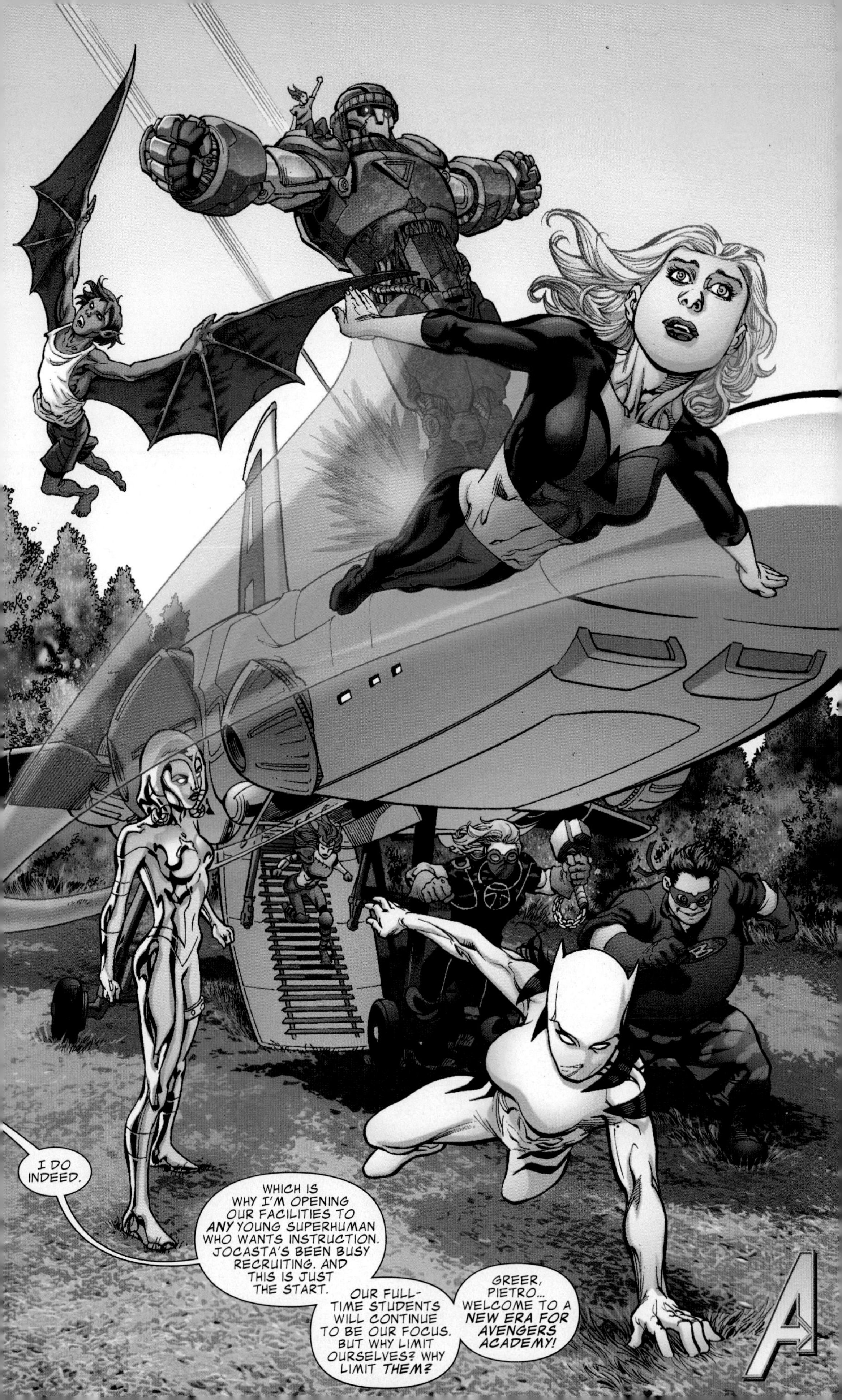
I DO INDEED.
WHICH IS WHY I'M OPENING OUR FACILITIES TO ANY YOUNG SUPERHUMAN WHO WANTS INSTRUCTION. JOCASTA'S BEEN BUSY RECRUITING. AND THIS IS JUST THE START.
OUR FULL-TIME STUDENTS WILL CONTINUE TO BE OUR FOCUS. BUT WHY LIMIT OURSELVES? WHY LIMIT THEM?
GREER, PIETRO... WELCOME TO A NEW ERA FOR AVENGERS ACADEMY!

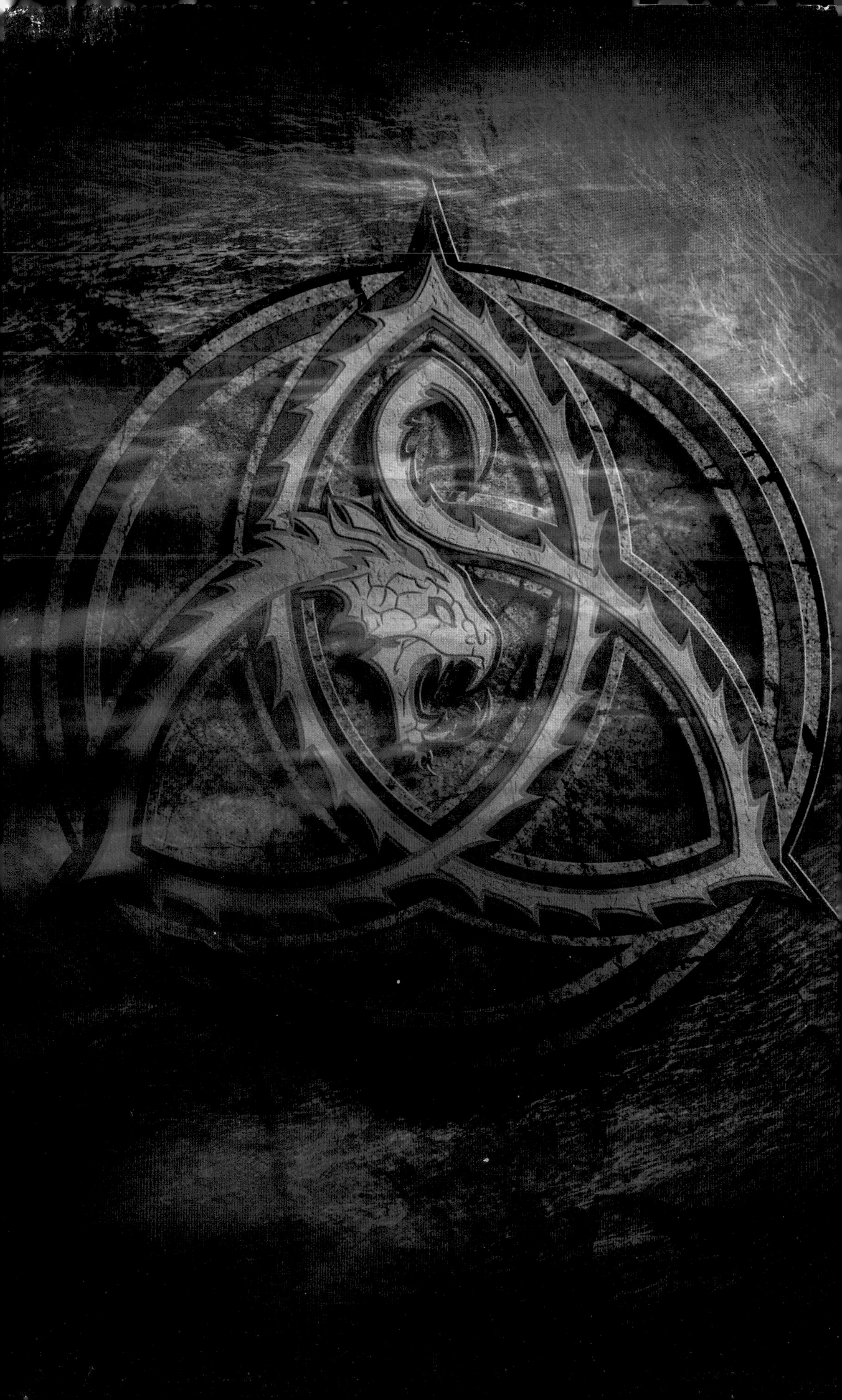

Siege HC/TP

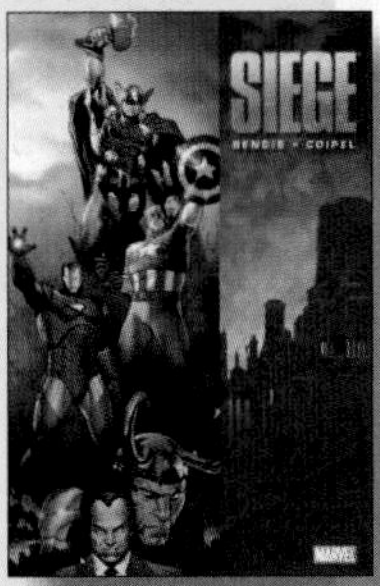
SIEGE
BENDIS • COIPEL

lects *Siege* #1-4, *Siege: The bal* and *Siege: Digital Prologue*

Brian Michael Bendis, Olivier ipel and Michael Lark

s is it! The culmination of Bendis' en-year story arc that started with engers Disassembled!

: APR100649 • 978-0-7851-4810-4
AUG100700 • 978-0-7851-4079-5

➤ New Avengers: Siege HC/TP

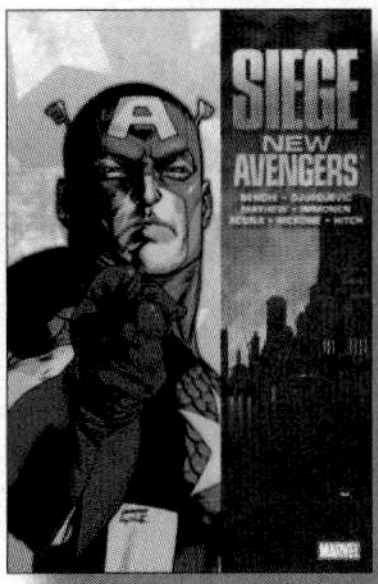
SIEGE
NEW AVENGERS

Collects *New Avengers* #61-64, *Annual* #3, *New Avengers Finale* and more!

By Brian Michael Bendis, Stuart Immonen, Marko Djurdjevic, Bryan Hitch and more

Steve Rogers returns to a world with Norman Osborn in charge!

HC: JUN100659 • 978-0-7851-4577-6
TP: NOV100669 • 978-0-7851-4578-3

AVENGERS THE INITIATIVE

Avengers: The Initiative Vol. Basic Training HC/TP

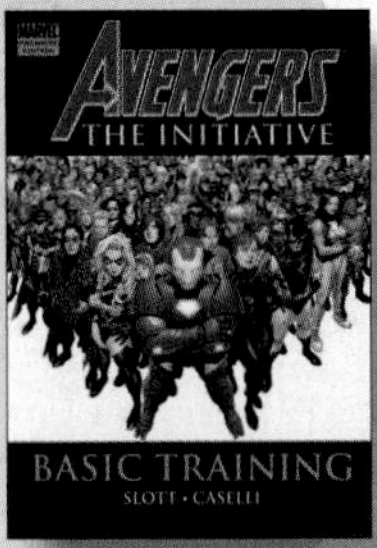
AVENGERS
THE INITIATIVE
BASIC TRAINING
SLOTT • CASELLI

llects *Avengers: The Initiative* #1-6

Dan Slott and Stefano Caselli

s is the new face of the Marvel iverse!

: SEP072268 • 978-0-7851-2160-2
: JAN082220 • 978-0-7851-2516-7

➤ Avengers: The Initiative – Disassembled HC/TP

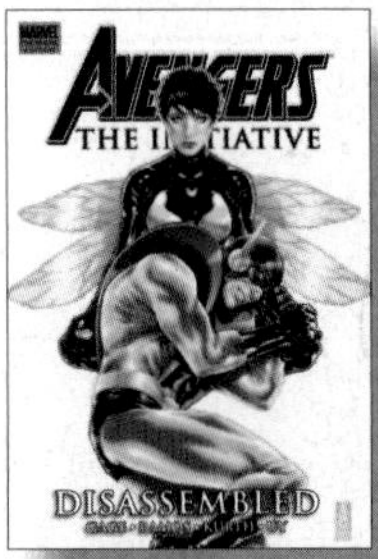
AVENGERS
DISASSEMBLED

Collects *Avengers: The Initiative* #20-25 and *Avengers: The Initiative Featuring Reptyl*

By Dan Slott, Christos N. Gage, Steve Kurth and Humberto Ramos

The Skrull plot that set up the Initiative is now exposed. Can the Initiative survive?

HC: JUN090624 • 978-0-7851-3151-9
TP: SEP090533 • 978-0-7851-3168-7

Avengers: The Initiative Vol. Killed in Action HC/TP

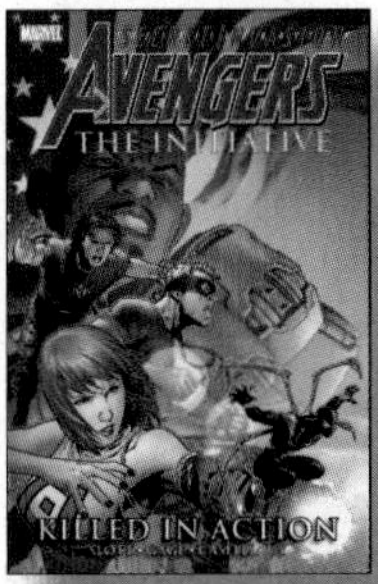
AVENGERS
KILLED IN ACTION

llects *Avengers: The Initiative* #7- , *Annual* #1

Dan Slott, Christos Gage, efano Caselli and more!

me cadets will graduate. Some l wash out. Some will die!

: APR082354 • 978-0-7851-2868-7
: SEP082454 • 978-0-7851-2861-8

➤ Avengers: The Initiative – Dreams & Nightmares HC/TP

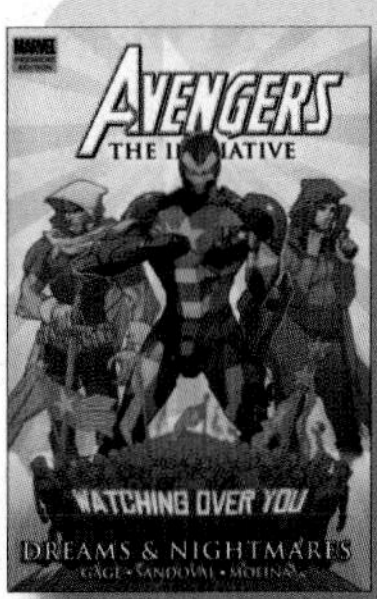
AVENGERS
WATCHING OVER YOU
DREAMS & NIGHTMARES

Collects *Avengers: The Initiative* #26-30

By Christos N. Gage, Rafa Sandoval and Jorge Molina

Initiative! Report for duty! Your new commanders? Taskmaster and the Hood!

HC: JAN100660 • 978-0-7851-3904-1
TP: MAY108107 • 978-0-7851-3905-8

Avengers: The Initiative Vol. Secret Invasion HC/TP

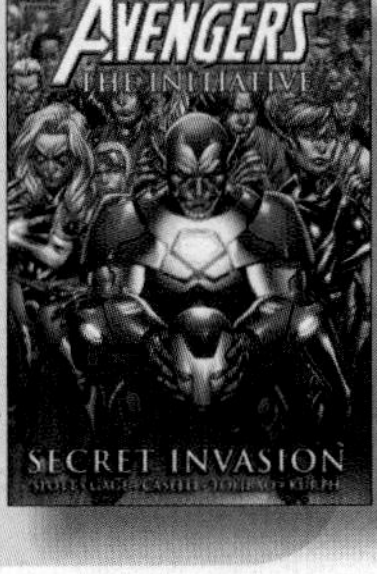
AVENGERS
THE INITIATIVE
SECRET INVASION

llects *Avengers: The Initiative* #14-19

Dan Slott, Christos N. Gage, efano Caselli and Harvey Talibao

e Initiative gets sucked into Skrull- nia!

: DEC082426 • 978-0-7851-3150-2
: MAR092648 • 978-0-7851-3167-0

➤ Siege: Avengers – The Initiative HC/TP

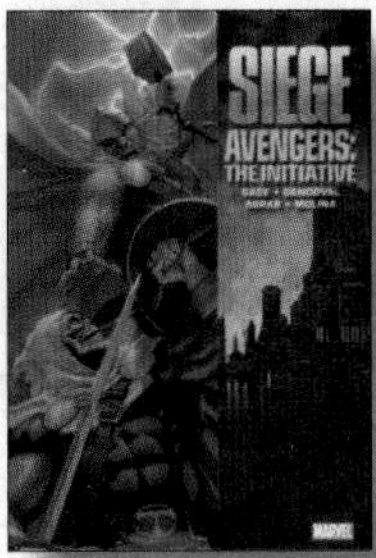
SIEGE
AVENGERS:
THE INITIATIVE

Collects *Avengers: The Initiative* #31-35 and *Avengers: The Initiative Special*

By Christos N. Gage and Rafa Sandoval

The Avengers Resistance face the Initiative in a drama-filled series conclusion!

HC: JUN100658 • 978-0-7851-4817-3
TP: OCT100696 • 978-0-7851-4818-0

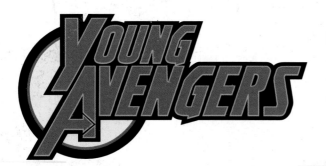

Who are the Young Avengers? Their role models are Captain America, Hawkeye, Thor, the Vision, and Hulk, but they are not who you think!

➤ Young Avengers Vol. 1: Sidekicks TP

YOUNG AVENGERS
SIDEKICKS

Collects *Young Avengers* #1-6

By Allan Heinberg and Jim Cheung

You think you know who these kids are…but you don't!

FEB062085 • 978-0-7851-2018-6

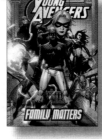

➤ Young Avengers Vol. 2: Family Matters TP

YOUNG AVENGERS
FAMILY MATTERS

Collects *Young Avengers* #7-12 and *Special* #1

By Allan Heinberg, Jim Cheung and Andrea Divito

The Young Avengers find themselves in the middle of a new Kree/Skrull War!

FEB072207 • 978-0-7851-1557-1

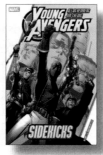

➤ Young Avengers Vol. 1 HC

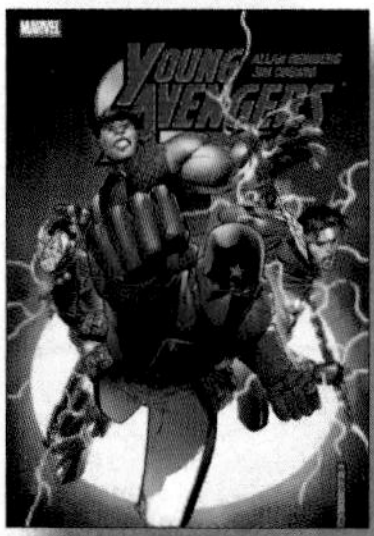

Oversized hardcover collects *Young Avengers* #1-12 and *Special* #1

HC: NOV072209 • 978-0-7851-3033-8

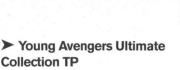

➤ Young Avengers Ultimate Collection TP

Trade paperback collects *Young Avengers* #1-12 and *Special* #1

TP: MAY100705 • 978-0-7851-4907-1

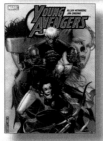

➤ Civil War: Young Avengers & Runaways TP

YOUNG AVENGERS & RUNAWAYS
CIVIL WAR

Collects *Civil War: Young Avengers & Runaways* #1-4

By Zeb Wells and Stefano Caselli

Choosing a side was never easy for this band of rebellious kids!

JAN072440 • 978-0-7851-2317-0

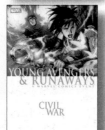

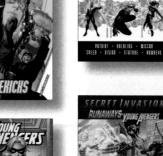

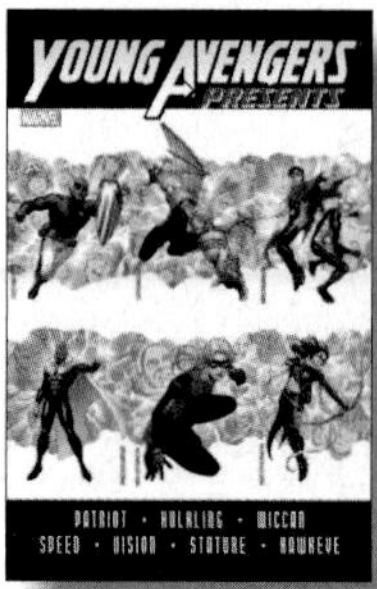

➤ Young Avengers Presents

YOUNG AVENGERS PRESENTS

Collects *Young Avengers Presen* #1-6

By Ed Brubaker, Brian Reed, Matt Fraction, Alan Davis, Mark Brooks and more!

The origins of your favorite team teen heroes!

AUG082461 • 978-0-7851-2975

➤ Secret Invasion: Runaways/Young Avengers TP

SECRET INVASION
RUNAWAYS YOUNG AVENGERS

Collects *Secret Invasion: Runaways/Young Avengers* #1-3 and more!

By Christopher Yost and Takeshi Miyazawa

The kids team up again – but is there a Skrull amongst them?

DEC082443 • 978-0-7851-3266

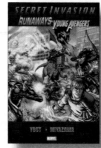

➤ Dark Reign: Young Avengers TP

Collects *Dark Reign: Young Avengers* #1-5

By Paul Cornell and Mark Brook

The Young Avengers meet… the Young Avengers? The most unexpected Marvel story of the ye

OCT090628 • 978-0-7851-3909

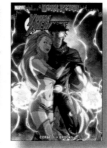

➤ Siege: Battlefield HC/TP

SIEGE
BATTLEFIELD

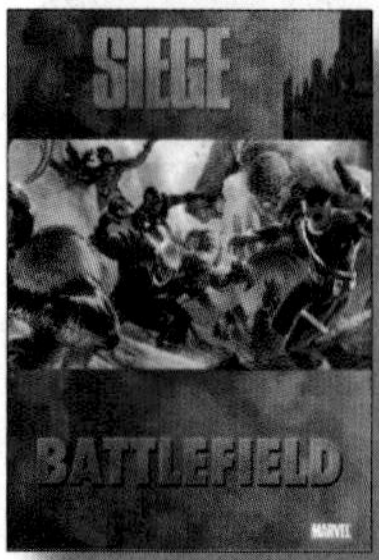

Collects *Siege: Young Avengers, Spider-Man, Loki, Captain Americ* and *Secret Warriors*

By Christos N. Gage, Sean McKeever, Jonathan Hickman, Mahmud Asrar and more

The Young Avengers take their tu in fighting Siege on Asgard!

MAY100677 • 978-0-7851-4598-

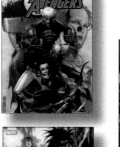